6 00
Atari

From **COMPUTE!** Books and
Optimized Systems Software, Inc.

The Atari® BASIC SOURCE BOOK

Compiled by Bill Wilkinson
Optimized Systems Software, Inc.
With the assistance of
Kathleen O'Brien and Paul Laughton

COMPUTE!™ Publications, Inc. abc
A Subsidiary Of American Broadcasting Companies, Inc.

COMPUTE! Books is a division of COMPUTE! Publications, Inc., a subsidiary of American Broadcasting Companies, Inc.

Editorial mailing address is:
PO Box 5406
Greensboro, NC 27403 USA
(919) 275-9809

Optimized Systems Services, Inc., is located at:
10379 Lansdale Avenue
Cupertino, CA 95014 USA
(408) 446-3099

All reasonable care has been taken in the writing, testing, and correcting of the text and of the software within this book. There is, however, no expressed or implied warranty of any kind from the authors or publishers with respect to the text or software herein contained. In the event of any damages resulting from the use of the text or the software in this book, or from undocumented or documented manufacturer's changes in Atari BASIC made before or after the publication of this book, the authors or publishers shall be in no sense liable.

Printed in the United States of America

ISBN 0-942386-15-9

10 9 8 7 6 5 4 3 2 1

Table of Contents

Appendices

Publisher's Foreword

It's easy to take a computer language like Atari BASIC for granted. But every PEEK and POKE, every FOR-NEXT loop and IF-THEN branch, is really a miniprogram in itself. Taken together, they become a powerful tool kit. And, as Atari owners know, there are few home-computer languages as powerful and versatile — from editing to execution — as Atari BASIC.

With this book, the Atari BASIC tool kit is unlocked. The creators of Atari BASIC and COMPUTE! Publications now offer you, for the first time, a detailed, inside look at exactly how a major computer manufacturer's primary language works.

For intermediate programmers, the thorough and careful explanations in Parts 1 and 2 will help you understand exactly what is happening in your Atari computer as you edit and run your programs.

For advanced programmers, Part 3 provides a complete listing of the source code for Atari BASIC, so that your machine language programs can make use of the powerful routines built into that 8K cartridge.

And for programmers at all levels, by the time you're through studying this book you'll feel that you've seen a whole computer language at work.

Special thanks are due to Bill Wilkinson, the creative force behind Atari BASIC and many other excellent programs for Atari and other computers, for his willingness to share copyrighted materials with computer users. Readers of COMPUTE! Magazine already know him as a regular columnist, and in this book he continues his tradition of clear explanations and understandable writing.

Acknowledgments

As far as we know, this is the first time that the actual source listing of a major manufacturer's primary computer language has been made available to the general public.

As with our previous *COMPUTE!* Publications book *Inside Atari DOS,* this book contains much more than simply a source listing. All major routines are examined and explained. We hope that when you finish reading this book you will have a better understanding of and appreciation for the design and work which go into as sophisticated a program as Atari BASIC.

This book is the result of the efforts of many people. The initial credit must go to Richard Mansfield of *COMPUTE!* Publications for serving as our goad and go-between. Without his (and *COMPUTE!*'s) insistence, this book might never have been written. Without his patience and guidance, the contents of this book might not have been nearly as interesting.

To Kathleen O'Brien and Paul Laughton must go the lion's share of the authoring credits. Between them, they have done what I believe is a very creditable job of explaining a very difficult subject, the internal workings of Atari BASIC. In fact, Part I of this book is entirely their work. Of course, their ability to explain the listing may not be so surprising. After all, between them they wrote almost all of the original code for Atari BASIC. So, even though Paul and Kathleen are not associated with Optimized Systems Software, we were pleased to have their invaluable help in writing this book and hope that they receive some of the credit which has long been due them.

Mike Peters was responsible for taking our old, almost unreadable copies of the source code diskettes for Atari BASIC and converting them to another machine, using another assembler, and formatting the whole thing into an acceptable form for this book. This isn't surprising either, since Mike keypunched the original (yes, on cards).

And I am Bill Wilkinson, the one responsible for the rest of this book. In particular, I hope you will find that a good amount of the material in Part II will aid you in understanding how to make the best use of this book.

The listing of Atari BASIC is reproduced here courtesy of OSS, Inc., which now owns its copyright and most other associated rights.

Preface

In 1978, Atari, Inc., purchased a copy of Microsoft BASIC for the 6502 microprocessor (similar to the version from which Applesoft is derived). After laboring for quite some time, the people of Atari still couldn't make it do everything they wanted it to in the ROM space they had available. And there was a deadline fast approaching: the January 1979 Las Vegas Consumer Electronics Show (CES).

At that time, Kathleen, Paul, Mike and I all worked for Shepardson Microsystems, Inc. (SMI). Though little known by the public, SMI was reasonably successful in producing some very popular microcomputer software, including the original Apple DOS, Cromemco's 16K and 32K BASICs, and more. So it wasn't too surprising that Atari had heard of us.

And they asked us: Did we want to try to fix Microsoft BASIC for them? Well, not really. Did we think we could write an all-new BASIC in a reasonable length of time? *Yes.* And would we bet a thousand dollars a week on our ability to do so?

While Bob Shepardson negotiated with Atari and I wrote the preliminary specifications for the language (yes, I'm the culprit), time was passing all too rapidly. Finally, on 6 October 1978, Atari's Engineering Department gave us the okay to proceed.

The schedule? Produce *both* a BASIC and a Disk File Manager (which became Atari DOS) in only six months. And, to make sure the pressure was intense, they gave us a $1000-a-week incentive (if we were early) or penalty (if we were late).

But Paul Laughton and Kathleen O'Brien plunged into it. And, although the two of them did by far the bulk of the work, there was a little help from Paul Krasno (who implemented the transcendental routines), Mike Peters (who did a lot of keypunching and operating), and me (who designed the floating point scheme and stood around in the way a lot). Even Bob Shepardson got into the act, modifying his venerable IMP-16 assembler to accept the special syntax table mnemonics that Paul invented (and which we paraphrase in the current listing via macros).

Atari delivered the final signed copy of the purchase order on 28 December 1978, two and a half months into the project. But it didn't really matter: Paul and Kathy were on vacation, having delivered the working product more than a week before!

So Atari took Atari BASIC to CES, and Shepardson Microsystems faded out of the picture. As for the bonus for early delivery — there was a limit on how much the incentive could be. Darn.

The only really unfortunate part of all this was that Atari got the BASIC so early that they moved up their ROM production schedule and committed to a final product before we had a chance to do a second round of bug fixing.

And now? Mike and I are running Optimized Systems Software, Inc. And even though Paul and Kathleen went their own way, we have kept in touch enough to make this book possible.

Part One

How Atari BASIC Works

Atari BASIC:
A High-Level Language Translator

The programming language which has become the *de facto* standard for the Atari Home Computer is the Atari 8K BASIC Cartridge, known simply as Atari BASIC. It was designed to serve the programming needs of both the computer novice and the experienced programmer who is interested in developing sophisticated applications programs. In order to meet such a wide range of programming needs, Atari BASIC was designed with some unique features.

In this chapter we will introduce the concepts of high level language translators and examine the design features of Atari BASIC that allow it to satisfy such a wide variety of needs.

Language Translators

Atari BASIC is what is known as a *high level language translator.*

A *language,* as we ordinarily think of it, is a system for communication. Most languages are constructed around a set of symbols and a set of rules for combining those symbols.

The English language is a good example. The symbols are the words you see on this page. The rules that dictate how to combine these words are the patterns of English grammar. Without these patterns, communication would be very difficult, if not impossible: Out sentence this believe, of make don't this trying if sense you to! If we don't use the proper symbols, the results are also disastrous: @twu2 yeggopt gjsiem, keorw?

In order to use a computer, we must somehow communicate with it. The only language that our machine really understands is that strange but logical sequence of ones and zeros known as machine language. In the case of the Atari, this is known as 6502 machine language.

When the 6502 central processing unit (CPU) "sees" the sequence 01001000 in just the right place according to its rules of syntax, it knows that it should push the current contents of the accumulator onto the CPU stack. (If you don't know what an "accumulator" or a "CPU stack" is, don't worry about it. For the discussion which follows, it is sufficient that you be aware of their existence.)

Language translators are created to make it simpler for humans to communicate with computers. There are very few 6502 programmers, even among the most expert of them, who would recognize 01001000 as the push-the-accumulator instruction. There are more 6502 programmers, but still not very many, who would recognize the hexadecimal form of 01001000, $48, as the push-the-accumulator instruction. However, most, if not all, 6502 programmers will recognize the symbol PHA as the instruction which will cause the 6502 to push the accumulator.

PHA, $48, and even 01001000, to some extent, are translations from the machine's language into a language that humans can understand more easily. We would like to be able to communicate to the computer in symbols like PHA; but if the machine is to understand us, we need a language translator to translate these symbols into machine language.

The Debug Mode of Atari's Editor/Assembler cartridge, for example, can be used to translate the symbols $48 and PHA to the ones and zeros that the machine understands. The debugger can also translate the machine's ones and zeros to $48 and PHA. The assembler part of the Editor/Assembler cartridge can be used to translate entire groups of symbols like PHA to machine code.

Assemblers

An assembler — for example, the one contained in the Assembler/Editor cartridge — is a program which is used to translate symbols that a human can easily understand into the ones and zeros that the machine can understand. In order for the assembler to know what we want it to do, we must communicate with it by using a set of symbols arranged according to a set of rules. The assembler is a translator, and the language it understands is 6502 assembly language.

The purpose of 6502 assembly language is to aid program authors in writing machine language code. The designers of the 6502 assembly language created a set of symbols and rules that matches 6502 machine language as closely as possible.

This means that the assembler retains some of the

disadvantages of machine language. For instance, the process of adding two large numbers takes dozens of instructions in 6502 machine language. If human programmers had to code those dozens of instructions in the ones and zeros of machine language, there would be very few human programmers.

But the process of adding two large numbers in 6502 assembly language also takes dozens of instructions. The assembly language instructions are easier for a programmer to read and remember, but they still have a one-to-one correspondence with the dozens of machine language instructions. The programming is easier, but the process remains the same.

High Level Languages

High level languages, like Atari BASIC, Atari PILOT, and Atari Pascal, are simpler for people to use because they more closely approximate human speech and thought patterns. However, the computer still understands only machine language. So the high level languages, while seeming simple to their users, are really much more complex in their internal operations than assembly language.

Each high level language is designed to meet the specific need of some group of people. Atari Pascal is designed to implement the concept of structured programming. Atari PILOT is designed as a teaching tool. Atari BASIC is designed to serve both the needs of the novice who is just learning to program a computer and the needs of the expert programmer who is writing a sophisticated application program, but wants the program to be accessible to a large number of users.

Each of these languages uses a different set of symbols and symbol-combining rules. But all these language translators were themselves written in assembly language.

Language Translation Methods

There are two different methods of performing language translation — *compilation* and *interpretation*. Languages which translate via interpretation are called *interpreters*. Languages which translate via compilation are called *compilers*.

Interpreters examine the program source text and simulate the operations desired. Compilers translate the program source text into machine language for direct machine execution.

The compilation method tends to produce faster, more efficient programs than does the interpretation method. However, the interpretation method can make programming easier.

Problems with the Compiler Method

The compiler user first creates a program source file on a disk, using a text editing program. Then the compiler carefully examines the source program text and generates the machine language as required. Finally, the machine language code is loaded and executed. While this three-step process sounds fairly simple, it has several serious "gotchas."

Language translators are very particular about their symbols and symbol-combining rules. If a symbol is misspelled, if the wrong symbol is used, or if the symbol is not in exactly the right place, the language translator will reject it. Since a compiler examines the entire program in one gulp, one misplaced symbol can prevent the compiler from understanding any of the rest of the program — even though the rest of the program does not violate any rules! The result is that the user often has to make several trips between the text editor and the compiler before the compiler successfully generates a machine language program.

But this does not guarantee that the program will work. If the programmer is very good or very lucky, the program will execute perfectly the very first time. Usually, however, the user must debug the program.

This nearly always involves changing the source program, usually many times. Each change in the source program sends the user back to step one: after the text editor changes the program, the compiler still has to agree that the changes are valid, and then the machine code version must be tested again. This process can be repeated dozens of times if the program is very complex.

Faster Programming or Faster Programs?

The interpretation method of language translation avoids many of these problems. Instead of translating the source code into machine language during a separate compiling step, the interpreter does all the translation *while the program is running*. This means that whenever you want to test the program you're writing, you merely have to tell the interpreter to run it. If things don't work right, stop the program, make a few changes, and run the program again at once.

You must pay a few penalties for the convenience of using the interpreter's interactive process, but you can generally develop a complex program much more quickly than the compiler user can.

However, an interpreter is similar to a compiler in that the source code fed to the interpreter must conform to the rules of the language. The difference between a compiler and an interpreter is that a compiler has to verify the symbols and symbol-combining rules only once — when the program is compiled. No evaluation goes on when the program is running. The interpreter, however, must verify the symbols and symbol-combining rules every time it attempts to run the program. If two identical programs are written, one for a compiler and one for an interpreter, the compiled program will generally execute at least ten to twenty times faster than the interpreted program.

Pre-compiling Interpreter

Atari BASIC has been incorrectly called an interpreter. It does have many of the advantages and features of an interpretive language translator, but it also has some of the useful features of a compiler. A more accurate term for Atari's BASIC Language Translator is *pre-compiling interpreter.*

Atari BASIC, like an interpreter, has a text editor built into it. When the user enters a source line, though, the line is not stored in text form, but is translated into an intermediate code, a set of symbols called *tokens*. The program is stored by the editor in token form as each program line is entered. Syntax and symbol errors are weeded out at that time.

Then, when you run the program, these tokens are examined and their functions simulated; but because much of the evaluation has already been done, the execution of an Atari BASIC program is faster than that of a pure interpreter. Yet Atari BASIC's program-building process is much simpler than that of a compiler.

Atari BASIC has advantages over compilers and interpreters alike. With Atari BASIC, every time you enter a line it is verified for language correctness. You don't have to wait until compilation; you don't even have to wait until a test run. When you type RUN you already know there are no syntax errors in your program.

Chapter Two

Internal Design Overview

Atari BASIC is divided into two major functional areas: the Program Constructor and the Program Executor. The Program Constructor is used when you enter and edit a BASIC program. The source line pre-compiler, also part of the Program Constructor, translates your BASIC program source text lines into tokenized lines. The Program Executor is used to execute the tokenized program — when you type RUN, the Program Executor takes over.

Both the Program Constructor and the Program Executor are designed to use data tables. Some of these tables are already contained in BASIC's ROM (read-only memory). Others are constructed by BASIC in the user RAM (random-access memory). Understanding these various tables is an important key to understanding the design of Atari BASIC.

Tokens

In Atari BASIC, tokens are the intermediate code into which the source text is translated. They represent source-language symbols that come in various lengths — some as long as 100 characters (a long variable name) and others as short as one character ("+" or "-"). Every token, however, is exactly one eight-bit byte in length.

Since most BASIC Language Symbols are more than one character long, the representation of a multi-character BASIC Language Symbol with a single-byte token can mean a considerable saving of program storage space.

A single-byte token symbol is also easier for the Program Executor to recognize than a multi-character symbol, since it can be evaluated by machine language routines much more quickly. The SEARCH routine — 76 bytes long — located at $A462 is a good example of how much assembly language it takes to recognize a multi-character symbol. On the other hand, the two instructions located at $AB42 are enough to determine if a one-byte token is a variable. Because routines to recognize Atari BASIC's one-byte tokens take so much less machine language, they execute relatively quickly.

The 256 possible tokens are divided into logical numerical groups that also make them simpler to deal with in assembly language. For example, any token whose value is 128 ($80) or greater represents a variable name. The logical grouping of the token values also means faster execution speeds, since, in effect, the computer only has to check bit 7 to recognize a variable.

The numerical grouping of the tokens is shown below:

Token Value (Hex)	**Description**
00-0D	Unused
0E	Floating Point Numeric Constant. The next six bytes will hold its value.
0F	String Constant. The next byte is the string length. A string of that length follows.
10-3C	Operators. See table starting at $A7E3 for specific operators and values.
3D-54	Functions. See table starting at $A820 for specific functions and values.
55-7F	Unused.
80-FF	Variables.

In addition to the tokens listed above, there is another set of single-byte tokens, the Statement Name Tokens. Every statement in BASIC starts with a unique statement name, such as LET, PRINT, and POKE. (An assignment statement such as "A=B+C," without the word LET, is considered to begin with an implied LET.) Each of these unique statement names is represented by a unique Statement Name Token.

The Program Executor does not confuse Statement Name Tokens with the other tokens because the Statement Name Tokens are always located in the same place in every statement — at the beginning. The Statement Name Token value is derived from its entry number, starting with zero, in the Statement Name Table at $A4AF.

Tables

A table is a systematic arrangement of data or information. Tables in Atari BASIC fall into two distinct types: tables that are part of the Atari BASIC ROM and tables that Atari BASIC builds in the user RAM area.

ROM Tables

The following is a brief description of the various tables in the Atari BASIC ROM. The detailed use of these tables will be explained in subsequent chapters.

Statement Name Table ($A4AF). The first two bytes in each entry point to the information in the Statement Syntax Table for this statement. The rest of the entry is the name of the statement name in ATASCII. Since name lengths vary, the last character of the statement name has the most significant bit turned on to indicate the end of the entry. The value of the Statement Name Token is derived from the relative (from zero) entry number of the statement name in this table.

Statement Execution Table ($AA00). Each entry in this table is the two-byte address of the 6502 machine language code which will simulate the execution of the statement. This table is organized with the statements in the same order as the statements in the Statement Name Table. Therefore, the Statement Name Token can be used as an index to this table.

Operator Name Table ($A7E3). Each entry comprises the ATASCII text of an Operator Symbol. The last character of each entry has the most significant bit turned on to indicate the end of the entry. The relative (from zero) entry number, plus 16 ($10), is the value of the token for that entry. Each of the entries is also given a label whose value is the value of the token for that symbol. For example, the ";" symbol at $A7E8 is the fifth (from zero) entry in the table. The label for the ";" token is CSC, and the value of CSC is $15, or 21 decimal (1*16+5).

Operator Execution Table ($AA70). Each two-byte entry points to the address, minus one, of the routine which simulates the execution of an operator. The token value, minus 16, is used to access the entries in this table during execution time. The entries in this table are in the same order as in the Operator Name Table.

Operator Precedence Table ($AC3F). Each entry represents the relative execution precedence of an individual operator. The table entries are accessed by the operator tokens, minus 16. Entries correspond with the entries in the Operator Name Table. (See Chapter 7.)

Statement Syntax Table ($A60D). Entries in this table are used in the process of translating the source program to tokens. The address pointer in the first part of each entry in the Statement Name Table is used to access the specific syntax information for that statement in this table. (See Chapter 5.)

RAM Tables

The tables that BASIC builds in the user RAM area will be explained in detail in Chapter 3. The following is a brief description of these tables:

Variable Name Table. Each entry contains the source ATASCII text for the corresponding user variable symbol in the program. The relative (from zero) entry number of each entry in this table, plus 128, becomes the value of the token representing the variable.

Variable Value Table. Each entry either contains or points to the current value of a variable. The entries are accessed by the token value, minus 128.

Statement Table. Each entry is one tokenized BASIC program line. The tokenized lines are kept in this table in ascending numerical order by line number.

Array/String Table. This table contains the current values for all strings and numerical arrays. The location of the specific values for each string and/or array variable is accessed from information in the Variable Value Table.

Runtime Stack. This is the LIFO Runtime Stack, used to control the execution of GOSUB/RETURN and similar statements.

Pre-compiler

Atari BASIC translates the BASIC source lines from text to tokens as soon as they are entered. To do this, Atari BASIC must recognize the symbols of the BASIC Language. BASIC also requires that its symbols be combined in certain specific patterns. If the symbols don't follow the required patterns, then Atari BASIC cannot translate the line. The process of checking a source line for the required symbol patterns is called *syntax checking.*

BASIC performs syntax checking as part of the tokenizing process. When the Program Editor receives a completed line of input, the editor hands the line to the syntax routine, which examines the first word of the line for a statement name. If a valid statement name is not found, then the line is assumed to be an implied LET statement.

The grammatical rules for each statement are contained in the Statement Syntax Table. A special section of code examines the symbols in the source line, under the direction of the grammatical rules set forth in the Statement Syntax Table. If the source line does not conform to the rules, then it is reported back as an error. Otherwise, the line is translated to tokens. The result of this process is returned to the Program Editor for further processing.

Program Editor

When Atari BASIC is not executing statements, it is in the edit mode. When the user enters a source line and hits return, the editor accepts the line into a line buffer, where it is examined by the pre-compiler. The pre-compiler returns either tokens or an error text line.

If the line started with a line number, the editor inserts the tokenized line into the Statement Table. If the Statement Table already contains a line with the same line number, then the old line is removed from the Statement Table. The new line is then inserted just after the statement with the next lower line number and just before the statement with the next higher line number.

If the line has no line number, the editor inserts the line at the end of the Statement Table. It then passes control to the Program Executor, which will carry out the statement(s) in the line at the end of the Statement Table.

Program Executor

The Program Executor has a pointer to the statement that it is to execute. When control is passed to the executor, the pointer points to the direct (command) line at the end of the statement table. If that statement causes some other line to be executed (RUN, GOTO, GOSUB, etc.), the pointer is changed to the new line. Lines continue to be executed as long as nothing stops that execution (END, STOP, error, etc.). When the program execution is stopped, the Program Executor returns control to the editor.

When a statement is to be executed, the Statement Name Token (the first code in the statement) directs the interpreter to the specific code that executes that statement. For instance, if that token represents the PRINT statement, the PRINT execution code is called. The execution code for each statement then examines the other tokens and simulates their operations.

Execute Expression

Arithmetic and logical expressions (A+B, C/D+E, F<G, etc.) are simulated with the Execute Expression code. Expression operators (+,-,*, etc.) have execution precedence — some operators must be executed before some others. The expression 1+3*4 has a value of 13 rather than 16 because * had a higher precedence than +. To properly simulate expressions, BASIC rearranges the expression with higher precedence first.

BASIC uses two temporary storage areas to hold parts of the rearranged expression. One temporary storage area, the Argument Stack, holds arguments — values consisting of constants, variables, and temporary values resulting from previous operator simulations. The other temporary storage area, the Operator Stack, holds operators. Both temporary storage areas are managed as Last-In/First-Out (LIFO) stacks.

LIFO Stacks

A LIFO (Last In/First Out) stack operates on the principle that the last object placed in the stack storage area will be the first object removed from it. If the letters A, B, C, and D, in that order, were placed in a LIFO stack, then D would be the first letter removed, followed by C, B, and A. The operations required to rearrange the expression using these stacks will be explained in Chapter 7.

BASIC also uses another LIFO stack, the Runtime Stack, in the simulation of statements such as GOSUB and FOR. GOSUB requires that BASIC remember where in the statement table the GOSUB was located so it will return to the right spot when RETURN is executed. If more than one GOSUB is executed before a RETURN, BASIC returns to the statement after the most recent GOSUB.

Memory Usage

Many of BASIC's functions are controlled by a set of tables built in RAM not already occupied by BASIC or the Operating System (OS). Figure 3.1 is a diagram of memory use by both programs. Every time a BASIC programmer enters a statement, memory requirements for the RAM tables change. Memory use by the OS also varies. Different graphics modes, for example, require different amounts of memory.

These changing memory requirements are monitored, and this series of pointers keeps BASIC and the OS from overlaying each other in memory:

- High memory address (HMADR) at location $02E5
- Application high memory (APHM) at location $000E
- Low memory address (LMADR) at location $02E7

When a graphics mode requires larger screen space, the OS checks the application high memory address (APHM) that has been set by BASIC. If there is enough room for the new screen, the OS uses the upper portion of space and sets the pointer HMADR to the bottom of the screen to tell the application how much space the OS is now using.

BASIC builds its table toward high memory from low memory. The pointer to the lowest memory available to an application, called LMADR in the BASIC listing, is set by the OS to tell BASIC the lowest memory address that BASIC can use. When BASIC needs more room for one of its tables, BASIC checks HMADR. If there is enough room, BASIC uses the space and puts the highest address it has used into APHM for OS.

BASIC's operation consists primarily of building, reading, and modifying tables. Pointers to the RAM tables are kept in consecutive locations in zero page starting at $80. These tables are, in order,

- Multipurpose Buffer
- Variable Name Table
- Variable Value Table
- String/Array Table

- Statement Table
- Runtime Stack

BASIC reserves space for a buffer at LMADR. It then builds the tables contiguously (without gaps), starting at the top of the buffer and extending as far as necessary towards APHM. When a new entry needs to be added to a table, all data in the tables above is moved upward the exact amount needed to fit the new entry into the right place.

Figure 3-1. Memory Usage

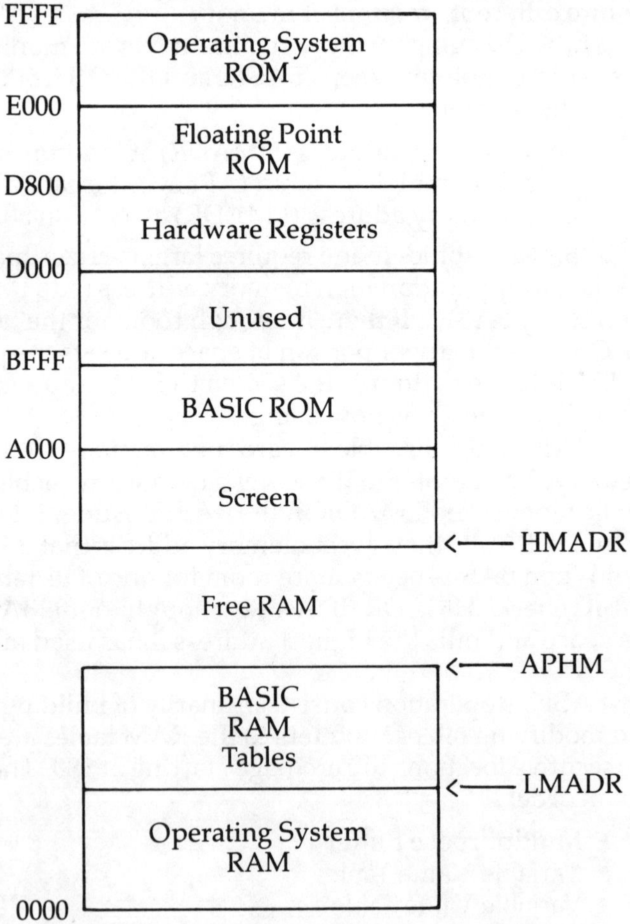

Variable Name Table

The Variable Name Table (VNT) is built during the pre-compile process. It is read, but not modified, during execution — but only by the LIST statement. The VNT contains the names of the variables used in the program in the order in which they were entered.

The length of entries in the Variable Name Table depends on the length of the variable name. The high order bit of the last character of the name is on. For example, the ATASCII code for the variable name ABC is 41 42 43 (expressed in hexadecimal). In the Variable Name Table it looks like this:

41 42 C3

The $ character of a string name and the (character of an array element name are stored as part of the variable name. The table entries for variables C, AA$, and X(3) would look like this:

C	C3
AA$	41 41 A4
X(3)	58 A8

It takes only two bytes to store X(3) because this table stores only X(.

A variable is represented in BASIC by a token. The value of this token is the position (relative to zero) of the variable name in the Variable Name Table, plus $80. BASIC references an entry in the table by using the token, minus $80, as an index. The Variable Name Table is not changed during execution time.

The zero page pointer to the Variable Name Table is called VNTP in the BASIC listing.

Variable Value Table

The Variable Value Table (VVT) is also built during the pre-compile process. It is both read and modified during execution. There is a one-to-one correspondence in the order of entries between the Variable Name Table and the Variable Value Table. If XXX is the fifth variable in the Variable Name Table, then XXX's value is the fifth entry in the Variable Value Table. BASIC references a table entry by using the variable token, minus $80, as an index.

Each entry in the Variable Value Table consists of eight bytes. The first two bytes have the following meaning:

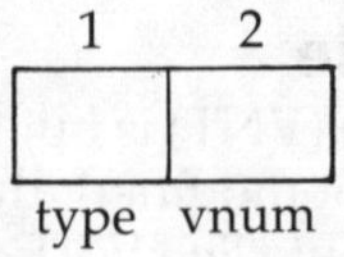

type = one byte, which indicates the type of variable
$00 for floating point variable
$40 for array variable
$80 for string variable

vnum = one byte, which indicates the relative position of the variable in the tables

The meaning of the next six bytes varies, depending on the type of variable (floating point, string, or array). In all three cases, these bytes are initialized to zero during syntaxing and during the execution of the RUN or CLR.

When the variable is a floating point number, the six bytes represent its value.

When the variable is an array, the remaining six bytes have the following format:

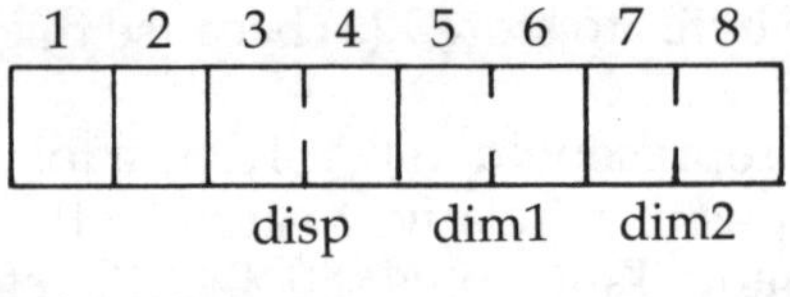

disp = the two-byte displacement into string/array space of this array variable

dim 1 = two bytes indicating the first dimension value

dim2 = two bytes indicating the second dimension value

All three of these values are set appropriately when the array is DIMensioned during execution.

When the variable is a string, the remaining six bytes have the following meaning:

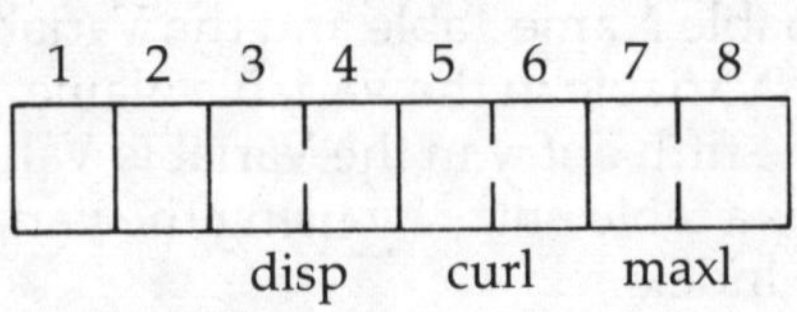

disp = the two-byte displacement into string/array space of this string variable. This value is set when the string is DIMensioned during execution.
curl = the two-byte current length of the string. This value changes as the length of the string changes during execution.
maxl = the two-byte maximum possible length of this string. This value is set to the DIM value during execution.

When either a string or an array is DIMensioned during execution, the low-order bit in the type byte is turned on, so that the array type is set to $41 and the string type to $81.

The zero page pointer to the Variable Value Table is called VVTP in the BASIC listing.

Statement Table

The Statement Table, built as each statement is entered during editing, contains tokenized forms of the statements that were entered. This table determines what happens during execution.

The format of a Statement Table entry is shown in Figure 3-2. There can be several tokens per statement and several statements per line.

Figure 3-2. Format of a Statement Table Entry

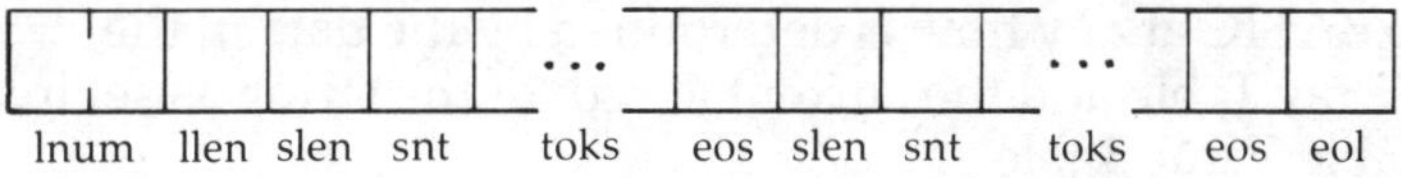

lnum = the two-byte line number (low-order, high-order)
llen = the one-byte line length (the displacement to the next line in the table)
slen = the one-byte statement length (the displacement to the next statement in the line)
snt = the one-byte Statement Name Token
toks = the other tokens that make up the statement (this is variable in length)
eos = the one-byte end of statement token
eol = the one-byte end of line token

The zero page pointer to the Statement Table is called STMTAB in the BASIC listing.

String/Array Table

The String/Array Table (also called String/Array Space) is created and modified during execution. Strings and arrays can be intermixed in the table, but they have different formats. Each array or string is pointed to by an entry in the Variable Value Table. The entry in the String/Array Table is created when the string or array is DIMensioned during execution. The data in the entry changes during execution as the value of the string or an element of the array changes.

An entry in the String/Array Table is not initialized to any particular value when it is created. The elements of arrays and the characters in a string cannot be counted upon to have any particular value. They can be zero, but they can also be garbage — data previously stored at those locations.

Array Entry

For an array, the String/Array Table contains one six-byte entry for each array element. Each element is a floating point number, stored in raveled order. For example, the entry in the String/Array Table for an array that was dimensioned as A(1,2) contains six elements, in this order:

A(0,0)   A(0,1)   A(0,2)   A(1,0)   A(1,1)   A(1,2)

String Entry

A string entry in the String/Array Table is created during execution, when the string is DIMensioned. The size of the entry is determined by the DIM value. The "value" of the string to BASIC at any time is determined by the data in the String/Array Table and the current length of the string as set in the Variable Value Table.

The zero page pointer to the String/Array Table is called STARP in the BASIC listing.

The Runtime Stack is created during execution. BASIC uses this LIFO stack to control processing of FOR/NEXT loops and GOSUBs. When either a FOR or a GOSUB statement is encountered during execution, an entry is put on the Runtime Stack. When a NEXT, RETURN, or a POP statement is encountered, entries are pulled off the stack.

Both the FOR entry and the GOSUB entry have a four-byte header:

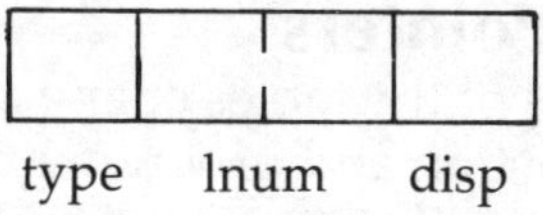

type = one byte indicating the type of element
GOSUB type = 0
FOR type = non-zero

lnum = the two-byte number of the line which contains the statement (low-order, high-order)

disp = one byte indicating the displacement into the line in the Statement Table of the token which caused this stack entry.

The FOR-type byte is actually the token representing the loop control variable from the FOR statement. (In the statement FOR I=1 to 10, I is the loop control variable.) So the FOR-type byte will have a value of $80 through $FF — the possible values of a variable token.

The FOR entry contains 12 additional bytes, formatted like this:

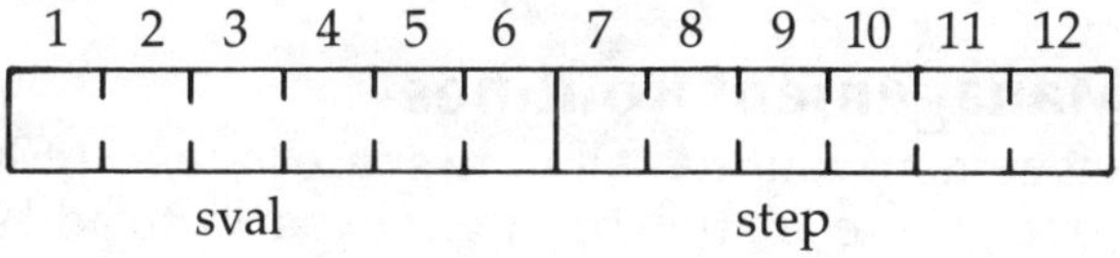

sval = the six-byte (floating point) limit value at which to stop the loop

step = the six-byte (floating point) STEP value to increment by

The GOSUB entry consists entirely of the four-byte header. The LIST and READ statements also put a GOSUB type entry on the Runtime Stack, so that the line containing the LIST or READ can be found again when the statement has finished executing.

The zero page pointer to the Runtime Stack is called RUNSTK in the BASIC listing.

Zero Page Table Pointers

The starting addresses of the tables change dynamically during both program construction and program execution. BASIC keeps the current start addresses of the tables and other pointers required to manage memory space in contiguous zero-page cells. Each pointer is a two-byte address, low byte first.

Since these zero page cell addresses remain constant, BASIC is always able to find the tables. Here are the zero page pointers used in memory management, their names in the BASIC listing, and their addresses:

Multipurpose Buffer		$80, $81
Variable Name Table	VNTP	$82, $83
VNT dummy end	VNTD	$84, $85
Variable Value Table	VVTP	$86, $87
Statement Table	STMTAB	$88, $89
Current Statement Pointer	STMCUR	$8A, $8B
String/Array Table	STARP	$8C, $8D
Runtime Stack	RUNSTK	$8E, $8F
Top of used memory	MEMTOP	$90, $91

Memory Management Routines

Memory Management routines allocate space to the BASIC tables as needed. There are two routines: expand, to add space, and contract, to delete space. Each routine has one entry point for cases in which the number of bytes to be added or deleted is less than 256, and another when it is greater than or equal to 256.

The EXPAND and CONTRACT routines often move many thousands of bytes each time they are called. The 6502 microprocessor is designed to move fewer than 256 bytes of data very quickly. When larger blocks of data are moved, the additional 6502 instructions required can make the process very slow. The EXPAND and CONTRACT routines circumvent this by using the less-than-256-byte fast-move capabilities in the movement of thousands of bytes. The end result is a set of very fast and very complex data movement routines.

All of this complexity does have a drawback. The infamous Atari BASIC lock-up problem lives in these two routines. If an EXPAND or CONTRACT requires that an exact multiple of 256 bytes be moved, then the routines move things from the wrong place in memory to the wrong place in memory, whereupon the computer locks up and won't respond. The only way to avoid losing hours of work this way is to SAVE to disk or cassette frequently.

EXPAND ($A881)

Parameters at entry:

register

X	=	the zero page address containing the pointer to the location after which space is to be added
Y	=	the low-order part of the number of bytes to expand
A	=	the high-order part of the number of bytes to expand

The routine creates a hole in the table memory, starting at a requested location and continuing the requested number of bytes.

The routine first checks to see that there is enough free memory space to satisfy the request.

It adds the requested expand size to each of the zero-page table pointers between the one pointed to by the X register and MEMTOP. Then each pointer will point to the correct address when EXPAND is done.

EXPAND then creates space at the address indicated by the X register. The number of bytes required is contained in the Y and A registers. (Y contains the least significant byte, while A contains the most significant.) All data from the requested address to the address pointed to by MEMTOP is moved toward high memory by the requested number of bytes. This creates a hole of the proper size.

The routine then sets Application High Memory (APHM) to the value in MEMTOP. This tells the OS the highest memory address that BASIC is currently using.

EXPLOW ($A87F)

Parameters at entry:

register

X	=	zero page address containing the pointer to the location after which space is to be added
Y	=	number of bytes to expand (low-order byte only)

This is an additional entry point for the EXPAND routine. It is used when the number of bytes to be added to the table is less than 256.

This routine first loads the 6502 accumulator with zero to indicate the most significant byte of the expand length. It then functions exactly like EXPAND.

CONTRACT ($A8FD)

Parameters at entry:

register

X	=	zero page address containing the pointer to the starting location where space is to be removed
Y	=	the low-order part of the number of bytes to contract
A	=	the high-order part of the number of bytes to contract

This routine removes a requested number of bytes at a requested location by moving all the data from higher in the tables downward the exact amount needed to replace the unwanted bytes.

It subtracts the requested contract size from each of the zero page table pointers between the one pointed to by the X register and MEMTOP. Then each pointer will point to the correct address when CONTRACT is done.

The routine sets application high memory (APHM) to the value in MEMTOP to indicate to the OS the highest memory address that BASIC is currently using.

The block of data to be moved downward is defined by starting at the address pointed to by the zero-page address pointed to in X, *plus* the offset number stored in Y and A, and then continuing to the address specified at MEMTOP. Each byte of data in that block is moved downward in memory by the number of bytes specified in Y and A, effectively erasing all the data between the specified address and that address plus the requested offset.

CONTLOW ($A8FB)

Parameters at entry:

register

X	=	the zero page address containing the pointer to the location at which space is to be removed

Y = the number of bytes to contract (low-order byte only)

This routine is used to remove fewer than 256 bytes from the tables at a requested location by moving all the data from higher in the tables downward the exact amount needed to replace the unwanted bytes.

This routine first loads the 6502 accumulator with zero to serve as the most significant byte of the contract length. It then functions exactly like CONTRACT.

Miscellaneous Memory Allocations

Besides the tables, which change dynamically, BASIC also uses buffers and stacks at fixed locations.

The Argument/Operator Stack is allocated at BASIC's low memory address and occupies 256 bytes. During pre-compiling it is used as the output buffer for the tokens. During execution, it is used while evaluating an expression. This buffer/stack is referenced by a pointer at location $80. This pointer has several names in the BASIC listing: LOMEM, ARGOPS, ARGSTK, and OUTBUFF.

The Syntax Stack is used during the process of syntaxing a statement. It is referenced directly — that is, not through a pointer. It is located at $480 and is 256 bytes long.

The Line Buffer is the storage area where the statement is placed when it is ENTERed. It is the input buffer for the edit and pre-compile processes. It is 128 bytes long and is referenced directly as LBUFF. Often the address of LBUFF is also put into INBUFF so that the buffer can be referenced through a pointer, though INBUFF can point to other locations during various phases of BASIC's execution.

Program Editor

The Atari keyboard is the master control panel for Atari BASIC. Everything BASIC does has its origins at this control panel. The Program Editor's job is to service the control panel and respond to the commands that come from it.

The editor gets a line from the user at the keyboard; does some preliminary processing on the line; passes the line to the pre-compiler for further processing; inserts, deletes, or replaces the line in the Statement Table; calls the Program Executor when necessary; and then waits to receive the user's next line input.

Line Processing

The Program Editor, which starts at $A060, begins its process by resetting the 6502 CPU stack. Resetting the CPU stack is a drastic operation that can only occur at the beginning of a logical process. Each time Atari BASIC prepares to get a new line from the user, it restarts its entire logical process.

Getting a Line

The Program Editor gets a user's line by calling CIO. The origin of the line is transparent to the Program Editor. The line may have been typed in at the keyboard or entered from some external device like the disk (if the ENTER command was given). The Program Editor simply calls CIO and asks it to put a line of not more than 255 bytes into the buffer pointed to by INBUFF ($F3). INBUFF points to the 128-byte area defined at LBUFF ($580).

The OS's screen editor, which is involved in getting a line from the keyboard, will not pass BASIC a line that is longer than 120 bytes. Normally, then, the 128-byte buffer at LBUFF is big enough to contain the user's line.

Sometimes, however, if a line was originally entered from the keyboard with few blanks and many abbreviations, then LISTed to and re-ENTERed from the disk, an input line may be longer than 128 bytes. When this happens, data in the $600 page is overlaid. A LINE TOO LONG error will not necessarily occur at this point. A LINE TOO LONG error occurs only if the Pre-compiler exceeds its stack while processing the line or if the tokenized line OUTBUFF exceeds 256 bytes. These overflows depend on the complexity of the line rather than on its actual length.

When CIO has put a line into the line buffer (LBUFF) and the Program Editor has regained control, it checks to see if the user has changed his mind and hit the break key. If the user did indeed hit break, the Program Editor starts over and asks CIO for another line.

Flags and Indices

In order to help control its processing, the Program Editor uses flags and indices. These must be given initial values.

CIX and COX. The index CIX ($F2) is used to access the user's input line in the line buffer (LBUFF), while COX ($94) is used to access the tokenized statement in the output buffer (OUTBUFF). These buffers and their indices are also used by the pre-compiler. The indices are initialized to zero to indicate the beginning of the buffers.

DIRFLG. This flag byte ($A6) is used by the editor to remember whether a line did or did not have a line number, and also to remember if the pre-compiler found an error in that line. DIRFLG is initialized to zero to indicate that the line has a line number and that the pre-compiler has not found an error.

MAXCIX. This byte ($9F) is maintained in case the line contains a syntax error. It indicates the displacement into LBUFF of the error. The character at this location will then be displayed in inverse video. The Program Editor gives this byte the same initial value as CIX, which is zero.

SVVNTP. The pointer to the current top of the Variable Name Table (VNTD) is saved as SVVNTP ($AD) so that if there is a syntax error in this line, any variables that were added can be removed. If a user entered an erroneous line, such as 100 A=XAND B, the variable XAND would already have been added to the variable tables before the syntax error was discovered. The user probably meant to enter 100 A=X AND B, and, since there can only be 128 variables in BASIC, he probably does not want the variable XAND using up a place in the variable tables. The Program Editor uses SVVNTP to find the entry in the Variable Name Table so it can be removed.

SVVVTE. The process used to indicate which variable entries to remove from the Variable Value Table in case of error is different. The number of new variables in the line (SVVVTE,$B1) is initialized to zero. The Program Pre-compiler increments the value every time it adds a variable to the Variable Value Table. If a syntax error is detected, this number is multiplied by eight (the number of bytes in each entry on the Variable Value Table) to get the number of bytes to remove, counting backward from the most recent value entered.

Handling Blanks

In many places in the BASIC language, blanks are not significant. For example,

100 IFX=6THENGOTO500

has the same meaning as

100 IF X = 6 THEN GOTO 500.

The Program Editor, using the SKIPBLANK routine ($DBA1), skips over unnecessary blanks.

Processing the Line Number

Once the editor has skipped over any leading blanks, it begins to examine the input line, starting with the line number. The floating point package is called to determine if a line number is present, and, if so, to convert the ATASCII line number to a floating point number. The floating point number is converted to an integer, saved in TSLNUM for later use, and stored in the tokenized line in the output buffer (OUTBUFF).

The routine used to store data into OUTBUFF is called :SETCODE ($A2C8). When :SETCODE stores a byte into OUTBUFF, it also increments COX, that buffer's index.

BASIC could convert the ATASCII line number directly to an integer, but the routine to do this would not be used any other time. Routines to convert ATASCII to floating point and floating point to integer already exist in BASIC for other purposes. Using these existing routines conserves ROM space.

An interesting result of this sequence is that it is valid to enter a floating point number as a line number. For example, 100.1, 10.9, or 2.05E2 are valid line numbers. They would be converted to 100, 11, and 205 respectively.

If the input line does not start with a line number, the line is considered to be a direct statement. DIRFLG is set to $80 so that the editor can remember this fact. The line number is set to 32768 ($8000). This is one larger than the largest line number a user is allowed to enter. BASIC later makes use of this fact in processing the direct statement.

Line length. The byte after the line number in the tokenized line in OUTBUFF is reserved so that the line length (actually the displacement to the next line) can be inserted later. (See Chapter 2.) The routine :SETCODE is called to reserve the byte by incrementing (COX) to indicate the next byte.

Saving erroneous lines. In the byte labeled STMSTRT, the Program Editor saves the index into the line buffer (LBUFF) of the first non-blank character after the line number. This index is used only if there is a syntax error, so that all the characters in the erroneous line can be moved into the tokenized line buffer and from there into the Statement Table.

There are advantages to saving an erroneous line in the Statement Table, because you can LIST the error line later. The advantage is greatest, not when entering a program at the keyboard, but when entering a program originally written in a different BASIC on another machine (via a modem, perhaps). Then, when a line that is not correct in Atari BASIC is entered, the line is flagged and stored — not discarded. The user can later list the program, find the error lines, and re-enter them with the correct syntax for Atari BASIC.

Deleting lines. If the input line consists solely of a line number, the Program Editor deletes the line in the Statement Table which has that line number. The deletion is done by pointing to the line in the Statement Table, getting its length, and calling CONTRACT. (See Chapter 3.)

Statement Processing

The user's input line may consist of one or more statements. The Program Editor repeats a specific set of functions for each statement in the line.

Initializing

The current index (COX) into the output buffer (OUTBUFF) is saved in a byte called STMLBD. A byte is reserved in OUTBUFF by the routine :SETCODE. Later, the value in

STMLBD will be used to access this byte, and the statement length (the displacement to the next statement) will be stored here.

Recognizing the Statement Name

After the editor calls SKBLANK to skip blanks, it processes the statement name, now pointed to by the input index (CIX). The editor calls the routine SEARCH ($A462) to look for this statement name in the Statement Name Table. SEARCH saves the table entry number of this statement name into location STENUM.

The entry number is also the Statement Name Token value, and it is stored into the tokenized output buffer (OUTBUFF) as such by :SETCODE. The SEARCH routine also saves the address of the entry in SRCADR for use by the pre-compiler.

If the first word in the statement was not found in the Statement Name Table, the editor assumes that the statement is an implied LET, and the appropriate token is stored. It is left to the pre-compiler to determine if the statement has the correct syntax for LET.

The editor now gives control to the pre-compiler, which places the appropriate tokens in OUTBUFF, increments the indices CIX and COX to show current locations, and indicates whether a syntax error was detected by setting the 6502 carry flag on if there was an error and clearing the carry flag if there was not. (See Chapter 5.)

If a Syntax Error Is Detected

If the 6502 carry flag is set when the editor regains control, the editor does error processing.

In MAXCIX, the pre-compiler stored the displacement into LBUFF at which it detected the error. The Program Editor changes the character at this location to inverse video.

The character in inverse video may not be the point of error from your point of view, but it is where the pre-compiler detected an error. For example, assume you entered X=YAND Z. You probably meant to enter X=Y AND Z, and therefore would consider the error to be between Y and AND. However, since YAND is a valid variable name, X=YAND is a valid BASIC statement.

The pre-compiler doesn't know there is an error until it encounters B. The value of highlighting the error with inverse video is that it gives the user an approximation of where the error is. This can be a big advantage, especially if the input line contained multiple statements or complex expressions.

The next thing the editor does when a syntax error has been detected is set a value in DIRFLG to indicate this fact for future reference. Since the DIRFLG byte also indicates whether this is a direct statement, the error indicator of $40 is ORed with the value already in DIRFLG.

The editor takes the value that it saved in STMSTRT and puts it into CIX so that CIX now points to the start of the first statement in the input line in LBUFF. STMLBD is set to indicate the location of the first statement length byte in OUTBUFF. (A length will be stored into OUTBUFF at this displacement at a later time.)

The editor sets the index into OUTBUFF (COX) to indicate the Statement Name Token of the first statement in OUTBUFF, and stores a token at that location to indicate that this line has a syntax error. The entire line (after the line number) is moved into OUTBUFF. At this point COX indicates the end of the line in OUTBUFF. (Later, the contents of OUTBUFF will be moved to the Statement Table.)

This is the end of the special processing for an erroneous line. The process that follows is done for both correct and erroneous lines.

Final Statement Processing

During initial line processing, the Program Editor saved in STMLBD a value that represents the location in OUTBUFF at which the statement length (displacement to the next statement) should be stored. The Program Editor now retrieves that value from STMLBD. Using this value as an index, the editor stores the value from COX in OUTBUFF as the displacement to the next statement.

The Program Editor checks the next character in LBUFF. If this character is not a carriage return (indicating end of the line), then the statement processing is repeated. When the carriage return is found, COX will be the displacement to the next line. The Program Editor stores COX as the line length at a displacement of two into OUTBUFF.

Statement Table Processing

The final tokenized form of the line exists in OUTBUFF at this point. The Program Editor's next task is to insert or replace the line in the Statement Table.

The Program Editor first needs to create the correct size hole in the Statement Table. The editor calls the GETSTMT routine ($A9A2) to find the address where this line should go in the Statement Table. If a line with the same line number already exists, the routine returns with the address in STMCUR and with the 6502 carry flag off. Otherwise, the routine puts the address where the new line should be inserted in the Statement Table into STMCUR and turns *on* the 6502 carry flag. (See Chapter 6.)

If the line does not exist in the Statement Table, the editor loads zero into the 6502 accumulator. If the line does exist, the editor calls the GETLL routine ($A9DD) to put the line length into the accumulator. The editor then compares the length of the line already in the Statement Table (old line) with the length of the line in OUTBUFF (new line).

If more room is needed in the Statement Table, the editor calls the EXPLOW ($A87F; see Chapter 3). If less space is needed for the new line, it calls a routine to point to the next line (GNXTL, at location $A9D0; see Chapter 6), and then calls the CONTLOW ($A8FB; see Chapter 3).

Now that we have the right size hole, the tokenized line is moved from OUTBUFF into the Statement Table at the location indicated by STMCUR.

Line Wrap-up

After the line has been added to the Statement Table, the editor checks DIRFLG for the syntax error indicator. If the second most significant bit ($40) is on, then there is an error.

Error Wrap-up

If there is an error, the editor removes any variables that were added by this line by getting the number of bytes that were added to the Variable Name Table and the Variable Value Table from SVVNTP and SVVVTE. It then calls CONTRACT ($A8FD) to remove the bytes from each table.

Next, the editor lists the line. The Statement Name Token, which was set to indicate an error, causes the word "ERROR" to be printed. An inverse video character indicates where the error was detected. The editor now waits for you to enter another line.

Handling Correct Lines

If the line was syntactically correct, the editor again examines DIRFLG. In earlier processing, the most significant bit ($80) of this byte was set on if the line was a direct statement. If it is not a direct statement, then the editor is finished with the line, and it waits for another input line.

If the line *is* a direct statement, earlier processing already assigned it a line number of 32768 ($8000), one larger than the largest line number a user can enter. Since lines are arranged in the Statement Table in ascending numerical order, this line will have been inserted at the end of the table. The current statement pointer (STMCUR—$8A, $8B) points to this line.

The Program Editor transfers control to a Program Executor routine, Execution Control (EXECNL at location $A95F), which will handle the execution of the direct statement. (See Chapter 6.)

The Pre-compiler

The symbols and symbol-combining rules of Atari BASIC are coded into Syntax Tables, which direct the Program Pre-compiler in examining source code and producing tokens. The information in the Syntax Tables is a transcription of a meta-language definition of Atari BASIC.

The Atari BASIC Meta-language

A meta-language is a language which describes or defines another language. Since a meta-language is itself a language, it also has symbols and symbol-combining rules — which define with precision the symbols and symbol-combining rules of the subject language.

Atari BASIC is precisely defined with a specially developed meta-language called the Atari BASIC Meta-language, or ABML. (ABML was derived from a commonly used compiler-technology meta-language called BNF.) The symbols and symbol-combining rules of ABML were intentionally kept very simple.

Making Up a Language

To show you how ABML works, we'll create an extremely simple language called SAP, for Simple Arithmetic Process. SAP symbols consist of variables, constants, and operators.

- Variables: The letters A, B, and C only.
- Constants: The numbers 1,2,3,4,5,6,7,8, and 9 only.
- Operators: The characters +, −, *, /, and ! only. Of course, you already know the functions of all the operators except "!". The character ! is a pseudo-operator of the SAP language used to denote the end of the expression, like the period that ends this sentence.

The grammar of the SAP language is precisely defined by the ABML definition in Figure 5-1.

Figure 5-1. The SAP Language Expressed in ABML

SAP := <expression>!
<expression> := <value><operation>|
<operation> := <operator><expression>
<value> := <constant> | <variable>
<constant> := 1 | 2 | 3 | 4 | 5 | 6 | 7 | 8 | 9
<variable> := A | B | C
<operator> := + | - | * | /

The ABML symbols used to define the SAP language in Figure 5-1 are:

:= *is defined as* — Whatever is on the left of := is defined as consisting of whatever is on the right of :=, and in that order.

| *or* — The symbol | allows choices for what something *is defined as*. For instance, in the sixth line <variable> can be A *or* B *or* C. If | does not appear between two symbols, then there is no choice. For example, in the second line <expression> must have both <value> *and* <operation>, in that order, to be valid.

< > *label* — Whatever comes between < and > is an ABML label. All labels, as non-terminal symbols, must be defined at some point, though the definitions can be circular — notice that <operation> is part of the definition of <expression> in the second line, while in the third line <expression> is part of the definition of <operation>.

terminal symbols — Symbols used in definitions, which are not enclosed by < and > and are also not one of the ABML symbols, are terminal symbols in the language being defined by ABML. In SAP, some terminal symbols are A, !, B, *, and 1. They cannot be defined as consisting of other symbols — they are themselves the symbols that the SAP language manipulates, and must appear exactly as they are shown to be valid in SAP. In effect, they are the vocabulary of the SAP language.

Statement Generation

The ABML description of SAP can be used to generate grammatically correct statements in the SAP language. To do this, we merely start with the first line of the definition and replace the non-terminal symbols with the definitions of those symbols. The replacement continues until only terminal symbols remain. These remaining terminal symbols constitute a grammatically correct SAP statement.

Since the *or* statement requires that one and only one of the choices be used, we will have to arbitrarily replace the non-terminal with the one valid choice.

Figure 5-2 illustrates the ABML statement generation process.

Figure 5-2. The Generation of One Possible SAP Statement

(1) SAP := <expression>!
(2) SAP := <value><operation>!
(3) SAP := <variable><operation>!
(4) SAP := B<operation>!
(5) SAP := B<operator><expression>!
(6) SAP := B*<expression>!
(7) SAP := B*<value><operation>!
(8) SAP := B*<constant><operation>!
(9) SAP := B*4<operation>!
(10) SAP := B*4<operator><expression>!
(11) SAP := B*4+<expression>!
(12) SAP := B*4+<value><operation>!
(13) SAP := B*4+<variable><operation>!
(14) SAP := B*4+C<operation>!
(15) SAP := B*4+C!

In (2), <value><operation> replaces <expression> because the ABML definition of SAP (Figure 5-1) defines <expression> as <value><operation>.

In (3), the non-terminal <value> is replaced with

<variable>. The definition of <value> gives two choices for the substitution of <value>. We happened to choose <variable>.

In (4), we reach a terminal symbol, and the process of defining <value> ends. We happened to choose **B** to replace <variable>.

In (5), we go back and start defining <operation>. There are two choices for the replacement of <operation>, either <operator> <expression> or nothing at all (since there is nothing to the right of | in the second line of Figure 5-1). If nothing had been chosen, then (5) would have been: SAP := B! The statement B! has no further non-terminals; the process would have been finished, and a valid statement would have been produced. Instead we happened to choose <operator> <expression>.

The SAP definition for <expression> is <value> <operation>. If we replace <operation> with its definition we get:

<expression> := <value> <operator> <expression>

The definition of <expression> includes <expression> as part of its definition. If the <operator> <expression> choice were always made for <operation>, then the process of replacement would never stop. A SAP statement can be infinitely long by definition. The only thing which prevents us from *always* having an infinitely long SAP statement is that there is a second choice for the replacement of <operation> : nothing.

The replacements in (5) and (10) reflect the repetitive choices of defining <expression> in terms of itself. The choice in (15) reflects the *nothing* choice and thus finishes the replacement process.

Computerized Statement Generation

If we slightly modify our procedure for generating statements, we will have a process that could be easily programmed into a computer. Instead of arbitrarily replacing the definition of non-terminals, we can think of the non-terminal as a GOSUB. When we see <X> := <Y> <Z>, we can think of <Y> as being a subroutine-type procedure:

(a) Go to the line that has <Y> on the left side.
(b) Process the definition (right side) of <Y>.

(c) If while processing the definition of <Y>, other non-terminals are found, GOSUB to them.
(d) If while processing the definition of <Y> we encounter a terminal, output the terminal symbol as the next symbol of the generated statement.
(e) When the definition of <Y> is finished, return to the place that <Y> was called from and continue.

Since ABML is structured so that it can be programmed, a fascinating exercise is to design a simple English sentence grammar with ABML, then write a BASIC program to generate valid English sentences at random. The randomness of the sentences would be derived by using the RND function to select from the definitions *or* choices. An example of such a grammar is shown in Figure 5-3. (The programming exercise is left to you.)

Figure 5-3. A Simple English Sentence Grammar in ABML

SENTENCE	:= <subject> <adverb> <verb> <object>.
<subject>	:= The <adjective> <noun>
<verb>	:= eats | sleeps | drinks | talks | hugs
<adverb>	:= quickly | silently | slowly | viciously | lovingly | sadly |
<object>	:= at home | in the car | at the table | at school | <subject>
<noun>	:= boy | girl | dog | programmer | computer | teacher
<adjective>	:= happy | sad | blue | light | round | smart | cool | nice |

Syntactical Analysis

The process of examining a language statement for grammatical correctness is called *syntactical analysis*, or *syntaxing*.

Statement verification is similar to statement generation. Instead of arbitrarily choosing which *or* definition to use, however, the choices are already made, and we must check to see whether the statement symbols are used in valid patterns. To do this, we must process through each *or* definition until we find a matching valid terminal symbol.

The result of statement generation is a valid, grammatically correct statement, but the result of statement verification is a statement validity indication, which is a simple *yes* or *no.* Either the statement is grammatically correct or it is not. Failure occurs when some statement symbol cannot be matched with a valid terminal symbol under the rules of the grammar.

The Reporting System

To use the *pass/fail* result of statement verification, we must build a reporting system into the non-terminal checking process. Whenever we, in effect, GOSUB to a non-terminal definition, that non-terminal definition must report its *pass/fail* status.

A *fail* status is generated and returned by a non-terminal definition when it finds no matching terminal for the current statement symbol. If the current statement symbol is B and the <constant> definition in the SAP language is called, then <constant> would report a *fail* status to the routine that called it.

A *pass* status is returned when a terminal symbol is found which matches the current statement symbol. If our current statement symbol had been 7 instead of B, then <constant> would have reported *pass.*

Whenever such a match does occur, we return to the statement, and the next symbol to the right becomes the new current symbol for examination and verification.

Cycling Through the Definitions

In SAP, the <constant> definition is called from the <value> definition. If <constant> reports *fail,* then we examine the next *or* choice, which is <variable>. The current symbol is B, so <variable> reports *pass.*

Since at least one of the *or* choices of <value> has reported *pass,* <value> will report *pass* to its caller. If both <constant> and <variable> had reported *fail,* then <value> would report *fail* to its caller.

The caller of <value> is <expression>. If <value> reports *pass,* <operation> is called. If <operation> reports *pass,* then <expression> can report *pass* to its caller. If either <value> or <operation> reports *fail,* then <expression> must report *fail,* since there are no other *or* choices for <expression>.

The definition of <operation> contains a special *pass/fail* property. If either <operator> or <expression> reports *fail,* then the *or* choice must be examined. In this case the *or* choice is *nothing*. The *or nothing* means something special: report *pass*, but do not advance to the next symbol.

The final *pass/fail* report is generated from the first line of the definition. If <expression> reports *pass* and the next symbol is !, then SAP reports *pass*. If either one of these conditions has a *fail* status, then SAP must report *fail* to whatever called SAP from outside the language.

Backing Up

Sometimes it is necessary to back up over symbols which have already been processed. Let's assume that there was a definition of the type <X> := <Y>|<Z>. It is possible that while <Y> is attempting to complete its definition, it will find a number of valid matching terminal symbols before it discovers a symbol that it cannot match. In this case, <Y> would have consumed a number of symbols before it decided to report *fail*. All of the symbols that <Y> consumed must be *un*consumed before <Z> can be called, since <Z> will need to check those same symbols.

The process of unconsuming symbols is called *backup*. Backup is usually performed by the caller of <Y>, which remembers which source symbol was current when it called <Y>. If <Y> reports *fail*, then the caller of <Y> restores the current symbol pointer before calling <Z>.

Locating Syntax Error

When a final report of *fail* is given for a statement, it is often possible to guess where the error occurred. In a left-to-right system, the symbol causing the failure is usually the symbol which follows the rightmost symbol found to be valid. If we keep track of the rightmost valid symbol during the various backups, we can report a best guess as to where the failure-causing error is located. This is exactly what Atari BASIC does with the inverse video character in the ERROR line.

For simplicity, our example was coded for SAP, but the syntactical analysis we have just described is essentially the process that the Atari BASIC pre-compiler uses to verify the grammar of a source statement. The Syntax Tables are an ABML description of Atari BASIC. The pre-compiler, also known as the *syntaxer*, contains the routines which verify BASIC statements.

Statement Syntax Tables

There is one entry in the Syntax Tables for each BASIC statement. Each statement entry in the Syntax Table is a transcription of an ABML definition of the grammar for that particular statement. The starting address of the table entry for a particular statement is pointed to by that statement's entry in the Statement Name Table.

The data in the Syntax Tables is very much like a computer machine language. The pseudo-computer which executes this pseudo-machine language is the pre-compiler code. Like any machine language, the pseudo-machine language of the Syntax Tables has instructions and instruction operands. For example, an ABML non-terminal symbol is transcribed to a code which the pre-compiler executes as a type of "GOSUB and report *pass/fail*" command.

Here are the pseudo-instruction codes in the Syntax Tables; each is one byte in length.

Absolute Non-Terminal Vector

Name: ANTV
Code: $00

This is one of the forms of the non-terminal GOSUB. It is followed by the address, minus 1, of the non-terminal's definition within the Syntax Table. The address is two bytes long, with the least significant byte first.

External Subroutine Call

Name: ESRT
Code: $01

This instruction is a special type of terminal symbol checker. It is followed by the address, minus 1, of a 6502 machine language routine. The address is two bytes long, with the least significant byte first. The ESRT instruction is a *deus ex machina* — the "god from the machine" who solved everybody's problems at the end of classical Greek plays. There are some terminals whose definition in ABML would be very complex and require a great many instructions to describe. In these cases, we go outside the pseudo-machine language of the Syntax Tables and get help from 6502 machine language routines — the *deus ex machina* that quickly gives the desired result. A numeric constant is one example of where this outside help is required.

ABML *or*

Name: OR
Value: $02

This is the familiar ABML *or* symbol (|). It provides for an alternative definition of a non-terminal.

Return

Name: RTN
Value: $03

This code signals the end of an ABML definition line. When we write an ABML statement on paper, the end of a definition line is obvious — there is no further writing on the line. When ABML is transcribed to machine codes, the definitions are all pushed up against each other. Since the function that is performed at the end of a definition is a return, the end of definition is called return (RTN).

Unused (Codes $04 through $0D are unused.)

Expression Non-Terminal Vector

Name: VEXP
Value: $0E

The ABML definition for an Atari BASIC expression is located at $A60D. Nearly every BASIC statement definition contains the possibility of having <expression> as part of it. VEXP is a single-byte call to <expression>, to avoid wasting the two extra bytes that ANTV would take. The pseudo-machine understands that this instruction is the same as an ANTV call to <expression> at $A60D.

Change Last Token

Name: CHNG
Value: $0F

This instruction is followed by a one-byte *change to* token value. The operator token instructions cause a token to be placed into the output buffer. Sometimes it is necessary to change the token that was just produced. For example, there are several = operators. One = operator is for the *assignment* statement LET X=4. Another = operator is for *comparison* operations like IF Y=5. The pseudo-machine will generate the *assignment* = token when it matches =. The context of the grammar at that point may have required a *comparison* = token. The CHNG instruction rectifies this problem.

Operator Token

Name: (many)
Value: $10 through $7F

These instructions are terminal codes for the Atari BASIC Operators. The code values are the values of each operator token. The values, value names, and operator symbols are defined in the Operator Name Table (see Chapter 2).

When the pseudo-machine sees these terminal symbol representations, it compares the symbol it represents to the current symbol in the source statement. If the symbols do not match, then *fail* status is generated. If the symbols match, then *pass* status is generated, the token (instruction value) is placed in the token output buffer, and the next statement source symbol becomes the current symbol for verification.

Relative Non-Terminal Vectors

Name: (none)
Value: $80 — $BF (Plus)
$C0 — $FF (Minus)

This instruction is similar to ANTV, except that it is a single byte. The upper bit is enough to signal that this one-byte code is a non-terminal GOSUB. The destination address of the GOSUB is given as a position relative to the current table location. The values $80 through $BF correspond to an address which is at the current table address *plus* $00 through $3F. The values $C0 through $FF correspond to an address which is at the current table address *minus* $01 through $3F.

Pre-compiler Main Code Description

The pre-compiler, which starts at SYNENT ($A1C3), uses the pseudo-instructions in the Syntax Tables to verify the correctness of the source line and to generate the tokenized statements.

Syntax Stack

The pre-compiler uses a LIFO stack in its processing. Each time a non-terminal vector (''GOSUB'') is executed, the pre-compiler must remember where the call was made from. It must also remember the current locations in the input buffer (source statement) and the output buffer (tokenized statement) in case the called routine reports *fail* and backup is required. This LIFO stack is called the Syntax Stack.

The Syntax Stack starts at $480 at the label SIX. The stack is 256 bytes in size. Each entry in the stack is four bytes long. The stack can hold 64 levels of non-terminal calls. If a sixty-fifth stack entry is attempted, the LINE TOO LONG error is reported. (This error should be called LINE TOO COMPLEX, but the line is most likely too long also.)

The first byte of each stack entry is the current input index (CIX). The second byte is the current output index (COX). The final two bytes are the current address within the syntax tables.

The current stack level is managed by the STKLVL ($A9) cell. STKLVL maintains a value from $00 to $FC, which is the displacement to the current top of the stack entry.

Initialization

The editor has saved an address in SRCADR ($96). This address is the address, minus 1, of the current statement's ABML instructions in the Syntax Tables. The current input index (CIX) and the current output index (COX) are also preset by the editor.

The initialization code resets the syntax stack manager (STKLVL) to zero and loads the first stack entry with the values in CIX, COX, and CPC — the current program counter, which holds the address of the next pseudo-instruction in the Syntax Tables.

PUSH

Values are placed on the stack by the PUSH routine ($A228). PUSH is entered with the new current pseudo-program counter value on the CPU stack. PUSH saves the current CIX, COX, and CPC on the syntax stack and increments STKLVL. Next, it sets a new CPC value from the data on the CPU stack. Finally, PUSH goes to NEXT.

POP

Values are removed from the stack with the POP routine ($A252). POP is entered with the 6502 carry flag indicating *pass/fail*. If the carry is clear, then *pass* is indicated. If the carry is set, then *fail* is indicated.

POP first checks STKLVL. If the current value is zero, then the pre-compiler is done. In this case, POP returns to the editor via RTS. The carry bit status informs the editor of the *pass/fail* status.

If STKLVL is not zero, POP decrements STKLVL.

At this point, POP examines the carry bit status. If the carry is clear *(pass)*, POP goes to NEXT. If the carry is set *(fail)*, POP goes to FAIL.

NEXT and the Processes It Calls

After initialization is finished and after each Syntax Table instruction is processed, NEXT is entered to process the next syntax instruction.

NEXT starts by calling NXSC to increment CPC and get the next syntax instruction into the A register. The instruction value is then tested to determine which syntax instruction code it is and where to go to process it.

If the Syntax Instruction is OR ($02) or RTN ($03), then exit is via POP. When POP is called due to these two instructions, the carry bit is always clear, indicating *pass*.

ERNTV. If the instruction is RNTV (''GOSUB'' $80 – $FF), then ERNTV ($A201) is entered. This code calculates the new CPC value, then exits via PUSH.

GETADR. If the instruction is ANTV ($00) or the *deus ex machina* ESRT ($01) instruction, then GETADR is called. GETADR obtains the following two-byte address from the Syntax Table.

If the instruction was ANTV, then GETADR exits via PUSH.

If the instruction was ESRT, then GETADR calls the external routine indicated. The external routine will report *pass/fail* via the carry bit. The *pass/fail* condition is examined at $A1F0. If *pass* is indicated, then NEXT is entered. If *fail* is indicated, then FAIL is entered.

TERMTST. If the instruction is VEXP ($0E), then the code at $A1F9 will go to TERMTST ($A2A9), which will cause the code at $A2AF to be executed for VEXP. This code obtains the address, minus 1, of the ABML for the <expression> in the Syntax Table and exits via PUSH.

ECHNG. If the instruction was CHNG ($0F), then ECHNG ($A2BA) is entered via tests at $A1F9 and $A2AB. ECHNG will increment CPC and obtain the *change-to* token which will then replace the last previously generated token in OUTBUFF. ECHNG exits via RTS, which will take control back to NEXT.

SRCONT. The Operator Token Instructions ($10-$7F) are handled by the SRCONT routine. SRCONT is called via tests at $A1F9 and $A2AD. SRCONT will examine the current source symbol to see if it matches the symbol represented by the operator token. When SRCONT has made its determination, it will return to the code at $A1FC. This code will examine the *pass/fail* (carry clear/set) indicator returned by SRCONT and take the appropriate action. (The SRCONT routine is detailed on the next page.)

FAIL

If any routine returns a *fail* indicator, the FAIL code at $A26C will be entered. FAIL will sequentially examine the instructions, starting at the Syntax Table address pointed to by CPC, looking for an OR instruction.

If an OR instruction is found, the code at $A27D will be entered. This code first determines if the current statement symbol is the rightmost source symbol to be examined thus far. If it is, it will update MAXCIX. The editor will use MAXCIX to set the inverse video flag if the statement is erroneous. Second, the code restores CIX and COX to their before-failure values and goes to NEXT to try this new OR choice.

If, while searching for an OR instruction, FAIL finds a RTN instruction, it will call POP with the carry set. Since the carry is set, POP will re-enter FAIL once it has restored things to the previous calling level.

All instruction codes other than OR and RTN are skipped over by FAIL.

Pre-compiler Subroutine Descriptions

SRCONT ($A2E6)

The SRCONT code will be entered when an operator token instruction is found in the Syntax Tables by the main pre-compiler code. The purpose of the routine is to determine if the current source symbol in the user's line matches the terminal symbol represented by the operator token. If the symbols match, the token is placed into the output buffer and *pass* is returned. If the symbols do not match, *fail* is returned.

SRCONT uses the value of the operator token to access the terminal symbol name in the Operator Name Table. The characters in the source symbol are compared to the characters in the terminal symbol. If all the characters match, *pass* is indicated.

TNVAR, TSVAR ($A32A)

These *deus ex machina* routines are called by the ESRT instruction. The purpose of the routines is to determine if the current source symbol is a valid numeric (TNVAR) or string (TSVAR) variable. If the source symbol is not a valid variable, *fail* is returned.

When *pass* is indicated, the routine will put a variable token into the output buffer. The variable token ($80-$FF) is an index into the Variable Name Table and the Variable Value Table, plus $80.

The Variable Name Table is searched. If the variable is already in the table, the token value for the existing variable is used. If the variable is not in the table, it will be inserted into both tables and a new token value will be used.

A source symbol is considered a valid variable if it starts with an alphabetic character and it is not a symbol in the Operator Name Table, which includes all the reserved words.

The variable is considered to be a string if it ends with $; otherwise it is a numeric variable. If it is a string variable, $ is stored with the variable name characters.

The routine also determines if the variable is an array by looking for **(**. If the variable is an array, **(** is stored with the variable name characters in the Variable Name Table. As a result, ABC, ABC$, and ABC(n) are all recognized as different variables.

TNCON ($A400)
TNCON is called by the ESRT instruction. Its purpose is to examine the current source symbol for a numeric constant, using the floating point package. If the symbol is not a numeric constant, the routine returns *fail*.

If the symbol is a numeric constant, the floating point package has converted it to a floating point number. The resulting six-byte constant is placed in the output buffer preceded by the $0E numeric constant token. The routine then exits with *pass* indicated.

TSCON ($A428)
TSCON is called by the ESRT instruction. Its purpose is to examine the current symbol for a string constant. If the symbol is not a string constant, the routine returns *fail*.

If the first character of the symbol is '', the symbol is a string constant. The routine will place the string constant token ($0F) into the output buffer, followed by a string length byte, followed by the string characters.

The string constant consists of all the characters that follow the starting double quote up to the ending double quote. If the EOL character ($9B) is found before the ending double quote, an ending double quote is assumed. The EOL is not part of the string. The starting and ending double quotes are not saved with the string. All 256 character codes except $9B (EOL) and $22 ('') are allowed in the string.

SEARCH ($A462)
This is a general purpose table search routine used to find a source symbol character string in a table.

The table to be searched is assumed to have entries which consist of a fixed length part (0 to 255 bytes) followed by a variable length ATASCII part. The last character of the ATASCII part is assumed to have the most significant bit ($80) on. The last table entry is assumed to have the first ATASCII character as $00.

Upon entry, the X register contains the length of the fixed part of the table (0 to 255). The A, Y register pair points to the start of the table to be searched. The source string for comparison is pointed to by INBUFF plus the value in CIX.

Upon exit, the 6502 carry flag is clear if a match was found, and set if no match was found. The X register points to the end of the symbol, plus 1, in the buffer. The SRCADR ($95) two-byte cell points to the matched table entry. STENUM ($AF) contains the number, relative to zero, of the matched table entry.

SETCODE (A2C8)
The SETCODE routine is used to place a token in the next available position in the output (token) buffer. The value in COX determines the current displacement into the token buffer. After the token is placed in the buffer, COX is incremented by one. If COX exceeds 255, the LINE TOO LONG error message is generated.

Execution Overview

During the editing and pre-compiling phase, the user's statements were checked for correct syntax, tokenized, and put into the Statement Table. Then direct statements were passed to the Program Executor for immediate processing, while program statements awaited later processing by the Program Executor.

We now enter the execution phase of Atari BASIC. The Program Executor consists of three parts: routines which simulate the function of individual statement types; an expression execution routine which processes expressions (for example, A+B+3, A$(1,3), "HELP", A(3)+7.26E-13); and the Execution Control routine, which manages the whole process.

Execution Control

Execution Control is invoked in two situations. If the user has entered a direct statement, Execution Control does some initial processing and then calls the appropriate statement execution routine to simulate the requested operation. If the user has entered RUN as a direct statement, the statement execution routine for RUN instructs Execution Control to start processing statements from the beginning of the statement table.

When the editor has finished processing a direct statement, it initiates the Execution Control routine EXECNL ($A95F). Execution Control's job is to manage the process of statement simulation.

The editor has saved the address of the statement it processed in STMCUR and has put the statement in the Statement Table. Since this is a direct statement, the line number is $8000, and the statement is saved as the last line in the Statement Table.

The fact that a direct statement is always the last statement in the Statement Table gives a test for the end of a user's program.

The high-order byte of the direct statement line number ($8000) has its most significant bit on. Loading this byte ($80) into the 6502 accumulator will set the minus flag on. The line number of any program statement is less than or equal to $7FFF. Loading the high order byte ($7F or less) of a program line number into the accumulator will set the 6502 minus flag off. This gives a simple test for a direct statement.

Initialization

Execution Control uses several parameters to help it manage the task of statement execution.

STMCUR holds the address in the Statement Table of the line currently being processed.

LLNGTH holds the length of the current line.

NXTSTD holds the displacement in the current line of the next statement to process.

STMCUR already contains the correct value when Execution Control begins processing. SETLN1 ($B81B) is called to store the correct values into LLNGTH and NXTSTD.

Statement Execution

Since the user may have changed his or her mind about execution, the routine checks to see if the user hit the break key. If the user did hit BREAK, Execution Control carries out XSTOP ($B793), the same routine that is executed when the STOP statement is encountered. At the end of its execution, the XSTOP routine gives control to the beginning of the editor.

If the user did not hit BREAK, Execution Control checks to see whether we are at the end of the tokenized line. Since this is the first statement in the line, we can't be at the end of the line. So why do the test? Because this part of the routine is executed once for each statement in the line in order to tell us when we do reach the end of the line. (The end-of-line procedure will be discussed later in this chapter.)

The statement length byte (the displacement to the next statement in the line) is the first byte in a statement. (See Chapter 3.) The displacement *to* this byte was saved in NXTSTD. Execution Control now loads this new statement's displacement using the value in NXTSTD.

The byte after the statement length in the line is the statement name token. Execution Control loads the statement name token into the A register. It saves the displacement to the next byte, the first of the statement's tokens, in STINDEX for the use of the statement simulation routines.

The statement name token is used as an index to find this statement's entry in the Statement Execution Table. Each table entry consists of the address, minus 1, of the routine that will simulate that statement. This simulation routine is called by pushing the address from the table onto the 6502 CPU stack and doing an RTS. Later, when a simulation routine is finished, it can do an RTS and return to Execution Control. (The name of most of the statement simulation routines in the BASIC listing is the statement name preceded by an X: XFOR, XRUN, XLIST.)

Most of the statement simulation routines return to Execution Control after processing.

Execution Control again tests for BREAK and checks for the end of the line. As long as we are not at end-of-line, it continues to execute statements. When we reach end-of-line, it does some end-of-line processing.

End-of-line Handling in a Direct Statement

When we come to the end of the line in a direct statement, Execution Control has done its job and jumps to SNX3. The READY message is printed and control goes back to the Program Editor.

End-of-line Handling during Program Execution

Program execution is initiated when the user types RUN. Execution Control handles RUN like any other direct statement. The statement simulation routine for RUN initializes STMCUR, NXTSTD, and LLNGTH to indicate the first statement of the first line in the Statement Table, then returns to Execution Control. Execution Control treats this first program statement as the next statement to be executed, picking up the statement name tokens and calling the simulation routines.

Usually, Execution Control is unaware of whether it is processing a direct statement or a program statement. End-of-line is the only time the routine needs to make a distinction.

At the end of every program line, Execution Control gets the length of the current line and calls GNXTL to update the address in STMCUR to make the next line in the Statement Table the new current line. Then it calls TENDST ($A9E2) to test the new line number to see if it is another program line or a direct statement. If it is a direct statement, we are at the end of the user's program.

Since the direct statement includes the RUN command that started program execution, Execution Control does not execute the line. Instead, Execution Control calls the same routine that would have been called if the program had contained an END statement (XEND, at $B78D). XEND does some end-of-program processing, causes READY to be printed, and returns to the beginning of the editor.

If we are not at the end of the user's program, processing continues with the new current line.

Execution Control Subroutines

TENDST ($A9E2)

Exit parameters: The minus flag is set on if we are at the end of program.

This routine checks for the end of the user's program in the Statement Table.

The very last entry in the Statement Table is always a direct statement. Whenever the statement indicated by STMCUR is the direct statement, we have finished processing the user's program.

The line number of a direct statement is $8000. The line number of any other statement is $7FFF or less. TENDST determines if the current statement is the direct statement by loading the high-order byte of the line number into the A register. This byte is at a displacement of one from the address in STMCUR. If this byte is $80 (a direct statement), loading it turns the 6502 minus flag on. Otherwise, the minus flag is turned off.

GETSTMT ($A9A2)

Entry parameters: TSLNUM contains the line number of the statement whose address is required.

Exit parameters: If the line number is found, the STMCUR contains the address of the statement and the carry flag is set off (clear). If the line number does not exist, STMCUR contains the address where a statement with that line number should be, and the carry flag is set on (set).

The purpose of this routine is to find the address of the statement whose line number is contained in TSLNUM.

The routine saves the address currently in STMCUR into SAVCUR and then sets STMCUR to indicate the top of the

Statement Table. The line whose address is in STMCUR is called the current line or statement.

GETSTMT then searches the Statement Table for the statement whose line number is in TSLNUM. The line number in TSLNUM is compared to the line number of the current line. If they are equal, then the required statement has been found. Its address is in STMCUR, so GETSTMT clears the 6502 carry flag and is finished.

If TSLNUM is smaller than the current statement line number, GETSTMT gets the length of the current statement by executing GETLL ($A9DD). GNXTL ($A9D0) is executed to make the next line in the statement table the current statement by putting its address into STMCUR. GETSTMT then repeats the comparison of TSLNUM and the line number of the current line in the same manner.

If TSLNUM is greater than the current line number, then a line with this line number does not exist. STMCUR already points to where the line should be, the 6502 carry flag is already set, and the routine is done.

GETLL ($A9DD)
Entry parameters: STMCUR indicates the line whose length is desired.

Exit parameters: Register A contains the length of the current line.

GETLL gets the length of the current line (that is, the line whose address is in STMCUR).

The line length is at a displacement of two into the line. GETLL loads the length into the A register and is done.

GNXTL ($A9D0)
Entry parameters: STMCUR contains the address of the current line, and register A contains the length of the current line.

Exit parameters: STMCUR contains the address of the next line.

This routine gets the next line in the statement table and makes it the current line.

GNXTL adds the length of the current line (contained in the A register) to the address of the current line in STMCUR. This process yields the address of the next line in the statement table, which replaces the value in STMCUR.

SETLN1 ($B81B)

Entry parameters: STMCUR contains the address of the current line.

Exit parameters: LLNGTH contains the length of the current line. NXTSTD contains the displacement in the line to the next statement to be executed (in this case, the first statement in the line).

This routine initializes several line parameters so that Execution Control can process the line.

The routine gets the length of the line, which is at a displacement of two from the start of the line.

SETLN1 loads a value of three into the Y register to indicate the displacement into the line of the first statement and stores the value into NXTSTD as the displacement to the next statement for execution.

SETLINE ($B818)

Entry parameters: TSLNUM contains the line number of a statement.

Exit parameters: STMCUR contains the address of the statement whose line number is in TSLNUM. LLNGTH contains the length of the line. NXTSTD contains the displacement in the line to the next statement to be executed (in this case, the first statement in the line). Carry is set if the line number does not exist.

This routine initializes several line parameters so that execution control can process the line.

SETLINE first calls GETSTMT ($A9A2) to find the address of the line whose number is in TSLNUM and put that address into STMCUR. It then continues exactly like SETLN1.

Execute Expression

The Execute Expression routine is entered when the Program Executor needs to evaluate a BASIC expression within a statement. It is also the executor for the LET and implied LET statements.

Expression operators have an order of precedence; some must be simulated before others. To properly evaluate an expression, Execute Expression rearranges it during the evaluation.

Expression Rearrangement Concepts

Operator precedence rules in algebraic expressions are so simple and so unconscious that most people aren't aware of following them. When you evaluate a simple expression like $Y=AX^2+BX+C$, you don't think: "Exponentiation has a higher precedence than multiplication, which has a higher precedence than addition; therefore, I will first square the X, then perform the multiplication." You just do it.

Computers don't develop habits or common sense — they have to be specifically commanded. It would be nice if we could just type $Y=AX^2+BX+C$ into our machine and have the computer understand, but instead we must separate all our variables with operators. We also have to learn a few new operators, such as * for multiply and ^ for exponentiation.

Given that we are willing to adjust our thinking this much, we enter Y=A*X^2+B*X+C. The new form of expression does not quite have the same feel as $Y=AX^2+BX+C$; we have translated normal human patterns halfway into a form the computer can use.

Even the operation X^2 causes another problem for the computer. It would really prefer that we give it the two values first, then tell it what to do with them. Since the computer still needs separators between items, we should write X^2 as X,2,^.

Now we have something the computer can work with. It can obtain the two values X,2, apply the operator ^, and get a result without having to look ahead.

If we were to transcribe X^2*A in the same manner, we would have X,2,^,A,*. The value returned by X,2,^ is the first value to multiply, so the value pair for multiplication is (X,2,^) and A. Again we have two values followed by an operator, and the computer can understand.

If we continue to transcribe the expression by pairing values and operators, we find that we don't want to add the value X^2*A to B; we want to add the value X^2*A to B*X. Therefore, we need to tell the computer X,2,^,A,*,B,X,*,+. The value pair for the operator + is (X,2,^,A,*) and (B,X,*).

The value pair for the final operation, =, is (X,2,^,A,*,B,X,*,+,C,+) and Y. So the complete translation of $Y=AX^2+BX+C$ is X,2,^,A,*,B,X,*,+,C,+,Y,=.

Very few people other than Forth programmers put up with this form of expression transcription. Therefore, Atari BASIC was designed to perform this translation for us, provided we use the correct symbols, like * and ^.

The Expression Rearrangement Algorithm

The algorithm for expression rearrangement requires two LIFO stacks for temporary storage of the rearranged terms. The Operator Stack is used for temporarily saving operators; the Argument Stack is used for saving arguments. Arguments are values consisting of variables, constants, and the constant-like values resulting from previous expression operations.

Operator Precedence Table

The *Atari BASIC User's Manual* lists the operators by precedence. The highest-precedence operators, like <, >, and =<, are at the top of the list; the lowest-precedence operator, OR, is at the bottom. The operators at the top of the list get executed before the operators at the bottom of the list.

The operators in the precedence table are arranged in the same order as the Operator Name Table. Thus the token values can be used as direct indices to obtain an operator precedence value.

The entry for each operator in the Operator Precedence Table contains two precedence values, the *go-onto-stack* precedence and the *come-off-stack* precedence. When a new operator has been plucked from an expression, its go-onto-stack precedence is tested in relation to the top-of-stack operator's come-off-stack precedence.

Expression Rearrangement Procedure

The symbols of the expression (the arguments and the operators) are accessed sequentially from left to right, then rearranged into their correct order of precedence by the following procedure:

1. Initialize the Operator Stack with the Start Of Expression (SOE) operator.
2. Get the next symbol from the expression.
3. If the symbol is an argument (variable or constant), place the argument on the top of the Argument Stack. Go to step 2.
4. If the symbol is an operator, save the operator in the temporary save cell, SAVEOP.
5. Compare the go-onto-stack precedence of the operator in SAVEOP to the come-off stack precedence of the operator on the top of the Operator Stack.
6. If the top-of-stack operator's precedence is less than the precedence of the SAVEOP operator, then the SAVEOP operator is pushed onto the Operator Stack. When the push is done, go back to step 2.
7. If the top-of-stack operator's precedence is equal to or greater than the precedence of the SAVEOP operator, then pop the top-of-stack operator and execute it. When the execution is done, go back to step 5 and continue.

The Expression Rearrangement Procedure has one apparent problem. It seems that there is no way to stop it. There are no exits for the ''evaluation done'' condition. This problem is handled by enclosing the expression with two special operators: the Start Of Expression (SOE) operator, and the End Of Expression (EOE) operator. Remember that SOE was the first operator placed on the Operator Stack, in step 1. Execution code for the SOE operator will cause the procedure to be exited in step 7, when SOE is popped and executed. The EOE operator is never executed. EOE's function is to force the execution of SOE.

The precedence values of SOE and EOE are set to insure that SOE is executed only when the expression evaluation is finished. The SOE come-off-stack precedence is set so that its value is always less than all the other operators' go-onto-stack precedence values. The EOE go-onto-stack precedence is set so that its value is always equal to or less than all the other operators' (including SOE's) come-off-stack precedence values.

Because SOE and EOE precedence are set this way, no operator other than EOE can cause SOE to be popped and executed. Second, EOE will cause all stacked operators, including SOE, to be popped and executed. Since SOE is always at the start of the expression and EOE is always at the end of the expression, SOE will not be executed until the expression is fully evaluated.

In actual practice, the SOE operator is not physically part of the expression in the Statement Table. The Expression Rearrangement Procedure initializes the Operator Stack with the SOE operator before it begins to examine the expression.

There is no single operator defined as the End Of Expression (EOE) operator. Every BASIC expression is followed by a symbol like :, THEN, or the EOL character. All of these symbols function as operators with precedence equivalent to the precedence of our phantom EOE operator. The THEN token, for example, serves a dual purpose. It not only indicates the THEN action, but also acts as the EOE operator when it follows an expression.

Expression Rearrangement Example

To illustrate how the expression evaluation procedure works, including expression rearrangement, we will evaluate our Y=A*X^2+B*X+C example and see how the expression is rearranged to X,2,^,A,*,B,X,*,+,C,+,Y,= with a correct result. To work our example, we need to establish a precedence table for the operators. The values in Figure 7-1 are similar to the actual values of these operators in Atari BASIC. The lowest precedence value is zero; the highest precedence value is $0F.

Figure 7-1. Example Precedence Table

operator symbol	go-on-stack precedence	come-off-stack precedence
SOE	NA	$00
+	$09	$09
*	$0A	$0A
^	$0C	$0C
=	$0F	$01
! (EOE)	$00	NA

Symbol values and notations. In the example steps, the term PS*n* refers to step *n* in the Expression Rearrangement Procedure (page 57). Step 5, for instance, will be called PS5.

In the actual expression, the current symbol will be underlined. If B is the current symbol, then the actual expression will appear as Y=A*X 2+**B***X+C . In the rearranged expression, the symbols which have been evaluated up to that point will also be underlined.

The values of the variables are:

A=2 C=6
B=4 X=3

The variable values are assumed to be accessed when the variable arguments are popped for operator execution.

The end-of-expression operator is represented by ! .

Example step 1.

Actual Expression: Y=A*X^2+B*X+C!
Rearranged Expression: X,2,^,A,*,B,X,*,+,C,+,Y,=,!
Argument Stack:
Operator Stack: SOE
SAVEOP:

PS1 has been executed. The Operator Stack has been initialized with the SOE operator. We are ready to start processing the expression symbols.

Example step 2.

Actual Expression: **Y**=A*X^2+B*X+C!
Rearranged Expression: X,2,^,A,*,B,X,*,+,C,+,Y,=,!
Argument Stack: Y
Operator Stack: SOE
SAVEOP:

The first symbol, Y, has been obtained and stacked in the Argument Stack according to PS2 and PS3.

Example step 3.

Actual Expression: Y**=**A*X^2+B*X+C!
Rearranged Expression: X,2,^,A,*,B,X,*,+,C,+,Y,=,!
Argument Stack: Y
Operator Stack: SOE,=
SAVEOP: =

Operator = has been obtained via PS2. The relative precedences of SOE ($00) and = ($0F) dictate that the = be placed on the Operator Stack via PS6.

Example step 4.

Actual Expression: Y=**A***X∧2+B*X+C!
Rearranged Expression: X,2,∧,A,*,B,X,*,+,C,+,Y,=,!
Argument Stack: Y,A
Operator Stack: SOE,=
SAVEOP:

The next symbol is A. This symbol is pushed onto the Argument Stack via PS3.

Example step 5.

Actual Expression: Y=A*****X∧2+B*X+C!
Rearranged Expression: X,2,∧,A,*,B,X,*,+,C,+,Y,=,!
Argument Stack: Y,A
Operator Stack: SOE,=,*
SAVEOP: *

The next symbol is the operator *. The relative precedence of * and = dictates that * be pushed onto the Operator Stack.

Example step 6.

Actual Expression: Y=A***X**∧2+B*X+C!
Rearranged Expression: X,2,∧,A,*,B,X,*,+,C,+,Y,=,!
Argument Stack: Y,A,X
Operator Stack: SOE,=,*
SAVEOP:

The next symbol is the variable X. This symbol is stacked on the Argument Stack according to PS3.

Example step 7.

Actual Expression: Y=A*X**∧**2+B*X+C!
Rearranged Expression: X,2,∧,A,*,B,X,*,+,C,+,Y,=,!
Argument Stack: Y,A,X
Operator Stack: SOE,=,*,∧
SAVEOP: ∧

The next symbol is ∧ . The relative precedence of the and the * dictate that ∧ be stacked via PS6.

Example step 8.

Actual Expression: Y=A*X^ 2+B*X+C!
Rearranged Expression: X,2,^,A,*,B,X,*,+,C,+,Y,=,!
Argument Stack: Y,A,X,2
Operator Stack: SOE,=,*,^
SAVEOP:

The next symbol is 2. This symbol is stacked on the Argument Stack via PS3.

Example step 9.

Actual Expression: Y=A*X^ 2+B*X+C!
Rearranged Expression: **X,2,^,**A,*,B,X,*,+,C,+,Y,=,!
Argument Stack: Y,A,9
Operator Stack: SOE,=,*
SAVEOP: +

The next symbol is the operator +. The precedence of the operator that was at the top of the stack, ^ , is greater than the precedence of +. PS7 dictates that the top-of-stack operator be popped and executed.

The ^ operator is popped. Its execution causes arguments X and 2 to be popped from the Argument Stack, replacing the variable with the value that it represents and operating on the two values yielded: X^ 2=3^ 2=9. The resulting value, 9, is pushed onto the Argument Stack. The + operator remains in SAVEOP. We continue at PS5.

Note that in the rearranged expression the first symbols, X,2, ^, have been evaluated according to plan.

Example step 10.

Actual Expression: Y=A*X^ 2+B*X+C!
Rearranged Expression: **X,2,^,A,*,**B,X,*,+,C,+,Y,=,!
Argument Stack: Y,18
Operator Stack: SOE,=
SAVEOP: +

This step originates at PS5. The SAVEOP operator, +, has a precedence that is less than the operator which was at the top of the stack, *. Therefore, according to PS7, the * is popped and executed.

The execution of * results in A*9=2*9=18. The resulting value is pushed onto the Argument Stack.

Example step 11.

Actual Expression: Y=A*X^2+B*X+C!
Rearranged Expression: **X,2,^,A,***,B,X,*,+,C,+,Y,=,!
Argument Stack: Y,18
Operator Stack: SOE,=,+
SAVEOP:

When step 10 finished, we went to PS5. The operator in SAVEOP was +. Since + has a higher precedence than the top-of-stack operator, =, the + operator was pushed onto the Operator Stack via PS6.

Example step 12.

Actual Expression: Y=A*X^2+B*X+C!
Rearranged Expression: **X,2,^,A,***,B,X,*,+,C,+,Y,=,!
Argument Stack: Y,18,B
Operator Stack: SOE,=,+
SAVEOP:

The next symbol is the variable B, which is pushed onto the Argument Stack via PS3.

Example step 13.

Actual Expression: Y=A*X^2+B*X+C!
Rearranged Expression: **X,2,^,A,***,B,X,*,+,C,+,Y,=,!
Argument Stack: Y,18,B
Operator Stack: SOE,=,+,*
SAVEOP: *

The next symbol is the operator *. Since * has a higher precedence than the top-of-stack +, * is pushed onto the stack via PS6.

Example step 14.

Actual Expression: Y=A*X^2+B*X+C!
Rearranged Expression: **X,2,^,A,***,B,X,*,+,C,+,Y,=,!
Argument Stack: Y,18,B,X
Operator Stack: SOE,=,+,*
SAVEOP:

The variable X is pushed onto the Argument Stack via PS3.

Example step 15.

Actual Expression: Y=A*X^2+B*X+C!
Rearranged Expression: **X,2,^,A,*,B,X,***,+,C,+,Y,=,!

Argument Stack: Y,18,12
Operator Stack: SOE, =, +
SAVEOP: +

The operator + is retrieved from the expression. Since + has a lower precedence than * which is at the top of the stack, * is popped and executed.

The execution of * causes B*X=4*3=12. The resulting value of 12 is pushed onto the Argument Stack. We will continue at PS5 via the PS7 exit rule.

Example step 16.

Actual Expression: Y=A*X^2+B*X+C!
Rearranged Expression: **X,2,^,A,*,B,X,*,+,**C,+,Y,=,!
Argument Stack: Y,30
Operator Stack: SOE, =
SAVEOP: +

This step starts at PS5. The SAVEOP operator, +, has precedence that is equal to the precedence of the top-of-stack operator, also +. Therefore, + is popped from the operator stack and executed. The results of the execution cause 18+12, or 30, to be pushed onto the Argument Stack. PS5 is called.

Example step 17.

Actual Expression: Y=A*X^2+B*X+C!
Rearranged Expression: **X,2,^,A,*,B,X,*,+,**C,+,Y,=,!
Argument Stack: Y,30
Operator Stack: SOE, =, +
SAVEOP:

This step starts at PS5. The SAVEOP is +. The top-of-stack operator, =, has a lower precedence than +; therefore, + is pushed onto the stack via PS6.

Example step 18.

Actual Expression: Y=A*X^2+B*X+**C**!
Rearranged Expression: **X,2,^,A,*,B,X,*,+,**C,+,Y,=,!
Argument Stack: Y,30,C
Operator Stack: SOE, =, +
SAVEOP:

The variable C is pushed onto the Argument Stack via PS3.

Example step 19.

Actual Expression: Y=A*X^2+B*X+C!
Rearranged Expression: **X,2,^,A,*,B,X,*,+,C,+,**Y,=,!
Argument Stack: Y,36
Operator Stack: SOE,=
SAVEOP: !

The EOE operator ! is plucked from the expression. The EOE has a lower precedence than the top-of-stack + operator. Therefore, + is popped and executed. The resulting value of 30+6, 36, is pushed onto the Argument Stack. PS5 will execute next.

Example step 20.

Actual Expression: Y=A*X^2+B*X+C!
Rearranged Expression: **X,2,^,A,*,B,X,*,+,C,+,Y,=,**!
Argument Stack:
Operator Stack: SOE
SAVEOP: !

This step starts at PS5. The ! operator has a lower precedence than the top-of-stack = operator, which is popped and executed. The execution of = causes the value 36 to be assigned to Y. This leaves the Argument Stack empty. PS5 will be executed next.

Example step 21.

Actual Expression: Y=A*X^2+B*X+C!
Rearranged Expression: **X,2,^,A,*,B,X,*,+,C,+,Y,=,!**
Argument Stack:
Operator Stack:
SAVEOP: !

The ! operator in SAVEOP causes the SOE operator to be popped and executed. The execution of SOE terminates the expression evaluation.

Note that the rearranged expression was executed exactly as predicted.

Mainline Code

The Execute Expression code implements the Expression Rearrangement Procedure. The mainline code starts at the EXEXPR label at $AAE0. The input to EXEXPR starts at the current token in the current statement. STMCUR points to the current statement. STINDEX contains the displacement to the current token in the STMCUR statement. The output of EXEXPR is whatever values remain on the top of the argument stack when the expression evaluation is finished.

In the following discussion, PS*n* refers to the procedure step *n* in the Expression Rearrangement Procedure.

PS1, initialization, occurs when EXEXPR is entered. EXPINT is called to initialize the operator and argument stacks. EXPINT places the SOE operator on the operator stack.

PS2, which obtains the next token, directly follows initialization at EXNXT ($AAE3). The code calls EGTOKEN to get the next expression symbol and classify it. If the token is an argument, the carry will be set. If the token is an operator, the carry will be clear.

If the token is an argument, PS3 is implemented via a call to ARGPUSH. After the argument is pushed onto the argument stack, EXNXT (PS2) will receive control.

If the token was an operator, then the code at EXOT ($AAEE) will be executed. This code implements PS4 by saving the token in EXSVOP.

PS5, which compares the precedents of the EXSVOP token and the top-of-stack token, follows EXOT at EXPTST ($AAFA). This code also executes the SOE operator. If SOE is popped, then Execute Expression finishes via RTS.

If the top-of-stack operator precedence is less than the EXSVOP operator precedence, PS6 is implemented at EOPUSH ($AB15). EOPUSH pushes EXSVOP onto the operator stack and then goes to EXNXT (PS2).

If the top-of-stack operator precedence is greater than or equal to the EXSVOP operator precedence, then PS7 is implemented at EXOPOP ($AB0B). EXOPOP will pop the top-of-stack operator and execute it by calling EXOP. When EXOP is done, control passes to EXPTST (PS5).

Expression Evaluation Stacks

The two expression evaluation stacks, the Argument Stack and the Operator Stack, share a single 256-byte memory area. The Argument Stack grows upward from the lower end of the 256-byte area. The Operator Stack grows downward from the upper end of the 256-byte area.

The 256-byte stack area is the multipurpose buffer at the start of the RAM tables. The buffer is pointed to by the

ARGSTK (also ARGOPS) zero-page pointer at $80. The current index into the Argument Stack is maintained by ARSLVL ($AA). When the Argument Stack is empty, ARSLVL is zero.

The OPSTKX cell maintains the current index into the Operator Stack. When the Operator Stack is initialized with the SOE operator, OPSTKX is initialized to $FF. As operators are added to the Operator Stack, OPSTKX is decremented. As arguments are added to the Argument Stack, ARSLVL is incremented.

Since the two stacks share a single 256-byte memory area, there is a possibility that the stacks will run into each other. The code at $ABC1 is used to detect a stack collision. It does this by comparing the values in ARSLVL and OPSTKX. If ARSLVL is greater than or equal to OPSTKX, then a stack collision occurs, sending the STACK OVERFLOW error to the user.

Operator Stack

Each entry on the Operator Stack is a single-byte operator-type token. Operators are pushed onto the stack at EXOPUSH ($AB15) and are popped from the stack at EXOPOP ($AB0B).

Argument Stack

Each entry on the Argument Stack is eight bytes long. The format of these entries is described in Figures 7-2, 7-3, and 7-4, and are the same as the formats for entries in the Variable Value Table.

Unlike the Variable Value Table, the Argument Stack must deal with both variables and constants. In Figure 7-2, we see that VNUM is used to distinguish variable entries from constant entries.

The SADR and AADR fields in the entries for strings and arrays are of special interest. (See Figures 7-3 and 7-4.) When a string or array variable is dimensioned, space for the variable is created in the string/array space. The displacement to the start of the variable's area within the string/array space is placed in the SADR/AADR fields at that time. A displacement is used rather than an absolute address because the absolute address can change if any program changes are made after the DIM statement is executed.

Execute Expression needs these values to be absolute address values within the 6502 address space. When a string/array variable is retrieved from the Variable Value Table, the displacement is transformed to an absolute address. When (and if) the variable is put back into the Variable Value Table, the absolute address is converted back to a displacement.

The entries for string constants also deserve some special attention. String constants are the quoted strings within the user program. These strings become part of the tokenized statements in the Statement Table. When Execute Expression gets a string token, it will create a string constant Argument Stack entry. This entry's SADR is an absolute address pointer to the string in the Statement Table. SLEN and SDIM are set to the actual length of the quoted string.

Argument Work Area

An argument which is currently being examined by Execute Expression is kept in a special zero-page Argument Work Area (AWA). The AWA starts at the label VTYPE at $D2.

Figure 7-2. Argument Stack Entry

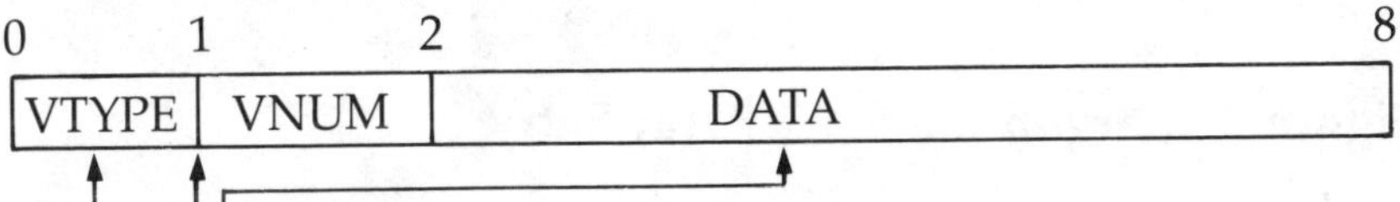

Data Field. Format depends on VTYPE.

If VNUM = 0, the entry is a constant.
If VNUM > 0, the entry is a variable. In this case, the VNUM value is the entry number in the Variable Value Table. The token representing this variable is VNUM + $80.

$00 = Data is a six-byte floating point constant.
$80 = Data represents an undimensioned string.
$81 = Data represents a dimensioned string with a relative address pointer.
$83 = Data represents a dimensioned string with an absolute address pointer.
$40 = Data represents an undimensioned array.
$41 = Data represents a dimensioned array with a relative address pointer.
$43 = Data represents a dimensioned array with an absolute address pointer.

Figure 7-3. Argument Stack String Entry

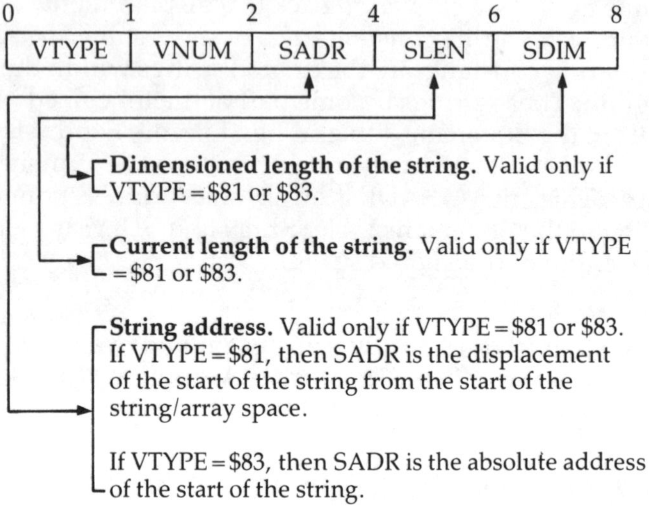

Figure 7-4. Argument Stack Array Entry

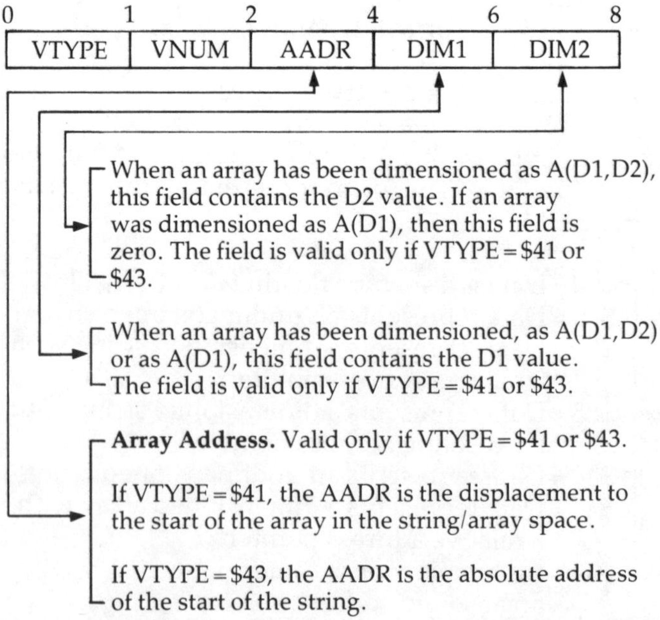

Operator Executions

An operator is executed when it is popped from the Operator Stack. Execute Expression calls EXOP at $AB20 to start this execution. The EXOP routine uses the operator token value as an index into the Operator Execution Table ($AA70). The operator execution address from this table, minus 1, is placed on the 6502 CPU stack. An RTS is then executed to begin executing the operator's code.

The names of the operator execution routines all begin with the characters *XP*.

All the Atari BASIC functions, such as PEEK, RND, and ABS, are executed as operators.

Most routines for the execution of the operators are very simple and straightforward. For example, the * operator routine, XPMUL ($AC96), pops two arguments, multiplies them via the floating point package, pushes the result onto the argument stack, and returns.

String, Array, DIM, and Function Operations

Any array reference in an expression may be found in one of two forms: A(*x*) or A(*x*,*y*). The indices *x* and *y* may be any valid expression. The intent of the indices is to reference a specific array element.

Before the specific element reference can take place, the *x* and/or *y* index expressions must be fully evaluated. To do this, the characters '(' ',' and ')' are made operators. The precedence of these operators forces things to happen in the correct sequence. Figure 7-5 shows the relative precedence of these operators for an array.

Figure 7-5. Array Operator Precedence

operator symbol	go-on-stack precedence	come-off-stack precedence
(	$0F	$02
, *(comma)*	$04	$03
)	$04	$0E

As a result of these precedence values, (has a high enough precedence to go onto the stack, no matter what other operator is on the top of the stack.

The *comma*'s go-on-stack precedence will force all operators except (to be popped and executed. As a result, the *x* index sub-expression, in the expression A(*x*,*y*), will be fully evaluated and the final *x* index value will be pushed onto the Argument Stack.

The *comma* will then be placed onto the Operator Stack. Its come-off-stack precedence is such that no other operator, except) , will pop it off.

The) operator precedence will force any *y* index expression to be fully evaluated and the *y* index result value to be placed onto the Argument Stack.

It will then force the *comma* operator to be popped and executed. This action results in a *comma* counter being incremented.

The) will then force the (to be popped and executed. The execution of (results in the proper array element being referenced. The (operator will pop the indices from the Argument Stack. The number of indices (either zero or one) to be popped is governed by the *comma* counter, which was incremented by one for each *comma* that was popped and executed.

Atari BASIC has numerous (tokens, and each causes a different (routine to be executed. These (operators are *array* (CALPRN), *string* (CSLPRN), *array DIM* (CDLPRN), *string DIM* (CDSLPR), *function* (CFLPRN), and the expression grouping CLPRN operator. The Syntax Table pseudo-instruction CHNG is used to change the CLPRN token to the other (tokens in accordance with the context of the grammar.

The expression operations for each of these various (operators in relation to *commas* and (is exactly the same. When (is executed, the *comma* count will show how many arguments the operator's code must pop from the argument stack. Each of these arguments will have been evaluated down to a single value in the form of a constant.

Execution Boundary Conditions

BASIC Language statements can be divided into groups with related functions. The execution boundary statements, RUN, STOP, CONT and END, cause a BASIC program to start or stop executing. The routines which simulate these statements are XRUN, XSTOP, XCONT, and XEND.

Program Termination Routines

Any BASIC statement can be used as either a direct statement or a program statement, but some only make sense in one mode. The STOP statement has no real meaning when entered as a direct statement. When the statement simulation routine for STOP is asked to execute in direct mode, it does as little processing as possible and exits. Useful processing occurs only when STOP is a program statement.

STOP ($B7A7). The XSTOP and XEND routines are similar and perform some of the same tasks. The tasks common to both are handled by the STOP routine.

If this statement is not a direct statement, the STOP routine saves the line number of the current line in STOPLN. This line number is used later for printing the STOPed message. It is also used by the CONT simulation routine (XCONT) to determine where to restart program execution. (Since XEND also uses this routine, it is possible to CONTinue after an END statement in the middle of a program.)

The STOP routine also resets the LIST and ENTER devices to the screen and the keyboard.

XSTOP ($B793). XSTOP does the common STOP processing and then calls :LPRTOKEN($B535) to print the STOPed message. It then calls one of the error printing routines, :ERRM2 ($B974), to output the AT LINE *nnn* portion. The :ERRM2 routine will not print anything if this was a direct statement. When :ERRM2 is finished, it jumps back to the start of the editor.

XEND ($B78D). XEND calls the STOP routine to save the current line number. It then transfers to the start of the editor via the SNX1 entry point. This turns off the sound, closes any open IOCBs, and prints the READY message. XEND also leaves values on the 6502 CPU stack. These values are thrown away when the editor resets the stack.

END OF PROGRAM. A user may have neglected to include an END statement in his program. In this case, when Execution Control comes to the end of the Statement Table it calls XEND, and the program is terminated exactly as if the last statement in the program were an END.

Program Initiation Routines

The statements that cause a user's program to begin execution are RUN and CONT. These statements are simulated by XRUN and XCONT.

XCONT ($B7BE). The CONT statement has no meaning when encountered as a program statement, so its execution has no effect.

When the user enters CONT as a direct statement, XCONT uses the line number that was saved in STOPLN to set Execution Control's line parameters (STMCUR, NXTSTD, and LLNGTH). This results in the current line being the line following the one whose line number is in STOPLN. This means that any statement following STOP or END on a line will not be executed; therefore, STOP and END should always be the last statement in the line.

If we are at the end of the Statement Table, XCONT terminates as if an END statement had been encountered in the program. If there are more lines to process, XCONT returns to Execution Control, which resumes processing at the line whose address was just put into STMCUR.

XRUN ($B74D). The RUN statement comes in two formats, RUN and RUN <filespec>. In the case of RUN <filespec>, XRUN executes XLOAD to load a saved program, which replaces the current one in memory. The process then proceeds like RUN.

XRUN sets up Execution Control's line pointers to indicate the first line in the Statement Table. It clears some flags used to control various other BASIC statements; for example, it resets STOPLN to 0. It closes all IOCBs and executes XCLR to reset all the variables to zero and get rid of any entries in the String/Array Table or the Runtime Stack.

If there is no program, so the only thing in the Statement Table is the direct statement, then XRUN does some clean-up, prints READY, and returns to the start of the editor, which resets the 6502 CPU stack.

If there is a program, XRUN returns to Execution Control, which starts processing the first statement in the table as the current statement.

When RUN <filespec> is used as a program statement, it performs the useful function of chaining to a new program, but if RUN alone is used as a program statement, an infinite loop will probably result.

Error Handling Routine

There are other conditions besides the execution boundary statements that terminate a program's execution. The most familiar are errors.

There are two kinds of errors that can occur during execution: Input/Output errors and BASIC language errors.

Any BASIC routine that does I/O calls the IOTEST routine ($BCB3) to check the outcome of the operation. If an error that needs to be reported to the user is indicated, IOTEST gets the error number that was returned by the Operating System and joins the Error Handling Routine, ERROR ($B940), which finishes processing the error.

When a BASIC language error occurs, the error number is generated by the Error Handling Routine. This routine calculates the error by having an entry point for every BASIC language error. At each entry point, there is a 6502 instruction that increments the error number. By the time the main routine, ERROR, is reached, the error number has been generated.

The Error Handling Routine calls STOP ($B7A7) to save the line number of the line causing the error in STOPLN. It tests TRAPLN to see if errors are being TRAPed. The TRAP option is on if TRAPLN contains a valid line number. In this case, the Error Handler does some clean-up and joins XGOTO, which transfers processing to the desired line.

If the high-order byte of the line number is $80 (not a valid line number), then we are not TRAPing errors. In this case, the Error Handler prints the four-part error message, which consists of ERROR, the error number, AT LINE, and finally the line number. If the line in error was a direct statement, the AT LINE part is not printed. The error handler resets ERRNUM to zero and is finished.

The Error Handling Routine does not do an orderly return, but jumps back to the start of the editor at the SYNTAX entry point where the 6502 stack is reset, clearing it of the now-unwanted return addresses.

Program Flow Control Statements

Execution Control always processes the statement in the Statement Table that follows the one it thinks it has just finished. This means that statements in a BASIC program are usually processed in sequential order.

Several statements, however, can change that order: GOTO, IF, TRAP, FOR, NEXT, GOSUB, RETURN, POP, and ON. They trick Execution Control by changing the parameters that it maintains.

Simple Flow Control Statements

XGOTO ($B6A3)

The simplest form of flow control transfer is the GOTO statement, simulated by the XGOTO routine.

Following the GOTO token in the tokenized line is an expression representing the line number of the statement that the user wishes to execute next. The first thing the XGOTO routine does is ask Execute Expression to evaluate the expression and convert it to a positive integer. XGOTO then calls the GETSTMT routine to find this line number in the Statement Table and change Execution Control's line parameters to indicate this line.

If the line number does not exist, XGOTO restores the line parameters to indicate the line containing the original GOTO, and transfers to the Error Handling Routine via the ERNOLN entry point. The Error Handling Routine processes the error and jumps to the start of the editor.

If the line number was found, XGOTO jumps to the beginning of Execution Control (EXECNL) rather than returning to the point in the routine from which it was called. This leaves garbage on the 6502 CPU stack, so XGOTO first pulls the return address off the stack.

XIF ($B778)

The IF statement changes the statement flow based on a condition. The simulation routine, XIF, begins by calling a subroutine of Execute Expression to evaluate the condition. Since this is a logical (rather than an arithmetic) operation, we are only interested in whether the value is zero or non-zero. If the expression was false (non-zero), XIF modifies Execution Control's line parameters to indicate the end of this line and then returns. Execution Control moves to the next line, skipping any remaining statements on the original IF statement line.

If the expression is true (zero), things get a little more complicated. Back during syntaxing, when a statement of the form IF <expression> THEN <statement> was encountered, the pre-compiler generated an end-of-statement token after THEN. XIF now tests for this token. If we are at the end of the statement, XIF returns to Execution Control, which processes what it thinks is the next statement in the current line, but which is actually the THEN <statement> part of the IF statement.

If XIF does not find the end-of-statement token, then the statement must have had the form IF <expression> THEN <line number>. XIF jumps to XGOTO, which finishes processing by changing Execution Control's line parameters to indicate the new line.

XTRAP ($B7E1)

The TRAP statement does not actually change the program flow when it is executed. Instead, the XTRAP simulation routine calls a subroutine of Execute Expression to evaluate the line number and then saves the result in TRAPLN ($BC).

The program flow is changed only if there is an error. The Error Handling Routine checks TRAPLN. If it contains a valid line number, the error routine does some initial set-up and joins the XGOTO routine to transfer to the new line.

Runtime Stack Routines

The rest of the Program Flow Control Statements use the Runtime Stack. They put items on the stack, inspect them, and/or remove them from the stack.

Every item on the Runtime Stack contains a four-byte header. This header consists of a one-byte type indication, a two-byte line number, and a one-byte displacement to the Statement Name Token. (See pages 18-19.) The type byte is the last byte placed on the stack for each entry. This means that the pointer to the top of the Runtime Stack (RUNSTK) points to the type byte of the most recent entry on the stack. A zero type byte indicates a GOSUB-type entry. Any non-zero type byte represents a FOR-type entry.

A GOSUB entry consists solely of the four-byte header. A FOR entry contains twelve additional bytes: a six-byte limit value and a six-byte step value.

Several routines are used by more than one of the statement simulation routines.

PSHRSTK ($B683) This routine expands the Runtime Stack by calling EXPLOW and then storing the type byte, line number, and displacement of the Statement Name Token on the stack.

POPRSTK ($B841) This routine makes sure there really is an entry on the Runtime Stack. POPRSTK saves the displacement to the statement name token in SVDISP, saves the line number in TSLNUM, and puts the type/variable number in the 6502 accumulator. It then removes the entry by calling the CONTLOW routine.

:GETTOK ($B737) This routine first sets up Execution Control's line parameters to point to the line whose number is in the entry just pulled from the Runtime Stack. If the line was found, :GETTOK updates the line parameters to indicate that the statement causing this entry is now the current statement. Finally, it loads the 6502 accumulator with the statement name token from the statement that created this entry and returns to its caller.

If the line number does not exist, :GETTOK restores the current statement address and exits via the ERGFDEL entry point in the Error Handling Routine.

Now let's look at the simulation routines for the statements that utilize the Runtime Stack.

XFOR ($B64B)

XFOR is the name of the simulation routine which executes a FOR statement.

In the statement FOR I=1 TO 10 STEP 2:
I is the *loop control variable*

1 is its *initial value*
10 is the *limit value*
2 is the *step value*

XFOR calls Execute Expression, which evaluates the initial value and puts it in the loop control variable's entry in the Variable Value Table.

Then it calls a routine to remove any currently unwanted stack entries — for example, a previous FOR statement that used the same loop control variable as this one.

XFOR calls a subroutine of Execute Expression to evaluate the limit and step values. If no step value was given, a value of 1 is assigned. It expands the Runtime Stack using EXPLOW and puts the values on the stack.

XFOR uses PSHRSTK to put the header entry on the stack. It uses the variable number of the loop control variable (machine-language ORed with $80) as the type byte. XFOR now returns to Execution Control, which processes the statement following the FOR statement.

The FOR statement does not change program flow. It just sets up an entry on the Runtime Stack so that the NEXT statement can change the flow.

XNEXT ($B6CF)

The XNEXT routine decides whether to alter the program flow, depending on the top Runtime Stack entry. XNEXT calls the POPRSTK routine repeatedly to remove four-byte header entries from the top of the stack until an entry is found whose variable number (type) matches the NEXT statement's variable token. If the top-of-stack or GOSUB-type entry is encountered, XNEXT transfers control to an Error Handling Routine via the ERNOFOR entry point.

To compute the new value of the loop variable, XNEXT calls a subroutine of Execute Expression to retrieve the loop control variable's current value from the Variable Value Table, then gets the step value from the Runtime Stack, and finally adds the step value to the variable value. XNEXT again calls an Execute Expression subroutine to update the variable's value in the Variable Value Table.

XNEXT gets the limit value from the stack to determine if the variable's value is at or past the limit. If so, XNEXT returns to Execution Control without changing the program flow, and the next sequential statement is processed.

If the variable's value has not reached the limit, XNEXT returns the entry to the Runtime Stack and changes the program flow. POPRSTK already saved the line number of the FOR statement in TSLNUM and the displacement to the statement name token in SVDISP. XNEXT calls the :GETTOK routine to indicate the FOR statement as the current statement.

If the token at the saved displacement is not a FOR statement name token, then the Error Handling Routine is given control at the ERGFDEL entry point. Otherwise, XNEXT returns to Execution Control, which starts processing with the statement following the FOR statement.

XGOSUB ($B6A0)

The GOSUB statement causes an entry to be made on the Runtime Stack and also changes program flow.

The XGOSUB routine puts the GOSUB-type indicator (zero) into the 6502 accumulator and calls PSHRSTK to put a four-byte header entry on the Runtime Stack for later use by the simulation routine for RETURN. XGOSUB then processes exactly like XGOTO.

XRTN ($B719)

The RETURN statement causes an entry to be removed from the Runtime Stack. The XRTN routine uses the information in this entry to determine what statement should be processed next.

The XRTN first calls POPRSTK to remove a GOSUB-type entry from the Runtime Stack. If there are no GOSUB entries on the stack, then the Error Handling Routine is called at ERBRTN. Otherwise, XRTN calls :GETTOK to indicate that the statement which created the Runtime Stack entry is now the current statement.

If the statement name token at the saved displacement is not the correct type, then XRTN exits via the Error Handling Routine's ERGFDEL entry point. Otherwise, control is returned to the caller. When Execution Control was the caller, then GOSUB must have created the stack entry, and processing will start at the statement following the GOSUB.

Several other statements put a GOSUB-type entry on the stack when they need to mark their place in the program. They do not affect program flow and will be discussed in later chapters.

XPOP ($B841)
The XPOP routine uses POPRSTK to remove an entry from the Runtime Stack. A user might want to do this if he decided not to RETURN from a GOSUB.

XON ($B7ED)
The ON statement comes in two versions: ON-GOTO and ON-GOSUB. Only ON-GOSUB uses the Runtime Stack.

The XON routine evaluates the variable and converts it to an integer (MOD 256). If the value is zero, XON returns to Execution Control without changing the program flow.

If the value is non-zero and this is an ON-GOSUB statement, XON puts a GOSUB-type entry on the Runtime Stack for RETURN to use later.

From this point, ON-GOSUB and ON-GOTO perform in exactly the same manner. XON uses the integer value calculated earlier to index into the tokenized statement line to the correct GOTO or GOSUB line number. If there is no line number corresponding to the index, XON returns to Execution Control without changing program flow. Otherwise, XON joins XGOTO to finish processing.

Tokenized Program Save and Load

The tokenized program can be saved to and reloaded from a peripheral device, such as a disk or a cassette. The primary statement for saving the tokenized program is SAVE. The saved program is reloaded into RAM with the LOAD statement. The CSAVE and the CLOAD statements are special versions of SAVE and LOAD for use with a cassette.

Saved File Format

The tokenized program is completely contained within the Variable Name Table, the Variable Value Table, and the Statement Table. However, since these tables vary in size, we must also save some information about the size of the tables.

The SAVE file format is shown in Figure 10-1. The first part consists of seven fields, each of them two bytes long, which tell where each table starts or ends. Part two contains the saved program's Variable Name Table (VNT), Variable Value Table (VVT), and Statement Table (ST).

The displacement value in all the part-one fields is actually the displacement *plus* 256. We must subtract 256 from each displacement value to obtain the true displacement.

The VNT starts at relative byte zero in the file's second part. The second field in part one holds that value *plus* 256.

The DVVT field in part one contains the displacement, minus 256, of the VVT from the start of part two.

The DST value, minus 256, gives the displacement of the Statement Table from the start of part two.

The DEND value, minus 256, gives the end-of-file displacement from the start of part two.

Figure 10-1. SAVE File Format

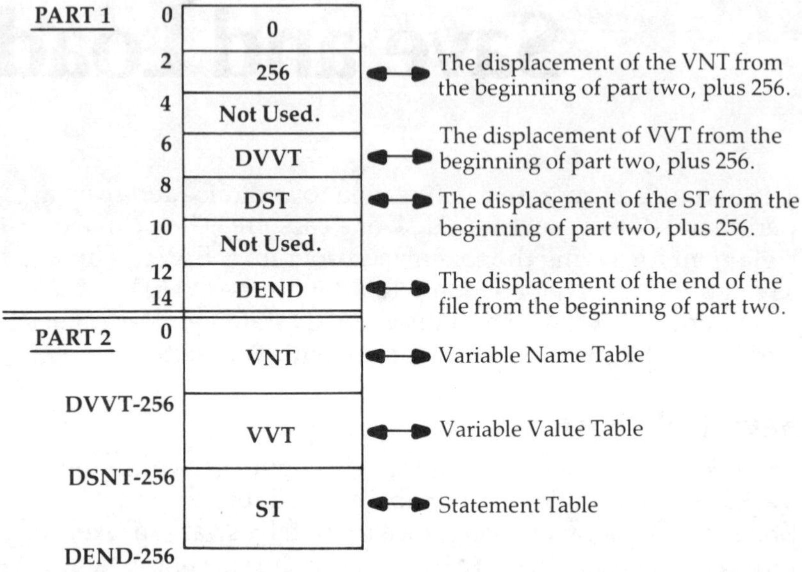

XSAVE ($BB5D)

The code that implements the SAVE statement starts at the XSAVE ($BB5D) label. Its first task is to open the specified output file, which it does by calling ELADVC.

The next operation is to move the first seven RAM table pointers from $80 to a temporary area at $500. While these pointers are being moved, the value contained in the first pointer is subtracted from the value in each of the seven pointers, including the first.

Since the first pointer held the absolute address of the first RAM table, this results in a list of displacements from the first RAM table to each of the other tables. These seven two-byte displacements are then written from the temporary area to the file via IO3. These are the first fourteen bytes of the SAVE file. (See Figure 10-1.)

The first RAM table is the 256-byte buffer, which will not be SAVEd. This is why the seven two-byte fields at the beginning of the SAVEd file hold values exactly 256 more than the true displacement of the tables they point to. (The LOAD procedure will resolve the 256-byte discrepancy.)

The next operation is to write the three needed RAM tables. The total length of these tables is determined from the value in the seventh entry in the displacement list, minus 256. To write the three entries, we point to the start of the Variable Name Table and call IO4, with the length of the three tables. This saves the second part of the file format.

The file is then closed and XSAVE returns to Execution Control.

XLOAD ($BAFB)

The LOAD statement is implemented at the XLOAD label located at $BAFB.

XLOAD first opens the specified load file for input by calling ELADVC. BASIC reads the first fourteen bytes from the file into a temporary area starting at $500. These fourteen bytes are the seven RAM table displacements created by SAVE.

The first two bytes will always be zero, according to the SAVE file format. (See Figure 10-1.) BASIC tests these two bytes for zero values. If these bytes are not zero, BASIC assumes the file is not a valid SAVE file and exits via the ERRNSF, which generates error code 21 (Load File Error).

If this is a valid SAVE file, the value in the pointer at $80 (Low Memory Address) is added to each of the seven displacements in the temporary area. These values will be the memory addresses of the three RAM tables, if and when they are read into memory.

The seventh pointer in the temporary area contains the address where the end of the Statement Table will be. If this address exceeds the current system high memory value, the routine exits via ERRPTL, which generates error code 19 (Load Program Too Big).

If the program will fit, the seven addresses are moved from the temporary area to the RAM table pointers at $80. The second part of the file is then loaded into the area now pointed to by the Variable Name Table pointer $82. The file is closed, CLR is executed, and a test for RUN is made.

If RUN called XLOAD, then a value of $FF was pushed onto the CPU stack. If RUN did not call XLOAD, then $00 was pushed onto the CPU stack. If RUN was the caller, then an RTS is done.

If XLOAD was entered as a result of a LOAD or CLOAD statement, then XLOAD exits directly to the Program Editor, not to Execution Control.

CSAVE and CLOAD

The CSAVE and CLOAD statements are special forms of SAVE and LOAD. These two statements assume that the SAVE/LOAD device is the cassette device.

CSAVE is not quite the same as SAVE "C:". Using SAVE with the "C:" device name will cause the program to be saved using long cassette inter-record gaps. This is a time waster, and CSAVE uses short inter-record gaps.

CSAVE starts at XCSAVE ($BBAC). CLOAD starts at XCLOAD ($BBA4).

The LIST and ENTER Statements

LIST can be used to store a program on an external device and ENTER can retrieve it. The difference between LOAD-SAVE and LIST-ENTER is that LOAD-SAVE deals with the tokenized program, while LIST-ENTER deals with the program in its source (ATASCII) form.

The ENTER Statement

BASIC is in ENTER mode whenever a program is not RUNning. By default the Program Editor looks for lines to be ENTERed from the keyboard, but the editor handles all ENTERed lines alike, whether they come from the keyboard or not.

The Enter Device

To accomplish transparency of all input data (not just ENTERed lines), BASIC maintains an enter device indicator, ENTDTD ($B4). When a BASIC routine (for example, the INPUT simulation routine) needs data, an I/O operation is done to the IOCB specified in ENTDTD. When the value in ENTDTD is zero, indicating IOCB 0, input will come from the keyboard. When data is to come from some other device, ENTDTD contains a number indicating the corresponding IOCB. During coldstart initialization, the enter device is set to IOCB 0. It is also reset to 0 at various other times.

XENTER ($BACB)

The XENTER routine is called by Execution Control to simulate the ENTER statement. XENTER opens IOCB 7 for input using the specified <filespec>, stores a 7 in the enter device ENTDTD, and then jumps to the start of the editor.

Entering from a Device

When the Program Editor asks GLGO, the get line routine ($BA92), for the next line, GLGO tells CIO to get a line from the device specified in ENTDTD — in this case, from IOCB 7. The editor continues to process lines from IOCB 7 until an end-of-file error occurs. The IOTEST routine detects the EOF condition, sees that we are using IOCB 7 for ENTER, closes device 7, and jumps to SNX2 to reset the enter device (ENTDTD) to 0 and print the READY message before restarting at the beginning of the editor.

The LIST Statement

The routine which simulates the LIST statement, XLIST, is actually another example of a language translator, complete with symbols and symbol-combining rules. XLIST translates the tokens generated by Atari BASIC back into the semi-English BASIC statements in ATASCII. This translation is a much simpler task than the one done by the pre-compiler, since XLIST can assume that the statement to be translated is syntactically correct. All that is required is to translate the tokens and insert blanks in the appropriate places.

The List Device

BASIC maintains a list device indicator, LISTDTD ($B5), similar to the enter device indicator discussed earlier. When a BASIC routine wants to output some data (an error message, for example), the I/O operation is done to the device (IOCB) specified in LISTDTD.

During coldstart initialization and at various other times, LISTDTD is set to zero, representing IOCB 0, the editor, which will place the output on the screen. Routines such as XPRINT or XLIST can change the LIST device to indicate some other IOCB. Thus the majority of the BASIC routines need not be concerned about the output's destination.

Remember that IOCB 0 is always open to the editor, which gets input from the keyboard and outputs to the screen. IOCB 6 is the S: device, the direct access to graphics screen, which is used in GRAPHICS statements. Atari BASIC uses IOCB 7 for I/O commands that allow different devices, like SAVE, LOAD, ENTER, and LIST.

XLIST ($B483)

The XLIST routine considers the output's destination in its initialization process and then forgets about it. It looks at the first expression in the tokenized line. If it is the <filespec>

string, XLIST calls a routine to open the specified device using IOCB 7 and to store a 7 in LISTDTD. All of XLIST's other processing is exactly the same, regardless of the LISTed data's final destination.

XLIST marks its place in the Statement Table by calling a subroutine of XGOSUB to put a GOSUB type entry on the Runtime Stack. Then XLIST steps through the Statement Table in the same way that Execution Control does, using Execution Control's line parameters and subroutines. When XLIST is finished, Execution Control takes the entry off the Runtime Stack and continues.

The XLIST routine, assuming it is to LIST all program statements, sets default starting and ending line numbers of 0 (in TSLNUM) and $7FFF (in LELNUM).

XLIST then determines whether line numbers were specified in the tokenized line that contained the LIST statement. XLIST compares the current index into the line (STINDEX) to the displacement to the next statement (NXTSTD). If STINDEX is not pointing to the next statement, at least one line number is specified. In this case, XLIST calls a subroutine of Execute Expression to evaluate the line number and convert it to a positive integer, which XLIST stores in TSLNUM as the starting line number.

If a second line number is specified, XLIST calls Execute Expression again and stores the value in LELNUM as the final line to LIST. If there is no second line number, then XLIST makes the ending line number equal to the starting line number, and only one line will be LISTed. If no line numbers were present, then TSLNUM and LELNUM still contain their default values, and all the program lines will be LISTed.

XLIST gets the first line to be LISTed by calling the Execution Control subroutine GETSTMT to initialize the line parameters to correspond to the line number in TSLNUM. If we are not at the end of the Statement Table, and if the current line's number is less than or equal to the final line number to be LISTed, XLIST calls a subroutine :LLINE to list the line.

After LISTing the line, XLIST calls Execution Control's subroutines to point to the next line. LISTing continues in this manner until the end of the Statement Table is reached or until the final line specified has been printed.

When XLIST is finished, it exits via XRTN at $B719, which makes the LIST statement the current statement again and then returns to Execution Control.

LIST Subroutines

:LLINE ($B55C)

The :LLINE routine LISTs the current line (the line whose address is in STMCUR).

:LLINE gets the line number from the beginning of the tokenized line. The floating point package is called to convert the integer to floating point and then to printable ATASCII. The result is stored in the buffer indicated by INBUFF. :LLINE calls a subroutine to print the line number and then a blank.

For every statement in the line, :LLINE sets STINDEX to point to the statement name token and calls the :LSTMT routine ($B590) to LIST the statement. When all statements have been LISTed, :LLINE returns to its caller, XLIST.

:LSTMT ($B590)

The :LSTMT routine LISTs the statement which starts at the current displacement (in STINDEX) into the current line. This routine does the actual language translation from tokens to BASIC statements.

:LSTMT uses two subroutines, :LGCT and :LGNT, to get the current and next token, respectively. If the end of the statement has been reached, these routines both pull the return address of their caller off the 6502 CPU stack and return to :LSTMT's caller, :LLINE. Otherwise, they return the requested token from the tokenized statement line.

The first token in a statement is the statement name token. :LSTMT calls a routine which prints the corresponding statement name by calling :LSCAN to find the entry and :LPRTOKEN to print it.

In the discussion of the Program Editor we saw that an erroneous statement was given a statement name of ERROR and saved in the Statement Table. If the current statement is this ERROR statement or is REM or DATA, :LSTMT picks up each remaining character in the statement and calls PRCHAR ($BA9F) to print the character.

Each type of token is handled differently. :LSTMT determines the type (variable, numeric constant, string constant, or operator) and goes to the proper code to translate it.

Variable Token. A variable token has a value greater than or equal to $80. When :LSTMT encounters a variable token, it turns off the most significant bit to get an index into the Variable Name Table. :LSTMT asks the :LSCAN routine to get the address of this entry. :LSTMT then calls :LPRTOKEN ($B535) to print the variable name. If the last character of the name is (, the next token is an array left parenthesis operator, and :LSTMT skips it.

Numeric Constant Token. A numeric constant is indicated by a token of $0E. The next six bytes are a floating point number. :LSTMT moves the numeric constant from the tokenized line to FRO ($D4) and asks the floating point package to convert it to ATASCII. The result is in a buffer pointed to by INBUFF. :LSTMT moves the address of the ATASCII number to SRCADR and tells :LPRTOKEN to print it.

String Constant Token. A string constant is indicated by a token of $0F. The next byte is the length of the string followed by the actual string data. Since the double quotes are not stored with a string constant, :LSTMT calls PRCHAR ($BA9F) to print the leading double quote. The string length tells :LSTMT how many following characters to print without translation. :LSTMT repeatedly gets a character and calls PRCHAR to print it until the whole string constant has been processed. It then asks PRCHAR to print the ending double quote.

Operator Token. An operator token is any token greater than or equal to $10 and less than $80. By subtracting $10 from the token value, :LSTMT creates an index into the Operator Name Table. :LSTMT calls :LSCAN to find the address of this entry. If the operator is a function (token value greater than or equal to $3D), :LPROTOKEN is called to print it. If this operator is not a function but its name is alphabetic (such as AND), the name is printed with a preceding and following blank. Otherwise, :LPRTOKEN is called to print just the operator name.

:LSCAN ($B50C)

This routine scans a table until it finds the translation of a token into an ATASCII name. A token's value is based on its table entry number; therefore, the entry number can be derived by modifying the token. For example, a variable token is created by machine-language ORing the table entry number of the variable name with $80. The entry number can be produced by ANDing out the high-order bit of the token. It is this entry number, stored in SCANT, that the :LSCAN routine uses.

The tables scanned by :LSCAN have a definite structure. Each entry consists of a fixed length portion followed by a variable length ATASCII portion. The last character in the ATASCII portion has the high-order bit on. Using these facts, :LSCAN finds the entry corresponding to the entry number in SCANT and puts the address of the ATASCII portion in SCRADR.

:LPRTOKEN ($B535)
This routine's task is to print the string of ATASCII characters whose address is in SCRADR. :LPRTOKEN makes sure the most significant bit is off (except for a carriage return) and prints the characters one at a time until it has printed the last character in the string (the one with its most significant bit on).

Atari Hardware Control Statements

The Atari Hardware Control Statements allow easy access to some of the computer's graphics and audio capabilities. The statements in this group are COLOR, GRAPHICS, PLOT, POSITION, DRAWTO, SETCOLOR, LOCATE, and SOUND.

XGR ($BA50)
The GRAPHICS statement determines the current graphics mode. The XGR simulation routine executes the GRAPHICS statement. The XGR routine first closes IOCB 6. It then calls an Execute Expression subroutine to evaluate the graphics mode value and convert it to an integer.

XGR sets up to open the screen by putting the address of a string "S:" into INBUFF. It creates an AUX1 and AUX2 byte from the graphics mode integer. XGR calls a BASIC I/O routine which sets up IOCB 6 and calls CIO to open the screen for the specified graphics mode. Like all BASIC routines that do I/O, XGR jumps to the IOTEST routine, which determines what to do next based on the outcome of the I/O.

XCOLOR ($BA29)
The COLOR statement is simulated by the XCOLOR routine. XCOLOR calls a subroutine of Execute Expression to evaluate the color value and convert it to an integer. XCOLOR saves this value (MOD 256) in BASIC memory location COLOR ($C8). This value is later retrieved by XPLOT and XDRAWTO.

XSETCOLOR ($B9B7)
The routine that simulates the SETCOLOR statement, XSETCOLOR, calls a subroutine of Execute Expression to evaluate the color register specified in the tokenized line. The Execute Expression routine produces a one-byte integer. If the value is not less than 5 (the number of color registers), XSETCOLOR exits via the Error Handling Routine at entry point ERVAL. Otherwise, it calls Execute Expression to get two more integers from the tokenized line.

To calculate the color value, XSETCOLOR multiplies the first integer (MOD 256) by 16 and adds the second (MOD 256). Since the operating system's five color registers are in consecutive locations starting at $2C4, XSETCOLOR uses the register value specified as an index to the proper register location and stores the color value there.

XPOS ($BA16)
The POSITION statement, which specifies the X and Y coordinates of the graphics cursor, is simulated by the XPOS routine.

XPOS uses a subroutine of Execute Expression to evaluate the X coordinate of the graphics window cursor and convert it to an integer value. The two-byte result is stored in the operating system's X screen coordinate location (SCRX at $55). This is the column number or horizontal position of the cursor.

XPOS then calls another Execute Expression subroutine to evaluate the Y coordinate and convert it to a one-byte integer. The result is stored in the Y screen coordinate location (SCRY at $54). This is the row number, or vertical position.

XLOCATE ($BC95)
XLOCATE, which simulates the LOCATE statement, first calls XPOS to set up the X and Y screen coordinates. Next it initializes IOCB 6 and joins a subroutine of XGET to do the actual I/O required to get the screen data into the variable specified.

XPLOT ($BA76)
XPLOT, which simulates the PLOT statement, first calls XPOS to set the X and Y coordinates of the graphics cursor. XPLOT gets the value that was saved in COLOR ($C8) and joins a PUT subroutine (PRCX at $BAA1) to do the I/O to IOCB 6 (the screen).

XDRAWTO ($BA31)
The XDRAWTO routine draws a line from the current X,Y screen coordinates to the X,Y coordinates specified in the statement. The routine calls XPOS to set the new X,Y coordinates. It places the value from BASIC's memory location COLOR into OS location SVCOLOR ($2FB). XDRAWTO does some initialization of IOCB 6 specifying the *draw* command ($11). It then calls a BASIC I/O routine which finishes the

initialization of IOCB 6 and calls CIO to draw the line. Finally, XDRAWTO jumps to the IOTEST routine, which will determine what to do next based on the outcome of the I/O.

XSOUND ($B9DD)

The Atari computer hardware uses a set of memory locations to control sound capabilities. The SOUND statement gives the user access to some of these capabilities. The XSOUND routine, which simulates the SOUND statement, places fixed values in some of the sound locations and user specified values in others.

The XSOUND routine uses Execute Expression to get four integer values from the tokenized statement line. If the first integer (voice) is greater than or equal to 4, the Error Handling Routine is invoked at ERVAL.

The OS audio control bits are all turned off by storing a 0 into $D208. Any bits left on from previous serial port usage are cleared by storing 3 in $D20F.

The Atari has four sound registers (one for each voice) starting at $D200. The first byte of each two-byte register determines the pitch (frequency). In the second byte, the four most significant bits are the distortion, and the four least significant bits are the volume.

The voice value mentioned earlier is multiplied by 2 and used as an index into the sound registers. The second value from the tokenized line is stored as the pitch in the first byte of one of the registers ($D200, $D202, $D204, or $D206), depending on the voice index. The third value from the tokenized line is multiplied by 16 and the fourth value is added to it to create the value to be stored as distortion/volume. The voice, times 2, is again used as an index to store this value in the second byte of a sound register ($D201, $D203, $D205, or $D207). The XSOUND routine then returns to Execution Control.

External Data I/O Statements

The external data I/O statements allow data which is not part of the BASIC source program to flow into and out of BASIC. External data can come from the keyboard, a disk, or a cassette. BASIC can also create external information by sending data to external devices such as the screen, a printer, or a disk.

The INPUT and GET statements are the primary statements used for obtaining information from external devices. The PRINT and PUT statements are the primary statements for sending data to external devices.

XIO, LPRINT, OPEN, CLOSE, NOTE, POINT and STATUS are specialized I/O statements. LPRINT is used to print a single line to the "P:" device. The other statements assist in the I/O process.

XINPUT ($B316)

The execution of the INPUT statement starts at XINPUT ($B316).

Getting the Input Line. The first action of XINPUT is to read a line of data from the indicated device. A line is any combination of up to 255 characters terminated by the EOL character ($9B). This line will be read into the buffer located at $580.

If the INPUT statement contained was followed by # <expression>, the data will be read from the IOCB whose number was specified by <expression>. If there was no # <expression>, IOCB 0 will be used. IOCB 0 is the screen editor and keyboard device (E:). If IOCB 0 is indicated, the prompt character (?) will be displayed before the input line request is made; otherwise, no prompt is displayed.

Line Processing. Once the line has been read into the buffer, processing of the data in that line starts at XINA ($B335). The input line data is processed according to the tokens in the INPUT (or READ) statements. These tokens are numeric or string variables separated by commas.

Processing a Numeric Variable. If the new token is a numeric variable, the CVAFP routine is called to convert the next characters in the input line to a floating point number. If this conversion does not report an error, and if the next input line character is a comma or an EOL, the floating point value is processed.

The processing of a valid numeric input value consists of calling RTNVAR to return the variable and its new value to the Variable Value Table.

If there is an error, INPUT processing is aborted via the ERRINP routine. If there is no error, but the user has hit BREAK, the process is aborted via XSTOP. If there is no abort, XINX ($B389) is called to continue with INPUT's next task.

Processing a String Variable. If the next statement token is a string variable, it is processed at XISTR ($B35E). This routine is also used by the READ statement. If the calling statement is INPUT, then all input line characters from the current character up to but not including the EOL character are considered to be part of the input string data. If the routine was called by READ, all characters up to but not including the next comma or EOL are considered to be part of the input string.

The process of assigning the data to the string variable is handled by calling RISASN ($B386). If RISASN does not abort the process because of an error like DIMENSION TOO SMALL, XINX is called to continue with INPUT's next task.

XINX. The XINX ($B389) routine is entered after each variable token in an INPUT or a READ statement is processed.

If the next token in the statement is an EOL, the INPUT/READ statement processing terminates at XIRTS ($B3A1). XIRTS restores the line buffer pointer ($80) to the RAM table buffer. It then restores the enter device to IOCB 0 (in case it had been changed to some other input device). Finally, XIRTS executes an RTS instruction.

If the next INPUT/READ statement token is a comma, more input data is needed. If the next input line character is an EOL, another input line is obtained. If the statement was INPUT, the new line is obtained by entering XIN0 ($B326). If the statement was READ, the new line is obtained by entering XRD3 ($B2D0).

The processing of the next INPUT/READ statement variable token continues at XINA.

XGET ($BC7F)

The GET statement obtains one character from some specified device and assigns that character to a scalar (non-array) numeric variable.

The execution of GET starts at XGET ($BC7F) with a call to GIODVC. GIODVC will set the I/O device to whatever number is specified in the #<expression> or to IOCB zero if no # <expression> was specified. (If the device is IOCB 0 (E:), the user must type RETURN to force E: to terminate the input.)

The single character is obtained by calling IO3. The character is assigned to the numeric variable by calling ISVAR1 ($BD2D). ISVAR1 also terminates the GET statement processing.

PRINT

The PRINT statement is used to transmit text data to an external device. The arguments in the PRINT statement are a list of numeric and/or string expressions separated by commas or semicolons. If the argument is numeric, the floating point value is converted to text form. If the argument is a string, the string value is transmitted as is.

If an argument separator is a comma, the arguments are output in tabular fashion: each new argument starts at the next tab stop in the output line, with blanks separating the arguments.

If the argument separator is a semicolon, the transmitted arguments are appended to each other without separation.

The transmitted line is terminated with an EOL, unless a semicolon or comma directly precedes the statement's EOL or statement separator (:).

XPRINT ($B3B6). The PRINT routine begins at XPRINT ($B3B6). The tab value is maintained in the PTABW ($C9) cell. The cell is initialized with a value of ten during BASIC's cold start, so that commas in the PRINT line cause each argument to be displaced ten positions after the beginning of the last argument. The user may POKE PTABW to set a different tab value.

XPRINT copies PTABW to SCANT ($AF). SCANT will be used to contain the next multiple-of-PTABW output line displacement — the column number of the next tab stop.

COX is initialized to zero and is used to maintain the current output column or displacement.

XPR0. XPRINT examines the next statement token at XPR0 ($B3BE), classifies it, and executes the proper routine.

 # Token. If the next token is #, XPRIOD ($B437) is entered. This routine modifies the list device to the device specified in the #<expression>. XPR0 is then entered to process the next token.

, Token. The XPTAB ($B419) routine is called to process the , token. Its job is to tab to the next tab column.

If COX (the current column) is greater than SCANT, we must skip to the next available tab position. This is done by continuously adding PTABW to SCANT until COX is less than or equal to SCANT. When COX is less than SCANT, blanks ($20) are transmitted to the output device until COX is equal to SCANT.

The next token is then examined at XPR0.

EOL and : Tokens. The XPEOS ($B446) routine is entered for EOL and : tokens. If the previous token was a ; or , token, PRINT exits at XPRTN ($B458). If the previous token was not a ; or , token, an EOL character is transmitted before exiting via XPRTN.

; Token. No special action is taken for the ; token except to go to XPR0 to examine the next token.

Numbers and Strings. If the next token is not one of the above tokens, Execute Expression is called to evaluate the expression. The resultant value is popped from the argument stack and its type is tested for a number or a string.

If the argument popped was numeric, it will be converted to text form by calling CVFASC. The resulting text is transmitted to the output device from the buffer pointed to by INBUFF ($F3). XPR0 is then entered to process the next token.

If the argument popped was a string, it will be transmitted to the output device by the code starting at :XPSTR ($B3F8). This code examines the argument parameters to determine the current length of the string. When the string has been transmitted, XPR0 is entered to process the next token.

XLPRINT ($B464)

LPRINT, a special form of the PRINT statement, is used to print a line to the printer device (P:).

The XLPRINT routine starts at $B464 by opening IOCB 7 for output to the P: device. XPRINT is then called to do the printing. When the XPRINT is done, IOCB 7 is closed via CLSYS1 and LPRINT is terminated.

XPUT ($BC72)
The PUT statement sends a single byte from the expression in the PUT statement to a specified external device.

Processing starts at XPUT ($BC72) with a call to GIODVC. GIODVC sets the I/O device to the IOCB specified in # <expression>. If a #<expression> does not exist, the device will be set to IOCB zero (E:).

The routine then calls GETINT to execute PUT's expression and convert the resulting value to a two-byte integer. The least significant byte of this integer is then sent to the PUT device via PRCX. PRCX also terminates the PUT processing.

XXIO ($BBE5)
The XIO statement, a general purpose I/O statement, is intended to be used when no other BASIC I/O statement will serve the requirements. The XIO parameters are an IOCB I/O command, an IOCB specifying expression, an AUX1 value, an AUX2 value, and finally a string expression to be used as a filespec parameter.

XIO starts at XXIO ($BBE5) with a call to GIOCMD. GIOCMD gets the IOCB command parameter. XIO then continues at XOP1 in the OPEN statement code.

XOPEN ($BBEB)
The OPEN statement is used to open an external device for input and/or output. OPEN has a #<expression>, the *open type* parameter (AUX1), an AUX2 parameter, and a string expression to be used as a filespec.

OPEN starts at XOPEN at $BBEB. It loads the open command code into the A register and continues at XOP1.

XOP1. XOP1 continues the OPEN and XIO statement processing. It starts at $BBED by storing the A register into the IOCMD cell. Next it obtains the AUX1 (open type) and AUX2 values from the statement.

The next parameter is the filespec string. In order to insure that the filespec has a proper terminator, SETSEOL is called to place a temporary EOL at the end of the string.

The XIO or OPEN command is then executed via a call to IO1. When IO1 returns, the temporary EOL at the end of the string is replaced with its previous value by calling RSTSEOL.

OPEN and XIO terminate by calling IOTEST to insure that the command was executed without error.

XCLOSE ($BC1B)

The CLOSE statement, which closes the specified device, starts at XCLOSE ($BC1B). It loads the IOCB close command code into the A register and continues at GDVCIO.

GDVCIO. GDVCIO ($BC1D) is used for general purpose device I/O. It stores the A register into the IOCMD cell, calls GIODVC to get the device from #<expression>, then calls IO7 to execute the I/O. When IO7 returns, IOTEST is called to test the results of the I/O and terminate the routine.

XSTATUS ($BC28)

The STATUS statement executes the IOCB status command. Processing starts at XSTATUS ($BC28) by calling GIODVC to get the device number from #<expression>. It then calls IO8 with the status command in the A register. When IO8 returns, the status returned in the IOCB status cell is assigned to the variable specified in the STATUS statement by calling ISVAR1. ISVAR1 also terminates the STATUS statement processing.

XNOTE ($BC36)

The NOTE statement is used specifically for disk random access. NOTE executes the Disk Device Dependent Note Command, $26, which returns two values representing the current position within the file for which the IOCB is open.

NOTE begins at XNOTE at $BC36. The code loads the command value, $26, into the A register and calls GDVCIO to do the I/O operation. When GDVCIO returns, the values are moved from AUX3 and AUX4 to the first variable in the NOTE statement. The next variable is assigned the value from AUX5.

XPOINT ($BC4D)

The POINT statement is used to position a disk file to a previously NOTEd location. Processing starts at XPOINT ($BC4D). This routine converts the first POINT parameter to an integer and stores the value in AUX3 and AUX4. The second parameter is then converted to an integer and its value stored in AUX5. The POINT command, $25, is executed by calling GDIO1, which is part of GDVCIO.

Miscellaneous I/O Subroutines

IOTEST. IOTEST ($BCB3) is a general purpose routine that examines the results of an I/O operation. If the I/O processing has returned an error, IOTEST processes that error.

IOTEST starts by calling LDIOSTA to get the status byte from the IOCB that performed the last I/O operation. If the byte value is positive (less than 128), IOTEST returns to the caller.

If the status byte is negative, the I/O operation was abnormal and processing continues at SICKIO.

If the I/O aborted due to a BREAK key depression, BRKBYT ($11) is set to zero to indicate BREAK. If a LOAD was in progress when BREAK was hit, exit is via COLDSTART; otherwise IOTEST returns to its caller.

If the error was not from IOCB 7 (the device BASIC uses), the error status value is stored in ERRNUM and ERROR is called to print the error message and abort program execution.

If the error was from IOCB 7, then IOCB 7 is closed and ERROR is called with the error status value in ERRNUM — unless ENTER was being executed, and the error was an end-of-file error. In this case, IOCB 7 is closed, the enter device is reset to IOCB 0, and SNX2 is called to return control to the Program Editor.

I/O Call Routine. All I/O is initiated from the routine starting at IO1 ($BD0A). This routine has eight entry points, IO1 through IO8, each of which stores predetermined values in an IOCB. All IO*n* entry points assume that the X register contains the IOCB value, times 16.

IO1 sets the buffer length to 255.

IO2 sets the buffer length to zero.

IO3 sets the buffer length to the value in the Y register plus a most-significant length byte of zero.

IO4 sets the buffer length from the values in the Y,A register pair, with the A register being the most-significant value.

IO5 sets the buffer address from the value in the INBUFF cell ($F3).

IO6 sets the buffer address from the Y,A register pair. The A register contains the most significant byte.

IO7 sets the I/O command value from the value in the IOCMD cell.

IO8 sets the I/O command from the value in the A register.

All of this is followed by a call to the operating system CIO entry point. This call executes the I/O. When CIO returns, the general I/O routine returns to its caller.

Internal I/O Statements

The READ, DATA, and RESTORE statements work together to allow the BASIC user to pass predetermined information to his or her program. This is, in a sense, internal I/O.

XDATA ($A9E7)
The information to be passed to the BASIC program is stored in one or more DATA statements. A DATA statement can occur any place in the program, but execution of a DATA statement has no effect.

When Execution Control encounters a DATA statement, it expects to process this statement just like any other. Therefore an XDATA routine is called, but XDATA simply returns to Execution Control.

XREAD ($B283)
The XREAD routine must search the Statement Table to find DATA. It uses Execution Control's subroutines and line parameters to do this. When XREAD is done, it must restore the line parameters to point to the READ statement. In order to mark its place in the Statement Table, XREAD calls a subroutine of XGOSUB to put a GOSUB-type entry on the Runtime Stack.

The BASIC program may need to READ some DATA, do some other processing, and then READ more DATA. Therefore, XREAD needs to keep track of just where it is in which DATA statement. There are two parameters that provide for this. DATALN ($B7) contains the line number at which to start the search for the next DATA statement. DATAD ($B6) contains the displacement of the next DATA element in the DATALN line. Both values are set to zero as part of RUN and CLR statement processing.

XREAD calls Execution Control's subroutine GETSTMT to get the line whose number is stored in DATALN. If this is the first READ in the program and a RESTORE has not set a different line number, DATALN contains zero, and GETSTMT will get the first line in the program. On subsequent READs, GETSTMT gets the last DATA statement that was processed by the previous READ.

After getting its first line, XREAD calls the XRTN routine to restore Execution Control's line parameters.

The current line number is stored in DATALN. XREAD steps through the line, statement by statement, looking for a DATA statement. If the line contains no DATA statement, then subsequent lines and statements are examined until a DATA statement is found.

When a DATA statement has been found, XREAD inspects the elements of the DATA statement until it finds the element whose displacement is in DATAD.

If no DATA is found, XREAD exits via the ERROOD entry point in the Error Handling Routine. Otherwise, a flag is set to indicate that a READ is being done, and XREAD joins XINPUT at :XINA. XINPUT handles the assignment of the DATA values to the variables. (See Chapter 13.)

XREST ($B26B)

The RESTORE statement allows the BASIC user to re-READ a DATA statement or change the order in which the DATA statements are processed. The XREST routine simulates RESTORE.

XREST sets DATALN to the line number given, or to zero if no line number is specified. It sets DATAD to zero, so that the next READ after a RESTORE will start at the first element in the DATA line specified in DATALN.

Miscellaneous Statements

XDEG ($B261) and XRAD ($B266)

The transcendental functions such as SIN or COS will work with either degrees or radians, depending on the setting of RADFLG ($FB). The DEG and RAD statements cause RADFLG to be set. These statements are simulated by the XDEG and XRAD routines, respectively.

The XDEG routine stores a six in RADFLG. XRAD sets it to zero. These particular values were chosen because they aid the transcendental functions in their calculations.

RADFLG is set to zero during BASIC's initialization process and also during simulation of the RUN statement.

XPOKE ($B24C)

The POKE statement is simulated by the XPOKE routine. XPOKE calls a subroutine of Execute Expression to get the address and data integers from the tokenized line. XPOKE then stores the data at the specified address.

XBYE ($A9E8)

The XBYE routine simulates the BYE statement. XBYE closes all IOCBs (devices and files) and then jumps to location $E471 in the Operating System. This ends BASIC and causes the memo pad to be displayed.

XDOS ($A9EE)

The DOS statement is simulated by the XDOS routine. The XDOS routine closes all IOCBs and jumps to whatever address is stored in location $0A. This will be the address of DOS if DOS has been loaded. If DOS has not been loaded, $0A will point to the memo pad.

XLET ($AAE0)

The LET and implied LET statements assign values to variables. They both invoke the XLET routine, which consists of the Execute Expression routines. (See Chapter 7.)

XREM ($A9E7)
The REM statement is for documentation purposes only and has no effect on the running program. The routine which simulates REM, XREM, simply executes an RTS instruction to return to Execution Control.

XERR ($B91E)
When a line containing a syntax error is entered, it is given a special statement name token to indicate the error. The entire line is flagged as erroneous no matter how many previously good statements are in the line. The line is then stored in the Statement Table.

The error statement is processed just like any other. Execution Control calls a routine, XERR, which is one of the entry points to the Error Handling Routine. It causes error 17 (EXECUTION OF GARBAGE).

XDIM ($B1D9)
The DIMension statement, simulated by the XDIM routine, reserves space in the String/Array Table for the DIMensioned variable.

The XDIM routine calls Execute Expression to get the variable to be DIMensioned from the Variable Value Table. The variable entry is put into a work area. In the process, Execute Expression gets the first and second DIMension values and sets a default of zero if only one value is specified.

XDIM checks to see if the variable has already been DIMensioned. If the variable was already DIMensioned, XDIM exits via the ERRDIM entry point in the Error Handling Routine. If not, a bit is set in the variable type byte in the work area entry to mark this variable as DIMensioned.

Next, XDIM calculates the amount of space required. This calculation is handled differently for strings and arrays.

DIMensioning an Array. XDIM first increments both dimension values by one and then multiplies them together to get the number of elements in the array. XDIM multiplies the result by 6 (the length of a floating point number) to get the number of bytes required. EXPAND is called to expand the String/Array Table by that amount.

XDIM must finish building the variable entry in the work area. It stores the first and second dimension values in the entry. It also stores the array's displacement into the

String/Array Table. It then calls an Execute Expression subroutine to return the variable to the Variable Value Table. (See Chapter 3.)

DIMensioning a String. Reserving space for a string in the String/Array Table is much simpler. XDIM merely calls the EXPAND routine to expand by the user-specified size.

XDIM must also build the Variable Value Table entry in the work area. It sets the current length to 0 and the maximum length to the DIMensioned value. The displacement of the string into the String/Array Table is also stored in the variable. XDIM then calls a subroutine of Execute Expression to return the variable entry to the Variable Value Table. (See Chapter 3.)

Initialization

When the Atari computer is powered up with the BASIC cartridge in place, the operating system does some processing and then jumps to a BASIC routine. Between the time that BASIC first gets control and the time it prints the READY message, initialization takes place. This initialization is called a cold start. No data or tables are preserved during a cold start.

Initialization is repeated if things go terribly awry. For example, if there is an I/O error while executing a LOAD statement, BASIC is totally confused. It gives up and begins all over again with the COLDSTART routine.

Sometimes a less drastic partial initialization is necessary. This process is handled by the WARMSTART routine, in which some tables are preserved.

Entering the NEW statement, simulated by the XNEW routine, has almost the same effect as a cold start.

COLDSTART ($A000)

Two flags, LOADFLG and WARMFLG, are used to determine if a cold or warm start is required.

The load flag, LOADFLG ($CA), is zero except during the execution of a LOAD statement. The XLOAD routine sets the flag to non-zero when it starts processing and resets it to zero when it finishes. If an I/O error occurs during that interval, IOTEST notes that LOADFLG is non-zero and jumps to COLDSTART.

The warm-start flag, WARMFLG ($08), is never set by BASIC. It is set by some other routine, such as the operating system or DOS. If WARMFLG is zero, a cold start is done. If it is non-zero, a warm start is done. During its power-up processing, before BASIC is given control, OS sets WARMFLG to zero to request a cold start. During System Reset processing, OS sets the flag to non-zero, indicating a warm start is desired.

If DOS has loaded any data into BASIC's program area during its processing, it will request a cold start.

The COLDSTART routine checks both WARMFLG and LOADFLG to determine whether to do a cold or warm start. If a cold start is required, COLDSTART initializes the 6502 CPU stack and clears the decimal flag. The rest of its processing is exactly the same as if the NEW statement had been entered.

XNEW ($A00C)
The NEW statement is simulated by the XNEW routine. XNEW resets the load flag, LOADFLG, to zero. It initializes the zero-page pointers to BASIC's RAM tables. It reserves 256 bytes at the low memory address for the multipurpose buffer and stores its address in the zero-page pointer located at $80. Since none of the RAM tables are to retain any data, their zero-page pointers ($82 through $90) are all set to low memory plus 256.

The Variable Name Table is expanded by one byte, which is set to zero. This creates a dummy end-of-table entry.

The Statement Table is expanded by three bytes. The line number of the direct statement ($8000) is stored there along with the length (three). This marks the end of the Statement Table.

A default tab value of 10 is set for the PRINT statement.

WARMSTART ($A04D)
A warm start is the least drastic of the three types of initialization. Everything the WARMSTART routine does is also done by COLDSTART and XNEW.

The stop line number (STOPLN), the error number (ERRNUM), and the DATA parameters (DATALN and DATAD) are all set to zero. The RADFLG flag is set to zero, indicating that transcendental functions are working in radians. The break byte (BRKBYT) is set *off* and $FF is stored in TRAPLN to indicate that errors are not being trapped.

All IOCBs (devices and files) are closed.

The enter and list devices (ENTDTD and LISTDTD) are set to zero to indicate the keyboard and the screen, respectively.

Finally, the READY message is printed and control passes to the Program Editor.

Part Two

Directly Accessing Atari BASIC

Introduction to Part Two

Congratulations! If you have read all of Part 1, you are through the hard stuff. In Part 2, we hope to teach you how to use at least some of the abundance of information presented in the Source Listing and in Part 1. In particular, we will show you how to examine the various RAM and ROM tables used by BASIC.

The examples and suggestions will be written in Atari BASIC. But those of you who are true-blue assembly language fanatics should have little trouble translating the concepts to machine code, especially with the source listing to guide you.

Would that we could present an example program or concept for each possible aspect of the BASIC interpreter, but space does not allow it — nor would it be appropriate. For example, although we will present here a program to list all keywords and token values used by BASIC, we will *not* explore the results (usually disastrous) of changing token values within a BASIC program.

Part 2 begins with a pair of introductory chapters. If you are experienced at hexadecimal-to-decimal conversions and with the concepts of word and byte PEEKs and POKEs, you may wish to skip directly to Chapter 3.

Chapter One

Hexadecimal Numbers

The word hexadecimal means, literally, ''of six and ten.'' It implies, however, a number notation which uses 16 as its base instead of 10. Hexadecimal notation is used as a sort of shorthand for the eight-digit binary numbers that the 6502 understands. If Atari BASIC understood hexadecimal numbers and we all had eight fingers on each hand, there would be no need for this chapter. Instead, to use this book you have to make many conversions back and forth between hexadecimal (''hex'') and decimal notation. Many BASIC users have never had to learn that process.

Virtually all the references to addresses and other values in this book are given in hexadecimal notation (or simply ''hex'' to us insiders). For example, we learn that the Atari BASIC ROM cartridge has $A000 for its lowest address and that location $80 contains a pointer to BASIC's current LOMEM. But what does all that mean?

First of all, if you are not familiar with 6502 assembly language, let me point out that there is a convention that a number preceded by a dollar sign ($80) is a hexadecimal number, even if it contains only decimal digits. Also, notice that in the Source Listing *all* numbers in the first three columns are hexadecimal, even though the dollar sign is not present. (To the right of those columns, though, only those numbers preceded by a dollar sign are in hex.)

Now, suppose I wanted to look at the contents of location $A4AF (SNTAB in the listing). Realistically, the only way to look at a memory location from BASIC is via the PEEK function (and see the next chapter if you are not sure how to use PEEK in this situation). But BASIC's language syntax requires a *decimal* number with PEEK — for instance, PEEK (15).

Obviously, we need some way to convert from hexadecimal to decimal. Aside from going out and buying one of the calculators made just for this purpose, the best way is probably to let your computer help you. And the computer can help you even if you only understand BASIC. As an example, here's a BASIC program that will convert hex to decimal notation:

```
10 DIM HEX$(23),NUM$(4)
20 HEX$="@ABCDEFGHI#######JKLMNO"
30 CVHEX=9000
100 PRINT :PRINT "GIVE ME A HEX NUMBER ";
110 INPUT NUM$
120 GOSUB CVHEX
130 PRINT "HEX ";NUM$;" = DECIMAL ";NUM
140 GOTO 100
9000 REM THE CONVERT HEX TO DECIMAL ROUTINE
9010 NUM=0
9020 FOR I=1 TO LEN(NUM$)
9030 NUM=NUM*16+ASC(HEX$(ASC(NUM$(I))-47))-64
9040 NEXT I:RETURN
```

Now, while this program might be handy for a few purposes, it would be much neater if we could simply use its capabilities anytime we wanted to examine or change a location (or its contents) referred to by a hex address or data. And so shall it be used.

If we remove lines 100 through 140, inclusive, then any BASIC program which incorporates the rest of the program may change a hex number into decimal by simply

1. placing the ATASCII form of the hex number in the variable NUM$,
2. calling the convert routine at line 9000 (via GOSUB CVHEX), and
3. using the result, which is returned in the variable NUM.

In the next chapter, we will immediately begin to make use of this routine. If you are not used to hex notation, you might do well to type in and play with this program before proceeding.

Finally, before we leave this subject, let's examine a routine which will allow us to go the other way — that is, convert decimal to hex:

```
40 DIM DEC$(16):DEC$="0123456789ABCDEF"
50 CVDEC=9100
100 PRINT :PRINT "GIVE ME A DECIMAL NUMBER ";
```

```
110 INPUT DEC:NUM=DEC
120 GOSUB CVDEC:REM 'NUM' is destroyed by this
130 PRINT DEC;" Decimal = ";NUM$;" Hex"
140 GOTO 100
9100 REM CONVERT DECIMAL TO HEX ROUTINE
9110 DIV=4096
9120 FOR I=1 TO 4
9130 N=INT(NUM/DIV):NUM$(I,I)=DEC$(N+1)
9140 NUM=NUM-DIV*N:DIV=DIV/16
9150 NEXT I
9160 RETURN
```

These lines are meant to be added to the previous program, though they can be used alone if you simply add this line:

10 DIM NUM$(4)

We will use portions of these programs in later chapters, but we may compress some of the code into fewer lines simply to save wear and tear on our fingers. If you study these routines, you'll recognize them in their transformed versions.

PEEKing and POKEing

In contrast to languages which include direct machine addressing capability, like "C" and Forth, and in contrast to "school" languages like Pascal and Fortran, which specifically prevent such addressing, BASIC provides a sort of halfway measure in machine accessibility.

POKE is a BASIC statement. Its syntax is POKE<address>,<data>. Naturally, both <address> and <data> may be constants, variables, or even full-blown expressions:

POKE 82,0: REM change left screen margin to zero

produces the same result as

LEFTMARGIN=82:POKE LEFTMARGIN,0

PEEK, on the other hand, is a BASIC function. It cannot stand alone as a statement. To use PEEK, we either PRINT the value (contents) of a PEEKed location, assign a PEEKed value to a variable, or test the value for some condition:

POKE 82, PEEK(82)+1 : REM move the left margin in a space

PRINT PEEK(106) : REM where is the top of system memory?

IF PEEK(195)=136 THEN PRINT "End of File"

In the first example, the number POKEd into 82 will be whatever number was stored before, *plus* 1. As explained in Part 1, the PEEK function is executed before the POKE.

An aside: Just where did I get those addresses I used in the PEEKs and POKEs? One way to find them is to peruse the listings of Atari's operating system, available in Atari's technical manuals set, and the listing of BASIC in this book. Another way would be to use a book (like COMPUTE! Books' *Mapping the Atari*) or a reference card designed specifically to tell you about such addresses.

And one more thing to consider before moving on. If we counted all of the bit patterns possible in a single 8-bit byte (like

01010101, 11110000, and 00000001, where each 1 or 0 represents a single *on* or *off* bit), we would discover that there are 256 unique combinations, ranging in value from 0 to 255. Since each memory location can hold only one byte, it is not surprising to learn that the PEEK function will always return a number from 0 to 255 ($00 to $FF). Similarly, BASIC will only POKE a data value that is an integer from 0 to 255. In fact, BASIC will convert any data to be POKEd to an integer number, rounding off any fractional parts.

So far so good. But suppose we want to examine a location which is actually a two-byte word, such as the line number where the last TRAPped error occurred, stored starting at location $BA hex or 186 decimal. PEEK only lets us look at one byte at a time. How do we look at two bytes? Simple: one byte at a time.

In most cases, words in a 6502-based machine are stored in memory with the least significant byte stored first. This means that the second byte of each word is a count of the number of 256's there are in its value, and the first byte is the leftovers. (Or we can more properly say that the first byte contains "the word's value modulo 256.") Confused? Let's try restating that.

In decimal arithmetic, we can count from 0 to 9 in a single digit. To go beyond 9, we have a convention that says the digit second from the right represents the number of 10's in the number, and so on.

If we consider bytes to be a computer's digits, which in many ways they are, and if we remember that each byte may represent any number from 0 to 255 (or $00 to $FF), then it is logical to say that the next byte is a count of the number of 256's in the number. The only thing illogical is that the higher byte comes after the lower byte (like reading 37 as "7 tens and 3 ones" instead of what we are used to).

Some examples might help:

a 6502 word in memory	as written in assembler	think of it as	decimal value
01 00	$0001	0*256 +1	1
00 01	$0100	1*256 +0	256
02 04	$0402	4*256 +2	1026
FF FF	$FFFF	255*256 +255	65535

So let's examine that error line location:

```
PRINT PEEK(186)+256 * PEEK(187)
```

Do you see it? Since the second byte is a count of the number of 256's in the value, we must multiply it by 256 to calculate its true value.

Now, in the case of line numbers, it is well and good that we print out a decimal value, since that is how we are used to thinking of them. But suppose you wished to print out some of BASIC's tables? You might very well wish to see the hex representations. The program presented here allows you to specify a hex address. It then presents you with the contents of the byte *and* the word found at that address, in both decimal and hex form.

```
10 DIM HEX$(23),NUM$(4)
20 HEX$="@ABCDEFGHI######JKLMNO"
30 CVHEX=9000
40 DIM DEC$(16):DEC$="0123456789ABCDEF"
50 CVDEC=9100
100 PRINT :PRINT "WHAT ADDRESS TO VIEW ";
110 INPUT NUM$:PRINT
120 PRINT "Address ";NUM$;" contains:"
130 GOSUB CVHEX:ADDR=NUM
140 NUM=PEEK(ADDR):GOSUB CVDEC
150 PRINT ,"byte ";PEEK(ADDR);" = $";NUM$(3)
160 WORD=PEEK(ADDR)+256*PEEK(ADDR+1)
170 NUM=WORD:GOSUB CVDEC
180 PRINT ,"word ";WORD;" = $";NUM$
190 GOTO 100
9000 REM THE CONVERT HEX TO DECIMAL ROUTINE
9010 NUM=0
9020 FOR I=1 TO LEN(NUM$)
9030 NUM=NUM*16+ASC(HEX$(ASC(NUM$(I))-47))-64
9040 NEXT I:RETURN
9100 REM CONVERT DECIMAL TO HEX ROUTINE
9110 DIV=4096
9120 FOR I=1 TO 4
9130 N=INT(NUM/DIV):NUM$(I,I)=DEC$(N+1)
9140 NUM=NUM-DIV*N:DIV=DIV/16
9150 NEXT I
9160 RETURN
```

You may have noticed that lines 10 through 50 and lines 9000 to the end are the same as those used in the example programs in the last chapter. And did you see line 160, where we obtained the word value by multiplying by 256?

As the last point of this chapter, we need to discuss how to *change* a word value. Obviously, in Atari BASIC we can't POKE both bytes of a word at once any more than we could retrieve both bytes at once (although BASIC A+ can, by using the DPOKE statement and DPEEK function). So we must invent a mechanism to do a double POKE.

Given that the variable ADDR contains the address at which we wish to POKE a word, and given that the variable WORD contains the value (in decimal) of the desired word, the following code fragment will perform the double POKE:

```
POKE ADDR+1,INT(WORD/256)
POKE ADDR,WORD-256*PEEK(ADDR+1)
```

This is kind of sneaky code, but calculating the most significant byte and POKEing the value in byte location ADDR+1 first allows us to also use it as a kind of temporary variable in calculating the least significant byte. By PEEKing the location that already holds the high-order byte, we can subtract it from the original value. The remainder is WORD modulo 256 — the low-order byte.

And that's about it. Hopefully, if you were not familiar with PEEK and POKE before, you now at least will not approach their use with too much caution. Generally, PEEKs will never harm either your running program or the machine, but don't be surprised if a stray POKE or two sends your computer off into never-never land. After all, you may have just told BASIC to start putting your program into ROM, or worse.

On the other hand, if you have removed your diskettes and turned off your cassette recorder, the worst that can happen from an erring POKE is that you'll have to turn the power off and back on again. So have at it. Happy PEEKing and POKEing.

Listing Variables in Use

Chapter 3 of Part 1 described the layout of the Variable Name Table and the Variable Value Table. In particular, we read that the Variable Name Table was built in a very simple fashion: Each new variable name, as it is encountered upon program entry, is simply added to the end of the list of names. The most significant bit of the last character of the name is turned on, to signal the end of that name. The contents of VNTP point to the beginning of the list of names, and the content of VNTD is the address of the byte after the end of the list.

Now, what does all that mean? What does it imply that we can do? Briefly, it implies that we can look at BASIC's memory and find out what variable names are in current use. Here's a program that will do exactly that:

```
32700 QQ=128:PRINT QQ,
32710 FOR Q=PEEK(130)+256*PEEK(131) TO PE
      EK(132)+256*PEEK(133)-1
32720 IF PEEK(Q)<128 THEN PRINT CHR$(PEEK
      (Q));:NEXT Q:STOP
32730 PRINT CHR$(PEEK(Q)-128):QQ=QQ+1:PRI
      NT QQ,:NEXT Q:STOP
```

Actually, this is not so much a program as it is a program fragment. It is intended that you will type NEW, type in the above fragment, and then LIST the fragment to a disk file (LIST "D:LVAR") or to a cassette (LIST "C:"). Then type NEW again and ENTER or LOAD the program whose variables you want to list. Finally, use ENTER to re-enter the fragment from disk (ENTER "D:LVAR") or cassette (ENTER "C:"). Then type GOTO 32700 to obtain your Variable Name Table listing.

Of course, if you had OPENed a channel to the printer (OPEN #1,8,0,"P:"), you could change the PRINTs to direct the listing to the printer (PRINT #1; CHR$ (<expression>)).

How does the fragment work? The reason for the start and end limits for the FOR loop are simple: word location 130 ($82) contains the pointer to the beginning of the Variable Name Table and word location 132 ($84) contains the pointer to the end of that same table, plus 1. So we simply traipse through that table, printing characters as we encounter them — except that when we encounter a character with its most significant bit on (IF PEEK(Q) > 127), we turn off that bit before printing it and start the next name on a new line.

Notice that we use the variable QQ to allow us to print out the token value for each variable name. We will use this information in some later chapters.

Also note that the variable names QQ and Q will appear in your variable name listing. Sorry. We *can* write a program which would accomplish the same thing without using variables, but it would be two or three times as big and much harder to understand. Of course, if you consistently use certain variable names, such as *I* and *J* in FOR-NEXT loops, you could use those names here instead, thus not affecting the count of variables in use.

Incidentally, the STOP at the end of the third line *should* be unnecessary, since the table is supposed to end with a character with its upper bit on. But I've learned not to take chances — things don't always go as they're supposed to.

Variable Values

In this chapter, we will show how you can determine the value of any variable by inspecting the Variable Value Table. Actually, in many respects this is a waste of effort. After all, if I need to know the value of the variable TOTAL, I can just type PRINT TOTAL.

But this book *is* supposed to be a guide, and there are a few uses for this information, particularly in assembly language subroutines, and it is instructive in that it gives us an inkling of what BASIC goes through to evaluate a variable reference.

It will probably be better to present the program first, and then explain what it does. Before doing so, though, note that the program fragment expects you to give it a valid variable token (128 through 255). No checks are made on the validity of that number, since we are all intelligent humans here and since we want to save program space. Enough. The program:

```
32500 PRINT :PRINT "WHAT VARIABLE NUMBER
      ";:INPUT Q
32505 Q=PEEK(134)+256*PEEK(135)+(Q-128)*
      8
32510 PRINT :PRINT "VARIABLE NUMBER ";PE
      EK(Q+1),
32515 ON INT(PEEK(Q)/64) GOTO 32600,3265
      0
32520 PRINT "IS A NUMBER, ":PRINT ,"VALU
      E ";
32525 QEXP=PEEK(Q+2):IF QEXP>127 THEN PR
      INT "-";:QEXP=QEXP-128
32530 QNUM=0:FOR QQ=Q+3 TO Q+7
32535 QNUM=QNUM*100+PEEK(QQ)-6*INT(PEEK(
      QQ)/16):NEXT QQ
32540 QEXP=QEXP-68:IF QEXP=0 THEN 32555
32545 FOR QQ=QEXP TO SGN(QEXP) STEP -SGN
      (QEXP)
```

```
32550 QNUM=(QEXP>0)*QNUM*100+(QEXP<0)*QN
      UM/100:NEXT QQ
32555 PRINT QNUM:PRINT :GOTO 32500
32570 IF PEEK(Q)/2<>INT(PEEK(Q)/2) THEN
      32580
32575 PRINT ,"AND IS NOT YET DIMENSIONED
      ":POP:GOTO 32500
32580 PRINT ,"ADDRESS IS ";PEEK(Q+2)+256
      *PEEK(Q+3):RETURN
32600 PRINT "IS AN ARRAY, ":GOSUB 32570
32610 PRINT ,"DIM 1 IS ";PEEK(Q+4)+256*P
      EEK(Q+5)
32615 PRINT ,"DIM 2 IS ";PEEK(Q+6)+256*P
      EEK(Q+7)
32620 GOTO 32500
32650 PRINT "IS A STRING, ":GOSUB 32570
32660 PRINT ,"LENGTH IS ";PEEK(Q+4)+256*
      PEEK(Q+5)
32665 PRINT ,"{3 SPACES}DIM IS ";PEEK(Q+
      6)+256*PEEK(Q+7)
32670 GOTO 32500
```

Did you get lost in all of that? I got lost several times as I wrote it, but it seems to work well. Shall we discuss it?

The first place where confusion may arise is when I ask you to give a variable token from 128 to 255, and then reveal that the entry in the Variable Value Table thinks variable numbers range from 0 to 127. Actually, there is no anomaly here. The variable token that you input is the token value of the variable in your program. The number in the table is its relative position. The numbers differ only in their uppermost bit.

The program uses the number you specify to form an address of an entry somewhere within the Variable Value Table. It then displays the internal variable number and examines the flag byte of the variable entry. Recall that the uppermost bit ($80, or 128) of the flag byte is on, if this variable is a string. The next bit ($40, or 64) is on if the variable is an array. If neither is on, the variable is a normal floating point number (or *scalar,* as it is sometimes called, to distinguish it from a floating point array). All this is decided and acted upon in line 32515.

Before examining what happens if the number is a scalar, let's look at strings and arrays. Both start out (lines 32600 and 32650) by identifying themselves and calling a subroutine which determines if the variable has been DIMensioned yet. If not, the subroutine tells us so, removes the GOSUB entry from the stack, and starts the whole shebang over again. If the variable is DIMensioned, though, we print its address before returning. Note that the address printed is the *relative address* within the String/Array Table.

If the DIMension check subroutine returns, both string and array variables have their vitals printed out before the program asks you for another variable number. In the case of a string, we see the current length (as would be obtained by the LENgth function) and its dimension. For an array, we see both dimensions. Note that array dimensions here are always one greater than the user program specified, so that a zero dimension value means "this dimension is unused."

Point of interest: this program will never print a zero for an array dimension. Why? Because Atari BASIC never places a zero in either dimension when the DIM statement is executed. In a way, this is a "feature" (a feature is a documented bug). It implies that we may code DIM XX(7) and yet use something like PRINT XX(N,0). In other words, a singly dimensioned array in Atari BASIC is exactly equivalent to a doubly dimensioned array with a 0 as the second subscript in the DIM statement.

Back to the listing. Fairly straightforward up until now. But look what happens if the variable is a scalar, a single floating point number.

First, we obtain the exponent byte; if its upper bit is on, the number is negative, so we print the minus sign before turning the bit off.

Second, we must loop through the five bytes of the mantissa, accumulating a value. The really strange part here is line 32535, so let's examine it closely. As we get each byte, we must multiply what we have gotten so far by 100 (remember, floating point numbers are in BCD format, so each byte represents a power of 100). Then, what we really want to do is add in 10 times the higher digit in the byte, plus the lower digit. We could have gotten those numbers as follows:

```
NEWBCDVALUE=OLDBCDVALUE*100
HIGHER=INT(PEEK(QQ)/16)
```

LOWER=PEEK(QQ)–16*HIGHER
BYTEVALUE=10*HIGHER+LOWER
NEWBCDVALUE=NEWBCDVALUE+BYTEVALUE
OLDBCDVALUE=NEWBCDVALUE

Hopefully, your algebra is up to understanding how line 32535 is just a simplification of all that. If not, don't worry about it. It works.

But we still haven't accounted for the exponent. Now, exponents in the Atari floating point format are powers of 100 in "excess 64" notation, which simply means that you subtract 64 from the exponent to get the real power of 100. But wait! The implied decimal point is all the way to the left of the number. So we must bias our "excess 64" by the five multiplies-by-100 we did in deriving the BCD value. All that is done in line 32540.

Finally, we simply count the exponent down to one or up to minus one, depending on what it started at. And line 32545 is tricky, but not too much so. I will leave its inner workings as an exercise for you, the reader.

And, hard though it may be to believe, we arrive at line 32555 with the number in hand. Then we PRINT it.

Did we really have to go through all that? Not really, but perhaps it gives you an idea of what BASIC's GETTOK routine ($AB3E) does when it encounters a variable name.

Finally, to test all this out, you should type it in, LIST it to disk or cassette, use NEW, and then enter or load your favorite program. Finally, re-ENTER this program fragment from disk or cassette and type GOTO 32500. Just for fun, you might try finding the variable values for the following program:

```
10 A = 12.34567890 : B = 9876543210
20 C = 0.0000556677
30 GOTO 60
40 D$ = "WILL NEVER BE EXECUTED"
50 E(7) = 1
60 DIM F$(30), G$(40), H(9,17), J(7)
70 G$="ONLY THIS STRING WILL HAVE LENGTH"
```

Type this little guy in, ENTER the variable value printer, and RUN the whole thing. Answer the variable number prompt with numbers from 128 to 135 and see what you get. It's interesting!

Examining the Statement Table

If you will recall, Chapter 3 in Part 1 discussed the various user tables that existed in Atari BASIC's RAM memory space. Specifically, it discussed the Variable Name Table, Variable Value Table, Statement Table, String/Array Table, and Runtime Stack.

In the last two chapters, we investigated the Variable Name Table and the Variable Value Table, showing how Atari BASIC can examine itself. So what is more logical than to now use Atari BASIC to display the contents of the Statement Table?

While we could write a program that would examine the tokenized program and produce source text, there is little incentive to do so. The task would be both very difficult and very redundant: BASIC's LIST command performs the same task very nicely, thank you.

What we can do, though, is write a program which will show the actual hex tokens used in a logical and almost readable form. Again, let's look at the program before decoding what it does.

```
10 DIM NUM$(4)
40 DIM DEC$(16):DEC$="0123456789ABCDEF"
50 CVDEC=9100
100 GOTO 32000
110 ERROR- THIS IS AN ERROR LINE
120 DATA AND, THIS, IS, DATA, 1,2,3
130 REM LINES 110 TO 130 ARE FOR DEMONST
    RATION PURPOSES ONLY
9100 REM CONVERT DECIMAL TO HEX
9110 DIV=4096
9120 FOR I=1 TO 4
9130 N=INT(NUM/DIV):NUM$(I,I)=DEC$(N+1)
9140 NUM=NUM-DIV*N:DIV=DIV/16
9150 NEXT I
9160 RETURN
```

```
32ØØØ QQ=PEEK(136)+256*PEEK(137)
32Ø1Ø Q=PEEK(QQ)+256*PEEK(QQ+1):QS=QQ:QQ
      =QQ+3
32Ø15 IF Q>32767 THEN PRINT "--END--":ST
      OP
32Ø2Ø QL=PEEK(QQ-1)+QS:PRINT "LINE NUMBE
      R ";Q,"LINE LENGTH ";PEEK(QQ-1)
32Ø3Ø QT=PEEK(QQ+1):PRINT "{2 SPACES}STM
      T LENGTH ";PEEK(QQ),"STMT CODE ";P
      EEK(QQ+1)
32Ø4Ø Q=PEEK(QQ)+QS:QQ=QQ+2
32Ø5Ø IF QQ<Q THEN 32Ø8Ø
32Ø6Ø IF Q<QL THEN PRINT :GOTO 32Ø3Ø
32Ø7Ø PRINT :GOTO 32Ø1Ø
32Ø8Ø IF QT>1 AND QT<55 THEN 3212Ø
32Ø9Ø PRINT "{2 SPACES}UNTOKENIZED::";
321ØØ PRINT CHR$(PEEK(QQ));:QQ=QQ+1:IF Q
      Q<Q THEN 321ØØ
3211Ø PRINT :GOTO 32Ø1Ø
3212Ø NUM=PEEK(QQ):GOSUB CVDEC
32125 IF PEEK(QQ)>127 THEN PRINT " V=";N
      UM$(3):GOTO 322ØØ
3213Ø IF PEEK(QQ)>15 THEN PRINT " ";NUM$
      (3);:GOTO 322ØØ
3214Ø IF PEEK(QQ)=14 THEN GOTO 3217Ø
3215Ø QQ=QQ+1:QN=PEEK(QQ):NUM=QN:GOSUB C
      VDEC
32155 PRINT " S,";NUM$(3);"=";:IF QN=Ø T
      HEN 322ØØ
3216Ø FOR QQ=QQ+1 TO QQ+QN-1:PRINT CHR$(
      PEEK(QQ));:NEXT QQ:GOTO 3219Ø
3217Ø PRINT " N=";
3218Ø FOR QQ=QQ+1 TO QQ+5:NUM=PEEK(QQ):G
      OSUB CVDEC:PRINT NUM$(3);:NEXT QQ
3219Ø QQ=QQ-1:PRINT
322ØØ QQ=QQ+1:IF QQ<Q THEN 3212Ø
3221Ø PRINT :IF QQ<QL THEN 32Ø3Ø
3222Ø PRINT :GOTO 32Ø1Ø
```

Now, even if you don't want to type all that in, there are a few points to be made about it. First, note that lines 10 through 50 and 9100 through 9160 are the decimal-to-hex converter from

Chapter 2. Then, let's start with line 32000 and do a functional description, with the line numbers denoting the portion we are examining.

32000. Decimal 136 is hex $88, the location of STMTAB, the pointer to the user's program space.

32010, 32020. In each line, the first two bytes are the line number; the next byte is the line length (actually, the offset to next line). Remember, line 32768 is actually the direct statement.

32030, 32040. Within a line, each statement begins with a statement length (the offset to the next statement from the beginning of the line) and a statement token.

32050-32070. Boundary conditions are checked for.

32080-32110. REM becomes statement token 0, DATA is token 1 and the error token is 55 ($37). All three of them simply store the user's input unchanged.

32120. Remember, any token with its upper bit on indicates a variable number token. They really don't need to be special cased in this program, but we do so for readability.

32130. Operator tokens have values of 16 to 127 ($10 to $7F).

32140-32160. For string constants (also called *string literals*), we simply print out the string length and its contents (the characters between the quote signs).

32170-32180. For numeric constants, we simply print the hex values of all six bytes.

32190-32200. Clean-up. We ensure that we return for all remaining tokens (if any) in each statement and for all remaining statements (if any) in each line.

Observe the FOR-NEXT loop controls in line 32180. Why QQ+1 TO QQ+5 if we want six values printed out? Ah, but this is a trick. Note that the loop termination value (QQ+5) involves the loop variable (QQ). The problem is, though, that the loop variable is changed by the prior implied assignment (QQ=QQ+1) *when the assignment takes place* — which is, of course, before the determination of the value of "QQ+5" takes place.

In other words, by the time we are ready to evaluate QQ+5, the variable QQ has already been changed from its original value to its new, loop controlling value (QQ+1).

Quite possibly, the proper general solution to using a FOR loop's variable in its own termination (or STEP) values is to assign it to a temporary variable, thusly:

QTEMP = QQ:FOR QQ = QTEMP + 1 TO QTEMP + 6

Did you notice that line 32160 actually has the same problem? Notice that we solved it there by adding –1 to the termination value to compensate for the + 1 in the initialization assignment.

One last comment before leaving the subject of strange FOR-NEXT loops. In Atari BASIC (and, indeed, in virtually all microcomputer BASICs), the termination (TO) value and the STEP value are determined when the FOR statement is first executed and are NOT changeable. Example:

```
10 X=7:Y=2
20 FOR I = 1 TO X STEP Y
30 X = X+1
40 Y = Y+X
50 NEXT I
```

This FOR loop will execute exactly four times (I = 1, 3, 5, and 7). The fact that X and Y change within the loop has no effect on the actual loop execution.

Viewing the Runtime Stack

The Runtime Stack is the last of the user RAM tables that we will discuss in Part 2.

Perhaps you noticed that we left out a discussion of the String/Array Table in Part 2. The omission was on purpose: there seems little purpose in PEEKing the contents of this table when BASIC's PRINT statement does an admirable job of letting you see all variable values. However, if you are so inclined, you could use the general purpose memory PEEKer program of Chapter 2 to view any portion of any memory, including the String/Array Table.

On the other hand, looking at the Runtime Stack is kind of fun and enlightening. And the program we will present here might even find use on occasion. If you are having trouble tracing a program's flow, through various GOSUBs and/or FOR loops, simply drop in the routine below and GOSUB to it at an appropriate place in your program. It will print out a LIFO (Last In, First Out) listing of all active GOSUB calls and FOR-NEXT loop beginnings.

```
10 FOR J=1 TO 3
20 GOSUB 30
30 FOR K=1 TO 5
40 GOSUB 50
50 JUNK=7:FOR Q=1 TO 2:GOSUB 32400
32400 QQ=PEEK(144)+256*PEEK(145)
32410 IF QQ<=PEEK(142)+256*PEEK(143) THE
      N PRINT "--END OF STACK--":STOP
32420 PRINT "AT LINE ";PEEK(QQ-3)+256*PE
      EK(QQ-2);
32430 PRINT ", OFFSET ";PEEK(QQ-1);
32440 IF PEEK(QQ-4)=0 THEN PRINT ", GOSU
      B":QQ=QQ-4:GOTO 32410
32450 PRINT ", FOR (#";PEEK(QQ-4);")":QQ
      =QQ-16:GOTO 32410
```

The first thing you might notice about this little routine is that, in contrast to all the programs we have used so far, it examines its portion of user RAM backward. That is, it starts at the top (high address) of the Runtime Stack area and works downward toward the bottom.

Again, nothing surprising. If you will recall the description of entries on this stack (pages 18-19 and 133-34), you will remember that every entry, whether a GOSUB or FOR, has a four-byte header. And, while FOR statements also have twelve bytes of termination and step value added, the four bytes are always at the *top* of each entry — they are the last items put on the stack.

Thus, we start at the top of the stack and examine four bytes. If the type byte is zero, it is a GOSUB entry, and all we must do is display the line number and statement offset. If we remove the four-byte header by subtracting 4 from our stack pointer, we are ready to examine the next entry.

In the case of a FOR entry, we similarly display the line number and statement offset. However, each FOR entry also has a variable token associated with it, so we also display that token's value. With the variable name lister of Chapter 2, you can find out which variable is controlling this FOR loop. Finally, note that after displaying a FOR loop entry, we remove sixteen bytes (the four-byte header and the two six-byte floating point values) in preparation for the next entry.

Incidentally, lines 10 through 50 are present as examples only. Add lines 32400 to 32450 to your own programs and see where you've come from.

Fixed Tokens

In the last chapter, we discussed the last of the tables in user RAM. Now we will see how and where BASIC stores its internal ROM-based tables.

As we noted in Chapter 5 of Part 1 (and viewed via the listing program of Chapter 5 in this Part), there are four kinds of tokens in an Atari BASIC program: (1) statement name tokens, (2) operator tokens, (3) variable tokens, and (4) constant tokens (string and numeric constants). Also, we learned in Part 1 how the tokenizing process works, converting the user's ATASCII source code into tokens. What we didn't learn, though, was exactly what token replaces what BASIC keyword.

In this chapter, we present a program which will list all of the fixed tokens (those in ROM). Actually, the program presents three listings, each consisting of a list of token values with their associated ATASCII strings. But wait a moment! Three listings? There are only *two* ROM-based tables — SNTAB and OPNTAB.

Yes, but it seems that this program is also capable of listing the Variable Name Table. Why list it again, when we did it so well in Chapter 3? Because we wanted to show you how BASIC itself does it. In many ways, this program emulates the functions of the SEARCH routine at address $A462 in the source listing. And, yes, BASIC uses a single routine to search all three of these same tables. You might want to examine BASIC's SEARCH routine at the same time you peruse this listing.

```
100 REM we make use of the general purpose
110 REM token lister three times:
200 PRINT :PRINT "A LIST OF VARIABLE TOKENS"
210 ADDR=PEEK(130)+256*PEEK(131)
220 SKIP=0:TOKEN=128:GOSUB 1000
300 PRINT :PRINT "A LIST OF STATEMENT TOKENS"
310 ADDR=42159:SKIP=2:TOKEN=0:GOSUB 1000
400 PRINT :PRINT "A LIST OF OPERATOR TOKENS"
410 ADDR=42979:SKIP=0:TOKEN=16:GOSUB 1000
420 STOP
1000 REM a general purpose token listing routine
```

```
1001 REM
1002 REM On entry to this routine, the following
1003 REM variables have meanings:
1004 REM ADDR = address of beginning of table
1005 REM SKIP = bytes per entry to skip
1006 REM TOKEN = starting token number
1007 REM
1100 ADDR=ADDR+SKIP:IF PEEK(ADDR)=0 THEN RETURN
1110 PRINT TOKEN,:TOKEN=TOKEN+1
1120 IF PEEK(ADDR)>127 THEN 1140
1130 PRINT CHR$(PEEK(ADDR));:ADDR=ADDR+1:GOTO 1120
1140 PRINT CHR$(PEEK(ADDR)-128):ADDR=ADDR+1:GOTO 1100
```

The main routine is actually lines 1100 through 1140 (while lines 1000 through 1007 simply explain it all). It's actually fairly simple. Each table is assumed to consist of a fixed number of bytes followed by a variable number of ATASCII bytes, the last of which has its upper bit on.

In line 1100, we skip over the fixed bytes (if any) and check for the end of the table. After that, we simply print the token value followed by the name.

Worth examining, though, are lines 200 through 420, where we call the main subroutine. First, note that the Variable Name Table has no bytes to skip and is located via its zero-page pointer. Naturally, the first variable token value is 128.

Each entry in the Statement Name Table (SNTAB, at location $A4AF) has two leading bytes (actually, the two-byte address, minus 1, of the syntax table entry for this statement). Statement name token values begin at zero, and 42159 is the decimal address of SNTAB.

Finally, the smallest-numbered operator token is 16 decimal (except for string and numeric constants, which are special cased). There are no leading bytes in the Operator Name Table, and it starts at location 42979 decimal (OPNTAB, at $A7E3).

Chapter Eight

What Takes Precedence?

There was one other ROM-based table mentioned in Part 1 which deserves some attention here. You may recall that when an expression is executed, the execution operators are given particular precedences, so that in BASIC, 2+3*4 equals 14, not 20. Chapter 7 of Part 1 does a particularly thorough job of explaining the concepts of precedence.

The program presented in this chapter prints out all of BASIC's operator tokens along with their token values and their dual precedence values. Actually, the program provides a visual readout of OPRTAB (Operator PRecedence TABle, at $AC3F).

In each pair of precedence values listed, the first number is the go-onto-stack value and the second is the come-off-stack value.

```
100 PRINT "A LIST OF OPERATOR TOKENS"
110 PRINT "  WITH THEIR PRECEDENCE TABLE VALUES"
220 SKIP=0:TOKEN=128:GOSUB 1000
1000 ADDR=42979:REM WHERE OP NAMES START
1010 TOKEN=16:REM LOWEST TOKEN VALUE
1020 REM NOW THE MAIN CODE LOOP
1100 IF PEEK(ADDR)=0 THEN STOP
1110 PRINT TOKEN,:PREC=PEEK(44095+TOKEN-16)
1120 PRINT INT(PREC/16);":";PREC-16*INT(PREC/16),
1130 PREC=PEEK(ADDR):ADDR=ADDR+1
1140 IF PREC<128 THEN PRINT CHR$(PREC);:GOTO 1130
1150 PRINT CHR$(PREC-128):TOKEN=TOKEN+1:GOTO 1100
```

If you closely examined the program in the last chapter, you will note a striking similarity to this program, especially lines 1100 through 1150. Actually, the only thing we have really added is the precedence printout of line 1120.

And note the form of the PEEK in line 1110. Then look at the line of code at address $AAF1 in the BASIC listing. Given the limitations of dissimilar languages, the code is identical. This is more evidence that you really can use BASIC as a tool to diagnose itself.

Using What We Know

Now that Atari BASIC stands revealed before you, what do you *do* with it? Many authors have, even without benefit of the listing in this book, either used or fooled BASIC in ways that we who designed it never dreamed of.

For example, consider what happens if you change BASIC's STARP pointer ($8C) to be equal to its ENDSTAR value ($8E). Remember, BASIC's SAVE command saves everything from the contents of VNTP to the contents of STARP (as documented in Chapter 10 of Part 1). So changing what is in STARP is tantamount to telling BASIC to SAVE more (or less) than what it normally would. Presto! We can now save the entire array and string space to disk or tape, also.

Is it useful? Here's one program that is, using the concepts we learned in the previous chapters.

```
30000 PRINT :PRINT "WHAT VARIABLE NUMBER
       DO YOU":PRINT,"WISH TO FIND ";
30010 INPUT QV
30020 QA=PEEK(130)+256*PEEK(131):QN=128
30030 IF QN=QV THEN 30060
30040 IF PEEK(QA)<128 THEN QA=QA+1:GOTO
      30040
30050 QN=QN+1:QA=QA+1:GOTO 30030
30060 IF PEEK(QA)<128 THEN PRINT CHR$(PE
      EK(QA));:QA=QA+1:GOTO 30060
30070 PRINT CHR$(PEEK(QA)-128);" IS THE
      VARIABLE"
30100 QA=PEEK(136)+256*PEEK(137)
30110 QN=PEEK(QA)+256*PEEK(QA+1):QL=PEEK
      (QA+2):QSV=QA:QA=QA+3
30120 IF QN>32767 THEN PRINT "--END--":E
      ND
30130 QS=PEEK(QA):QT=PEEK(QA+1):QA=QA+2:
      IF QT>1 AND QT<55 THEN 30150
```

```
30140 QA=QSV+QL:GOTO 30110
30150 IF PEEK(QA)=QV THEN PRINT "LINE ";
      QN:GOTO 30140
30160 IF PEEK(QA)>15 THEN 30200
30170 IF PEEK(QA)=14 THEN QA=QA+6:GOTO 3
      0200
30180 QA=QA+PEEK(QA+1)+1
30200 QA=QA+1:IF QA<QSV+QS THEN 30150
30210 IF QA<QSV+QL THEN 30130
30220 GOTO 30110
```

What does it do? It finds all the places in your program that you used a particular variable. And how do you use it? Type it in, LIST it to disk or cassette, and clear the user memory via NEW. Now type, ENTER, or LOAD the program you wish to investigate (and then SAVE it, if you haven't already done so). Finally, ENTER this program fragment from the disk or cassette where you LISTed it and type GOTO 30000.

Although the program asks you for a variable *number* (which you can get via the program of Chapter 3), it doesn't really matter if you don't know it. The program will print your chosen variable's name before giving all the references. If you chose wrong, try again.

And how does it work? Somewhat like the program token lister of Chapter 5, except that here we are simply skipping everything but variable name references. First, though, we use a modified Variable Name Table lister (lines 30020 through 30070) to tell you what name you chose.

Then, we start at the beginning of the program (line 30100) and check each user line number (30110 and 30120). Within each line, we loop through, checking all statements (30130), skipping entirely all REMs, DATA lines, and lines with syntax errors (line 30140). If we find ourselves in an expression, we check for a matching variable token reference (line 30150) and print it if found, after which we skip the rest of the line. We also skip over numeric and string constants (lines 30170 and 30180). Finally, we check to see if we are at the end of the statement (30200) or the end of a line (30210 and 30220).

This is a fairly large program fragment, and it will prove most useful in very large programs, where you can't remember, for example, how many places you are using the variable name LOOP. So you might want to try to leave room in memory for this aid; you may be very glad you did.

Part Three

Atari BASIC Source Code

Printed in the United States of America

Optimized Systems Software, Inc.
10379 Lansdale Avenue
Cupertino, California 95014 (U.S.A.)

Telephone: (408) 446-3099

Some Miscellaneous Equates

```
= ØØØ1      PATSIZ  EQU     $1          ; PATCH AREA SIZE
= ØØ2Ø      ZICB    EQU     $2Ø         ; zero PageIOCB
= ØØ8Ø      ZPG1    EQU     $8Ø         ; beginning of BASIC's zero page
= Ø48Ø      MISCR1  EQU     $48Ø        ; syntax stack, etc.
= Ø5ØØ      MISCRAM EQU     $5ØØ        ; other RAM usage

= E456      CIO     EQU     $E456       ; in OS ROMs
= Ø34Ø      IOCBORG EQU     $34Ø        ; where IOCBs start
= Ø3ØØ      DCBORG  EQU     $3ØØ        ; where DCB (for SIO) is

= AØØØ      ROM     EQU     $AØØØ       ; begin code here
= ØØD2      ZFP     EQU     $D2         ; begin fltg point work area

= ØØ9B      CR      EQU     $9B         ; ATASCII end of line

= Ø2E7      LMADR   EQU     $2E7        ; system lo mem
= Ø2E5      HMADR   EQU     $2E5        ; system high mem
= Ø2E5      HIMEM   EQU     HMADR

= D8ØØ      FPORG   EQU     $D8ØØ       ; fltg point in OS ROMs
= ØØ11      BRKBYT  EQU     $11
= ØØØ8      WARMFL  EQU     $Ø8         ; warmstart flag
= D2ØA      RNDLOC  EQU     $D2ØA       ; get a random byte here
= BFF9      CRTGI   EQU     $BFFC-3     ; cartridge init vector
= ØØ5D      EPCHAR  EQU     $5D         ; the "?" for INPUT statement
= E471      BYELOC  EQU     $E471       ; where to go for BYE
= ØØØA      DOSLOC  EQU     $ØA         ; via here to exit to DOS
= ØØ55      SCRX    EQU     $55         ; X AXIS
= ØØ54      SCRY    EQU     $54         ; Y AXIS
= Ø2C4      CREGS   EQU     $2C4        ; COLOR REGISTER
= Ø2FB      SVCOLOR EQU     $2FB        ; SAVE COLOR FOR CIO
= D2Ø8      SREG1   EQU     $D2Ø8       ; SOUND REG 1
= D2ØØ      SREG2   EQU     $D2ØØ       ; SOUND REG 2
= D2Ø1      SREG3   EQU     $D2Ø1       ; SOUND REG 3
= D2ØF      SKCTL   EQU     $D2ØF       ; sound control
= Ø27Ø      GRFBAS  EQU     $27Ø        ; 1ST GRAPHICS FUNCTION ADDR
= Ø2FE      DSPFLG  EQU     $2FE        ; ATARI DISPLAY FLAG
= ØØØE      APHM    EQU     $E          ; APPLICATION HIGH MEM
```

Zero Page

RAM Table Pointers

```
ØØØØ  = ØØ8Ø        ORG      ZPG1
ØØ8Ø            LOMEM                      ; LOW MEMORY POINTER
ØØ8Ø            ARGOPS                     ; ARGUMENT/OPERATOR STACK
ØØ8Ø            ARGSTK
ØØ8Ø  = ØØØ2    OUTBUFF  DS     2          ; SYNTAX OUTPUT BUFFER
ØØ82  = ØØØ2    VNTP     DS     2          ; VARIABLE NAME TABLE POINTER
ØØ84  = ØØØ2    VNTD     DS     2          ; VARIABLE NAME TABLE DUMMY END
ØØ86  = ØØØ2    VVTP     DS     2          ; VARIABLE VALUE TABLE POINTER
ØØ88            ENDVVT                     ; END VARIABLE VALUE TABLE
ØØ88  = ØØØ2    STMTAB   DS     2          ; STATEMENT TABLE [PROGRAM] ;
                                             POINTER
ØØ8A  = ØØØ2    STMCUR   DS     2          ; CURRENT PGM PTR
ØØ8C  = ØØØ2    STARP    DS     2          ; STRING/ARRAY TABLE POINTER
ØØ8E            ENDSTAR                    ; END STRING/ARRAY SPACE
ØØ8E  = ØØØ2    RUNSTK   DS     2          ; RUN TIME STACK
ØØ9Ø            TOPRSTK                    ; END RUN TIME STACK
ØØ9Ø  = ØØØ2    MEMTOP   DS     2          ; TOP OF USED MEMORY
ØØ92  = ØØØ1    MEOLFLG  DS     1          ; MODIFIED EOL FLAG
ØØ93  = ØØØ1             DS     1          ; ::SPARE::
```

Miscellaneous Zero Page RAM

```
                ;          USED FOR FREQUENTLY USED VALUES
                ;          TO DECREASE ROM SIZE AND INCREASE
                ;          EXECUTION SPEED.  ALSO USED FOR VARIOUS
                ;          INDIRECT ADDRESS POINTERS.
                ;
ØØ94  = ØØØ1    COX      DS    1        ; CURRENT OUTPUT INDEX
ØØ95            POKADR                  ; POKE ADDRESS
ØØ95  = ØØØ2    SRCADR   DS    2        ; SEARCH ADR
ØØ97            INDEX2                  ; ARRAY INDEX 2
ØØ97  = ØØØ2    SVESA    DS    2        ; SAVE EXPAND START ADR
ØØ99  = ØØØ2    MVFA     DS    2        ; MOVE FROM ADR
ØØ9B  = ØØØ2    MVTA     DS    2        ; MOVE TO ADR
ØØ9D            CPC                     ; CUR SYNTAX PGM COUNTER
ØØ9D  = ØØØ2    WVVTPT   DS    2        ; WORKING VAR TABLE PTR VALUE
ØØ9F            MAXCIX                  ; MAX SYNTAX CIX
ØØ9F  = ØØØ1    LLNGTH   DS    1        ; LINE LENGTH
ØØAØ  = ØØØ2    TSLNUM   DS    2        ; TEST LINE NO
ØØA2  = ØØØ2    MVLNG    DS    2        ; MOVE LENGTH
ØØA4  = ØØØ2    ECSIZE   DS    2        ; MOVE SIZE
ØØA6  = ØØØ1    DIRFLG   DS    1        ; DIRECT EXECUTE FLAG
ØØA7            STMLBD                  ; STMT LENGTH BYTE DISPL
ØØA7  = ØØØ1    NXTSTD   DS    1        ; NEXT STMT DISPL
ØØA8            STMSTRT                 ; STMT START CIX
ØØA8  = ØØØ1    STINDEX  DS    1        ; CURR STMT INDEX
ØØA9            STKLVL                  ; SYNTAX STACK LEVEL
ØØA9            IBUFFX                  ; INPUT BUFFER INDEX
ØØA9  = ØØØ1    OPSTKX   DS    1        ; OPERATOR STACK INDEX
ØØAA            ARSLVL
ØØAA            SRCSKP                  ; SEARCH SKIP FACTOR
ØØAA  = ØØØ1    ARSTKX   DS    1        ; ARG STACK INDEX
ØØAB            TSCOX                   ; TSCOW LENGTH BYTE PTR
ØØAB  = ØØØ1    EXSVOP   DS    1        ; SAVED OPERATOR
ØØAC            TVSCIX                  ; SAVE CIX FOR TVAT
ØØAC  = ØØØ1    EXSVPR   DS    1        ; SAVED OPERATOR PRECEDENCE
ØØAD            SVVNTP                  ; SAVE VAR NAME TBL PTR
ØØAD  = ØØØ2    LELNUM   DS    2        ; LIST END LINE #
ØØAF            ATEMP                   ; TEMP FOR ARRAYS
ØØAF            STENUM                  ; SEARCH TABLE ENTRY NUMBER
ØØAF  = ØØØ1    SCANT    DS    1        ; LIST SCAN COUNTER
ØØBØ            SVONTC                  ; SAVE ONT SRC CODE
ØØBØ  = ØØØ1    COMCNT   DS    1        ; COMMA COUNT FOR EXEXOR
ØØB1            SVVVTE                  ; SAVE VAR VALUE EXP SIZE
ØØB1  = ØØØ1    ADFLAG   DS    1        ; ASSIGN/DIM FLAG
ØØB2            SVONTL                  ; SAVE ONT SRC ARG LEN
ØØB2  = ØØØ1    SVDISP   DS    1        ; DISPL INTO LINE OF FOR/GOSUB
                                          TOKEN
ØØB3            ONLOOP                  ; LOOP CONTROL FOR OP
ØØB3            SVONTX                  ; SAVE ONT SRC INDEX
ØØB3  = ØØØ1    SAVDEX   DS    1        ; SAVE INDEX INTO STMT
ØØB4  = ØØØ1    ENTDTD   DS    1        ; ENTER DEVICE TB
ØØB5  = ØØØ1    LISTDTD  DS    1        ; LIST DEVICE TBL
ØØB6  = ØØØ1    DATAD    DS    1        ; DATA DISPL
ØØB7  = ØØØ2    DATALN   DS    2        ; DATA LINNO
ØØB9  = ØØØ1    ERRNUM   DS    1        ; ERROR #
ØØBA  = ØØØ2    STOPLN   DS    2        ; LINE # STOPPED AR [FOR CON]
ØØBC  = ØØØ2    TRAPLN   DS    2        ; TRAP LINE # [FOR ERROR]
ØØBE  = ØØØ2    SAVCUR   DS    2        ; SAVE CURRENT LINE ADDR
ØØCØ  = ØØØ1    IOCMD    DS    1        ; I/O COMMAND
ØØC1  = ØØØ1    IODVC    DS    1        ; I/O DEVICE
ØØC2  = ØØØ1    PROMPT   DS    1        ; PROMPT CHAR
ØØC3  = ØØØ1    ERRSAV   DS    1        ; ERROR # FOR USER
ØØC4  = ØØØ2    TEMPA    DS    2        ; TEMP ADDR CELL
ØØC6  = ØØØ2    ZTEMP2   DS    2        ; TEMP
ØØC8  = ØØØ1    COLOR    DS    1        ; SET COLOR FOR BASE
ØØC9  = ØØØ1    PTABW    DS    1        ; PRINT TAB WIDTH
ØØCA  = ØØØ1    LOADFLG  DS    1        ; LOAD IN PROGRESS FLAG
```

Argument Work Area (AWA)

Floating Point Work Area

```
00CB   = 00D2          ORG      ZFP
00D2                 TVTYPE                        ; VARIABLE TYPE
00D2   = 0001        VTYPE    DS      1            ; VARIABLE TYPE
00D3                 TVNUM                         ; VARIABLE NUMBER
00D3   = 0001        VNUM     DS      1            ; VARIABLE NUMBER
       = 0006        FPREC    EQU      6
       = 0005        FMPREC   EQU      FPREC-1     ; LENGTH OF FLOATING POINT
                                                   ; MANTISSA
00D4                 BININT                        ; FP REGO
00D4   = 0001        FR0      DS      1            ; FP REG0
00D5   = 0005        FR0M     DS      FPREC-1      ; FP REG0 MANTISSA

00DA   = 0006        FRE      DS      FPREC        ; FP REG0 EXP

00E0   = 0001        FR1      DS      1            ; FP REG 1
00E1   = 0005        FR1M     DS      FPREC-1      ; FP REG1 MANTISSA

00E6   = 0006        FR2      DS      FPREC        ; FP REG 2
00EC   = 0001        FRX      DS      1            ; FP SPARE
```

RAM for ASCII to Floating Point Conversion

```
00ED   = 0001        EEXP     DS      1            ; VALUE OF E
00EE                 FRSIGN                        ; FP SIGN
00EE   = 0001        NSIGN    DS      1            ; SIGN OF #
00EF                 SQRCNT
00EF                 PLYCNT
00EF   = 0001        ESIGN    DS      1            ; SIGN OF EXPONENT
00F0                 SGNFLG
00F0   = 0001        FCHRFLG  DS      1            ; 1ST CHAR FLAG
00F1                 XFMFLG
00F1   = 0001        DIGRT    DS      1            ; # OF DIGITS RIGHT OF DECIMAL
```

Input Buffer Controls

```
00F2   = 0001        CIX      DS      1            ; CURRENT INPUT INDEX
00F3   = 0002        INBUFF   DS      2            ; LINE INPUT BUFFER
```

Temps

```
00F5   = 0002        ZTEMP1   DS      2            ; LOW LEVEL ZERO PageTEMPS
00F7   = 0002        ZTEMP4   DS      2
00F9   = 0002        ZTEMP3   DS      2
```

Miscellany

```
00FB                 DEGFLG
00FB   = 0001        RADFLG   DS      1            ; 0=RADIANS, 6= DEGREES
       = 0000        RADON    EQU      0           ; INDICATE RADIANS
       = 0006        DEGON    EQU      6           ; INDICATES DEGREES
00FC   = 0002        FLPTR    DS      2            ; POLYNOMIAL POINTERS
00FE   = 0002        FPTR2    DS      2
```

Miscellaneous Non-Zero Page RAM

```
                     ;                USED FOR VALUES NOT ACCESSED FREQUENTLY
0100   = 0480          ORG      MISCR1
       = 0480        STACK    EQU      *           ; SYNTAX STACK
0480   = 0001        SIX      DS      1            ; INPUT INDEX
0481   = 0001        SOX      DS      1            ; OUTPUT INDEX
0482   = 0002        SPC      DS      2            ; PGM COUNTER
0484   = 057E          ORG      STACK+254
057E   = 0001        LBPR1    DS      1            ; LBUFF PREFIX 1
057F   = 0001        LBPR2    DS      1            ; BLUFF PREFIX 2
0580   = 0080        LBUFF    DS      128          ; LINE BUFFER
```

```
0600  = 05E0         ORG      LBUFF+$60
05E0  = 0006       PLYARG  DS      FPREC
05E6  = 0006       FPSCR   DS      FPREC
05EC  = 0006       FPSCR1  DS      FPREC
      = 05E6       FSCR    EQU     FPSCR
      = 05EC       FSCR1   EQU     FPSCR1
```

IOCB Area

```
05F2  = 0340         ORG      IOCBORG
```

IOCB — I/O Control Block

```
                   ;               THERE ARE 8 I/O CONTROL BLOCKS
                   ;               1 IOCB IS REQUIRED FOR EACH
                   ;               CURRENTLY OPEN DEVICE OR FILE.
                   ;
0340               IOCB
0340  = 0001       ICHID   DS      1             ; DEVICE HANDLER ID
0341  = 0001       ICDNO   DS      1             ; DEVICE NUMBER
0342  = 0001       ICCOM   DS      1             ; I/O COMMAND
0343  = 0001       ICSTA   DS      1             ; I/O STATUS
0344  = 0001       ICBAL   DS      1
0345  = 0001       ICBAH   DS      1             ; BUFFER ADR [H,L]
0346  = 0002       ICPUT   DS      2             ; PUT A BYTE VIA THIS
0348  = 0001       ICBLL   DS      1
0349  = 0001       ICBLH   DS      1             ; BUFFER LENGTH [H,L]
034A  = 0001       ICAUX1  DS      1             ; AUXILIARY 1
034B  = 0001       ICAUX2  DS      1             ; AUXILIARY 2
034C  = 0001       ICAUX3  DS      1             ; AUXILIARY 3
034D  = 0001       ICAUX4  DS      1             ; AUXILIARY 4
034E  = 0001       ICAUX5  DS      1             ; AUXILIARY 5
034F  = 0001           DS      1                 ; SPARE
      = 0010       ICLEN   EQU     *-IOCB
                   ;
0350  = 0070           DS      ICLEN*7           ; SPACE FOR 7 MORE IOCBS
```

ICCOM Value Equates

```
      = 0001       ICOIN   EQU     $01           ; OPEN INPUT
      = 0002       ICOOUT  EQU     $02           ; OPEN OUTPUT
      = 0003       ICOIO   EQU     $03           ; OPEN UN/OUT
      = 0004       ICGBR   EQU     $04           ; GET BINARY RECORD
      = 0005       ICGTR   EQU     $05           ; GET TEXT RECORDS
      = 0006       ICGBC   EQU     $06           ; GET BINARY CHAR
      = 0007       ICGTC   EQU     $07           ; GET TEXT CHAR
      = 0008       ICPBR   EQU     $08           ; PUT BINARY RECORD
      = 0009       ICPTR   EQU     $09           ; PUT TEXT RECORD
      = 000A       ICPBC   EQU     $0A           ; PUT BINARY CHAR
      = 000B       ICPTC   EQU     $0B           ; PUT TEXT CHAR
      = 000C       ICCLOSE EQU     $0C           ; CLOSE FILE
      = 000D       ICSTAT  EQU     $0D           ; GET STATUS
      = 000E       ICDDC   EQU     $0E           ; DEVICE DEPENDENT
      = 000E       ICMAX   EQU     $0E           ; MAX VALUE
      = 00FF       ICFREE  EQU     $FF           ; IOCB FREE INDICATOR
      = 001C       ICGR    EQU     $1C           ; OPEN GRAPHICS
      = 0011       ICDRAW  EQU     $11           ; DRAW TO
```

ICSTA Value Equates

```
      = 0001       ICSOK   EQU     $01           ; STATUS GOOD, NO ERRORS
      = 0002       ICSTR   EQU     $02           ; TRUNCATED RECORD
      = 0003       ICSEOF  EQU     $03           ; END OF FILE
      = 0080       ICSBRK  EQU     $80           ; BREAK KEY ABORT
      = 0081       ICSDNR  EQU     $81           ; DEVICE NOT READY
      = 0082       ICSNED  EQU     $82           ; NON-EXISTENT DEVICE
      = 0083       ICSDER  EQU     $83           ; DATA ERROR
      = 0084       ICSIVC  EQU     $84           ; INVALID COMMAND
      = 0085       ICSNOP  EQU     $85           ; DEVICE/FILE NOT OPEN
      = 0086       ICSIVN  EQU     $86           ; INVALID IOCB NUMBER
      = 0087       ICSWPE  EQU     $87           ; WRITE PROTECTION
```

Equates for Variables

```
                ;                        -IN VARIABLE VALUE TABLE
                ;                        -ON ARGUMENT STACK
                ;
= 0000          EVTYPE   EQU      0             ; VALUE TYPE CODE
= 0080          EVSTR    EQU      $80           ; - STRING
= 0040          EVARRAY  EQU      $40           ; - ARRAY
= 0002          EVSDTA   EQU      $02           ; - ON IF EVSADR IS ABS ADR
= 0001          EVDIM    EQU      $01           ; ON IF HAS BEEN DIM
= 0000          EVSCALER EQU      $00           ; - SCALER
                ;
= 0001          EVNUM    EQU      1             ; VARIABLE NUMBER [83 - FF]
                ;
= 0002          EVVALUE  EQU      2             ; SCALAR VALUE [6 BYTES]
                ;
= 0002          EVSADR   EQU      2             ; STRING DISPL [2]
= 0004          EVSLEN   EQU      4             ; STRING LENGTH [2]
= 0006          EVSDIM   EQU      6             ; STRING DIM [2]
                ;
= 0002          EVAADR   EQU      2             ; ARRAY DISPL [2]
= 0004          EVAD1    EQU      4             ; ARRAY DIM 1 [2]
= 0006          EVAD2    EQU      6             ; ARRAY DIM 2 [2]
```

Equates for Run Stack

```
= 0004          GFHEAD   EQU      4             ; LENGTH OF HEADER FOR FOR/GOSUB
= 000C          FBODY    EQU      12            ; LENGTH OF BODY OF FOR ELEMENT
= 0003          GFDISP   EQU      3             ; DISP TO SAVED LINE DISP
= 0001          GFLNO    EQU      1             ; DISPL TO LINE # IN HEADER
= 0000          GFTYPE   EQU      0             ; DISPL TO TYPE IN HEADER
= 0006          FSTEP    EQU      6             ; DISPL TO STEP IN FOR ELEMENT
= 0000          FLIM     EQU      0             ; DISPL TO LIMIT IN FOR ELEMENT
```

ROM Start

Cold Start

```
                        ;       COLD START - REINITIALIZES ALL MEMORY
                        ;                    WIPES OUT ANY EXISTING PROGRAM
A000                    COLDSTART
A000  A5CA                  LDA     LOADFLG         ;Y IN MIDDLE OF LOAD
A002  D004  ^A008           BNE     COLD1           ;DO COLDSTART
A004  A508                  LDA     WARMFLG         ; IF WARM START
A006  D045  ^A04D           BNE     WARMSTART       ; THEN BRANCH
A008                    COLD1
A008  A2FF                  LDX     #$FF            ; SET ENTRY STACK
A00A  9A                    TXS                     ; TO TOS
A00B  D8                    CLD                     ; CLEAR DECIMAL MODE
A00C                    XNEW
A00C  AEE702                LDX     LMADR           ;LOAD LOW
A00F  ACE802                LDY     LMADR+1         ;MEM VALUE
A012  8680                  STX     LOMEM           ; SET LOMEM
A014  8481                  STY     LOMEM+1
A016  A900                  LDA     #0              ; RESET MODIFIED
A018  8592                  STA     MEOLFLG         ; EOL FLAG
A01A  85CA                  STA     LOADFLG         ; RESET LOAD FLAG
A01C  C8                    INY                     ; ALLOW 256 FOR OUTBUFF
A01D  8A                    TXA                     ;VNTP
                        ;
A01E  A282                  LDX     #VNTP           ; GET ZPG DISPC TO VNTP
A020  9500              :CS1    STA     0,X         ; SET TABLE ADR LOW
A022  E8                    INX
A023  9400                  STY     0,X             ; SET TABLE ADR HIGH
A025  E8                    INX
A026  E092                  CPX     #MEMTOP+2       ; AT LIMIT
A028  90F6  ^A020           BCC     :CS1            ; BR IF NOT
                        ;
A02A  A286                  LDX     #VVTP           ; EXPAND VNT BY ONE
```

```
A02C  A001           LDY    #1              ; FOR END OF VNT
A02E  207FA8         JSR    EXPLOW          ; ZERO BYTE
A031  A28C           LDX    #STARP          ; EXPAND STMT TBL
A033  A003           LDY    #3              ; BY 3 BYTES
A035  207FA8         JSR    EXPLOW          ; GO DO IT
                ;
A038  A900           LDA    #0              ; SET 0
A03A  A8             TAY
A03B  9184           STA    [VNTD],Y        ; INTO VVTP
A03D  918A           STA    [STMCUR],Y      ; INTO STMCUR+0
A03F  C8             INY
A040  A980           LDA    #$80            ; $80 INTO
A042  918A           STA    [STMCUR],Y      ; STMCUR+1
A044  C8             INY
A045  A903           LDA    #$03            ; $03 INTO
A047  918A           STA    [STMCUR],Y      ; STMCUR+2
                ;
A049  A90A           LDA    #10             ; SET PRINT TAB
A04B  85C9           STA    PTABW           ; WIDTH TO 10
                ;
```

Warm Start

```
                ;       WARMSTART - BASIC RESTART
                ;                 DOES NOT DESTROY CURRENT PGM
A04D            WARMSTART
A04D  20F8B8         JSR    RUNINIT         ; INIT FOR RUN
A050  2041BD    SNX1JSR     CLSALL          ; GO CLOSE DEVICE 1-7
A053  2072BD    SNX2JSR     SETDZ           ; SET E/L DEVICE 0
A056  A592           LDA    MEOLFLG         ; IF AN EOL INSERTED
A058  F003 ^A05D     BEQ    SNX3
A05A  2099BD         JSR    RSTSEOL         ; THEN UN-INSERT IT
A05D  2057BD    SNX3    JSR     PREADY      ; PRINT READY MESSAGE
```

Syntax

```
A060                 LOCAL
```

Editor — Get Lines of Input

```
A060            SYNTAX
A060  A5CA           LDA    LOADFLG         ; IF LOAD IN PROGRESS
A062  D09C ^A000     BNE    COLDSTART       ; GO DO COLDSTART
A064  A2FF           LDX    #$FF            ; RESTORE STACK
A066  9A             TXS
A067  2051DA         JSR    INTLBF          ; GO INT LBUFF
A06A  A95D           LDA    #EPCHAR
A06C  85C2           STA    PROMPT
A06E  2092BA         JSR    GLGO            ;
A071  20F4A9         JSR    TSTBRK          ; TEST BREAK
A074  D0EA ^A060     BNE    SYNTAX          ; BR IF BREAK
                ;
A076  A900           LDA    #0              ; INIT CURRENT
A078  85F2           STA    CIX             ;INPUT INDEX TO ZERO
A07A  859F           STA    MAXCIX
A07C  8594           STA    COX             ;OUTPUT INDEX TO ZERO
A07E  85A6           STA    DIRFLG          ;SET DIRECT SMT
A080  85B3           STA    SVONTX          ; SET SAVE ONT CIX
A082  85B0           STA    SVONTC
A084  85B1           STA    SVVVTE          ; VALUE IN CASE
A086  A584           LDA    VNTD            ; OF SYNTAX ERROR
A088  85AD           STA    SVVNTP
A08A  A585           LDA    VNTD+1
A08C  85AE           STA    SVVNTP+1
                ;
A08E  20A1DB         JSR    SKBLANK         ;SKIP BLANKS
A091  209FA1         JSR    :GETLNUM        ;CONVERT AND PUT IN BUFFER
A094  20C8A2         JSR    :SETCODE        ; SET DUMMY FOR LINE LENGTH
A097  A5D5           LDA    BININT+1
A099  1002 ^A09D     BPL    :SYN0
A09B  85A6           STA    DIRFLG
```

```
A09D                    :SYN0
A09D  20A1DB               JSR      SKBLANKS        ; SKIP BLANKS
A0A0  A4F2                 LDY      CIX             ;GET INDEX
A0A2  84A8                 STY      STMSTRT         ;SAVE INCASE OF SYNTAX ERROR
A0A4  B1F3                 LDA      [INBUFF],Y      ;GET NEXT CHAR
A0A6  C99B                 CMP      #CR             ;IS IT CR
A0A8  D007 ^A0B1           BNE      :SYN1           ;BR NOT CR
A0AA  24A6                 BIT      DIRFLG          ; IF NO LINE NO.
A0AC  30B2 ^A060           BMI      SYNTAX          ; THEN NO. DELETE
A0AE  4C89A1               JMP      :SDEL           ;GO DELETE STMT
A0B1                    :SYN1
A0B1                    :XIF
A0B1  A594                 LDA      COX             ;SAVE COX
A0B3  85A7                 STA      STMLBD          ;AS PM TO STMT LENTGH BYTE
A0B5  20C8A2               JSR      :SETCODE        ; DUMMY FOR STMT LENGTH
                        ;
                        ;
A0B8  20A1DB               JSR      SKBLANK         ;GO SKIP BLANKS
A0BB  A9A4                 LDA      #SNTAB/256      ; SET UP FOR STMT
A0BD  A0AF                 LDY      #SNTAB&255      ;NAME SEARCH
A0BF  A202                 LDX      #2
A0C1  2062A4               JSR      SEARCH          ;AND DO IT
A0C4  86F2                 STX      CIX
A0C6  A5AF                 LDA      STENUM          ;GET STMT NUMBER
A0C8  20C8A2               JSR      :SETCODE        ;GO SET CODE
A0CB  20A1DB               JSR      SKBLANK
A0CE  20C3A1               JSR      :SYNENT         ;AND GO SYNTAX HIM
A0D1  9035 ^A108           BCC      :SYNOK          ;BR IF OK SYNTAX
                        ;                           ;ELSE SYNTAX ERROR
A0D3  A49F                 LDY      MAXCIX          ; GET MAXCIX
A0D5  B1F3                 LDA      [INBUFF],Y      ; LOAD MAXCIX CHAR
A0D7  C99B                 CMP      #CR             ; WAS IT CR
A0D9  D006 ^A0E1           BNE      :SYN3A          ; BR IF NOT CR
A0DB  C8                   INY                      ; MOVE CR RIGHT ONE
A0DC  91F3                 STA      [INBUFF],Y
A0DE  88                   DEY                      ; THEN PUT A
A0DF  A920                 LDA      #$20            ; BLANK IN IT'S PLACE
A0E1  0980              :SYN3A  ORA      #$80       ; SET MAXCIX CHAR
A0E3  91F3                 STA      [INBUFF],Y      ; TO FLASH
                        ;
A0E5  A940                 LDA      #$40            ;INDICATE SYNTAX ERROR
A0E7  05A6                 ORA      DIRFLG
A0E9  85A6                 STA      DIRFLG          ; IN DIRFLG
A0EB  A4A8                 LDY      STMSTRT         ;RESTORE STMT START
A0ED  84F2                 STY      CIX
A0EF  A203                 LDX      #3              ;SET FOR FIRST STMT
A0F1  86A7                 STX      STMLBD
A0F3  E8                   INX                      ;INC TO CODE
A0F4  8694                 STX      COX             ;AND SET COX
A0F6  A937                 LDA      #CERR           ; GARBAGE CODE
A0F8  20C8A2            :SYN3   JSR      :SETCODE   ;GO SET CODE
A0FB                    :XDATA
A0FB  A4F2                 LDY      CIX             ;GET INDEX
A0FD  B1F3                 LDA      [INBUFF],Y      ;GET INDEX CHAR
A0FF  E6F2                 INC      CIX             ;INC TO NXT
A101  C99B                 CMP      #CR             ;IS IT CR
A103  D0F3 ^A0F8           BNE      :SYN3           ;BR IF NOT
A105  20C8A2               JSR      :SETCODE
                        ;
A108  A594              :SYNOK  LDA      COX        ; GET DISPL TO END OF STMT
A10A  A4A7                 LDY      STMLBD
A10C  9180                 STA      [OUTBUFF],Y     ;SET LENGTH BYTE
                        ;
A10E  A4F2                 LDY      CIX             ;GET INPUT DISPL
A110  88                   DEY
A111  B1F3                 LDA      [INBUFF],Y      ;GET LAST CHAR
A113  C99B                 CMP      #CR             ;IS IT CR
A115  D09A ^A0B1           BNE      :SYN1           ;BR IF NOT
                        ;
A117  A002              :SYN4   LDY      #2         ; SET LINE LENGTH
A119  A594                 LDA      COX             ; INTO STMT
```

```
A11B  9180            STA       [OUTBUFF],Y
                ;
                ;
A11D  20A2A9    :SYN5    JSR     GETSTMT        ;GO GET STMT
A120  A900              LDA      #0
A122  B003 ^A127        BCS      :SYN6
                ;
A124            :SYN5A
A124  20DDA9            JSR      GETLL          ;GO GET LINE LENGTH
A127  38        :SYN6   SEC
A128  E594              SBC      COX            ;ACU=LENGTH[OLD-NEW]
A12A  F020 ^A14C        BEQ      :SYNIN         ; BR NEW=OLD
A12C  B013 ^A141        BCS      :SYNCON        ;BR OLD>NEW
                ;                               ;OLD<NEW
A12E  49FF              EOR      #$FF           ;COMPLEMENT RESULT
A130  A8                TAY
A131  C8                INY
A132  A28A              LDX      #STMCUR        ;POINT TO STMT CURRENT
A134  207FA8            JSR      EXPLOW         ;GO EXPAND
A137  A597              LDA      SVESA          ;RESET STMCUR
A139  858A              STA      STMCUR
A13B  A598              LDA      SVESA+1
A13D  858B              STA      STMCUR+1
A13F  D00B ^A14C        BNE      :SYNIN
                ;
A141  48        :SYNCON PHA      ; CONTRACT LENGTH
A142  20D0A9            JSR      GNXTL
A145  68                PLA
A146  A8                TAY
A147  A28A              LDX      #STMCUR        ;POINT TO STMT CURRENT
A149  20FBA8            JSR      CONTLOW        ;GO CONTRACT
                ;
A14C  A494      :SYNIN  LDY      COX            ; STMT LENGTH
A14E  88        :SYN7   DEY                     ; MINUS ONE
A14F  B180              LDA      [OUTBUFF],Y    ; GET BUFF CHAR
A151  918A              STA      [STMCUR],Y     ;PUT INTO STMT TBL
A153  98                TYA                     ; TEST END
A154  D0F8 ^A14E        BNE      :SYN7          ; BR IF NOT
A156  24A6              BIT      DIRFLG         ;TEST FOR SYNTAX ERROR
A158  502A ^A184        BVC      :SYN8          ;BR IF NOT
A15A  A5B1              LDA      SVVVTE         ; CONTRACT VVT
A15C                    ASLA
A15C +0A                ASL      A
A15D                    ASLA
A15D +0A                ASL      A
A15E                    ASLA
A15E +0A                ASL      A
A15F  A8                TAY
A160  A288              LDX      #ENDVVT
A162  20FBA8            JSR      CONTLOW
A165  38                SEC
A166  A584              LDA      VNTD           ; CONTRACT VNT
A168  E5AD              SBC      SVVNTP
A16A  A8                TAY
A16B  A585              LDA      VNTD+1
A16D  E5AE              SBC      SVVNTP+1
A16F  A284              LDX      #VNTD
A171  20FDA8            JSR      CONTRACT
A174  24A6              BIT      DIRFLG         ; IF STMT NOT DIRECT
A176  1006 ^A17E        BPL      :SYN9A         ; THE BRANCH
A178  2078B5            JSR      LDLINE         ; ELSE LIST DIRECT LINE
A17B  4C60A0            JMP      SYNTAX         ; THEN BACK TO SYNTAX
A17E  205CB5    :SYN9A  JSR      LLINE          ; LIST ENTIRE LINE
A181  4C60A0    :SYN9   JMP      SYNTAX
A184  10FB ^A181 :SYN8  BPL      :SYN9
A186  4C5FA9            JMP      EXECNL         ; GO TO PROGRAM EXECUTOR
                ;
A189  20A2A9    :SDEL   JSR      GETSTMT        ; GO GET LINE
A18C  B0F3 ^A181        BCS      :SYN9          ; BR NOT FOUND
A18E  20DDA9            JSR      GETLL          ;GO GET LINE LENGTH
A191  48                PHA                     ; Y
```

```
A192  20D0A9          JSR     GNXTL
A195  68              PLA
A196  A8              TAY
A197  A28A            LDX     #STMCUR          ;GET STMCUR DISPL
A199  20FBA8          JSR     CONTLOW          ; GO DELETE
A19C  4C60A0          JMP     SYNTAX           ;GO FOR NEXT LINE
```

Get a Line Number

```
                ;GETLNUM-GET A LINE NO FROM ASCLT IN INBUFF
                ;        TO BINARY INTO OUTBUFF
A19F            :GETLNUM
A19F  2000D8          JSR     CVAFP            ; GO CONVERT LINE #
A1A2  9008 ^A1AC      BCC     :GLNUM           ; BR IF GOOD LINE #
A1A4            :GLN1
                ;
A1A4  A900            LDA     #0               ; SET LINE #
A1A6  85F2            STA     CIX
A1A8  A080            LDY     #$80             ; =$8000
A1AA  3009 ^A1B5      BMI     :SLNUM
                ;
A1AC  2056AD    :GLNUM  JSR     CVFPI          ; CONVERT FP TO INT
A1AF  A4D5            LDY     BININT+1         ; LOAD RESULT
A1B1  30F1 ^A1A4      BMI     :GLN1            ; BR IF LNO>32767
A1B3  A5D4            LDA     BININT
                ;
A1B5            :SLNUM
A1B5  84A1            STY     TSLNUM+1         ; SET LINE # HIGH
A1B7  85A0            STA     TSLNUM           ; AND LOW
A1B9  20C8A2          JSR     :SETCODE         ; OUTPUT LOW
A1BC  A5A1            LDA     TSLNUM+1         ; OUTPUT HI
A1BE  85D5            STA     BININT+1
A1C0  4CC8A2          JMP     :SETCODE         ; AND RETURN
```

SYNENT

```
                ;         PERFORM LINE PRE-COMPILE
                ;
A1C3            :SYNENT
A1C3  A001            LDY     #1               ; GET PC HIGH
A1C5  B195            LDA     [SRCADR],Y
A1C7  859E            STA     CPC+1            ;SET PGM COUNTERS
A1C9  8D8304          STA     SPC+1
A1CC  88              DEY
A1CD  B195            LDA     [SRCADR],Y
A1CF  859D            STA     CPC
A1D1  8D8204          STA     SPC
A1D4  A900            LDA     #0               ;SET STKLUL
A1D6  85A9            STA     STKLVL           ;SET STKLUL
A1D8  A594            LDA     COX              ;MOVE
A1DA  8D8104          STA     SOX              ;COX TO SOX
A1DD  A5F2            LDA     CIX              ;MOVE
A1DF  8D8004          STA     SIX              ;CIX TO SIX
```

NEXT

```
                ;           GET NEXT SYNTAX CODE
                ;           AS LONG AS NOT FAILING
                ;
      = A1E2    :NEXT   EQU     *
A1E2  20A1A2          JSR     :NXSC            ; GET NEXT CODE
                ;
A1E5  301A ^A201      BMI     :ERNTV           ; BR IF REL-NON-TERMINAL
                ;
A1E7  C901            CMP     #1               ; TEST CODE=1
A1E9  902A ^A215      BCC     :GETADR          ; BR CODE=0 [ABS-NON-TERMINAL]
A1EB  D008 ^A1F5      BNE     :TSTSUC          ; BR CODE >1
                ;
A1ED  2015A2          JSR     :GETADR          ; CODE=1 [EXTERNAL SUBROUTINE]
A1F0  90F0 ^A1E2      BCC     :NEXT            ; BR IF SUB REPORTS SUCCESS
A1F2  4C6CA2          JMP     :FAIL            ; ELSE GO TO FAIL CODE
                ;
A1F5  C905      :TSTSUC CMP     #5             ; TEST CODE = 5
```

```
A1F7  9059 ^A252      BCC     :POP              ; CODE = [2,3,OR 4] POP UP TO
                                                ; NEXT SYNTAX CODE
A1F9  20A9A2          JSR     :TERMTST          ; CODE>5 GO TEST TERMINAL
A1FC  90E4 ^A1E2      BCC     :NEXT             ; BR IF SUCCESS
A1FE  4C6CA2          JMP     :FAIL             ; ELSE GO TO FAIL CODE
                ;
A201  38        :ERNTV  SEC                     ; RELATIVE NON TERMINAL
A202  A200            LDX     #Ø                ; TOKEN MINUS
A204  E9C1            SBC     #$C1
A206  BØØ2 ^A2ØA      BCS     :ERN1             ; BR IF RESULT PLUS
A208  A2FF            LDX     #$FF              ; ADD A MINUS
A20A  18        :ERN1   CLC
A20B  659D            ADC     CPC               ; RESULT PLUS CPC
A20D  48              PHA                       ; IS NEW CPC-1
A20E  8A              TXA
A20F  659E            ADC     CPC+1
A211  48              PHA                       ; SAVE NEW PC HIGH
A212  4C28A2          JMP     :PUSH             ; GO PUSH
      = A215    :GETADR EQU     *               ; GET DOUBLE BYTE ADR [-1]
A215  20A1A2          JSR     :NXSC             ; GET NEXT CODE
A218  48              PHA                       ; SAVE ON STACK
A219  20A1A2          JSR     :NXSC             ; GET NEXT CODE
A21C  48              PHA                       ; SAVE ON STACK
A21D  9009 ^A228      BCC     :PUSH             ; BR IF CODE =Ø
A21F  68              PLA                       ; EXCHANGE TOP
A220  A8              TAY                       ; 2 ENTRIES ON
A221  68              PLA                       ; CPU STACK
A222  AA              TAX
A223  98              TYA
A224  48              PHA
A225  8A              TXA
A226  48              PHA
A227  60              RTS                       ; ELSE GOTO EXTERNAL SRT VIA RTS
```

PUSH

```
                ;             PUSH TO NEXT STACK LEVEL
                ;
      = A228    :PUSH   EQU     *
A228  A6A9            LDX     STKLVL            ; GET STACK LEVEL
A22A  E8              INX                       ; PLUS 4
A22B  E8              INX
A22C  E8              INX
A22D  E8              INX
A22E  FØ1F ^A24F      BEQ     :SSTB             ;BR STACK TOO  BIG
A230  86A9            STX     STKLVL            ; SAVE NEW STACK LEVEL
                ;
A232  A5F2            LDA     CIX               ; CIX TO
A234  9D8004          STA     SIX,X             ; STACK IX
A237  A594            LDA     COX               ; COX TO
A239  9D8104          STA     SOX,X             ; STACK OX
A23C  A59D            LDA     CPC               ; CPC TO
A23E  9D8204          STA     SPC,X             ; STACK CPC
A241  A59E            LDA     CPC+1
A243  9D8304          STA     SPC+1,X
                ;
A246  68              PLA                       ; MOVE STACKED
A247  859E            STA     CPC+1             ; PC TO CPC
A249  68              PLA
A24A  859D            STA     CPC
A24C  4CE2A1          JMP     :NEXT             ; GO FOR NEXT
                ;
A24F  4C24B9    :SSTB   JMP     ERLTL
```

POP

```
                ;             LOAD CPC FROM STACK PC
                ;             AND DECREMENT TO PREV STACK LEVEL
                ;
      = A252    :POP    EQU     *
A252  A6A9            LDX     STKLVL            ; GET STACK LEVEL
A254  DØØ1 ^A257      BNE     :POP1             ; BR NOT TOP OF STACK
                ;
```

```
A256  60             RTS                     ; TO SYNTAX CALLER
                  ;
A257  BD8204      :POP1   LDA SPC,X          ; MOVE STACK PC
A25A  859D           STA     CPC             ; TO CURRENT PC
A25C  BD8304         LDA     SPC+1,X
A25F  859E           STA     CPC+1
                  ;
A261  CA             DEX                     ; X=X-4
A262  CA             DEX
A263  CA             DEX
A264  CA             DEX
A265  86A9           STX     STKLVL
                  ;
A267  B003 ^A26C     BCS     :FAIL           ; BR IF CALLER FAILING
A269  4CE2A1         JMP     :NEXT           ; ELSE GO TO NEXT
```

FAIL

```
                  ;          TERMINAL FAILED
                  ;          LOOK FOR ALTERNATIVE [OR] OR
                  ;          A RETURN INDICATOR
                  ;
     = A26C       :FAIL   EQU     *
A26C  20A1A2         JSR     :NXSC           ; GET NEXT CODE
                  ;
A26F  30FB ^A26C     BMI     :FAIL           ; BR IF RNTV
                  ;
A271  C902           CMP     #2              ; TEST CODE =2
A273  B008 ^A27D     BCS     :TSTOR          ; BR IF POSSIBLE OR
                  ;
A275  209AA2         JSR     :INCCPC         ; CODE = 0 OR 1
A278  209AA2         JSR     :INCCPC         ; INC PC BY TWO
A27B  D0EF ^A26C     BNE     :FAIL           ; AND CONTINUE FAIL PROCESS
                  ;
A27D  C903        :TSTOR  CMP     #3         ; TEST CODE=3
A27F  F0D1 ^A252     BEQ     :POP            ; BR CODE =3 [RETURN]
A281  B0E9 ^A26C     BCS     :FAIL           ; CODE>3 [RNTV] CONTINUE
                  ;
A283  A5F2           LDA     CIX             ; IF THIS CIX
A285  C59F           CMP     MAXCIX          ; IS A NEW MAX
A287  9002 ^A28B     BCC     :SCIX
A289  859F           STA     MAXCIX          ; THEN SET NEW MAX
A28B              :SCIX
A28B  A6A9           LDX     STKLVL          ; CODE=2 [OR]
A28D  BD8004         LDA     SIX,X           ; MOVE STACK INDEXES
A290  85F2           STA     CIX             ; TO CURRENT INDEXES
A292  BD8104         LDA     SOX,X
A295  8594           STA     COX
A297  4CE2A1         JMP     :NEXT           ; TRY FOR SUCCESS HERE
```

Increment CPC

```
                  ;       INCCPC - INC CPC BY ONE
                  ;
     = A29A       :INCCPC EQU     *
A29A  E69D           INC     CPC
A29C  D002 ^A2A0     BNE     :ICPCR
A29E  E69E           INC     CPC+1
A2A0  60          :ICPCR  RTS
```

NXSC

```
                  ;          GET NEXT SYNTAX CODE
                  ;
A2A1              :NXSC
A2A1  209AA2         JSR     :INCCPC         ; INC PC
A2A4  A200           LDX     #0
A2A6  A19D           LDA     [CPC,X]         ; GET NEXT CODE
A2A8  60             RTS                     ; RETURN
```

TERMTST

```
                         ;              TEST A TERMINAL CODE
                         ;
A2A9                     :TERMTST
A2A9  C90F                  CMP     #$0F              ; TEST CODE=F
A2AB  F00D ^A2BA            BEQ     :ECHNG            ; BR CODE < F
A2AD  B037 ^A2E6            BCS     :SRCONT           ; BR CODE > F
                         ;
A2AF  68                    PLA                       ; POP RTN ADR
A2B0  68                    PLA
A2B1  A90C                  LDA     #:EXP-1&255       ; PUSH EXP ADR
A2B3  48                    PHA                       ; FOR SPECIAL
A2B4  A9A6                  LDA     #:EXP/256         ; EXP ANTV CALL
A2B6  48                    PHA
A2B7  4C28A2                JMP     :PUSH             ; GO PUSH
                         ;
```

ECHNG

```
                         ;          EXTERNAL CODE TO CHANGE COX -1
                         ;
A2BA                     :ECHNG
A2BA  209AA2                JSR     :INCCPC           ; INC PC TO CODE
A2BD  A000                  LDY     #0
A2BF  B19D                  LDA     [CPC],Y           ; GET CODE
                         ;
A2C1  A494                  LDY     COX               ; GET COX
A2C3  88                    DEY                       ; MINUS 1
A2C4  9180                  STA     [OUTBUFF],Y       ; SET NEW CODE
A2C6  18                    CLC                       ; SET SUCCESS
A2C7  60                    RTS                       ; RETURN
```

SETCODE

```
                         ;       SET CODE IN ACV AT COX AND INC COX
                         ;
A2C8                     :SETCODE
A2C8  A494                  LDY     COX               ;GET COX
A2CA  9180                  STA     [OUTBUFF],Y       ;SET CHAR
A2CC  E694                  INC     COX               ;INC COX
A2CE  F001 ^A2D1            BEQ     :SCOVF            ;BR IF NOT ZERO
A2D0  60                    RTS                       ;DONE
A2D1  4C24B9             :SCOVF  JMP   ERLTL          ;GO TO LINE TOO LONG ERR
```

Exits for IF and REM

```
A2D4  A2FF               :EIF    LDX   #$FF           ; RESET STACK
A2D6  9A                    TXS
A2D7  A594                  LDA     COX               ; SET STMT LENGTH
A2D9  A4A7                  LDY     STMLBD
A2DB  9180                  STA     [OUTBUFF],Y
A2DD  4CB1A0                JMP     :XIF              ; GO CONTINUE IF
                         ;
A2E0                     :EREM
A2E0                     :EDATA
A2E0  A2FF                  LDX     #$FF              ; RESET STACK
A2E2  9A                    TXS
A2E3  4CFBA0                JMP     :XDATA            ;GO CONTINUE DATA
```

SRCONT

```
                         ;          SEARCH OP NAME TABLE AND TEST RESULT
                         ;
A2E6                     :SRCONT
A2E6  20A1DB                JSR     SKPBLANK          ; SKIP BLANKS
A2E9  A5F2                  LDA     CIX               ; GET CURRENT INPUT INDEX
A2EB  C5B3                  CMP     SVONTX            ; COMPARE WITH SAVED IX
A2ED  F016 ^A305            BEQ     :SONT1            ; BR IF SAVED IX SAME
A2EF  85B3                  STA     SVONTX            ; SAVE NEW IX
                         ;
A2F1  A9A7                  LDA     #OPNTAB/256       ; SET UP FOR ONT
A2F3  A0E3                  LDY     #OPNTAB&255       ; SEARCH
A2F5  A200                  LDX     #0
A2F7  2062A4                JSR     SEARCH            ; GO SEARCH
```

```
A2FA  B028 ^A324        BCS      :SONF          ; BR NOT FOUND
A2FC  86B2              STX      SVONTL         ; SAVE NEW CIX
A2FE  18                CLC
A2FF  A5AF              LDA      STENUM         ; ADD $10 TO
A301  6910              ADC      #$10           ; ENTRY NUMBER TO
A303  85B0              STA      SVONTC         ; GET OPERATOR CODE
                  ;
A305  A000        :SONT1  LDY       #0
A307  B19D              LDA      [CPC],Y        ; GET SYNTAX REQ CODE
A309  C5B0              CMP      SVONTC         ; DOES IT MATCH THE FOUND
A30B  F00E ^A31B        BEQ      :SONT2         ; BR IF MATCH
A30D  C944              CMP      #CNFNP         ; WAS REQ NFNP
A30F  D006 ^A317        BNE      :SONTF         ; BR IF NOT
A311  A5B0              LDA      SVONTC         ; GET WHAT WE GOT
A313  C944              CMP      #CNFNP         ; IS IT NFNA
A315  B002 ^A319        BCS      :SONTS         ; BR IF IT IS
A317              :SONTF
A317  38                SEC                     ; REPORT FAIL
A318  60                RTS
A319  A5B0        :SONTS  LDA       SVONTC      ; GET REAL CODE
                  ;
A31B  20C8A2      :SONT2  JSR       :SETCODE    ; GO SET CODE
A31E  A6B2              LDX      SVONTL         ; INC CIX BY
A320  86F2              STX      CIX
A322  18                CLC                     ; REPORT SUCCESS
A323  60                RTS                     ; DONE
A324  A900        :SONF   LDA       #0          ; SET ZERO AS
A326  85B0              STA      SVONTC         ; SAVED CODE
A328  38                SEC
A329  60                RTS                     ; DONE
```

TVAR

```
                  ;                 EXTERNAL SUBROUTINE FOR TNVAR & TSVAR
                  ;
A32A  A900        :TNVAR  LDA       #0          ; SET NUMERIC TEST
A32C  F002 ^A330        BEQ      :TVAR
                  ;
A32E  A980        :TSVAR  LDA       #$80        ; SET STR TEST
                  ;
A330  85D2        :TVAR   STA       TVTYPE      ; SAVE TEST TYPE
A332  20A1DB            JSR      SKPBLANK       ; SKIP LEADING BLANKS
A335  A5F2              LDA      CIX            ; GET INDEX
A337  85AC              STA      TVSCIX         ; FOR SAVING
                  ;
A339  20F3A3            JSR      :TSTALPH       ; GO TEST FIRST CHAR
A33C  B025 ^A363        BCS      :TVFAIL        ; BR NOT ALPHA
A33E  20E6A2            JSR      :SRCONT        ; IF THIS IS A
A341  A5B0              LDA      SVONTC         ; RESVD NAME
A343  F008 ^A34D        BEQ      :TV1           ; BR NOT RSVDNAME
A345  A4B2              LDY      SVONTL         ; IF NEXT CHAR AFTER
A347  B1F3              LDA      [INBUFF],Y     ; RESERVED NAME
A349  C930              CMP      #$30           ; NOT ALARM NUMERIC
A34B  9016 ^A363        BCC      :TVFAIL        ; THEN ERROR
                  ;
A34D  E6F2        :TV1    INC       CIX         ; INC TO NEXT CHAR
A34F  20F3A3            JSR      :TSTALPH       ; TEST ALPHA
A352  90F9 ^A34D        BCC      :TV1           ; BR IF ALPHA
A354  20AFDB            JSR      TSTNUM         ; TRY NUMBER
A357  90F4 ^A34D        BCC      :TV1           ; BR IF NUMBER
                  ;
A359  B1F3              LDA      [INBUFF],Y     ; GET OFFENDING CHAR
A35B  C924              CMP      #'$'           ; IS IT $
A35D  F006 ^A365        BEQ      :TVSTR         ; BR IF $ [STRING]
A35F  24D2              BIT      TVTYPE         ; THIS A NVAR SEARCH
A361  1009 ^A36C        BPL      :TVOK          ; BR IF NVAR
                  ;
A363  38          :TVFAIL SEC                   ; SET FAIL CODE
A364  60                RTS                     ; DONE
                  ;
A365  24D2        :TVSTR  BIT       TVTYPE      ; TEST SVAR SEARCH
A367  10FA ^A363        BPL      :TVFAIL        ; BR IF SVAR
```

```
A369  C8              INY                         ; INC OVER $
A36A  D00D ^A379      BNE      :TVOK2             ; BR ALWAYS
                   ;
A36C  B1F3         :TVOK   LDA     [INBUFF],Y      ; GET NEXT CHAR
A36E  C928            CMP      #'('               ; IS IT PAREN
A370  D007 ^A379      BNE      :TVOK2             ; BR NOT PAREN
A372  C8              INY                         ; INC OVER PAREN
A373  A940            LDA      #$40               ; OR IN ARRAY
A375  05D2            ORA      TVTYPE             ; CODE TO TVTYPE
A377  85D2            STA      TVTYPE
                   ;
A379  A5AC         :TVOK2  LDA     TVSCIX         ; GET SAVED CIX
A37B  85F2            STA      CIX                ; PUT BACK
A37D  84AC            STY      TVSCIX             ; SAVE NEW CIX
                   ;
A37F  A583            LDA      VNTP+1             ; SEARCH VNT
A381  A482            LDY      VNTP               ; FOR THIS GUY
A383  A200            LDX      #0
A385  2062A4          JSR      SEARCH
A388               :TVRS
A388  B00A ^A394      BCS      :TVS0              ; BR NOT FOUND
A38A  E4AC            CPX      TVSCIX             ; FOUND RIGHT ONE
A38C  F04D ^A3DB      BEQ      :TVSUC             ; BR IF YES
A38E  2090A4          JSR      SRCNXT             ; GO SEARCH MORE
A391  4C88A3          JMP      :TVRS              ; TEST THIS RESULT
                   ;
A394               :TVS0
A394  38              SEC                         ; SIGH:
A395  A5AC            LDA      TVSCIX             ; VAR LENGTH IS
A397  E5F2            SBC      CIX                ; NEW CIX-OLD CIX
A399  85F2            STA      CIX
                   ;
A39B  A8              TAY                         ; GO EXPAND VNT
A39C  A284            LDX      #VNTD              ; BY VAR LENGTH
A39E  207FA8          JSR      EXPLOW
A3A1  A5AF            LDA      STENUM             ; SET VARIABLE NUMBER
A3A3  85D3            STA      TVNUM
                   ;
A3A5  A4F2            LDY      CIX                ; AND
A3A7  88              DEY
A3A8  A6AC            LDX      TVSCIX             ; GET DISPL TO EQU+1
A3AA  CA              DEX
A3AB  BD8005       :TVS1   LDA     LBUFF,X        ; MOVE VAR TO
A3AE  9197            STA      [SVESA],Y
A3B0  CA              DEX
A3B1  88              DEY
A3B2  10F7 ^A3AB      BPL      :TVS1
                   ;
A3B4  A4F2            LDY      CIX                ;TURN ON MSB
A3B6  88              DEY                         ;OF LAST CHAR
A3B7  B197            LDA      [SVESA],Y          ;IN VTVT ENTRY
A3B9  0980            ORA      #$80
A3BB  9197            STA      [SVESA],Y
                   ;
A3BD  A008            LDY      #8                 ; THEN EXPAND
A3BF  A288            LDX      #STMTAB            ; VVT BY 8
A3C1  207FA8          JSR      EXPLOW
A3C4  E6B1            INC      SVVVTE             ; INC VVT EXP SIZE
                   ;
A3C6  A002            LDY      #2                 ; CLEAR VALUE
A3C8  A900            LDA      #0                 ; PART OF
A3CA  99D200       :TVS1A  STA     TVTYPE,Y       ; ENTRY
A3CD  C8              INY
A3CE  C008            CPY      #8
A3D0  90F8 ^A3CA      BCC      :TVS1A
A3D2  88              DEY                         ; AND THEN
A3D3  B9D200       :TVS2   LDA     TVTYPE,Y       ; PUT IN VAR TABLE
A3D6  9197            STA      [SVESA],Y          ; ENTRY
A3D8  88              DEY
A3D9  10F8 ^A3D3      BPL      :TVS2
                   ;
```

```
A3DB  24D2        :TVSUC  BIT     TVTYPE        ; WAS THERE A PAREN
A3DD  5002 ^A3E1          BVC     :TVNP         ; BR IF NOT
A3DF  C6AC                DEC     TVSCIX        ; LET SYNTAX SEE PAREN
                  ;
A3E1  A5AC        :TVNP   LDA     TVSCIX        ; GET NEW CIX
A3E3  85F2                STA     CIX           ; TO CIX
                  ;
A3E5  A5AF                LDA     STENUM        ; GET TABLE ENTRY NO
A3E7  3007 ^A3F0          BMI     :TVFULL       ; BR IF > $7F
A3E9  0980                ORA     #$80          ; MAKE IT > $7F
A3EB  20C8A2              JSR     :SETCODE      ; SET CODE TO OUTPUT BUFFER
A3EE  18                  CLC                   ; SET SUCCESS CODE
A3EF  60                  RTS                   ; RETURN
                  ;
A3F0  4C38B9      :TVFULL JMP     ERRVSF        ; GO TO ERROR RTN
```

TSTALPH

```
                  ;               TEST CIX FOR ALPHA
                  ;
A3F3              :TSTALPH
A3F3  A4F2                LDY     CIX
A3F5  B1F3                LDA     [INBUFF],Y
A3F7              TSTALPH
A3F7  C941                CMP     #'A
A3F9  9003 ^A3FE          BCC     :TAFAIL
A3FB  C95B                CMP     #$5B
A3FD  60                  RTS
                  ;
A3FE  38          :TAFAIL SEC
A3FF  60                  RTS
```

TNCON

```
                  ;               EXTERNAL SUBROUTINE TO CHECK FOR NUMBER
                  ;
A400              :TNCON
A400  20A1DB              JSR     SKBLANK
A403  A5F2                LDA     CIX
A405  85AC                STA     TVSCIX
A407  2000D8              JSR     CVAFP         ; GO TEST AND CONV
A40A  9005 ^A411          BCC     :TNC1         ; BR IF NUMBER
A40C  A5AC                LDA     TVSCIX
A40E  85F2                STA     CIX
A410  60                  RTS                   ; RETURN FAIL
                  ;
A411  A90E        :TNC1   LDA     #$0E          ; SET NUMERIC CONST
A413  20C8A2              JSR     :SETCODE
                  ;
A416  A494                LDY     COX
A418  A200                LDX     #0
A41A  B5D4        :TNC2   LDA     FR0,X         ; MOVE CONST TO STMT
A41C  9180                STA     [OUTBUFF],Y
A41E  C8                  INY
A41F  E8                  INX
A420  E006                CPX     #6
A422  90F6 ^A41A          BCC     :TNC2
A424  8494                STY     COX
A426  18                  CLC
A427  60                  RTS
```

TSCON

```
                  ;               EXT SRT TO CHECK FOR STR CONST
                  ;
A428              :TSCON
A428  20A1DB              JSR     SKBLANK
A42B  A4F2                LDY     CIX           ; GET INDEX
A42D  B1F3                LDA     [INBUFF],Y    ; GET CHAR
A42F  C922                CMP     #$22          ; IS IT DQUOTE
A431  F002 ^A435          BEQ     :TSC1         ; BR IF DQ
A433  38                  SEC                   ; SET FAIL
A434  60                  RTS                   ; RETURN
                  ;
```

```
A435  A90F          :TSC1  LDA     #$0F          ; SET SCON CODE
A437  20C8A2               JSR     :SETCODE
A43A  A594                 LDA     COX           ; SET COX
A43C  85AB                 STA     TSCOX         ; SAVE FOR LENGTH
A43E  20C8A2               JSR     :SETCODE      ; SET DUMMY FOR NOW
                    ;
A441  E6F2          :TSC2  INC     CIX           ; NEXT INPUT CHAR
A443  A4F2                 LDY     CIX
A445  B1F3                 LDA     [INBUFF],Y
A447  C99B                 CMP     #CR           ; IS IT CR
A449  F00C ^A457           BEQ     :TSC4         ; BR IF CR
A44B  C922                 CMP     #$22          ; IS IT DQ
A44D  F006 ^A455           BEQ     :TSC3         ; BR IF DQ
A44F  20C8A2               JSR     :SETCODE      ; OUTPUT IT
A452  4C41A4               JMP     :TSC2         ; NEXT
                    ;
A455  E6F2          :TSC3  INC     CIX           ; INC CIX OVER DQ
A457  18            :TSC4  CLC
A458  A594                 LDA     COX           ; LENGTH IS COX MINUS
A45A  E5AB                 SBC     TSCOX         ; LENGTH BYTE COX
A45C  A4AB                 LDY     TSCOX
A45E  9180                 STA     [OUTBUFF],Y   ; SET LENGTH
                    ;
A460  18                   CLC                   ; SET SUCCESS
A461  60                   RTS                   ; DONE
```

Search a Table

```
                    ;          TABLE FORMAT:
                    ;             GARBAGE TO SKIP  [N]
                    ;             ASCII CHAR       [N]
                    ;               WITH LEAST SIGNIFICANT BYTE HAVING
                    ;               MOST SIGNIFICANT BIT ON
                    ;          LAST TABLE ENTRY MUST HAVE FIRST ASCII
                               CHAR = 0
                    ;
                    ;          ENTRY PARMS:
                    ;             X = SKIP LENGTH
                    ;             A,Y = TABLE ADR [HIGH LOW]
                    ;             ARGUMENT = INBUFF + CIX
                    ;          EXIT PARMS:
                    ;             CARRY = CLEAR IF FOUND
                    ;             X = FOUND ARGUMENT END CIX+1
                    ;             SRCADR = TABLE ENTRY ADR
                    ;             STENUM = TABLE ENTRY NUMBER
                    ;
A462                SEARCH
A462  86AA                 STX     SRCSKP        ; SAVE SKIP FACTOR
                    ;
A464  A2FF                 LDX     #$FF          ; SET ENTRY NUMBER
A466  86AF                 STX     STENUM        ; TO ZERO
                    ;
A468  8596          :SRC1  STA     SRCADR+1      ; SET SEARCH ADR
A46A  8495                 STY     SRCADR
A46C  E6AF                 INC     STENUM        ; INC ENTRY NUMBER
A46E  A6F2                 LDX     CIX           ; GET ARG DISPL
A470  A4AA                 LDY     SRCSKP        ; GET SKIP LENGTH
A472  B195                 LDA     [SRCADR],Y    ; GET FIRST CHAR
A474  F027 ^A49D           BEQ     :SRCNF        ; BR IF EOT
A476  A900                 LDA     #0            ; SET STATUS = EQ
A478  08                   PHP                   ; AND PUSH IT
                    ;
A479  BD8005        :SRC2  LDA     LBUFF,X       ; GET INPUT CHAR
A47C  297F                 AND     #$7F          ; TURN OFF MSB
A47E  C92E                 CMP     #'.'          ; IF WILD CARD
A480  F01D ^A49F           BEQ     :SRC5         ; THEN BR
A482                :SRC2A
A482  5195                 EOR     [SRCADR],Y    ; EX-OR WITH TABLE CHAR
A484                       ASLA                  ; SHIFT MSB TO CARRY
A484 +0A                   ASL     A
A485  F002 ^A489           BEQ     :SRC3         ; BR IF [ARG=TAB] CHAR
                    ;
```

```
A487  68              PLA                        ; POP STATUS
A488  Ø8              PHP                        ; PUSH NE STATUS
                 ;
A489  C8         :SRC3   INY                     ;INC TABLE INDEX
A48A  E8              INX                        ;INC ARG INDEX
A48B  9ØEC ^A479      BCC      :SRC2             ; IF TABLE MSB OFF, CONTINUE
                 ;                               ;ELSE END OF ENTRY
A48D  28              PLP                        ;GET STATUS
A48E  FØØB ^A49B      BEQ      :SRCFND           ;BR IF NO MIS MATCH
                 ;
A49Ø             SRCNXT
A49Ø  18              CLC
A491  98              TYA                        ;ACV=ENTRY LENGTH
A492  6595            ADC      SRCADR            ;PLUS START ADR [L]
A494  A8              TAY                        ;TO Y
A495  A596            LDA      SRCADR+1          ;ETC
A497  69ØØ            ADC      #Ø
A499  DØCD ^A468      BNE      :SRC1             ;BR ALLWAYS
                 ;
A49B  18         :SRCFND CLC                     ;INDICATE FOUND
A49C  6Ø              RTS
                 ;
A49D  38         :SRCNF  SEC                     ;INDICATE NOT FOUND
A49E  6Ø              RTS
                 ;
A49F  A9Ø2       :SRC5   LDA      #2             ; IF NOT
A4A1  C5AA            CMP      SRCSKP            ; STMT NAME TABLE
A4A3  DØDD ^A482      BNE      :SRC2A            ; THEN IGNORE
A4A5  B195       :SRC6   LDA      [SRCADR],Y     ;TEST MSB OF TABLE
A4A7  3ØØ3 ^A4AC      BMI      :SRC7             ; IF ON DONE
A4A9  C8              INY                        ; ELSE
A4AA  DØF9 ^A4A5      BNE      :SRC6             ; LOOK AT NEXT CHAR
A4AC  38         :SRC7   SEC                     ; INDICATE MSB ON
A4AD  BØDA ^A489      BCS      :SRC3             ; AND RE-ENTER CODE
```

Statement Name Table

```
                 ;
                 ; SNTAB- STATEMENT NAME TABLE
                 ;        EACH ENTRY HAS SYNTAX TABLE ADR PTR
                 ;        FOLLOWED BY STMT NAME
                 ;
A4AF             SNTAB
                 ;
A4AF  C7A7            DW       :SREM-1
A4B1  5245CD          DC       'REM'
                 ;
A4B4  CAA7            DW       :SDATA-1
A4B6  444154C1        DC       'DATA'
                 ;
A4BA  F3A6            DW       :SINPUT-1
A4BC  494E5Ø55D4      DC       'INPUT'
                 ;
A4C1  BCA6            DW       :SCOLOR-1
A4C3  434F4C4FD2      DC       'COLOR'
                 ;
A4C8  32A7            DW       :SLIST-1
A4CA  4C4953D4        DC       'LIST'
                 ;
A4CE  23A7            DW       :SENTER-1
A4DØ  454E5445D2      DC       'ENTER'
A4D5  BFA6            DW       :SLET-1
A4D7  4C45D4          DC       'LET'
                 ;
A4DA  93A7            DW       :SIF-1
A4DC  49C6            DC       'IF'
                 ;
A4DE  D1A6            DW       :SFOR-1
A4EØ  464FD2          DC       'FOR'
                 ;
A4E3  E9A6            DW       :SNEXT-1
```

```
A4E5   4E4558D4           DC       'NEXT'
                  ;
A4E9   BCA6               DW       :SGOTO-1
A4EB   474F54CF           DC       'GOTO'
                  ;
A4EF   BCA6               DW       :SGOTO-1
A4F1   474F2Ø54CF         DC       'GO TO'
                  ;
A4F6   BCA6               DW       :SGOSUB-1
A4F8   474F5355C2         DC       'GOSUB'
                  ;
A4FD   BCA6               DW       :STRAP-1
A4FF   545241DØ           DC       'TRAP'
                  ;
                  ;
A5Ø3   BDA6               DW       :SBYE-1
A5Ø5   4259C5             DC       'BYE'
                  ;
A5Ø8   BDA6               DW       :SCONT-1
A5ØA   434F4ED4           DC       'CONT'
                  ;
A5ØE   5FA7               DW       :SCOM-1
A51Ø   434FCD             DC       'COM'
                  ;
                  ;
A513   2ØA7               DW       :SCLOSE-1
A515   434C4F53C5         DC       'CLOSE'
                  ;
A51A   BDA6               DW       :SCLR-1
A51C   434CD2             DC       'CLR'
A51F   BDA6               DW       :SDEG-1
A521   4445C7             DC       'DEG'
                  ;
A524   5FA7               DW       :SDIM-1
A526   4449CD             DC       'DIM'
                  ;
A529   BDA6               DW       :SEND-1
A52B   454EC4             DC       'END'
                  ;
A52E   BDA6               DW       :SNEW-1
A53Ø   4E45D7             DC       'NEW'
                  ;
A533   19A7               DW       :SOPEN-1
A535   4F5Ø45CE           DC       'OPEN'
A539   23A7               DW       :SLOAD-1
A53B   4C4F41C4           DC       'LOAD'
A53F   23A7               DW       :SSAVE-1
A541   534156C5           DC       'SAVE'
A545   4ØA7               DW       :SSTATUS-1
A547   5354415455         DC       'STATUS'
       D3
A54D   49A7               DW       :SNOTE-1
A54F   4E4F54C5           DC       'NOTE'
A553   49A7               DW       :SPOINT-1
A555   5Ø4F494ED4         DC       'POINT'
A55A   17A7               DW       :SXIO-1
A55C   5849CF             DC       'XIO'
                  ;
A55F   62A7               DW       :SON-1
A561   4FCE               DC       'ON'
                  ;
A563   5CA7               DW       :SPOKE-1
A565   5Ø4F4BC5           DC       'POKE'
                  ;
A569   FBA6               DW       :SPRINT-1
A56B   5Ø52494ED4         DC       'PRINT'
                  ;
A57Ø   BDA6               DW       :SRAD-1
A572   5241C4             DC       'RAD'
                  ;
A575   F4A6               DW       :SREAD-1
```

```
A577   524541C4           DC      'READ'
                     ;
A57B   EEA6               DW      :SREST-1
A57D   524553544F         DC      'RESTORE'
       52C5
                     ;
A584   BDA6               DW      :SRET-1
A586   5245545552         DC      'RETURN'
       CE
                     ;
A58C   26A7               DW      :SRUN-1
A58E   5255CE             DC      'RUN'
                     ;
A591   BDA6               DW      :SSTOP-1
A593   53544FDØ           DC      'STOP'
                     ;
A597   BDA6               DW      :SPOP-1
A599   5Ø4FDØ             DC      'POP'
                     ;
A59C   FBA6               DW      :SPRINT-1
A59E   BF                 DC      '?'
                     ;
A59F   E7A6               DW      :SGET-1
A5A1   4745D4             DC      'GET'
A5A4   B9A6               DW      :SPUT-1
A5A6   5Ø55D4             DC      'PUT'
A5A9   BCA6               DW      :SGR-1
A5AB   4752415Ø48         DC      'GRAPHICS'
       4943D3
                     ;
A5B3   5CA7               DW      :SPLOT-1
A5B5   5Ø4C4FD4           DC      'PLOT'
                     ;
A5B9   5CA7               DW      :SPOS-1
A5BB   5Ø4F534954         DC      'POSITION'
       494FCE
                     ;
A5C3   BDA6               DW      :SDOS-1
A5C5   444FD3             DC      'DOS'
                     ;
A5C8   5CA7               DW      :SDRAWTO-1
A5CA   4452415754         DC      'DRAWTO'
       CF
                     ;
A5DØ   5AA7               DW      :SSETCOLOR-1
A5D2   534554434F         DC      'SETCOLOR'
       4C4FD2
                     ;
A5DA   E1A6               DW      :SLOCATE-1
A5DC   4C4F434154         DC      'LOCATE'
       C5
                     ;
A5E2   58A7               DW      :SSOUND-1
A5E4   534F554EC4         DC      'SOUND'
A5E9   FFA6               DW      :SLPRINT-1
A5EB   4C5Ø52494E         DC      'LPRINT'
       D4
A5F1   BDA6               DW      :SCSAVE-1
A5F3   43534156C5         DC      'CSAVE'
A5F8   BDA6               DW      :SCLOAD-1
A5FA   434C4F41C4         DC      'CLOAD'
A5FF   BFA6               DW      :SILET-1
A6Ø1   ØØ                 DB      Ø
A6Ø2   8ØØØ               DB      $8Ø,ØØ
A6Ø4   2A4552524F         DB      '*ERROR- '
       522D2Ø
A6ØC   AØ                 DB      $AØ
```

Syntax Tables

Syntax Table OP Codes

```
= 0000        :ANTV   EQU     $00         ; ABSOLUTE NON TERMINAL VECTOR
              ;                                 FOLLOWED BY 2 BYTE ADR -1
= 0001        :ESRT   EQU     $01         ; EXTERNAL SUBROUTINE CALL
              ;                                 FOLLOWED BY 2 BYTE ADR -1
= 0002        :OR     EQU     $02         ; ALTERNATIVE, BNF OR (])
= 0003        :RTN    EQU     $03         ; RETURN, (#)
= 0004        :NULL   EQU     $04         ; ACCEPT TO THIS POINT (&)
= 000E        :VEXP   EQU     $0E         ; SPECIAL NTV FOR EXP (<EXP>)
= 000F        :CHNG   EQU     $0F         ; CHANGE LAST OUTPUT TOKEN
```

<EXP> = (<EXP>)<NOP> | <UNARY><EXP> | <NV><NOP>#

```
A60D                 :EXP    SYN      CLPRN
A60D +2B                   DB      CLPRN
A60E                     SYN       JS,:EXP
A60E +BF                 DB       $80+(((:EXP-*)&$7F) XOR $40 )
A60F                     SYN       CRPRN
A60F +2C                   DB      CRPRN
A610                     SYN       JS,:NOP
A610 +DE                 DB       $80+(((:NOP-*)&$7F) XOR $40 )
A611                     SYN       :OR
A611 +02                   DB      :OR
A612                     SYN       JS,:UNARY
A612 +C6                 DB       $80+(((:UNARY-*)&$7F) XOR $40 )
A613                     SYN       JS,:EXP
A613 +BA                 DB       $80+(((:EXP-*)&$7F) XOR $40 )
A614                     SYN       :OR
A614 +02                   DB      :OR
A615                     SYN       JS,:NV
A615 +CD                 DB       $80+(((:NV-*)&$7F) XOR $40 )
A616                     SYN       JS,:NOP
A616 +D8                 DB       $80+(((:NOP-*)&$7F) XOR $40 )
A617                     SYN       :RTN
A617 +03                   DB      :RTN
```

<UNARY> = + | - | NOT#

```
                     ;
A618                 :UNARY  SYN      CPLUS
A618 +25                   DB      CPLUS
A619                     SYN       :CHNG,CUPLUS
A619 +0F                   DB      :CHNG
A61A +35                   DB      CUPLUS
A61B                     SYN       :OR
A61B +02                   DB      :OR
A61C                     SYN       CMINUS
A61C +26                   DB      CMINUS
A61D                     SYN       :CHNG,CUMINUS
A61D +0F                   DB      :CHNG
A61E +36                   DB      CUMINUS
A61F                     SYN       :OR
A61F +02                   DB      :OR
A620                     SYN       CNOT
A620 +28                   DB      CNOT
A621                     SYN       :RTN
A621 +03                   DB      :RTN
```

<NV> = <NFUN> | <NVAR> | <NCON> | <STCOMP>#

```
A622                 :NV     SYN      JS,:NFUN,:OR
A622 +FD                 DB       $80+(((:NFUN-*)&$7F) XOR $40 )
A623 +02                   DB      :OR
A624                     SYN       JS,:NVAR,:OR
A624 +E8                 DB       $80+(((:NVAR-*)&$7F) XOR $40 )
A625 +02                   DB      :OR
A626                     SYN       :ESRT,AD,:TNCON-1,:OR
A626 +01                   DB      :ESRT
```

```
A627 +FFA3              DW     (:TNCON-1)
A629 +02                DB     :OR
A62A                   SYN      :ANTV,AD,:STCOMP-1
A62A +00                DB     :ANTV
A62B +7DA6              DW     (:STCOMP-1)
A62D                   SYN      :RTN
A62D +03                DB     :RTN
```

<NOP> = <OP> <EXP> | &#

```
A62E               :NOP    SYN       JS,:OP
A62E +C4               DB      $80+(((:OP-*)&$7F) XOR $40 )
A62F                   SYN      JS,:EXP
A62F +9E               DB      $80+(((:EXP-*)&$7F) XOR $40 )
A630                   SYN      :OR
A630 +02                DB     :OR
A631                   SYN      :RTN
A631 +03                DB     :RTN
```

<OP> = ** | * | / | < = | S= | < > | < | > | = | AND | OR#

```
A632               :OP     SYN       CEXP,:OR
A632 +23                DB     CEXP
A633 +02                DB     :OR
A634                   SYN      CPLUS,:OR
A634 +25                DB     CPLUS
A635 +02                DB     :OR
A636                   SYN      CMINUS,:OR
A636 +26                DB     CMINUS
A637 +02                DB     :OR
A638                   SYN      CMUL,:OR
A638 +24                DB     CMUL
A639 +02                DB     :OR
A63A                   SYN      CDIV,:OR
A63A +27                DB     CDIV
A63B +02                DB     :OR
A63C                   SYN      CLE,:OR
A63C +1D                DB     CLE
A63D +02                DB     :OR
A63E                   SYN      CGE,:OR
A63E +1F                DB     CGE
A63F +02                DB     :OR
A640                   SYN      CNE,:OR
A640 +1E                DB     CNE
A641 +02                DB     :OR
A642                   SYN      CLT,:OR
A642 +20                DB     CLT
A643 +02                DB     :OR
A644                   SYN      CGT,:OR
A644 +21                DB     CGT
A645 +02                DB     :OR
A646                   SYN      CEQ,:OR
A646 +22                DB     CEQ
A647 +02                DB     :OR
A648                   SYN      CAND,:OR
A648 +2A                DB     CAND
A649 +02                DB     :OR
A64A                   SYN      COR
A64A +29                DB     COR
A64B                   SYN      :RTN
A64B +03                DB     :RTN
```

<NVAR> = <TNVAR> <NMAT>#

```
A64C               :NVAR   SYN       :ESRT,AD,:TNVAR-1
A64C +01                DB     :ESRT
A64D +29A3              DW     (:TNVAR-1)
A64F                   SYN      JS,:NMAT
A64F +C2               DB      $80+(((:NMAT-*)&$7F) XOR $40 )
A650                   SYN      :RTN
A650 +03                DB     :RTN
```

<NMAT> = (<EXP> <NMAT2>) | &#

```
A651                :NMAT   SYN      CLPRN,:CHNG,CALPRN
A651 +2B                 DB     CLPRN
A652 +ØF                 DB     :CHNG
A653 +38                 DB     CALPRN
A654                   SYN      :VEXP
A654 +ØE                 DB     :VEXP
A655                   SYN      JS,:NMAT2
A655 +C4               DB       $8Ø+(((:NMAT2-*)&$7F) XOR $4Ø )
A656                   SYN      CRPRN
A656 +2C                 DB     CRPRN
A657                   SYN      :OR
A657 +Ø2                 DB     :OR
A658                   SYN      :RTN
A658 +Ø3                 DB     :RTN
```

<NMAT2> = ,<EXP> | &#

```
A659                :NMAT2  SYN      CCOM,:CHNG,CACOM
A659 +12                 DB     CCOM
A65A +ØF                 DB     :CHNG
A65B +3C                 DB     CACOM
A65C                   SYN      :VEXP
A65C +ØE                 DB     :VEXP
A65D                   SYN      :OR
A65D +Ø2                 DB     :OR
A65E                   SYN      :RTN
A65E +Ø3                 DB     :RTN
```

<NFUN> = <NFNP> <NFP> | <NFSP> <SFP> | <NFUSR> #

```
A65F                :NFUN   SYN      CNFNP
A65F +44                 DB     CNFNP
A66Ø                   SYN      JS,:NFP
A66Ø +D2               DB       $8Ø+(((:NFP-*)&$7F) XOR $4Ø )
A661                   SYN      :OR
A661 +Ø2                 DB     :OR
A662                   SYN      :ANTV,AD,:NFSP-1
A662 +ØØ                 DB     :ANTV
A663 +CDA7               DW     (:NFSP-1)
A665                   SYN      JS,:SFP
A665 +D3               DB       $8Ø+(((:SFP-*)&$7F) XOR $4Ø )
A666                   SYN      :OR
A666 +Ø2                 DB     :OR
A667                   SYN      JS,:NFUSR
A667 +C2               DB       $8Ø+(((:NFUSR-*)&$7F) XOR $4Ø )
A668                   SYN      :RTN
A668 +Ø3                 DB     :RTN
```

<NFUSR> = USR (<PUSR>) #

```
A669                :NFUSR  SYN      CUSR
A669 +3F                 DB     CUSR
A66A                   SYN      CLPRN,:CHNG,CFLPRN
A66A +2B                 DB     CLPRN
A66B +ØF                 DB     :CHNG
A66C +3A                 DB     CFLPRN
A66D                   SYN      :ANTV,AD,:PUSR-1
A66D +ØØ                 DB     :ANTV
A66E +D9A7               DW     (:PUSR-1)
A67Ø                   SYN      CRPRN
A67Ø +2C                 DB     CRPRN
A671                   SYN      :RTN
A671 +Ø3                 DB     :RTN
```

<NFP> = (<EXP>) #

```
A672                :NFP    SYN      CLPRN,:CHNG,CFLPRN
A672 +2B                 DB     CLPRN
A673 +ØF                 DB     :CHNG
A674 +3A                 DB     CFLPRN
A675                   SYN      :VEXP
```

```
A675 +ØE                  DB     :VEXP
A676                    SYN       CRPRN
A676 +2C                  DB     CRPRN
A677                    SYN        :RTN
A677 +Ø3                  DB     :RTN
```

<SFP> = <STR>)#

```
A678              :SFP     SYN          CLPRN,:CHNG,CFLPRN
A678 +2B                  DB     CLPRN
A679 +ØF                  DB     :CHNG
A67A +3A                  DB     CFLPRN
A67B                    SYN       JS,:STR
A67B +C7                DB       $8Ø+(((:STR-*)&$7F) XOR $4Ø )
A67C                    SYN       CRPRN
A67C +2C                  DB     CRPRN
A67D                    SYN        :RTN
A67D +Ø3                  DB     :RTN
```

<STCOMP> = <STR> <SOP> <STR>#

```
A67E              :STCOMP SYN         JS,:STR
A67E +C4                DB       $8Ø+(((:STR-*)&$7F) XOR $4Ø )
A67F                    SYN       JS,:SOP
A67F +E3                DB       $8Ø+(((:SOP-*)&$7F) XOR $4Ø )
A68Ø                    SYN       JS,:STR
A68Ø +C2                DB       $8Ø+(((:STR-*)&$7F) XOR $4Ø )
A681                    SYN       :RTN
A681 +Ø3                  DB     :RTN
```

<STR> = <SFUN> | <SVAR> | <SCON>#

```
A682              :STR     SYN          JS,:SFUN
A682 +C8                DB       $8Ø+(((:SFUN-*)&$7F) XOR $4Ø )
A683                    SYN       :OR
A683 +Ø2                  DB     :OR
A684                    SYN       JS,:SVAR
A684 +CB                DB       $8Ø+(((:SVAR-*)&$7F) XOR $4Ø )
A685                    SYN       :OR
A685 +Ø2                  DB     :OR
A686                    SYN       :ESRT,AD,:TSCON-1
A686 +Ø1                  DB     :ESRT
A687 +27A4                DW     (:TSCON-1)
A689                    SYN       :RTN
A689 +Ø3                  DB     :RTN
```

<SFUN> = SFNP<NFP>#

```
A68A              :SFUN    SYN          :ANTV,AD,:SFNP-1
A68A +ØØ                  DB     :ANTV
A68B +D5A7                DW     (:SFNP-1)
A68D                    SYN       JS,:NFP
A68D +A5                DB       $8Ø+(((:NFP-*)&$7F) XOR $4Ø )
A68E                    SYN       :RTN
A68E +Ø3                  DB     :RTN
```

<SVAR> = <TSVAR> <SMAT>#

```
A68F              :SVAR    SYN          :ESRT,AD,:TSVAR-1
A68F +Ø1                  DB     :ESRT
A69Ø +2DA3                DW     (:TSVAR-1)
A692                    SYN       JS,:SMAT
A692 +C2                DB       $8Ø+(((:SMAT-*)&$7F) XOR $4Ø )
A693                    SYN       :RTN
A693 +Ø3                  DB     :RTN
```

<SMAT> = (<EXP> <SMAT2>) | &#

```
                  ;
A694              :SMAT    SYN          CLPRN,:CHNG,CSLPRN
A694 +2B                  DB     CLPRN
A695 +ØF                  DB     :CHNG
A696 +37                  DB     CSLPRN
```

```
A697                    SYN      :VEXP
A697 +ØE                  DB    :VEXP
A698                    SYN      JS,:SMAT2
A698 +C4                DB      $8Ø+(((:SMAT2-*)&$7F) XOR $4Ø )
A699                    SYN      CRPRN
A699 +2C                  DB    CRPRN
A69A                    SYN      :OR
A69A +Ø2                  DB    :OR
A69B                    SYN      :RTN
A69B +Ø3                  DB    :RTN
```

<SMAT2> = , <EXP> | &#

```
A69C               :SMAT2  SYN      CCOM,:CHNG,CACOM
A69C +12                  DB    CCOM
A69D +ØF                  DB    :CHNG
A69E +3C                  DB    CACOM
A69F                    SYN      :VEXP
A69F +ØE                  DB    :VEXP
A6AØ                    SYN      :OR
A6AØ +Ø2                  DB    :OR
A6A1                    SYN      :RTN
A6A1 +Ø3                  DB    :RTN
```

<SOP> = < > <#

```
A6A2               :SOP
A6A2                    SYN      CLE,:CHNG,CSLE,:OR
A6A2 +1D                  DB    CLE
A6A3 +ØF                  DB    :CHNG
A6A4 +2F                  DB    CSLE
A6A5 +Ø2                  DB    :OR
A6A6                    SYN      CNE,:CHNG,CSNE,:OR
A6A6 +1E                  DB    CNE
A6A7 +ØF                  DB    :CHNG
A6A8 +3Ø                  DB    CSNE
A6A9 +Ø2                  DB    :OR
A6AA                    SYN      CGE,:CHNG,CSGE,:OR
A6AA +1F                  DB    CGE
A6AB +ØF                  DB    :CHNG
A6AC +31                  DB    CSGE
A6AD +Ø2                  DB    :OR
A6AE                    SYN      CLT,:CHNG,CSLT,:OR
A6AE +2Ø                  DB    CLT
A6AF +ØF                  DB    :CHNG
A6BØ +32                  DB    CSLT
A6B1 +Ø2                  DB    :OR
A6B2                    SYN      CGT,:CHNG,CSGT,:OR
A6B2 +21                  DB    CGT
A6B3 +ØF                  DB    :CHNG
A6B4 +33                  DB    CSGT
A6B5 +Ø2                  DB    :OR
A6B6                    SYN      CEQ,:CHNG,CSEQ
A6B6 +22                  DB    CEQ
A6B7 +ØF                  DB    :CHNG
A6B8 +34                  DB    CSEQ
A6B9                    SYN      :RTN
A6B9 +Ø3                  DB    :RTN
```

<PUT> = <D1>,<EXP> <EOS>#

```
A6BA               :SPUT
A6BA                    SYN      CPND,:VEXP
A6BA +1C                  DB    CPND
A6BB +ØE                  DB    :VEXP
A6BC                    SYN      CCOM
A6BC +12                  DB    CCOM
```

< > = <EXP> <EOS>#

```
                        ;
A6BD                    :STRAP
A6BD                    :SGOTO
A6BD                    :SGOSUB
A6BD                    :SGR
A6BD                    :SCOLOR
A6BD                    :XEOS    SYN        :VEXP
A6BD +ØE                          DB     :VEXP
```

< > = <EOS>#

```
A6BE                    :SCSAVE
A6BE                    :SCLOAD
A6BE                    :SDOS
A6BE                    :SCLR
A6BE                    :SRET
A6BE                    :SEND
A6BE                    :SSTOP
A6BE                    :SPOP
A6BE                    :SNEW
A6BE                    :SBYE
A6BE                    :SCONT
A6BE                    :SDEG
A6BE                    :SRAD
A6BE                         SYN      JS,:EOS
A6BE +FA                     DB       $8Ø+(((:EOS-*)&$7F) XOR $4Ø )
A6BF                         SYN       :RTN
A6BF +Ø3                       DB     :RTN
```

<LET> = <NVAR> = <EXP> <EOS> | <SVAR> = <STR> <EOS>#

```
A6CØ                    :SLET
A6CØ                    :SILET
A6CØ                         SYN       :ANTV,AD,:NVAR-1
A6CØ +ØØ                       DB     :ANTV
A6C1 +4BA6                     DW     (:NVAR-1)
A6C3                         SYN       CEQ,:CHNG,CAASN
A6C3 +22                       DB     CEQ
A6C4 +ØF                       DB     :CHNG
A6C5 +2D                       DB     CAASN
A6C6                         SYN       :VEXP
A6C6 +ØE                       DB     :VEXP
A6C7                         SYN       JS,:EOS
A6C7 +F1                     DB       $8Ø+(((:EOS-*)&$7F) XOR $4Ø )
A6C8                         SYN       :OR
A6C8 +Ø2                       DB     :OR
                        ;
A6C9                         SYN       JS,:SVAR
A6C9 +86                     DB       $8Ø+(((:SVAR-*)&$7F) XOR $4Ø )
A6CA                         SYN       CEQ,:CHNG,CSASN
A6CA +22                       DB     CEQ
A6CB +ØF                       DB     :CHNG
A6CC +2E                       DB     CSASN
A6CD                         SYN       :ANTV,AD,:STR-1
A6CD +ØØ                       DB     :ANTV
A6CE +81A6                     DW     (:STR-1)
A6DØ                         SYN       JS,:EOS
A6DØ +E8                     DB       $8Ø+(((:EOS-*)&$7F) XOR $4Ø )
A6D1                         SYN       :RTN
A6D1 +Ø3                       DB     :RTN
```

<FOR> = <TNVAR> = <EXP> TO <EXP> <FSTEP> <EOS>#

```
A6D2                    :SFOR    SYN        :ESRT,AD,:TNVAR-1
A6D2 +Ø1                       DB     :ESRT
A6D3 +29A3                     DW     (:TNVAR-1)
A6D5                         SYN       CEQ,:CHNG,CAASN
A6D5 +22                       DB     CEQ
A6D6 +ØF                       DB     :CHNG
A6D7 +2D                       DB     CAASN
```

```
A6D8                    SYN     :VEXP
A6D8 +ØE                  DB    :VEXP
A6D9                    SYN     CTO
A6D9 +19                  DB    CTO
A6DA                    SYN     :VEXP
A6DA +ØE                  DB    :VEXP
A6DB                    SYN     JS,:FSTEP
A6DB +C3                DB      $8Ø+(((:FSTEP-*)&$7F) XOR $4Ø )
A6DC                    SYN     JS,:EOS
A6DC +DC                DB      $8Ø+(((:EOS-*)&$7F) XOR $4Ø )
A6DD                    SYN     :RTN
A6DD +Ø3                  DB    :RTN
```

<FSTEP> = STEP <EXP> | &

```
A6DE               :FSTEP
A6DE                    SYN     CSTEP
A6DE +1A                  DB    CSTEP
A6DF                    SYN     :VEXP
A6DF +ØE                  DB    :VEXP
A6EØ                    SYN     :OR
A6EØ +Ø2                  DB    :OR
A6E1                    SYN     :RTN
A6E1 +Ø3                  DB    :RTN
```

<LOCATE> = <EXP>,<EXP>,<TNVAR> <EOL>#

```
A6E2               :SLOCATE
A6E2                    SYN     :VEXP
A6E2 +ØE                  DB    :VEXP
A6E3                    SYN     CCOM
A6E3 +12                  DB    CCOM
A6E4                    SYN     :VEXP
A6E4 +ØE                  DB    :VEXP
A6E5                    SYN     CCOM
A6E5 +12                  DB    CCOM
A6E6                    SYN     JS,:SNEXT
A6E6 +C4                DB      $8Ø+(((:SNEXT-*)&$7F) XOR $4Ø )
A6E7                    SYN     :RTN
A6E7 +Ø3                  DB    :RTN
```

<GET> = <D1>,<TNVAR>#

```
A6E8               :SGET
A6E8                    SYN     JS,:D1
A6E8 +DD                DB      $8Ø+(((:D1-*)&$7F) XOR $4Ø )
A6E9                    SYN     CCOM
A6E9 +12                  DB    CCOM
```

<NEXT> = <TNVAR> <EOS>#

```
                   ;
A6EA               :SNEXT  SYN      :ESRT,AD,:TNVAR-1
A6EA +Ø1                  DB    :ESRT
A6EB +29A3                DW    (:TNVAR-1)
A6ED                    SYN     JS,:EOS
A6ED +CB                DB      $8Ø+(((:EOS-*)&$7F) XOR $4Ø )
A6EE                    SYN     :RTN
A6EE +Ø3                  DB    :RTN
```

<RESTORE> = <EXP> <EOS> | <EOS>#

```
A6EF               :SREST  SYN      :VEXP
A6EF +ØE                  DB    :VEXP
A6FØ                    SYN     JS,:EOS
A6FØ +C8                DB      $8Ø+(((:EOS-*)&$7F) XOR $4Ø )
A6F1                    SYN     :OR
A6F1 +Ø2                  DB    :OR
A6F2                    SYN     JS,:EOS
A6F2 +C6                DB      $8Ø+(((:EOS-*)&$7F) XOR $4Ø )
A6F3                    SYN     :RTN
A6F3 +Ø3                  DB    :RTN
```

<INPUT> = <OPD> <READ>#

```
A6F4            :SINPUT SYN      JS,:OPD
A6F4 +F8            DB      $8Ø+(((:OPD-*)&$7F) XOR $4Ø )
```

<READ> = <NSVARL> <EOS>#

```
A6F5            :SREAD  SYN      JS,:NSVRL
A6F5 +DB            DB      $8Ø+(((:NSVRL-*)&$7F) XOR $4Ø )
A6F6                SYN      JS,:EOS
A6F6 +C2            DB      $8Ø+(((:EOS-*)&$7F) XOR $4Ø )
A6F7                SYN      :RTN
A6F7 +Ø3              DB    :RTN
```

EOS = : | CR#

```
A6F8            :EOS    SYN      CEOS
A6F8 +14              DB    CEOS
A6F9                SYN      :OR
A6F9 +Ø2              DB    :OR
A6FA                SYN      CCR
A6FA +16              DB    CCR
A6FB                SYN      :RTN
A6FB +Ø3              DB    :RTN
```

<PRINT> = <D1> <EOS> | <D1> <PR1> <EOS>

```
A6FC            :SPRINT
A6FC                SYN      JS,:D1
A6FC +C9            DB      $8Ø+(((:D1-*)&$7F) XOR $4Ø )
A6FD                SYN      JS,:EOS
A6FD +BB            DB      $8Ø+(((:EOS-*)&$7F) XOR $4Ø )
A6FE                SYN      :OR
A6FE +Ø2              DB    :OR
A6FF                SYN      JS,:OPD
A6FF +ED            DB      $8Ø+(((:OPD-*)&$7F) XOR $4Ø )
A7ØØ            :SLPRINT
A7ØØ                SYN      :ANTV,AD,:PR1-1
A7ØØ +ØØ              DB    :ANTV
A7Ø1 +9FA7            DW    (:PR1-1)
A7Ø3                SYN      JS,:EOS
A7Ø3 +B5            DB      $8Ø+(((:EOS-*)&$7F) XOR $4Ø )
A7Ø4                SYN      :RTN
A7Ø4 +Ø3              DB    :RTN
```

<D1> = <CPND> <EXP>#

```
A7Ø5            :D1     SYN      CPND
A7Ø5 +1C              DB    CPND
A7Ø6                SYN      :VEXP
A7Ø6 +ØE              DB    :VEXP
A7Ø7                SYN      :RTN
A7Ø7 +Ø3              DB    :RTN
```

<NSVAR> = <NVAR> | <SVAR>#

```
A7Ø8            :NSVAR  SYN      :ESRT,AD,:TNVAR-1
A7Ø8 +Ø1              DB    :ESRT
A7Ø9 +29A3            DW    (:TNVAR-1)
A7ØB                SYN      :OR
A7ØB +Ø2              DB    :OR
A7ØC                SYN      :ESRT,AD,:TSVAR-1
A7ØC +Ø1              DB    :ESRT
A7ØD +2DA3            DW    (:TSVAR-1)
A7ØF                SYN      :RTN
A7ØF +Ø3              DB    :RTN
```

<NSVRL> = <NSVAR> <NSV2> | &#

```
A71Ø            :NSVRL  SYN      JS,:NSVAR
A71Ø +B8            DB      $8Ø+(((:NSVAR-*)&$7F) XOR $4Ø )
A711                SYN      JS,:NSV2
```

```
A711 +C3            DB      $80+(((:NSV2-*)&$7F) XOR $40 )
A712                SYN      :OR,:RTN
A712 +02              DB    :OR
A713 +03              DB    :RTN
```

<NSV2> = ,<NSVRL> | &#

```
A714            :NSV2   SYN       CCOM
A714 +12              DB    CCOM
A715                SYN      JS,:NSVRL
A715 +BB            DB      $80+(((:NSVRL-*)&$7F) XOR $40 )
A716                SYN      :OR,:RTN
A716 +02              DB    :OR
A717 +03              DB    :RTN
```

<XIO> = <AEXP>,<D2S><FS>,<AEXP><EOS>#

```
A718            :SXIO
A718                SYN      :VEXP
A718 +0E              DB    :VEXP
A719                SYN      CCOM
A719 +12              DB    CCOM
```

<OPEN> = <D1>,<EXP>,<EXP>,<FS>,<EOS>#

```
A71A            :SOPEN
A71A                SYN      JS,:D1
A71A +AB            DB      $80+(((:D1-*)&$7F) XOR $40 )
A71B                SYN      CCOM
A71B +12              DB    CCOM
A71C                SYN      JS,:TEXP
A71C +F9            DB      $80+(((:TEXP-*)&$7F) XOR $40 )
A71D                SYN      CCOM
A71D +12              DB    CCOM
A71E                SYN      JS,:FS
A71E +F3            DB      $80+(((:FS-*)&$7F) XOR $40 )
A71F                SYN      JS,:EOS
A71F +99            DB      $80+(((:EOS-*)&$7F) XOR $40 )
A720                SYN      :RTN
A720 +03              DB    :RTN
```

<CLOSE> = <D1><EOS>#

```
A721            :SCLOSE
A721                SYN      JS,:D1
A721 +A4            DB      $80+(((:D1-*)&$7F) XOR $40 )
A722                SYN      JS,:EOS
A722 +96            DB      $80+(((:EOS-*)&$7F) XOR $40 )
A723                SYN      :RTN
A723 +03              DB    :RTN
```

< > = <FS><EOS>#

```
A724            :SENTER
A724            :SLOAD
A724            :SSAVE
A724                SYN      JS,:FS
A724 +ED            DB      $80+(((:FS-*)&$7F) XOR $40 )
A725                SYN      JS,:EOS
A725 +93            DB      $80+(((:EOS-*)&$7F) XOR $40 )
A726                SYN      :RTN
A726 +03              DB    :RTN
```

<RUN> = <FS><EOS2> | <EOS2>#

```
A727            :SRUN
A727                SYN      JS,:FS
A727 +EA            DB      $80+(((:FS-*)&$7F) XOR $40 )
A728                SYN      JS,:EOS
A728 +90            DB      $80+(((:EOS-*)&$7F) XOR $40 )
A729                SYN      :OR
A729 +02              DB    :OR
```

```
A72A                        SYN      JS,:EOS
A72A +8E                    DB      $8Ø+(((:EOS-*)&$7F) XOR $4Ø )
A72B                        SYN      :RTN
A72B +Ø3                      DB      :RTN
```

<OPD> = <D1>, | #

```
A72C                   :OPD
A72C                        SYN      JS,:D1
A72C +99                    DB      $8Ø+(((:D1-*)&$7F) XOR $4Ø )
A72D                   :OPDX    SYN       CCOM
A72D +12                      DB     CCOM
A72E                        SYN      :OR
A72E +Ø2                      DB     :OR
A72F                        SYN      JS,:D1
A72F +96                    DB      $8Ø+(((:D1-*)&$7F) XOR $4Ø )
A73Ø                        SYN      CSC
A73Ø +15                      DB     CSC
A731                        SYN      :OR
A731 +Ø2                      DB     :OR
A732                        SYN      :RTN
A732 +Ø3                      DB     :RTN
```

<LIST> = <FS>;<L2> | <L2>#

```
A733                   :SLIST
A733                        SYN      JS,:FS
A733 +DE                    DB      $8Ø+(((:FS-*)&$7F) XOR $4Ø )
A734                        SYN      JS,:EOS
A734 +84                    DB      $8Ø+(((:EOS-*)&$7F) XOR $4Ø )
A735                        SYN      :OR
A735 +Ø2                      DB     :OR
A736                        SYN      JS,:FS
A736 +DB                    DB      $8Ø+(((:FS-*)&$7F) XOR $4Ø )
A737                        SYN      CCOM
A737 +12                      DB     CCOM
A738                        SYN      JS,:LIS
A738 +C4                    DB      $8Ø+(((:LIS-*)&$7F) XOR $4Ø )
A739                        SYN      :OR
A739 +Ø2                      DB     :OR
A73A                        SYN      JS,:LIS
A73A +C2                    DB      $8Ø+(((:LIS-*)&$7F) XOR $4Ø )
A73B                        SYN      :RTN
A73B +Ø3                      DB     :RTN
```

<LIS> = <L1> <EOS2>#

```
A73C                   :LIS
A73C                        SYN      :ANTV,AD,:L1-1
A73C +ØØ                      DB     :ANTV
A73D +BFA7                    DW     (:L1-1)
A73F                        SYN      JS,:EOS2
A73F +F4                    DB      $8Ø+(((:EOS2-*)&$7F) XOR $4Ø )
A74Ø                        SYN      :RTN
A74Ø +Ø3                      DB     :RTN
```

<STATUS> = <STAT> <EOS2>#

```
A741                   :SSTATUS
A741                        SYN      JS,:STAT
A741 +C3                    DB      $8Ø+(((:STAT-*)&$7F) XOR $4Ø )
A742                        SYN      JS,:EOS2
A742 +F1                    DB      $8Ø+(((:EOS2-*)&$7F) XOR $4Ø )
A743                        SYN      :RTN
A743 +Ø3                      DB     :RTN
```

<STAT> = <D1>,<NVAR>#

```
A744                   :STAT
A744                        SYN      JS,:D1
A744 +81                    DB      $8Ø+(((:D1-*)&$7F) XOR $4Ø )
```

```
A745                    SYN     CCOM
A745  +12                 DB    CCOM
A746                    SYN     :ANTV,AD,:NVAR-1
A746  +00                 DB    :ANTV
A747  +4BA6               DW    (:NVAR-1)
A749                    SYN     :RTN
A749  +03                 DB    :RTN
```

< > = <STAT>,<NVAR><EOS2>#

```
A74A                  :SNOTE
A74A                  :SPOINT
A74A                    SYN     JS,:STAT
A74A  +BA               DB      $80+(((:STAT-*)&$7F) XOR $40 )
A74B                    SYN     CCOM
A74B  +12                 DB    CCOM
A74C                    SYN     :ANTV,AD,:NVAR-1
A74C  +00                 DB    :ANTV
A74D  +4BA6               DW    (:NVAR-1)
A74F                    SYN     JS,:EOS2
A74F  +E4               DB      $80+(((:EOS2-*)&$7F) XOR $40 )
A750                    SYN     :RTN
A750  +03                 DB    :RTN
```

<FS> = <STR>

```
A751                  :FS
A751                    SYN     :ANTV,AD,:STR-1
A751  +00                 DB    :ANTV
A752  +81A6               DW    (:STR-1)
A754                    SYN     :RTN
A754  +03                 DB    :RTN
```

<TEXP> = <EXP>,<EXP>#

```
                      ;
A755                  :TEXP
A755                    SYN     :VEXP
A755  +0E                 DB    :VEXP
A756                    SYN     CCOM
A756  +12                 DB    CCOM
A757                    SYN     :VEXP
A757  +0E                 DB    :VEXP
A758                    SYN     :RTN
A758  +03                 DB    :RTN
```

<SOUND> = <EXP>,<EXP>,<EXP>,<EXP><EOS>#

```
A759                  :SSOUND
A759                    SYN     :VEXP
A759  +0E                 DB    :VEXP
A75A                    SYN     CCOM
A75A  +12                 DB    CCOM
A75B                  :SSETCOLOR
A75B                    SYN     :VEXP
A75B  +0E                 DB    :VEXP
A75C                    SYN     CCOM
A75C  +12                 DB    CCOM
```

< > = <EXP>,<EXP><EOS>#

```
A75D                  :SPOKE
A75D                  :SPLOT
A75D                  :SPOS
A75D                  :SDRAWTO
A75D                    SYN     JS,:TEXP
A75D  +B8               DB      $80+(((:TEXP-*)&$7F) XOR $40 )
A75E                    SYN     JS,:EOS2
A75E  +D5               DB      $80+(((:EOS2-*)&$7F) XOR $40 )
A75F                    SYN     :RTN
A75F  +03                 DB    :RTN
```

<DIM> = <NSML> <EOS>#

```
A760                :SDIM
A760                :SCOM
A760                    SYN      JS,:NSML
A760 +EC                DB      $80+(((:NSML-*)&$7F) XOR $40 )
A761                    SYN      JS,:EOS2
A761 +D2                DB      $80+(((:EOS2-*)&$7F) XOR $40 )
A762                    SYN       :RTN
A762 +03                  DB     :RTN
```

<ON> = <EXP> <ON1> <EXPL> <EOS>#

```
A763                :SON     SYN       :VEXP
A763 +0E                  DB     :VEXP
A764                    SYN      JS,:ON1
A764 +C4                DB      $80+(((:ON1-*)&$7F) XOR $40 )
A765                    SYN      JS,:EXPL
A765 +C7                DB      $80+(((:EXPL-*)&$7F) XOR $40 )
A766                    SYN      JS,:EOS2
A766 +CD                DB      $80+(((:EOS2-*)&$7F) XOR $40 )
A767                    SYN       :RTN
A767 +03                  DB     :RTN
```

<ON1> = GOTO | GOSUB#

```
A768                :ON1     SYN       CGTO
A768 +17                  DB     CGTO
A769                    SYN       :OR
A769 +02                  DB     :OR
A76A                    SYN      CGS
A76A +18                  DB     CGS
A76B                    SYN       :RTN
A76B +03                  DB     :RTN
```

<EXPL> = <EXP> <EXPL1>#

```
A76C                :EXPL    SYN       :VEXP
A76C +0E                  DB     :VEXP
A76D                    SYN      JS,:EXPL1
A76D +C2                DB      $80+(((:EXPL1-*)&$7F) XOR $40 )
A76E                    SYN       :RTN
A76E +03                  DB     :RTN
```

<EXPL1> =, <EXPL> | &#

```
A76F                :EXPL1   SYN       CCOM
A76F +12                  DB     CCOM
A770                    SYN      JS,:EXPL
A770 +BC                DB      $80+(((:EXPL-*)&$7F) XOR $40 )
A771                    SYN       :OR
A771 +02                  DB     :OR
A772                    SYN       :RTN
A772 +03                  DB     :RTN
```

<EOS2> = CEOS | CCR#

```
A773                :EOS2
A773                    SYN      CEOS
A773 +14                  DB     CEOS
A774                    SYN       :OR
A774 +02                  DB     :OR
A775                    SYN      CCR
A775 +16                  DB     CCR
A776                    SYN       :RTN
A776 +03                  DB     :RTN
```

<NSMAT> = <TNVAR> (<EXP> <NMAT2>)

```
A777                :NSMAT
A777                    SYN       :ESRT,AD,:TNVAR-1
A777 +01                  DB     :ESRT
```

```
A778 +29A3             DW     (:TNVAR-1)
A77A                  SYN      CLPRN,:CHNG,CDLPRN
A77A +2B               DB     CLPRN
A77B +ØF               DB     :CHNG
A77C +39               DB     CDLPRN
A77D                  SYN      :VEXP
A77D +ØE               DB     :VEXP
A77E                  SYN      :ANTV,AD,:NMAT2-1
A77E +ØØ               DB     :ANTV
A77F +58A6             DW     (:NMAT2-1)
A781                  SYN      CRPRN
A781 +2C               DB     CRPRN
A782                  SYN      :OR
A782 +Ø2               DB     :OR
A783                  SYN      :ESRT,AD,:TSVAR-1
A783 +Ø1               DB     :ESRT
A784 +2DA3             DW     (:TSVAR-1)
A786                  SYN      CLPRN,:CHNG,CDSLPR
A786 +2B               DB     CLPRN
A787 +ØF               DB     :CHNG
A788 +3B               DB     CDSLPR
A789                  SYN      :VEXP
A789 +ØE               DB     :VEXP
A78A                  SYN      CRPRN
A78A +2C               DB     CRPRN
A78B                  SYN      :RTN
A78B +Ø3               DB     :RTN
```

<NSML> = <NSMAT> <NSML2> | &#

```
A78C              :NSML    SYN       JS,:NSMAT
A78C +AB              DB       $8Ø+(((:NSMAT-*)&$7F) XOR $4Ø )
A78D                  SYN       JS,:NSML2
A78D +C3              DB       $8Ø+(((:NSML2-*)&$7F) XOR $4Ø )
A78E                  SYN       :OR,:RTN
A78E +Ø2                DB     :OR
A78F +Ø3                DB     :RTN
```

<NSML2> =,<NSML> | &#

```
A79Ø              :NSML2   SYN        CCOM
A79Ø +12                DB     CCOM
A791                  SYN       JS,:NSML
A791 +BB              DB       $8Ø+(((:NSML-*)&$7F) XOR $4Ø )
A792                  SYN       :OR,:RTN
A792 +Ø2                DB     :OR
A793 +Ø3                DB     :RTN
```

<IF> = <EXP> THEN <IFA> <EOS>#

```
A794              :SIF     SYN        :VEXP
A794 +ØE                DB     :VEXP
A795                  SYN       CTHEN
A795 +1B                DB     CTHEN
A796                  SYN       JS,:IFA
A796 +C3              DB       $8Ø+(((:IFA-*)&$7F) XOR $4Ø )
A797                  SYN       JS,:EOS2
A797 +9C              DB       $8Ø+(((:EOS2-*)&$7F) XOR $4Ø )
A798                  SYN       :RTN
A798 +Ø3                DB     :RTN
```

<IFA> = <TNCON> | <EIF>

```
A799              :IFA     SYN        :ESRT,AD,:TNCON-1
A799 +Ø1                DB     :ESRT
A79A +FFA3              DW     (:TNCON-1)
A79C                  SYN       :OR
A79C +Ø2                DB     :OR
A79D                  SYN       :ESRT,AD,:EIF-1
A79D +Ø1                DB     :ESRT
A79E +D3A2              DW     (:EIF-1)
```

<PR1> = <PEL> | <PSL><PR2> | &#

```
A7A0                :PR1
A7A0                    SYN      JS,:PEL,:OR
A7A0 +C9                DB       $80+(((:PEL-*)&$7F) XOR $40 )
A7A1 +02                  DB     :OR
A7A2                    SYN      JS,:PSL
A7A2 +D4                DB       $80+(((:PSL-*)&$7F) XOR $40 )
A7A3                    SYN      JS,:PR2
A7A3 +C3                DB       $80+(((:PR2-*)&$7F) XOR $40 )
A7A4                    SYN       :OR
A7A4 +02                  DB     :OR
A7A5                    SYN       :RTN
A7A5 +03                  DB     :RTN
                    ;
```

<PR2> = <PEL> | &#

```
A7A6                :PR2    SYN      JS,:PEL
A7A6 +C3                DB       $80+(((:PEL-*)&$7F) XOR $40 )
A7A7                    SYN       :OR
A7A7 +02                  DB     :OR
A7A8                    SYN       :RTN
A7A8 +03                  DB     :RTN
```

<PEL> = <PES> <PELA>#

```
A7A9                :PEL    SYN      JS,:PES
A7A9 +C3                DB       $80+(((:PES-*)&$7F) XOR $40 )
A7AA                    SYN      JS,:PELA
A7AA +C8                DB       $80+(((:PELA-*)&$7F) XOR $40 )
A7AB                    SYN       :RTN
A7AB +03                  DB     :RTN
```

<PES> = <EXP> | <STR>

```
A7AC                :PES    SYN       :VEXP
A7AC +0E                  DB     :VEXP
A7AD                    SYN       :OR
A7AD +02                  DB     :OR
A7AE                    SYN       :ANTV,AD,:STR-1
A7AE +00                  DB     :ANTV
A7AF +81A6                DW     (:STR-1)
A7B1                    SYN       :RTN
A7B1 +03                  DB     :RTN
```

<PELA> = <PSL> <PEL> | &#

```
A7B2                :PELA   SYN      JS,:PSL
A7B2 +C4                DB       $80+(((:PSL-*)&$7F) XOR $40 )
A7B3                    SYN      JS,:PR2
A7B3 +B3                DB       $80+(((:PR2-*)&$7F) XOR $40 )
A7B4                    SYN       :OR
A7B4 +02                  DB     :OR
A7B5                    SYN       :RTN
A7B5 +03                  DB     :RTN
```

<PSL> = <PS> <PSLA>#

```
A7B6                :PSL    SYN      JS,:PS
A7B6 +C6                DB       $80+(((:PS-*)&$7F) XOR $40 )
A7B7                    SYN      JS,:PSLA
A7B7 +C2                DB       $80+(((:PSLA-*)&$7F) XOR $40 )
A7B8                    SYN       :RTN
A7B8 +03                  DB     :RTN
```

<PSLA> = <PSL> | &#

```
A7B9                :PSLA   SYN      JS,:PSL
A7B9 +BD                DB       $80+(((:PSL-*)&$7F) XOR $40 )
A7BA                    SYN       :OR
```

```
A7BA +02              DB     :OR
A7BB                 SYN      :RTN
A7BB +03              DB     :RTN
```

<PS> =, | , #

```
A7BC             :PS     SYN       CCOM
A7BC +12              DB     CCOM
A7BD                 SYN      :OR
A7BD +02              DB     :OR
A7BE                 SYN      CSC
A7BE +15              DB     CSC
A7BF                 SYN      :RTN
A7BF +03              DB     :RTN
```

<L1> = <EXP> <L2> | &#

```
A7C0             :L1     SYN       :VEXP
A7C0 +0E              DB     :VEXP
A7C1                 SYN     JS,:L2
A7C1 +C3             DB      $80+(((:L2-*)&$7F) XOR $40 )
A7C2                 SYN      :OR
A7C2 +02              DB     :OR
A7C3                 SYN      :RTN
A7C3 +03              DB     :RTN
```

<L2> =, <EXP> | &#

```
A7C4             :L2     SYN       CCOM
A7C4 +12              DB     CCOM
A7C5                 SYN      :VEXP
A7C5 +0E              DB     :VEXP
A7C6                 SYN      :OR
A7C6 +02              DB     :OR
A7C7                 SYN      :RTN
A7C7 +03              DB     :RTN
```

<REM> = <EREM>

```
A7C8             :SREM   SYN       :ESRT,AD,:EREM-1
A7C8 +01              DB     :ESRT
A7C9 +DFA2            DW     (:EREM-1)
```

<SDATA> = <EDATA>

```
A7CB             :SDATA  SYN       :ESRT,AD,:EDATA-1
A7CB +01              DB     :ESRT
A7CC +DFA2            DW     (:EDATA-1)
```

<NFSP> = ASC | VAL | LEN#

```
A7CE             :NFSP   SYN       CASC,:OR
A7CE +40              DB     CASC
A7CF +02              DB     :OR
A7D0                 SYN      CVAL,:OR
A7D0 +41              DB     CVAL
A7D1 +02              DB     :OR
A7D2                 SYN      CADR,:OR
A7D2 +43              DB     CADR
A7D3 +02              DB     :OR
A7D4                 SYN      CLEN
A7D4 +42              DB     CLEN
A7D5                 SYN      :RTN
A7D5 +03              DB     :RTN
                 ;
```

<SFNP> = STR | CHR#

```
                    ;
                    ;
A7D6                :SFNP   SYN      CSTR,:OR
A7D6 +3D                  DB    CSTR
A7D7 +Ø2                  DB    :OR
A7D8                    SYN      CCHR
A7D8 +3E                  DB    CCHR
A7D9                    SYN      :RTN
A7D9 +Ø3                  DB    :RTN
```

<PUSR> = <EXP><PUSR1>#

```
A7DA                :PUSR   SYN      :VEXP
A7DA +ØE                  DB    :VEXP
A7DB                    SYN     JS,:PUSR1
A7DB +C2                DB      $8Ø+(((:PUSR1-*)&$7F) XOR $4Ø )
A7DC                    SYN      :RTN
A7DC +Ø3                  DB    :RTN
```

<PUSR1> =,<PUSR> | &#

```
A7DD                :PUSR1  SYN      CCOM,:CHNG,CACOM
A7DD +12                  DB    CCOM
A7DE +ØF                  DB    :CHNG
A7DF +3C                  DB    CACOM
A7EØ                    SYN     JS,:PUSR
A7EØ +BA                DB      $8Ø+(((:PUSR-*)&$7F) XOR $4Ø )
A7E1                    SYN      :OR
A7E1 +Ø2                  DB    :OR
A7E2                    SYN      :RTN
A7E2 +Ø3                  DB    :RTN
```

OPNTAB — Operator Name Table

```
A7E3                OPNTAB
       = ØØØF       C        SET      $ØF          ;FIRST ENTRY VALUE=$1Ø
                    ;
       = ØØ1Ø       C        SET      C+1
       = ØØ1Ø       CDQ      EQU      C
A7E3   82                DB      $82               ;DOUBLE QUOTE
                    ;
       = ØØ11       C        SET      C+1
       = ØØ11       CSOE     EQU      C
A7E4   8Ø                DB      $8Ø               ; DUMMY FOR SOE
                    ;
       = ØØ12       C        SET      C+1
       = ØØ12       CCOM     EQU      C
A7E5   AC                DC      ','
                    ;
       = ØØ13       C        SET      C+1
       = ØØ13       CDOL     EQU      C
A7E6   A4                DC      '$'
                    ;
       = ØØ14       C        SET      C+1
       = ØØ14       CEOS     EQU      C
A7E7   BA                DC      ':'
                    ;
       = ØØ15       C        SET      C+1
       = ØØ15       CSC      EQU      C
A7E8   BB                DC      ';'
                    ;
       = ØØ16       C        SET      C+1
       = ØØ16       CCR      EQU      C            ;CARRIAGE RETURN
A7E9   9B                DB      CR
                    ;
       = ØØ17       C        SET      C+1
       = ØØ17       CGTO     EQU      C
A7EA   474F54CF          DC      'GOTO'
                    ;
```

```
      = ØØ18       C        SET      C+1
      = ØØ18       CGS      EQU      C
A7EE  474F5355C2        DC     'GOSUB'
                   ;
      = ØØ19       C        SET      C+1
      = ØØ19       CTO      EQU      C
A7F3  54CF              DC     'TO'
                   ;
      = ØØ1A       C        SET      C+1
      = ØØ1A       CSTEP    EQU      C
A7F5  535445DØ          DC     'STEP'
                   ;
      = ØØ1B       C        SET      C+1
      = ØØ1B       CTHEN    EQU      C
A7F9  544845CE          DC     'THEN'
                   ;
      = ØØ1C       C        SET      C+1
      = ØØ1C       CPND     EQU      C
A7FD  A3                DC     '#'
                   ;
      = ØØ1D       CSROP    EQU      C+1             ; START OF REAL OPS
                   ;
      = ØØ1D       C        SET      C+1
      = ØØ1D       CLE      EQU      C
A7FE  3CBD              DC     '<='
                   ;
      = ØØ1E       C        SET      C+1
      = ØØ1E       CNE      EQU      C
A8ØØ  3CBE              DC     '<>'
                   ;
      = ØØ1F       C        SET      C+1
      = ØØ1F       CGE      EQU      C
A8Ø2  3EBD              DC     '>='
                   ;
      = ØØ2Ø       C        SET      C+1
      = ØØ2Ø       CLT      EQU      C
A8Ø4  BC                DC     '<'
                   ;
      = ØØ21       C        SET      C+1
      = ØØ21       CGT      EQU      C
A8Ø5  BE                DC     '>'
                   ;
      = ØØ22       C        SET      C+1
      = ØØ22       CEQ      EQU      C
A8Ø6  BD                DC     '='
                   ;
      = ØØ23       C        SET      C+1
      = ØØ23       CEXP     EQU      C
A8Ø7  DE                DB       $5E+$8Ø        ;UP ARROW FOR EXP
                   ;
      = ØØ24       C        SET      C+1
      = ØØ24       CMUL     EQU      C
A8Ø8  AA                DC                 '*'
                   ;
      = ØØ25       C        SET      C+1
      = ØØ25       CPLUS    EQU      C
A8Ø9  AB                DC     '+'
                   ;
      = ØØ26       C        SET      C+1
      = ØØ26       CMINUS   EQU      C
A8ØA  AD                DC     '-'
                   ;
      = ØØ27       C        SET      C+1
      = ØØ27       CDIV     EQU      C
A8ØB  AF                DC     '/'
                   ;
      = ØØ28       C        SET      C+1
      = ØØ28       CNOT     EQU      C
A8ØC  4E4FD4            DC     'NOT'
                   ;
```

```
        = ØØ29      C         SET      C+1
        = ØØ29      COR       EQU      C
A8ØF    4FD2            DC       'OR'
                    ;
        = ØØ2A      C         SET      C+1
        = ØØ2A      CAND      EQU      C
A811    414EC4          DC       'AND'
                    ;
        = ØØ2B      C         SET      C+1
        = ØØ2B      CLPRN     EQU      C
A814    A8              DC       '('
                    ;
        = ØØ2C      C         SET      C+1
        = ØØ2C      CRPRN     EQU      C
A815    A9              DC       ')'
                    ;
                    ;
                    ; THE FOLLOWING ENTRIES ARE COMPRISED OF CHARACTERS
                    ; SIMILAR TO SOME OF THOSE ABOVE BUT HAVE
                    ; DIFFERENT SYNTACTICAL OR SEMANTIC MEANING
                    ;
        = ØØ2D      C         SET      C+1
        = ØØ2D      CAASN     EQU      C              ;ARITHMETIC ASSIGMENT
A816    BD              DC       '='
                    ;
        = ØØ2E      C         SET      C+1
        = ØØ2E      CSASN     EQU      C              ; STRING OPS
A817    BD              DC       '='
                    ;
        = ØØ2F      C         SET      C+1
        = ØØ2F      CSLE      EQU      C
A818    3CBD            DC       '<='
                    ;
        = ØØ3Ø      C         SET      C+1
        = ØØ3Ø      CSNE      EQU      C
A81A    3CBE            DC       '<>'
                    ;
        = ØØ31      C         SET      C+1
        = ØØ31      CSGE      EQU      C
A81C    3EBD            DC       '>='
                    ;
        = ØØ32      C         SET      C+1
        = ØØ32      CSLT      EQU      C
A81E    BC              DC       '<'
                    ;
        = ØØ33      C         SET      C+1
        = ØØ33      CSGT      EQU      C
A81F    BE              DC       '>'
                    ;
        = ØØ34      C         SET      C+1
        = ØØ34      CSEQ      EQU      C
A82Ø    BD              DC       '='
                    ;
        = ØØ35      C         SET      C+1
        = ØØ35      CUPLUS    EQU      C              ;UNARY PLUS
A821    AB              DC       '+'
                    ;
        = ØØ36      C         SET      C+1
        = ØØ36      CUMINUS   EQU      C              ; UNARY MINUS
A822    AD              DC       '-'
                    ;
        = ØØ37      C         SET      C+1
        = ØØ37      CSLPRN    EQU      C              ;STRING LEFT PAREN
A823    A8              DC       '('
                    ;
        = ØØ38      C         SET      C+1
        = ØØ38      CALPRN    EQU      C              ; ARRAY LEFT PAREN
A824    8Ø              DB       $8Ø                  ; DOES NOT PRINT
        = ØØ39      C         SET      C+1
        = ØØ39      CDLPRN    EQU      C              ; DIM LEFT PAREN
```

```
A825  80              DB      $80               ; DOES NOT PRINT
                 ;
      = 003A     C         SET     C+1
      = 003A     CFLPRN    EQU     C            ; FUNCTION LEFT PAREN
A826  A8              DC      '('
                 ;
      = 003B     C         SET     C+1
      = 003B     CDSLPR    EQU     C
A827  A8              DC      '('
                 ;
      = 003C     C         SET     C+1
      = 003C     CACOM     EQU     C            ; ARRAY COMMA
A828  AC              DC ','
```

Function Name Table

```
                 ;         PART OF ONTAB
                 ;
                 ;
A829             FNTAB
                 ;
      = 003D     C         SET     C+1
      = 003D     CFFUN     EQU     C            ;FIRST FUNCTION CODE
      = 003D     CSTR      EQU     C
A829  535452A4        DC      'STR$'
      = 003E     C         SET     C+1
      = 003E     CCHR      EQU     C
A82D  434852A4        DC      'CHR$'
      = 003F     C         SET     C+1
      = 003F     CUSR      EQU     C            ;USR FUNCTION CODE
A831  5553D2          DC      'USR'
      = 0040     C         SET     C+1
      = 0040     CASC      EQU     C
A834  4153C3          DC      'ASC'
      = 0041     C         SET     C+1
      = 0041     CVAL      EQU     C
A837  5641CC          DC      'VAL'
      = 0042     C         SET     C+1
      = 0042     CLEN      EQU     C
A83A  4C45CE          DC      'LEN'
      = 0043     C         SET     C+1
      = 0043     CADR      EQU     C
A83D  4144D2          DC      'ADR'
      = 0044     C         SET     C+1
      = 0044     CNFNP     EQU     C
A840  4154CE          DC      'ATN'
A843  434FD3          DC      'COS'
A846  504545CB        DC      'PEEK'
A84A  5349CE          DC      'SIN'
A84D  524EC4          DC      'RND'
A850  4652C5          DC      'FRE'
A853  4558D0          DC      'EXP'
A856  4C4FC7          DC      'LOG'
A859  434C4FC7        DC      'CLOG'
A85D  5351D2          DC      'SQR'
A860  5347CE          DC      'SGN'
A863  4142D3          DC      'ABS'
A866  494ED4          DC      'INT'
A869  504144444C      DC      'PADDLE'
      C5
A86F  53544943CB      DC      'STICK'
A874  50545249C7      DC      'PTRIG'
A879  53545249C7      DC      'STRIG'
                 ;
A87E  00              DB      $00
                 ;
                 ; END OF OPNTAB & FNTAB
```

Memory Manager

```
A87F                      LOCAL
                          ;
                          ;       MEMORY MANAGEMENT CONSISTS OF EXPANDING AND
                          ;       CONTRACTING TO INFORMATION AREA POINTED TO
                          ;       BY THE ZERO PAGE  POINTER TABLES.  ROUTINES
                          ;       MODIFY THE ADDRESS IN THE TABLES AND
                          ;       MOVE DATA AS REQUIRED.  THE TWO FUNDAMENTAL
                          ;       ROUTINES ARE 'EXPAND' AND 'CONTRACT'
```

EXPAND

```
                          ;               X = ZERO PAGE ADDRESS OF TABLE AT WHICH
                          ;               EXPANSION IS TO START
                          ;               Y = EXPANSION SIZE IN BYTES [LOW]
                          ;               A = EXPANSION SIZE IN BYTES [HIGH]
                          ;
                          ; EXPLOW - FOR EXPANSION < 256 BYTES
                          ;                SETS A = Ø
                          ;
A87F  A9ØØ                EXPLOW  LDA     #Ø
                          ;
A881                      EXPAND
A881  84A4                    STY     ECSIZE          ; SAVE EXPAND SIZE
A883  85A5                    STA     ECSIZE+1
                          ;
A885  38                      SEC
A886  A59Ø                    LDA     MEMTOP          ; TEST MEMORY TO BE FULL
A888  65A4                    ADC     ECSIZE
A88A  A8                      TAY                     ; MEMTOP+ECSIZE+1
A88B  A591                    LDA     MEMTOP+1
A88D  65A5                    ADC     ECSIZE+1        ; MUST BE LE
A88F  CDE6Ø2                  CMP     HIMEM+1
A892  9ØØC ^A8AØ              BCC     :EXP2           ; HIMEM
A894  DØØ7 ^A89D              BNE     :EXP1
A896  CCE5Ø2                  CPY     HIMEM
A899  9ØØ5 ^A8AØ              BCC     :EXP2
A89B  FØØ3 ^A8AØ              BEQ     :EXP2
A89D  4C3CB9              :EXP1   JMP     MEMFULL
                          ;
A8AØ                      :EXP2
A8AØ  38                      SEC                     ; FORM MOVE LENGTH [MVLNG]
A8A1  A59Ø                    LDA     MEMTOP          ; MOVE FROM ADR [MVFA]
A8A3  F5ØØ                    SBC     Ø,X             ; MVLNG = MEMTOP-EXPAND ADR
A8A5  85A2                    STA     MVLNG
A8A7  A591                    LDA     MEMTOP+1        ; MVFA[L] = EXP ADR [L]
A8A9  F5Ø1                    SBC     1,X
A8AB  85A3                    STA     MVLNG+1         ; MVFA[H] = EXP ADR[H] +
                                                        MVLNG[H]
A8AD  18                      CLC                     ; DURING MOVE MVLNG[L]
A8AE  75Ø1                    ADC     1,X             ; WILL BE ADDED SUCH
A8BØ  859A                    STA     MVFA+1          ; THAT MVFA = MEMTOP
                          ;
A8B2  B5ØØ                    LDA     Ø,X             ; SAVE PREMOVE EXPAND AT VALUE
A8B4  8599                    STA     MVFA            ; SET MVFA LOW
A8B6  8597                    STA     SVESA           ; FORM MOVE TO ADR [MVTA]
A8B8  65A4                    ADC     ECSIZE          ; MVTA[L] = EXP ADR[L] +
                                                        ECSIZE[L]
A8BA  859B                    STA     MVTA            ; MVTA[H] = [CARRY + EXP
                                                        AD-[H]
A8BC  B5Ø1                    LDA     1,X             ; +ECSIZE[H]] + MVLNG[H]
A8BE  8598                    STA     SVESA+1
A8CØ  65A5                    ADC     ECSIZE+1        ; DURING MOVE MVLNG[L]
A8C2  65A3                    ADC     MVLNG+1         ; WILL BE ADDED SUCH THAT
A8C4  859C                    STA     MVTA+1          ; MVTA = MEMTOP + ECSIZE
                          ;
A8C6                      :EXP3
```

```
A8C6  B500              LDA     0,X             ; ADD ECSIZE TO
A8C8  65A4              ADC     ECSIZE          ; ALL TABLE ENTRIES
A8CA  9500              STA     0,X             ; FROM EXPAND AT ADR
A8CC  B501              LDA     1,X             ; TO HIMEM
A8CE  65A5              ADC     ECSIZE+1
A8D0  9501              STA     1,X
A8D2  E8                INX
A8D3  E8                INX
A8D4  E092              CPX     #MEMTOP+2
A8D6  90EE ^A8C6        BCC     :EXP3
A8D8  850F              STA     APHM+1          ; SET NEW APL
A8DA  A590              LDA     MEMTOP          ; HI MEM TO
A8DC  850E              STA     APHM            ; MEMTOP
                  ;
A8DE  A6A3              LDX     MVLNG+1         ; X = MVLNG[H]
A8E0  E8                INX                     ; PLUS ONE
A8E1  A4A2              LDY     MVLNG           ; Y = MVLNG[L]
A8E3  D00B ^A8F0        BNE     :EXP6           ; TEST ZERO LENGTH
A8E5  F010 ^A8F7        BEQ     :EXP7           ; BR IF LOW = 0
                  ;
A8E7  88          :EXP4  DEY                    ; DEC MVLNG[L]
A8E8  C69A              DEC     MVFA+1          ; DEC MVFA[H]
A8EA  C69C              DEC     MVTA+1          ; DEC MVTA[H]
                  ;
A8EC  B199        :EXP5  LDA     [MVFA],Y       ; MVFA BYTE
A8EE  919B              STA     [MVTA],Y        ; TO MVTA
A8F0  88          :EXP6  DEY                    ; DEC COUNT LOW
A8F1  D0F9 ^A8EC        BNE     :EXP5           ; BR IF NOT ZERO
                  ;
A8F3  B199              LDA     [MVFA],Y        ; MOVE THE ZERO BYTE
A8F5  919B              STA     [MVTA],Y
                  ;
A8F7              :EXP7
A8F7  CA                DEX                     ; IF MVLNG[H] IS NOT
A8F8  D0ED ^A8E7        BNE     :EXP4           ; ZERO THEN MOVE 256 MORE
                  ;                               ELSE
A8FA  60                RTS                     ; DONE
```

CONTRACT

```
                  ;                 X = ZERO PAGE ADR OF TABLE AT WHICH
                  ;                     CONTRACTION WILL START
                  ;                 Y = CONTRACT SIZE IN BYTES [LOW]
                  ;                 A = CONTRACT SIZE IN BYTES [HI]
                  ;         CONTLOW
                  ;                 SETS A = 0
                  ;
A8FB  A900        CONTLOW LDA       #0
                  ;
A8FD              CONTRACT
A8FD  84A4              STY     ECSIZE          ; SAVE CONTRACT SIZE
A8FF  85A5              STA     ECSIZE+1
                  ;
A901  38                SEC                     ; FORM MOVE LENGTH [LOW]
A902  A590              LDA     MEMTOP
A904  F500              SBC     0,X             ; MVLNG[L] = $100-
A906  49FF              EOR     #$FF            ; [MEMTOP[L]] - CON AT
                                                ; VALUE [L]
A908  A8                TAY                     ; THIS MAKES START Y AT
A909  C8                INY                     ; MOVE HAVE A 2'S COMPLEMENT
A90A  84A2              STY     MVLNG           ; REMAINDER IN IT
                  ;
A90C  A591              LDA     MEMTOP+1        ; FORM MOVE LENGTH[HIGH]
A90E  F501              SBC     1,X
A910  85A3              STA     MVLNG+1
                  ;
A912  B500              LDA     0,X             ; FORM MOVE FROM ADR [MVFA]
A914  E5A2              SBC     MVLNG           ; MVFA = CON AT VALUE
A916  8599              STA     MVFA            ; MINUS MVLNG[L]
A918  B501              LDA     1,X             ; DURING MOVE MVLNG[L]
```

```
A91A  E900              SBC    #0              ; WILL BE ADDED BACK INTO
A91C  859A              STA    MVFA+1          ; MVFA IN [IND],Y INST
                  ;
A91E  869B              STX    MVTA            ; TEMP SAVE OF CON AT DISPL
                  ;
A920  38          :CONT1  SEC       ; SUBTRACT ECSIZE FROM
A921  B500              LDA    0,X             ; ALL TABLE ENTRY FROM
A923  E5A4              SBC    ECSIZE          ; CON AT ADR TO HIMEM
A925  9500              STA    0,X
A927  B501              LDA    1,X
A929  E5A5              SBC    ECSIZE+1
A92B  9501              STA    1,X
A92D  E8                INX
A92E  E8                INX
A92F  E092              CPX    #MEMTOP+2
A931  90ED ^A920        BCC    :CONT1
A933  850F              STA    APHM+1          ; SET NEW APL
A935  A590              LDA    MEMTOP          ; HI MEM TO
A937  850E              STA    APHM            ; MEMTOP
                  ;
A939  A69B              LDX    MVTA
                  ;
A93B  B500              LDA    0,X             ;FORM MOVE TO ADR [MVTA]
A93D  E5A2              SBC    MVLNG           ; MVTA = NEW CON AT VALUE
A93F  859B              STA    MVTA            ; MINUS MVLNG [L]
A941  B501              LDA    1,X             ; DURING MOVE MVLNG[L]
A943  E900              SBC    #0              ; WILL BE ADDED BACK INTO
A945  859C              STA    MVTA+1          ; MVTA IN [INO],Y INST
                  ;
A947              FMOVER
A947  A6A3              LDX    MVLNG+1         ; GET MOVE LENGTH HIGH
A949  E8                INX                    ; INC SO MOVE CAN BNE
A94A  A4A2              LDY    MVLNG           ; GET MOVE LENGTH LOW
A94C  D006 ^A954        BNE    :CONT2          ; IF NOT ZERO GO
A94E  F00B ^A95B        BEQ    :CONT4          ; BR IF LOW = 0
                  ;
A950  E69A        :CONT3  INC     MVFA+1       ;INC MVFA[H]
A952  E69C              INC    MVTA+1          ; INC MVTA[H]
                  ;
A954  B199        :CONT2  LDA      [MVFA],Y    ; GET MOVE FROM BYTE
A956  919B              STA    [MVTA],Y        ; SET MOVE TO BYTE
A958  C8                INY                    ; INCREMENT COUNT LOW
A959  D0F9 ^A954        BNE    :CONT2          ; BR IF NOT ZERO
                  ;
A95B              :CONT4
A95B  CA                DEX                    ; DECREMENT COUNT HIGH
A95C  D0F2 ^A950        BNE    :CONT3          ;BR IF NOT ZERO
A95E  60                RTS                    ; ELSE DONE
```

Execute Control

```
A95F                    LOCAL
```

EXECNL — Execute Next Line

```
                        ;   START PROGRAM EXECUTOR
                        ;
A95F              EXECNL
A95F  201BB8            JSR    SETLN1          ; SET UP LIN & NXT STMT
```

EXECNS — Execute Next Statement

```
A962              EXECNS
A962  20F4A9            JSR    TSTBRK          ; TEST BREAK
A965  D035 ^A99C        BNE    :EXBRK          ; BR IF BREAK
A967  A4A7              LDY    NXTSTD          ;GET PTR TO NEXT STMT L
A969  C49F              CPY    LLNGTH          ;AT END OF LINE
A96B  B01C ^A989        BCS    :EXEOL          ; BR IF EOL
                  ;
```

```
A96D  B18A              LDA      [STMCUR],Y      ;GET NEW STMT LENGTH
A96F  85A7              STA      NXTSTD          ;SAVE AS FUTURE STMT LENGTH
A971  98                TYA                      ;Y=DISPL TO THIS STMT LENGTH
A972  C8                INY                      ;PLUS 1 IS DISPL TO CODE
A973  B18A              LDA      [STMCUR],Y      ;GET CODE
A975  C8                INY                      ;INC TO STMT MEAT
A976  84A8              STY      STINDEX         ;SET WORK INDEX
                  ;
A978  207EA9            JSR      :STGO           ;GO EXECUTE
A97B  4C62A9            JMP      EXECNS          ;THEN DO NEXT STMT
                  ;
A97E              :STGO   ASLA                   ;TOKEN*2
A97E +0A                ASL      A
A97F  AA                TAX
A980  BD00AA            LDA      STETAB,X        ; GET ADR AND
A983  48                PHA                      ;PUSH TO STACK
A984  BD01AA            LDA      STETAB+1,X      ; AND GO TO
A987  48                PHA                      ;VIA
A988  60                RTS                      ;RTS
                  ;
A989              :EXEOL
A989  A001              LDY      #1
A98B  B18A              LDA      [STMCUR],Y
A98D  3010 ^A99F        BMI      :EXFD           ; BR IF DIR
                  ;
A98F  A59F              LDA      LLNGTH          ;GET LINE LENGTH
A991  20D0A9            JSR      GNXTL           ;INC STMCUR
A994  20E2A9            JSR      TENDST          ;TEST END STMT TABLE
A997  10C6 ^A95F        BPL      EXECNL          ;BR NOT END
                  ;
A999  4C8DB7      :EXDONE JMP      XEND          ; GO BACK TO SYNTAX
A99C  4C93B7      :EXBRK  JMP      XSTOP         ; BREAK, DO STOP
A99F  4C5DA0      :EXFD   JMP      SNX3          ; GO TO SYNTAX VIA READY MSG
```

GETSTMT — Get Statement in Statement Table

```
                  ;       SEARCH FOR STMT THAT HAS TSLNUM
                  ;       SET STMCUR TO POINT TO IT IF FOUND
                  ;       OR TO WHERE IT WOULD GO IF NOT FOUND
                  ;       CARRY SET IF NOT FOUND
A9A2              GETSTMT
                  ;
                  ;       SAVE CURRENT LINE ADDR
                  ;
A9A2  A58A              LDA      STMCUR
A9A4  85BE              STA      SAVCUR
A9A6  A58B              LDA      STMCUR+1
A9A8  85BF              STA      SAVCUR+1
A9AA  A589              LDA      STMTAB+1        ;START AT TOP OF TABLE
A9AC  A488              LDY      STMTAB
                  ;
A9AE  858B              STA      STMCUR+1        ;SET STMCUR
A9B0  848A              STY      STMCUR
                  ;
                  ;
A9B2  A001        :GS2    LDY      #1
A9B4  B18A              LDA      [STMCUR],Y      ;GET STMT LNO [HI]
A9B6  C5A1              CMP      TSLNUM+1        ;TEST WITH TSLNUM
A9B8  900D ^A9C7        BCC      :GS3            ;BR IF S<TS
A9BA  D00A ^A9C6        BNE      :GSRT1          ;BR IF S>TS
A9BC  88                DEY      :GS3            ;S=TS, TEST LOW BYTE
A9BD  B18A              LDA      [STMCUR],Y
A9BF  C5A0              CMP      TSLNUM
A9C1  9004 ^A9C7        BCC      :GS3            ;BR S<TS
A9C3  D001 ^A9C6        BNE      :GSRT1          ;BR S>TS
A9C5  18                CLC                      ;S=TS, CLEAR CARY
A9C6              :GSRT1
A9C6  60                RTS                      ;AND RETURN [FOUND]
                  ;
A9C7  20DDA9      :GS3    JSR      GETLL         ;GO GET THIS GUYS LENGTH
```

```
A9CA  20D0A9          JSR     GNXTL
A9CD  4CB2A9          JMP     :GS2
                ;
A9D0            GNXTL
A9D0  18              CLC
A9D1  658A            ADC     STMCUR          ;ADD LENGTH TO STMCUR
A9D3  858A            STA     STMCUR
A9D5  A8              TAY
A9D6  A58B            LDA     STMCUR+1
A9D8  6900            ADC     #0
A9DA  858B            STA     STMCUR+1
A9DC  60              RTS
A9DD  A002      GETLL   LDY     #2
A9DF  B18A            LDA     [STMCUR],Y
A9E1  60              RTS
```

TENDST — Test End of Statement Table

```
A9E2            TENDST
A9E2  A001            LDY     #1              ; INDEX TO CNO ['I]
A9E4  B18A            LDA     [STMCUR],Y      ; GET CNO [HI]
A9E6  60              RTS
A9E7            XREM
A9E7            XDATA
A9E7  60        TESTRTS RTS
```

XBYE — Execute BYE

```
A9E8            XBYE
A9E8  2041BD          JSR     CLSALL          ; CLOSE 1-7
A9EB  4C71E4          JMP     BYELOC          ; EXIT
```

XDOS — Execute DOS

```
A9EE            XDOS
A9EE  2041BD          JSR     CLSALL          ; CLOSE 1-7
A9F1  6C0A00          JMP     [DOSLOC]        ; GO TO DOS
```

TSTBRK — Test for Break

```
A9F4            TSTBRK
A9F4  A000            LDY     #0
                ;
A9F6  A511            LDA     BRKBYT          ; LOAD BREAK BYTE
A9F8  D004 ^A9FE      BNE     :TB2
A9FA  A0FF            LDY     #$FF
A9FC  8411            STY     BRKBYT
A9FE  98        :TB2    TYA                   ; SET COND CODE
A9FF  60              RTS                     ; DONE
```

Statement Execution Table

```
                ;STETAB-STATEMENT EXECUTION TABLE
                ;       -CONTAINS STMT EXECUTION ADR
                ;       -MUST BE IN SAME ORDER AS SNTAB
                ;
AA00            STETAB
AA00                  FDB     XREM-1
AA00  +A9E6           DW      REV (XREM-1)
AA02                  FDB     XDATA-1
AA02  +A9E6           DW      REV (XDATA-1)
      = 0001    CDATA   EQU     (*-STETAB)/2-1
AA04                  FDB     XINPUT-1
AA04  +B315           DW      REV (XINPUT-1)
AA06                  FDB     XCOLOR-1
AA06  +BA28           DW      REV (XCOLOR-1)
AA08                  FDB     XLIST-1
AA08  +B482           DW      REV (XLIST-1)
      = 0004    CLIST   EQU     (*-STETAB)/2-1
```

```
AAØA              FDB     XENTER-1
AAØA +BACA        DW      REV (XENTER-1)
AAØC              FDB     XLET-1
AAØC +AADF        DW      REV (XLET-1)
AAØE              FDB     XIF-1
AAØE +B777        DW      REV (XIF-1)
AA1Ø              FDB     XFOR-1
AA1Ø +B64A        DW      REV (XFOR-1)
     = ØØØ8   CFOR     EQU     (*-STETAB)/2-1
AA12              FDB     XNEXT-1
AA12 +B6CE        DW      REV (XNEXT-1)
AA14              FDB     XGOTO-1
AA14 +B6A2        DW      REV (XGOTO-1)
AA16              FDB     XGOTO-1
AA16 +B6A2        DW      REV (XGOTO-1)
AA18              FDB     XGOSUB-1
AA18 +B69F        DW      REV (XGOSUB-1)
     = ØØØC   CGOSUB   EQU     (*-STETAB)/2-1
AA1A              FDB     XTRAP-1
AA1A +B7EØ        DW      REV (XTRAP-1)
AA1C              FDB     XBYE-1
AA1C +A9E7        DW      REV (XBYE-1)
AA1E              FDB     XCONT-1
AA1E +B7BD        DW      REV (XCONT-1)
AA2Ø              FDB     XCOM-1
AA2Ø +B1D8        DW      REV (XCOM-1)
AA22              FDB     XCLOSE-1
AA22 +BC1A        DW      REV (XCLOSE-1)
AA24              FDB     XCLR-1
AA24 +B765        DW      REV (XCLR-1)
AA26              FDB     XDEG-1
AA26 +B26Ø        DW      REV (XDEG-1)
AA28              FDB     XDIM-1
AA28 +B1D8        DW      REV (XDIM-1)
AA2A              FDB     XEND-1
AA2A +B78C        DW      REV (XEND-1)
AA2C              FDB     XNEW-1
AA2C +AØØB        DW      REV (XNEW-1)
AA2E              FDB     XOPEN-1
AA2E +BBEA        DW      REV (XOPEN-1)
AA3Ø              FDB     XLOAD-1
AA3Ø +BAFA        DW      REV (XLOAD-1)
AA32              FDB     XSAVE-1
AA32 +BB5C        DW      REV (XSAVE-1)
AA34              FDB     XSTATUS-1
AA34 +BC27        DW      REV (XSTATUS-1)
AA36              FDB     XNOTE-1
AA36 +BC35        DW      REV (XNOTE-1)
AA38              FDB     XPOINT-1
AA38 +BC4C        DW      REV (XPOINT-1)
AA3A              FDB     XXIO-1
AA3A +BBE4        DW      REV (XXIO-1)
AA3C              FDB     XON-1
AA3C +B7EC        DW      REV (XON-1)
     = ØØ1E   CON      EQU     (*-STETAB)/2-1
AA3E              FDB     XPOKE-1
AA3E +B24B        DW      REV (XPOKE-1)
AA4Ø              FDB     XPRINT-1
AA4Ø +B3B5        DW      REV (XPRINT-1)
AA42              FDB     XRAD-1
AA42 +B265        DW      REV (XRAD-1)
AA44              FDB     XREAD-1
AA44 +B282        DW      REV (XREAD-1)
     = ØØ22   CREAD    EQU     (*-STETAB)/2-1
AA46              FDB     XREST-1
AA46 +B26A        DW      REV (XREST-1)
AA48              FDB     XRTN-1
AA48 +B718        DW      REV (XRTN-1)
AA4A              FDB     XRUN-1
AA4A +B74C        DW      REV (XRUN-1)
AA4C              FDB     XSTOP-1
```

```
AA4C +B792          DW       REV (XSTOP-1)
AA4E                FDB      XPOP-1
AA4E +B840          DW       REV (XPOP-1)
AA50                FDB      XPRINT-1
AA50 +B3B5          DW       REV (XPRINT-1)
AA52                FDB      XGET-1
AA52 +BC7E          DW       REV (XGET-1)
AA54                FDB      XPUT-1
AA54 +BC71          DW       REV (XPUT-1)
AA56                FDB      XGR-1
AA56 +BA4F          DW       REV (XGR-1)
AA58                FDB      XPLOT-1
AA58 +BA75          DW       REV (XPLOT-1)
AA5A                FDB      XPOS-1
AA5A +BA15          DW       REV (XPOS-1)
AA5C                FDB      XDOS-1
AA5C +A9ED          DW       REV (XDOS-1)
AA5E                FDB      XDRAWTO-1
AA5E +BA30          DW       REV (XDRAWTO-1)
AA60                FDB      XSETCOLOR-1
AA60 +B9B6          DW       REV (XSETCOLOR-1)
AA62                FDB      XLOCATE-1
AA62 +BC94          DW       REV (XLOCATE-1)
AA64                FDB      XSOUND-1
AA64 +B9DC          DW       REV (XSOUND-1)
AA66                FDB      XLPRINT-1
AA66 +B463          DW       REV (XLPRINT-1)
AA68                FDB      XCSAVE-1
AA68 +BBA3          DW       REV (XCSAVE-1)
AA6A                FDB      XCLOAD-1
AA6A +BBAB          DW       REV (XCLOAD-1)
AA6C                FDB      XLET-1
AA6C +AADF          DW       REV (XLET-1)
     = 0036     CILET    EQU      (*-STETAB)/2-1
AA6E                FDB      XERR-1
AA6E +B91D          DW       REV (XERR-1)
     = 0037     CERR     EQU      (*-STETAB)/2-1
```

Operator Execution Table

```
                ;        OPETAB - OPERATOR EXECUTION TABLE
                ;        - CONTAINS OPERATOR EXECUTION ADR
                ;        - MUST BE IN SAME ORDER AS OPNTAB
AA70            OPETAB
AA70                FDB      XPLE-1
AA70 +ACB4          DW       REV (XPLE-1)
AA72                FDB      XPNE-1
AA72 +ACBD          DW       REV (XPNE-1)
AA74                FDB      XPGE-1
AA74 +ACD4          DW       REV (XPGE-1)
AA76                FDB      XPLT-1
AA76 +ACC4          DW       REV (XPLT-1)
AA78                FDB      XPGT-1
AA78 +ACCB          DW       REV (XPGT-1)
AA7A                FDB      XPEQ-1
AA7A +ACDB          DW       REV (XPEQ-1)
AA7C                FDB      XPPOWER-1
AA7C +B164          DW       REV (XPPOWER-1)
AA7E                FDB      XPMUL-1
AA7E +AC95          DW       REV (XPMUL-1)
AA80                FDB      XPPLUS-1
AA80 +AC83          DW       REV (XPPLUS-1)
AA82                FDB XPMINUS-1
AA82 +AC8C          DW       REV (XPMINUS-1)
AA84                FDB      XPDIV-1
AA84 +AC9E          DW       REV (XPDIV-1)
AA86                FDB      XPNOT-1
AA86 +ACF8          DW       REV (XPNOT-1)
AA88                FDB      XPOR-1
AA88 +ACED          DW       REV (XPOR-1)
```

```
AA8A                FDB    XPAND-1
AA8A +ACE2          DW     REV (XPAND-1)
AA8C                FDB    XPLPRN-1
AA8C +AB1E          DW     REV (XPLPRN-1)
AA8E                FDB    XPRPRN-1
AA8E +AD7A          DW     REV (XPRPRN-1)
AA9Ø                FDB    XPAASN-1
AA9Ø +AD5E          DW     REV (XPAASN-1)
AA92                FDB    XSAASN-1
AA92 +AEA2          DW     REV (XSAASN-1)
AA94                FDB    XPSLE-1
AA94 +ACB4          DW     REV (XPSLE-1)
AA96                FDB    XPSNE-1
AA96 +ACBD          DW     REV (XPSNE-1)
AA98                FDB    XPSGE-1
AA98 +ACD4          DW     REV (XPSGE-1)
AA9A                FDB    XPSLT-1
AA9A +ACC4          DW     REV (XPSLT-1)
AA9C                FDB    XPSGT-1
AA9C +ACCB          DW     REV (XPSGT-1)
AA9E                FDB    XPEQ-1
AA9E +ACDB          DW     REV (XPEQ-1)
AAAØ                FDB    XPUPLUS-1
AAAØ +ACB3          DW     REV (XPUPLUS-1)
AAA2                FDB    XPUMINUS-1
AAA2 +ACA7          DW     REV (XPUMINUS-1)
AAA4                FDB    XPSLPRN-1
AAA4 +AE25          DW     REV (XPSLPRN-1)
AAA6                FDB    XPALPRN-1
AAA6 +AD85          DW     REV (XPALPRN-1)
AAA8                FDB    XPDLPRN-1
AAA8 +AD81          DW     REV (XPDLPRN-1)
AAAA                FDB    XPFLPRN-1
AAAA +AD7A          DW     REV (XPFLPRN-1)
AAAC                FDB    XDPSLP-1
AAAC +AD81          DW     REV (XDPSLP-1)
AAAE                FDB    XPACOM-1
AAAE +AD78          DW     REV (XPACOM-1)
               ;
AABØ                FDB    XPSTR-1
AABØ +BØ48          DW     REV (XPSTR-1)
AAB2                FDB    XPCHR-1
AAB2 +BØ66          DW     REV (XPCHR-1)
AAB4                FDB    XPUSR-1
AAB4 +BØB9          DW     REV (XPUSR-1)
AAB6                FDB    XPASC-1
AAB6 +BØ11          DW     REV (XPASC-1)
AAB8                FDB    XPVAL-1
AAB8 +AFFF          DW     REV (XPVAL-1)
AABA                FDB    XPLEN-1
AABA +AFC9          DW     REV (XPLEN-1)
AABC                FDB    XPADR-1
AABC +BØ1B          DW     REV (XPADR-1)
AABE                FDB    XPATN-1
AABE +B12E          DW     REV (XPATN-1)
AACØ                FDB    XPCOS-1
AACØ +B124          DW     REV (XPCOS-1)
AAC2                FDB    XPPEEK-1
AAC2 +AFEØ          DW     REV (XPPEEK-1)
AAC4                FDB    XPSIN-1
AAC4 +B11A          DW     REV (XPSIN-1)
AAC6                FDB    XPRND-1
AAC6 +BØ8A          DW     REV (XPRND-1)
AAC8                FDB    XPFRE-1
AAC8 +AFEA          DW     REV (XPFRE-1)
AACA                FDB    XPEXP-1
AACA +B14C          DW     REV (XPEXP-1)
AACC                FDB    XPLOG-1
AACC +B138          DW     REV (XPLOG-1)
AACE                FDB    XPL1Ø-1
AACE +B142          DW     REV (XPL1Ø-1)
```

```
AADØ                      FDB     XPSQR-1
AADØ +B156                DW      REV (XPSQR-1)
AAD2                      FDB     XPSGN-1
AAD2 +AD18                DW      REV (XPSGN-1)
AAD4                      FDB     XPABS-1
AAD4 +BØAD                DW      REV (XPABS-1)
AAD6                      FDB     XPINT-1
AAD6 +BØDC                DW      REV (XPINT-1)
AAD8                      FDB     XPPDL-1
AAD8 +BØ21                DW      REV (XPPDL-1)
AADA                      FDB     XPSTICK-1
AADA +BØ25                DW      REV (XPSTICK-1)
AADC                      FDB     XPPTRIG-1
AADC +BØ29                DW      REV (XPPTRIG-1)
AADE                      FDB     XPSTRIG-1
AADE +BØ2D                DW      REV (XPSTRIG-1)
```

Execute Expression

```
AAEØ                      LOCAL
```

EXEXPR — Execute Expression

```
AAEØ                XLET
AAEØ                EXEXPR
AAEØ   2Ø2EAB           JSR     EXPINT          ; GO INIT
                    ;
AAE3                :EXNXT
AAE3   2Ø3EAB           JSR     :EGTOKEN        ; GO GET TOKEN
AAE6   BØØ6 ^AAEE       BCS     :EXOT           ; BR IF OPERATOR
                    ;
AAE8   2ØBAAB           JSR     ARGPUSH         ; PUSH ARG
AAEB   4CE3AA           JMP     :EXNXT          ; GO FOR NEXT TOKEN
                    ;
AAEE   85AB         :EXOT   STA     EXSVOP      ; SAVE OPERATOR
AAFØ   AA               TAX
AAF1   BD2FAC           LDA     OPRTAB-16,X     ; GET OP PREC
AAF4                    LSRA                    ; SHIFT FOR GOES ON TO PREC
AAF4 +4A                LSR     A
AAF5                    LSRA
AAF5 +4A                LSR     A
AAF6                    LSRA
AAF6 +4A                LSR     A
AAF7                    LSRA
AAF7 +4A                LSR     A
AAF8   85AC             STA     EXSVPR          ; SAVE GOES ON PREC
                    ;
AAFA   A4A9         :EXPTST LDY     OPSTKX      ; GET OP STACK INDEX
AAFC   B18Ø             LDA     [ARGSTK],Y      ; GET TOP OP
AAFE   AA               TAX
AAFF   BD2FAC           LDA     OPRTAB-16,X     ; GET TOP OP PREC
ABØ2   29ØF             AND     #$ØF
ABØ4   C5AC             CMP     EXSVPR          ; [TOP OP]: [NEW OP]
ABØ6   9ØØD ^AB15       BCC     :EOPUSH         ; IF T<N, PUSH NEW
                    ;                           ;     ELSE POP
ABØ8   AA               TAX                     ; IF POP SOE
ABØ9   FØ14 ^AB1F       BEQ     :EXEND          ; THEN DONE
                    ;
ABØB                EXOPOP
ABØB   B18Ø             LDA     [ARGSTK],Y      ; RE-GET TOS OP
ABØD   E6A9             INC     OPSTKX          ; DEC OP STACK INDEX
ABØF   2Ø2ØAB           JSR     :EXOP           ; GET EXECUTE OP
AB12   4CFAAA           JMP     :EXPTST         ; GO TEST OP WITH NEW TOS
                    ;
AB15   A5AB         :EOPUSH LDA     EXSVOP      ; GET OP TO PUSH
AB17   88               DEY                     ; DEC TO NEXT ENTRY
AB18   918Ø             STA     [ARGSTK],Y      ; SET OP IN STACK
AB1A   84A9             STY     OPSTKX          ; SAVE NEW OP STACK INDEX
AB1C   4CE3AA           JMP     :EXNXT          ; GO GET NEXT TOKEN
                    ;
AB1F                XPLPRN
```

```
AB1F  60          :EXEND   RTS                  ; DONE EXECUTE EXPR
                  ;
AB20              :EXOP
AB20  38              SEC                       ; SUBSTRACT FOR REL Ø
AB21  E91D            SBC      #CSROP           ; VALUE OF FIRST REAL OP
AB23                  ASLA                      ; VALUE * 2
AB23 +ØA              ASL      A
AB24  AA              TAX
AB25  BD7ØAA          LDA      OPETAB,X         ; PUT OP EXECUTION
AB28  48              PHA                       ; ROUTINE ON STACK
AB29  BD71AA          LDA      OPETAB+1,X       ; AND GOTO
AB2C  48              PHA                       ; VIA
AB2D  6Ø              RTS                       ; RTS
```

Initialize Expression Parameters

```
AB2E              EXPINT
AB2E  AØFF            LDY      #$FF
AB3Ø  A911            LDA      #CSOE            ; OPERATOR
AB32  918Ø            STA      [ARGSTK],Y       ; STACK
AB34  84A9            STY      OPSTKX
AB36  C8              INY                       ; AND INITIALIZE
AB37  84BØ            STY      COMCNT
AB39  84AA            STY      ARSTKX           ; ARG STACK
AB3B  84B1            STY      ADFLAG           ; ASSIGN FLAG
AB3D  6Ø              RTS
```

GETTOK — Get Next Token and Classify

```
AB3E              GETTOK
AB3E              :EGTOKEN
AB3E  A4A8            LDY      STINDEX          ; GET STMT INDEX
AB4Ø  E6A8            INC      STINDEX          ; INC TO NEXT
AB42  B18A            LDA      [STMCUR],Y       ; GET TOKEN
AB44  3Ø43 ^AB89      BMI      :EGTVAR          ; BR IF VAR
                  ;
AB46  C9ØF            CMP      #$ØF             ; TOKEN: $ØF
AB48  9ØØ3 ^AB4D      BCC      :EGNC            ; BR IF $ØE, NUMERIC CONST
AB4A  FØ13 ^AB5F      BEQ      :EGSC            ; BR IF $ØF, STR CONST
AB4C  6Ø              RTS                       ; RTN IF OPERATOR
                  ;
AB4D              NCTOFRØ
AB4D  A2ØØ        :EGNC    LDX      #Ø
AB4F  C8          :EGT1    INY                  ; INC LINE INDEX
AB5Ø  B18A            LDA      [STMCUR],Y       ; GET VALUE FROM STMT TBL
AB52  95D4            STA      FRØ,X            ; AND PUT INTO FRØ
AB54  E8              INX
AB55  EØØ6            CPX      #6
AB57  9ØF6 ^AB4F      BCC      :EGT1
AB59  C8              INY                       ; INY Y BEYOND CONST
AB5A  A9ØØ            LDA      #EVSCALER        ; ACU=SCALER
AB5C  AA              TAX                       ; X = VAL NO Ø
AB5D  FØ22 ^AB81      BEQ      :EGST            ; GO SET REM
                  ;
AB5F  C8          :EGSC    INY                  ; INC Y TO LENGTH BYTE
AB6Ø  B18A            LDA      [STMCUR],Y       ; GET LENGTH
AB62  A28A            LDX      #STMCUR          ; POINT TO SMCUR
AB64              RISC
AB64  85D6            STA      VTYPE+EVSLEN     ; SET AS LENGTH
AB66  85D8            STA      VTYPE+EVSDIM     ; AND DIM
AB68  C8              INY
AB69  98              TYA                       ; ACU=DISPL TO STR
AB6A  18              CLC
AB6B  75ØØ            ADC      Ø,X              ; DISPL PLUS ADR
AB6D  85D4            STA      VTYPE+EVSADR     ; IS STR ADR
AB6F  A9ØØ            LDA      #Ø               ; SET = Ø
AB71  85D7            STA      VTYPE+EVSLEN+1   ; LENGTH HIGH
AB73  85D9            STA      VTYPE+EVSDIM+1   ; DIM HIGH
AB75  75Ø1            ADC      1,X              ; FINISH ADR
AB77  85D5            STA      VTYPE+EVSADR+1
                  ;
```

```
AB79  98              TYA                       ; ACU=DISPL TO STR
AB7A  65D6            ADC     VTYPE+EVSLEN      ; PLUS STR LENGTH
AB7C  A8              TAY                       ; IS NEW INDEX
AB7D  A200            LDX     #00               ; VAR NO = 0
AB7F  A983            LDA     #EVSTR+EVSDTA+EVDIM  ; TYPE = STR
                ;
AB81  85D2      :EGST   STA     VTYPE           ; SET TYPE
AB83  86D3            STX     VNUM              ; SET NUM
AB85  84A8            STY     STINDEX           ; SET NEW INDEX
AB87  18              CLC                       ; INDICATE VALUE
AB88  60        :EGRTS RTS                      ; RETURN
                ;
AB89            GETVAR
AB89            :EGTVAR
AB89  2028AC          JSR     GVVTADR           ; GET VVT ADR
AB8C  B19D      :EGT2   LDA     [WVVTPT],Y      ; MOVE VVT ENTRY
AB8E  99D200          STA     VTYPE,Y           ; TO FR0
AB91  C8              INY
AB92  C008            CPY     #8
AB94  90F6 ^AB8C      BCC     :EGT2
AB96  18              CLC                       ; INDICATE VALUE
AB97  60              RTS                       ; RETURN
```

AAPSTR — Pop String Argument and Make Address Absolute

```
AB98  20F2AB    AAPSTR  JSR     ARGPOP          ; GO POP ARG
```

GSTRAD — Get String [ABS] Address

```
AB9B            GSTRAD
AB9B  A902            LDA     #EVSDTA           ; LOAD TRANSFORMED BIT
AB9D  24D2            BIT     VTYPE             ; TEST STRING ADR TRANSFORM
AB9F  D015 ^ABB6      BNE     :GSARTS           ; BR IF ALREADY TRANSFORMED
ABA1  05D2            ORA     VTYPE             ; TURN ON TRANS BIT
ABA3  85D2            STA     VTYPE             ; AND SET
ABA5                  RORA                      ; SHIFT DIM BIT TO CARRY
ABA5 +6A              ROR     A
ABA6  900F ^ABB7      BCC     :GSND
                ;
ABA8  18              CLC
ABA9  A5D4            LDA     VTYPE+EVSADR      ; STRING ADR = STRING DISPL
                                                  + STARP
ABAB  658C            ADC     STARP
ABAD  85D4            STA     VTYPE+EVSADR
ABAF  A8              TAY
ABB0  A5D5            LDA     VTYPE+EVSADR+1
ABB2  658D            ADC     STARP+1
ABB4  85D5            STA     VTYPE+EVSADR+1
ABB6  60        :GSARTS RTS
ABB7  202EB9    :GSND   JSR     ERRDIM
```

ARGPUSH — Push FR0 to Argument Stack

```
ABBA            ARGPUSH
ABBA  E6AA            INC     ARSLVL            ; INC ARG STK LEVEL
ABBC  A5AA            LDA     ARSLVL            ; ACU = ARG STACK LEVEL
ABBE                  ASLA                      ; TIMES 8
ABBE +0A              ASL     A
ABBF                  ASLA
ABBF +0A              ASL     A
ABC0                  ASLA
ABC0 +0A              ASL     A
ABC1  C5A9            CMP     OPSTKX            ; TEST EXCEED MAX
ABC3  B00D ^ABD2      BCS     :APERR            ; BR IF GT MAX
ABC5  A8              TAY                       ; Y = NEXT ENTRY ADR
ABC6  88              DEY                       ; MINUS ONE
ABC7  A207            LDX     #7                ; X = 7 FOR 8
                ;
ABC9  B5D2      :APH1   LDA     VTYPE,X         ; MOVE FR0
ABCB  9180            STA     [ARGOPS],Y        ; TO ARGOPS
```

```
ABCD  88               DEY                        ; BACKWARDS
ABCE  CA               DEX
ABCF  10F8 ^ABC9       BPL      :APH1
ABD1  60               RTS                        ; DONE
                  ;
ABD2  4C2CB9      :APERR  JMP      ERRAOS         ; STACK OVERFLOW
```

GETPINT — Get Positive Integer from Expression

```
ABD5              GETPINT
ABD5  20E0AB           JSR      GETINT            ; GO GET INT
ABD8              GETPI0
ABD8  A5D5             LDA      FR0+1             ; GET HIGH BYTE
ABDA  3001 ^ABDD       BMI      :GPIERR           ; BR > 32767
ABDC  60               RTS                        ; DONE
ABDD  4C32B9      :GPIERR JMP      ERRLN
```

GETINT — Get Integer from Expression

```
ABE0  20E0AA      GETINT  JSR      EXEXPR         ; EVAL EXPR
ABE3              GTINTO
ABE3  20F2AB           JSR      ARGPOP            ; POP VALUE TO FR0
ABE6  4C56AD           JMP      CVFPI             ; GO CONVERT FR0 TO INT &
                                                    RETURN
```

GET1INT — Get One-Byte Integer from Expression

```
ABE9              GET1INT
ABE9  20D5AB           JSR      GETPINT           ; GET INT <32768
ABEC  D001 ^ABEF       BNE      :ERV1             ; IF NOT 1 BYTE, THEN ERROR
ABEE  60               RTS
ABEF              :ERV1
ABEF  203AB9           JSR      ERVAL
```

ARGPOP — Pop Argument Stack Entry to FR0 or FR1

```
ABF2              ARGPOP
ABF2  A5AA             LDA      ARSLVL            ; GET ARG STACK LEVEL
ABF4  C6AA             DEC      ARSLVL            ; DEC AS LEVEL
ABF6                   ASLA                       ; AS LEVEL * 8
ABF6 +0A               ASL      A
ABF7                   ASLA
ABF7 +0A               ASL      A
ABF8                   ASLA
ABF8 +0A               ASL      A
ABF9  A8               TAY                        ; Y = START OF NEXT ENTRY
ABFA  88               DEY                        ; MINUS ONE
ABFB  A207             LDX      #7                ; X = 7 FOR 8
                  ;
ABFD  B180        :APOP0  LDA      [ARGOPS],Y       ; MOVE ARG ENTRY
ABFF  95D2             STA      VTYPE,X
AC01  88               DEY                        ; BACKWARDS
AC02  CA               DEX
AC03  10F8 ^ABFD       BPL      :APOP0
AC05  60               RTS                        ; DONE
```

ARGP2 — Pop TOS to FR1,TOS-1 to FR0

```
AC06  20F2AB      ARGP2   JSR      ARGPOP         ; POP TOS TO FR0
AC09  20B6DD           JSR      MV0TO1            ; MOVE FR0 TO FR1
AC0C  4CF2AB           JMP      ARGPOP            ; POP TOS TO FR0 AND RETURN
```

POP1 — Get a Value in FR0

```
                  ;             - EVALUATE EXPRESSION IN STMT LINE &
                  ;               POP IT INTO FR0
                  ;
AC0F              POP1
AC0F  20E0AA           JSR      EXEXPR            ; EVALUATE EXPRESSION
AC12  20F2AB           JSR      ARGPOP            ; PUSH INTO FR0
AC15  60               RTS
```

RTNVAR — Return Variable to Variable Value Table from FR0

```
AC16                   RTNVAR
AC16   A5D3               LDA     VNUM              ; GET VAR NUMBER
AC18   2028AC             JSR     GVVTADR
AC1B   A200               LDX     #0
                       ;
AC1D   B5D2            :RV1     LDA      VTYPE,X    ; MOVE FR0 TO
AC1F   919D               STA     [WVVTPT],Y        ; VAR VALUE TABLE
AC21   C8                 INY
AC22   E8                 INX
AC23   E008               CPX     #8
AC25   90F6 ^AC1D         BCC     :RV1
AC27   60                 RTS                       ; DONE
```

GVVTADR — Get Value's Value Table Entry Address

```
AC28                   GVVTADR
AC28   A000               LDY     #0                ; CLEAR ADR HI
AC2A   849E               STY     WVVTPT+1
AC2C                      ASLA                      ; MULT VAR NO
AC2C +0A                  ASL     A
AC2D                      ASLA                      ; BY 8
AC2D +0A                  ASL     A
AC2E   269E               ROL     WVVTPT+1
AC30                      ASLA
AC30 +0A                  ASL     A
AC31   269E               ROL     WVVTPT+1
AC33   18                 CLC                       ; THEN
AC34   6586               ADC     VVTP              ; ADD VVTP VALUE
AC36   859D               STA     WVVTPT            ; TO FORM ENTRY
AC38   A587               LDA     VVTP+1            ; ADR
AC3A   659E               ADC     WVVTPT+1
AC3C   859E               STA     WVVTPT+1
AC3E   60                 RTS
```

Operator Precedence Table

```
                       ;                 - ENTRIES MUST BE IN SAME ORDER AS OPNTAB
                       ;                 - LEFT NIBBLE IS TO GO ON STACK PREC
                       ;                 - RIGHT NIBBLE IS COME OFF STACK PREC
                       ;
AC3F                   OPRTAB
AC3F   00                 DB      $00               ; CDQ
AC40   00                 DB      $00               ; CSOE
AC41   00                 DB      $00               ; CCOM
AC42   00                 DB      $00               ; CDOL
AC43   00                 DB      $00               ; CEOS
AC44   00                 DB      $00               ; CSC
AC45   00                 DB      $00               ; CCR
AC46   00                 DB      $00               ; CGTO
AC47   00                 DB      $00               ; CGS
AC48   00                 DB      $00               ; CTO
AC49   00                 DB      $00               ; CSTEP
AC4A   00                 DB      $00               ; CTHEN
AC4B   00                 DB      $00               ; CPND
AC4C   88                 DB      $88               ; CLE
AC4D   88                 DB      $88               ; CNE
AC4E   88                 DB      $88               ; CGE
AC4F   88                 DB      $88               ; CGT
AC50   88                 DB      $88               ; CLT
AC51   88                 DB      $88               ; CEQ
AC52   CC                 DB      $CC               ; CEXP
AC53   AA                 DB      $AA               ; CMUL
AC54   99                 DB      $99               ; CPLUS
AC55   99                 DB      $99               ; CMINUS
AC56   AA                 DB      $AA               ; CDIV
AC57   77                 DB      $77               ; CNOT
AC58   55                 DB      $55               ; COR
AC59   66                 DB      $66               ; CAND
AC5A   F2                 DB      $F2               ; CLPRN
```

```
AC5B  4E          DB      $4E        ; CRPRN
AC5C  F1          DB      $F1        ; CAASN
AC5D  F1          DB      $F1        ; CSASN
AC5E  EE          DB      $EE        ; CSLE
AC5F  EE          DB      $EE        ; CSNE
AC60  EE          DB      $EE        ; CSGE
AC61  EE          DB      $EE        ; CSLT
AC62  EE          DB      $EE        ; CSGT
AC63  EE          DB      $EE        ; CSEQ
AC64  DD          DB      $DD        ; CUPLUS
AC65  DD          DB      $DD        ; CUMINUS
AC66  F2          DB      $F2        ; CSLPRN
AC67  F2          DB      $F2        ; CALPRN
AC68  F2          DB      $F2        ; CDLPRN
AC69  F2          DB      $F2        ; CFLPRN
AC6A  F2          DB      $F2        ; CDSLPR
AC6B  43          DB      $43        ; CACOM
            ;
AC6C  F2          DB      $F2        ; FUNCTIONS
AC6D  F2          DB      $F2
AC6E  F2          DB      $F2
AC6F  F2          DB      $F2
AC70  F2          DB      $F2
AC71  F2          DB      $F2
AC72  F2          DB      $F2
AC73  F2          DB      $F2
AC74  F2          DB      $F2
AC75  F2          DB      $F2
AC76  F2          DB      $F2
AC77  F2          DB      $F2
AC78  F2          DB      $F2
AC79  F2          DB      $F2
AC7A  F2          DB      $F2
AC7B  F2          DB      $F2
AC7C  F2          DB      $F2
AC7D  F2          DB      $F2
AC7E  F2          DB      $F2
AC7F  F2          DB      $F2
AC80  F2          DB      $F2
AC81  F2          DB      $F2
AC82  F2          DB      $F2
AC83  F2          DB      $F2
```

Miscellaneous Operators

Miscellaneous Operators' Executors

```
AC84              XPPLUS
AC84  2006AC        JSR     ARGP2
AC87  203BAD        JSR     FRADD
AC8A  4CBAAB        JMP     ARGPUSH
AC8D              XPMINUS
AC8D  2006AC        JSR     ARGP2
AC90  2041AD        JSR     FRSUB
AC93  4CBAAB        JMP     ARGPUSH
AC96              XPMUL
AC96  2006AC        JSR     ARGP2
AC99  2047AD        JSR     FRMUL
AC9C  4CBAAB        JMP     ARGPUSH
AC9F              XPDIV
AC9F  2006AC        JSR     ARGP2
ACA2  204DAD        JSR     FRDIV
ACA5  4CBAAB        JMP     ARGPUSH
ACA8              XPUMINUS
ACA8  20F2AB        JSR     ARGPOP      ;GET ARGUMENT INTO FR0
ACAB  A5D4          LDA     FR0         ;GET BYTE WITH SIGN
ACAD  4980          EOR     #$80        ;FLIP SIGN BIT
ACAF  85D4          STA     FR0         ;RETURN BYTE WITH SIGN CHANGED
ACB1  4CBAAB        JMP     ARGPUSH     ;PUSH ON STACKS
ACB4              XPUPLUS
```

```
ACB4  60                    RTS
ACB5                  XPLE
ACB5                  XPSLE
ACB5  2026AD                JSR     XCMP
ACB8  304B ^AD05            BMI     XTRUE
ACBA  F049 ^AD05            BEQ     XTRUE
ACBC  1042 ^AD00            BPL     XFALSE
ACBE                  XPNE
ACBE                  XPSNE
ACBE  2026AD                JSR     XCMP
ACC1  F03D ^AD00            BEQ     XFALSE
ACC3  D040 ^AD05            BNE     XTRUE
ACC5                  XPLT
ACC5                  XPSLT
ACC5  2026AD                JSR     XCMP
ACC8  303B ^AD05            BMI     XTRUE
ACCA  1034 ^AD00            BPL     XFALSE
ACCC                  XPGT
ACCC                  XPSGT
ACCC  2026AD                JSR     XCMP
ACCF  302F ^AD00            BMI     XFALSE
ACD1  F02D ^AD00            BEQ     XFALSE
ACD3  1030 ^AD05            BPL     XTRUE
ACD5                  XPGE
ACD5                  XPSGE
ACD5  2026AD                JSR     XCMP
ACD8  3026 ^AD00            BMI     XFALSE
ACDA  1029 ^AD05            BPL     XTRUE
ACDC                  XPEQ
ACDC                  XPSEQ
ACDC  2026AD                JSR     XCMP
ACDF  F024 ^AD05            BEQ     XTRUE
ACE1  D01D ^AD00            BNE     XFALSE
                      ;
ACE3                  XPAND
ACE3  2006AC                JSR     ARGP2
ACE6  A5D4                  LDA     FR0
ACE8  25E0                  AND     FR1
ACEA  F014 ^AD00            BEQ     XFALSE
ACEC  D017 ^AD05            BNE     XTRUE
ACEE                  XPOR
ACEE  2006AC                JSR     ARGP2
ACF1  A5D4                  LDA     FR0
ACF3  05E0                  ORA     FR1
ACF5  F009 ^AD00            BEQ     XFALSE
ACF7  D00C ^AD05            BNE     XTRUE
ACF9                  XPNOT
ACF9  20F2AB                JSR     ARGPOP
ACFC  A5D4                  LDA     FR0
ACFE  F005 ^AD05            BEQ     XTRUE
                      ;         FALL THROUGH TO XFALSE
                      ;
                      ;
AD00                  XFALSE
AD00  A900                  LDA     #0
AD02  A8                    TAY
AD03  F004 ^AD09            BEQ     XTF
                      ;
AD05                  XTRUE
AD05  A940                  LDA     #$40
AD07                  XTI
AD07  A001                  LDY     #1
                      ;
AD09                  XTF
AD09  85D4                  STA     FR0
AD0B  84D5                  STY     FR0+1
AD0D  A2D6                  LDX     #FR0+2         ; POINT TO PART TO CLEAR
AD0F  A004                  LDY     #FPREC-2       ; GET # OF BYTES TO CLEAR
AD11  2048DA                JSR     ZXLY           ; CLEAR REST OF FR0
AD14  85D2                  STA     VTYPE
AD16                  XPUSH
AD16  4CBAAB                JMP     ARGPUSH
```

XPSGN — Sign Function

```
AD19                  XPSGN
AD19   20F2AB              JSR      ARGPOP
AD1C   A5D4                LDA      FRØ
AD1E   FØF6 ^AD16          BEQ      XPUSH
AD2Ø   1ØE3 ^ADØ5          BPL      XTRUE
AD22   A9CØ                LDA      #$CØ               ; GET MINUS EXPONENT
AD24   3ØE1 ^ADØ7          BMI      XTI
```

XCMP — Compare Executor

```
AD26                  XCMP
AD26   A4A9                LDY      OPSTKX             ; GET OPERATOR THAT
AD28   88                  DEY                         ; GOT US HERE
AD29   B18Ø                LDA      [ARGSTK],Y
AD2B   C92F                CMP      #CSLE              ; IF OP WAS ARITHMETIC
AD2D   9ØØ3 ^AD32          BCC      FRCMPP             ; THEN DO FP REG COMP
AD2F   4C81AF              JMP      STRCMP             ; ELSE DO STRING COMPARE
                      ;
AD32   2ØØ6AC         FRCMPP  JSR       ARGP2
```

FRCMP — Compare Two Floating Point Numbers

```
                      *        ON ENTRY   FRØ & FR1 CONTAIN FLOATING POINT #'S
                      *
                      *        ON EXIT    CC = + FRØ > FR1
                      *                   CC = - FRØ < FR1
                      *                   CC = Ø FREØ = FR1
                      *
                      *
AD35                  FRCMP
AD35   2Ø41AD              JSR      FRSUB              ; SUBTRACT FR1 FROM FRØ
                      ;
AD38   A5D4                LDA      FRØ                ; GET FRØ EXPONENT
AD3A   6Ø                  RTS                         ; RETURN WITH CC SET
```

FRADD — Floating Point Add

```
                      *        DOES NOT RETURN IF ERROR
                      *
AD3B                  FRADD
AD3B   2Ø66DA              JSR      FADD               ; ADD TWO #
AD3E   BØ13 ^AD53          BCS      :ERROV             ; BR IF ERROR
AD4Ø   6Ø                  RTS
```

FRSUB — Floating Point Subtract

```
                      *        DOES NOT RETURN IF ERROR
                      *
AD41                  FRSUB
AD41   2Ø6ØDA              JSR      FSUB               ; SUB TWO #
AD44   BØØD ^AD53          BCS      :ERROV             ; BR IF ERROR
AD46   6Ø                  RTS
```

FRMUL — Floating Point Multiply

```
                      *        DOES NOT RETURN IF ERROR
                      *
AD47                  FRMUL
AD47   2ØDBDA              JSR      FMUL               ; MULT TWO #
AD4A   BØØ7 ^AD53          BCS      :ERROV             ; BR IF ERROR
AD4C   6Ø                  RTS
```

FRDIV — Floating Point Divide

```
                      *        DOES NOT RETURN IF ERROR
                      *
AD4D                  FRDIV
AD4D   2Ø28DB              JSR      FDIV               ; DIVIDE TWO #
```

```
AD50  B001 ^AD53       BCS     :ERROV          ; BR IF ERROR
AD52  60               RTS
                 ;
                 ;
                 ;
AD53             :ERROV
AD53  202AB9           JSR     EROVFL
```

CVFPI — Convert Floating Point to Integer

```
                 *       DOES NOT RETURN IF ERROR
                 *
AD56             CVFPI
AD56  20D2D9           JSR     FPI             ; GO CONVERT TO INTEGER
AD59  B001 ^AD5C       BCS     :ERRVAL         ; IF ERROR, BR
AD5B  60               RTS                     ; ELSE RETURN
                 ;
                 ;
                 ;
AD5C             :ERRVAL
AD5C  203AB9           JSR     ERVAL           ; VALUE ERROR
```

XPAASN — Arithmetic Assignment Operator

```
AD5F             XPAASN
AD5F  A5A9             LDA     OPSTKX          ; GET OP STACK INDEX
AD61  C9FF             CMP     #$FF            ; AT STACK START
AD63  D00F ^AD74       BNE     :AAMAT          ; BR IF NOT, [MAT ASSIGN]
                 ;                                   DO SCALER ASSIGN
AD65  2006AC           JSR     ARGP2           ; GO POP TOP 2 ARGS
AD68  A205             LDX     #5              ; MOVE FR1 VALUE
AD6A  B5E0       :AASN1  LDA      FR1,X        ; TO FR0
AD6C  95D4             STA     FR0,X
AD6E  CA               DEX
AD6F  10F9 ^AD6A       BPL     :AASN1
AD71  4C16AC           JMP     RTNVAR          ; FR0 TO VVT & RETURN
                 ;
AD74             :AAMAT
AD74  A980             LDA     #$80            ; SET ASSIGN FLAG BIT ON
AD76  85B1             STA     ADFLAG          ; IN ASSIGN/DIM FLAG
AD78  60               RTS                     ; GO POP REM OFF OPS
```

XPACOM — Array Comma Operator

```
AD79             XPACOM
AD79  E6B0             INC     COMCNT          ; INCREMENT COMMA COUNT
```

XPRPRN — Right Parenthesis Operator

```
                 ;       XPFLPRN - FUNCTION RIGHT PAREN OPERATOR
                 ;
AD7B             XPRPRN
AD7B             XPFLPRN
AD7B  A4A9             LDY     OPSTKX          ; GET OPERATOR STACK TOP
AD7D  68               PLA
AD7E  68               PLA
AD7F  4C0BAB           JMP     EXOPOP          ; GO POP AND EXECUTE NEXT
                                                 OPERATOR
                 ;
```

XPDLPRN — DIM Left Parenthesis Operator

```
AD82             XDPSLP
AD82             XPDLPRN
AD82  A940             LDA     #$40            ; SET DIM FLAG BIT
AD84  85B1             STA     ADFLAG          ; IN ADFLAG
                                                     FALL THRU TO XPALPRN
```

XPALPRN — Array Left Parenthesis Operator

```
AD86                XPALPRN
AD86  24B1              BIT     ADFLAG            ; IF NOT ASSIGN
AD88  1006 ^AD90        BPL     :ALP1             ; THE BRANCH
                    ;                                    ELSE
AD8A  A5AA              LDA     ARSLVL            ; SAVE STACK LEVEL
AD8C  85AF              STA     ATEMP             ;OF THE VALUE ASSIGNMENT
AD8E  C6AA              DEC     ARSLVL            ; AND PSEUDO POP IT
                    ;
AD90  A900          :ALP1   LDA     #0            ; INIT FOR I2 = 0
AD92  A8                TAY
AD93  C5B0              CMP     COMCNT            ; IF COMMA COUNT =0 THEN
AD95  F00B ^ADA2        BEQ     :ALP2             ; BR WITH I2 = 0
                    ;                                    ELSE
AD97  C6B0              DEC     COMCNT
AD99  20E3AB            JSR     GTINTO            ; ELSE POP I2 AND MAKE INT
AD9C  A5D5              LDA     FR0+1
AD9E  3023 ^ADC3        BMI     :ALPER            ; ERROR IF > 32,767
ADA0  A4D4              LDY     FR0
                    ;
ADA2  8598          :ALP2   STA     INDEX2+1      ;SET 12 VALUE
ADA4  8497              STY     INDEX2
                    ;
ADA6  20E3AB            JSR     GTINTO            ; POP I2 AND MAKE INT
ADA9  A5D4              LDA     FR0               ; MOVE I1
ADAB  85F5              STA     ZTEMP1            ; TO ZTEMP1
ADAD  A5D5              LDA     FR0+1
ADAF  3012 ^ADC3        BMI     :ALPER            ; ERROR IF > 32,767
ADB1  85F6              STA     ZTEMP1+1
                    ;
ADB3  20F2AB            JSR     ARGPOP            ; POP THE ARRAY ENTRY
                    ;
ADB6  24B1              BIT     ADFLAG            ; IF NOT EXECUTING DIM
ADB8  5005 ^ADBF        BVC     :ALP3             ; THEN CONTINUE
ADBA  A900              LDA     #0                ; TURN OFF DIM BIT
ADBC  85B1              STA     ADFLAG            ; IN ADFLAG
ADBE  60                RTS                       ; AND RETURN
                    ;
ADBF                :ALP3
ADBF  66D2              ROR     VTYPE             ; IF ARRAY HAS BEEN
ADC1  B003 ^ADC6        BCS     :ALP4             ; DIMED THEN CONTINUE
ADC3  202EB9        :ALPER  JSR     ERRDIM        ; ELSE DIM ERROR
                    ;
ADC6                :ALP4
ADC6  A5F6              LDA     ZTEMP1+1          ; TEST INDEX 1
ADC8  C5D7              CMP     VTYPE+EVAD1+1     ; IN RANGE WITH
ADCA  9008 ^ADD4        BCC     :ALP5             ; DIM1
ADCC  D0F5 ^ADC3        BNE     :ALPER
ADCE  A5F5              LDA     ZTEMP1
ADD0  C5D6              CMP     VTYPE+EVAD1
ADD2  B0EF ^ADC3        BCS     :ALPER
                    ;
ADD4  A598          :ALP5   LDA     INDEX2+1      ;TEST INDEX 2
ADD6  C5D9              CMP     VTYPE+EVAD2+1     ; IN RANGE WITH
ADD8  9008 ^ADE2        BCC     :ALP6             ; DIM 2
ADDA  D0E7 ^ADC3        BNE     :ALPERR
ADDC  A597              LDA     INDEX2
ADDE  C5D8              CMP     VTYPE+EVAD2
ADE0  B0E1 ^ADC3        BCS     :ALPER
                    ;
ADE2  205DAF        :ALP6   JSR     AMUL1         ;INDEX1 = INDEX1
ADE5  A597              LDA     INDEX2            ;INDEX1 = INDEX1 + INDEX2
ADE7  A498              LDY     INDEX2+1
ADE9  2052AF            JSR     AADD
ADEC  2046AF            JSR     AMUL2             ; ZTEMP1 = ZTEMP1*6
ADEF  A5D4              LDA     VTYPE+EVAADR      ; ZTEMP1 = ZTEMP1 + DISPL
ADF1  A4D5              LDY     VTYPE+EVAADR+1
ADF3  2052AF            JSR     AADD
ADF6  A58C              LDA     STARP             ; ZTEMP1 = ZTEMP1 + ADR
```

```
ADF8  A48D              LDY     STARP+1
ADFA  2052AF            JSR     AADD
                  ;                                ZTEMP1 NOW POINTS
                  ;                                TO ELEMENT REQD
ADFD  24B1              BIT     ADFLAG           ; IF NOT ASSIGN
ADFF  1015 ^AE16        BPL     :ALP8            ; THEN CONTINUE
                  ;                                ELSE ASSIGN
AE01  A5AF              LDA     ATEMP            ;RESTORE ARG LEVEL
AE03  85AA              STA     ARSLVL           ; TO VALUE AND
AE05  20F2AB            JSR     ARGPOP           ; POP VALUE
                  ;
AE08  A005              LDY     #5
AE0A  B9D400      :ALP7 LDA       FR0,Y          ; MOVE VALUE
AE0D  91F5              STA     [ZTEMP1],Y       ; TO ELEMENT SPACE
AE0F  88                DEY
AE10  10F8 ^AE0A        BPL     :ALP7
AE12  C8                INY                      ; TURN OFF
AE13  84B1              STY     ADFLAG           ; ADFLAG
AE15  60                RTS                      ; DONE
                  ;
AE16  A005        :ALP8 LDY       #5
AE18  B1F5        :ALP9 LDA       [ZTEMP1],Y       ; MOVE ELEMENT TO
AE1A  99D400            STA     FR0,Y            ; FR0
AE1D  88                DEY
AE1E  10F8 ^AE18        BPL     :ALP9
                  ;
AE20  C8                INY
AE21  84D2              STY     VTYPE
AE23  4CBAAB            JMP     ARGPUSH          ; PUSH FR0 BACK TO STACK
                  ;                                AND RETURN
```

XPSLPRN — String Left Parenthesis

```
AE26              XPSLPRN
AE26  A5B0              LDA     COMCNT           ; IF NO INDEX 2
AE28  F007 ^AE31        BEQ     :XSLP2           ; THEN BR
                  ;
AE2A  2096AE            JSR     :XSPV            ; ELSE POP I2 AND
AE2D  8498              STY     INDEX2+1         ;SAVE IN INDEX 2
AE2F  8597              STA     INDEX2
                  ;
AE31  2096AE      :XSLP2 JSR      :XSPV          ; POP INDEX 1
AE34  38                SEC                      ; ADD DECREMENT BY ONE
AE35  E901              SBC     #1               ; AND PUT INTO ZTEMP1
AE37  85F5              STA     ZTEMP1
AE39  98                TYA
AE3A  E900              SBC     #0
AE3C  85F6              STA     ZTEMP1+1
                  ;
AE3E  20F2AB            JSR     ARGPOP           ; POP ARG STRING
                  ;
AE41  A5B1              LDA     ADFLAG           ; IF NOT A DEST STRING
AE43  100B ^AE50        BPL     :XSLP3           ; THEN BRANCH
AE45  05B0              ORA     COMCNT
AE47  85B1              STA     ADFLAG
AE49  A4D9              LDY     VTYPE+EVSDIM+1   ; INDEX 2 LIMIT
AE4B  A5D8              LDA     VTYPE+EVSDIM     ; IS DIM
AE4D  4C54AE            JMP     :XSLP4
                  ;
AE50  A5D6        :XSLP3 LDA      VTYPE+EVSLEN     ; INDEX 2 LIMIT
AE52  A4D7              LDY     VTYPE+EVSLEN+1   ; IS STRING LENGTH
                  ;
AE54  A6B0        :XSLP4 LDX      COMCNT         ; IF NO INDEX 2
AE56  F010 ^AE68        BEQ     :XSLP6           ; THEN BRANCH
AE58  C6B0              DEC     COMCNT           ; ELSE
AE5A  C498              CPY     INDEX2+1
AE5C  9035 ^AE93        BCC     :XSLER
AE5E  D004 ^AE64        BNE     :XSLP5           ; INDEX 2 LIMIT
AE60  C597              CMP     INDEX2
AE62  902F ^AE93        BCC     :XSLER
                  ;
```

```
AE64  A498          :XSLP5  LDY     INDEX2+1       ;USE INDEX 2
AE66  A597                  LDA     INDEX2         ;AS LIMIT
                    ;
AE68  38            :XSLP6  SEC                    ; LENGTH IS
AE69  E5F5                  SBC     ZTEMP1
AE6B  85D6                  STA     VTYPE+EVSLEN   ; LIMIT - INDEX 1
AE6D  AA                    TAX
AE6E  98                    TYA
AE6F  E5F6                  SBC     ZTEMP1+1
AE71  85D7                  STA     VTYPE+EVSLEN+1
AE73  901E ^AE93            BCC     :XSLER         ; LENGTH MUST BE
AE75  A8                    TAY                    ; GE ZERO
AE76  D003 ^AE7B            BNE     :XSLP7
AE78  8A                    TXA
AE79  F018 ^AE93            BEQ     :XSLER
                    ;
AE7B  209BAB        :XSLP7  JSR     GSTRAD         ; GET ABS ADR
                    ;
AE7E  18                    CLC
AE7F  A5D4                  LDA     VTYPE+EVSADR
AE81  65F5                  ADC     ZTEMP1         ; STRING ADR
AE83  85D4                  STA     VTYPE+EVSADR   ; STRING ADR + INDEX 1
AE85  A5D5                  LDA     VTYPE+EVSADR+1
AE87  65F6                  ADC     ZTEMP1+1
AE89  85D5                  STA     VTYPE+EVSADR+1
                    ;
AE8B  24B1                  BIT     ADFLAG         ; IF NOT ASSIGN
AE8D  1001 ^AE90            BPL     :XSLP8         ; THEN BR
AE8F  60                    RTS                    ; ELSE RETURN TO ASSIGN
                    ;
AE90  4CBAAB        :XSLP8  JMP     ARGPUSH        ; PUSH ARG AND RETURN
                    ;
AE93  2036B9        :XSLER  JSR     ERRSSL
```

XSPV — Pop Index Value as Integer and Insure Not Zero

```
AE96                :XSPV
AE96  20E3AB                JSR     GTINTO         ; GO GET THE INTEGER
AE99  A5D4                  LDA     FR0            ; GET VALUE LOW
AE9B  A4D5                  LDY     FR0+1          ; GET VALUE HI
AE9D  D003 ^AEA2    :XSPV1  BNE     :XSPVR         ; RTN IF VH NOT ZERO
AE9F  AA                    TAX                    ; TEST VL
AEA0  F0F1 ^AE93            BEQ     :XSLER         ; BR VL,VH = 0
AEA2  60            :XSPVR  RTS                    ; DONE
                    ;
```

XSAASN — String Assign Operator

```
AEA3                XSAASN
AEA3  2098AB                JSR     AAPSTR         ; POP STR WITH ABS ADR
AEA6                RISASN
AEA6  A5D4                  LDA     VTYPE+EVSADR   ; MVFA = ADR
AEA8  8599                  STA     MVFA
AEAA  A5D5                  LDA     VTYPE+EVSADR+1
AEAC  859A                  STA     MVFA+1
AEAE  A5D6                  LDA     VTYPE+EVSLEN
AEB0  85A2                  STA     MVLNG          ; MVLNG = LENGTH
AEB2  A4D7                  LDY     VTYPE+EVSLEN+1
AEB4  84A3                  STY     MVLNG+1
                    ;
AEB6  A4A9                  LDY     OPSTKX         ; IF AT TOP OF
AEB8  C0FF                  CPY     #$FF           ; OP STACK
AEBA  F00F ^AECB            BEQ     :XSA1          ; THEN BR
                    ;                                    ELSE
AEBC  A980                  LDA     #$80           ; SET ASSIGN BIT
AEBE  85B1                  STA     ADFLAG         ; IN ASSIGN/DIM FLAG
AEC0  200BAB                JSR     EXOPOP         ; AND PROCESS SUBSTRING
AEC3  A5D7                  LDA     VTYPE+EVSLEN+1 ; A,Y =
AEC5  A4D6                  LDY     VTYPE+EVSLEN   ; DEST LEN
AEC7  26B1                  ROL     ADFLAG         ; TURN OFF ASSIGN
AEC9  B007 ^AED2            BCS     :XSA2A         ; AND BR
```

```
                        ;
AECB  2098AB            :XSA1   JSR       AAPSTR          ; POP STR WITH ABS ADR
                        ;
AECE  A5D9              :XSA2   LDA       VTYPE+EVSDIM+1  ; A,Y = DEST LENGTH
AEDØ  A4D8                      LDY     VTYPE+EVSDIM
                        ;
AED2                    :XSA2A
AED2  C5A3                      CMP     MVLNG+1           ; IF DEST LENGTH
AED4  9006  ^AEDC               BCC     :XSA3             ; LESS THAN MOVE LENGTH
AED6  DØØ8  ^AEEØ               BNE     :XSA4
AED8  C4A2                      CPY     MVLNG             ; THEN
AEDA  BØØ4  ^AEEØ               BCS     :XSA4
AEDC  85A3              :XSA3   STA       MVLNG+1         ; SET MOVE LENGTH
AEDE  84A2                      STY     MVLNG             ; = DIST LENGTH
                        ;
AEEØ  18                :XSA4   CLC
AEE1  A5D4                      LDA     VTYPE+EVSADR      ; MOVE LENGTH PLUS
AEE3  65A2                      ADC     MVLNG             ; START ADR IS
AEE5  A8                        TAY                       ; END ADR
AEE6  A5D5                      LDA     VTYPE+EVSADR+1
AEE8  65A3                      ADC     MVLNG+1
AEEA  AA                        TAX
                        ;
AEEB  38                        SEC                       ; END ADR MINUS
AEEC  98                        TYA                       ; START OF STRING
AEED  E58C                      SBC     STARP             ; SPACE IS DISPL
AEEF  85F9                      STA     ZTEMP3            ; TO END OF STRING
AEF1  8A                        TXA                       ; WHICH WE SAVE
AEF2  E58D                      SBC     STARP+1           ; IN ZTEMP3
AEF4  85FA                      STA     ZTEMP3+1
                        ;
                        ;
AEF6  38                        SEC                       ; SET MOVE LENGTH LOW
AEF7  A9ØØ                      LDA     #Ø                ; = $1ØØ - MVL [L]
AEF9  E5A2                      SBC     MVLNG             ; BECAUSE OF THE WAY
AEFB  85A2                      STA     MVLNG             ; FMOVE WORKS
                        ;
AEFD  38                        SEC
AEFE  A599                      LDA     MVFA              ; ADJUST MVFA TO
AFØØ  E5A2                      SBC     MVLNG             ; CONFORM WITH MVL
AFØ2  8599                      STA     MVFA              ; CHANGE
AFØ4  A59A                      LDA     MVFA+1
AFØ6  E9ØØ                      SBC     #Ø
AFØ8  859A                      STA     MVFA+1
                        ;
AFØA  38                        SEC
AFØB  A5D4                      LDA     VTYPE+EVSADR      ; MOVE THE DEST
AFØD  E5A2                      SBC     MVLNG             ; STRING ADR TO
AFØF  859B                      STA     MVTA              ; MVTA AND
AF11  A5D5                      LDA     VTYPE+EVSADR+1    ; MAKE IT CONFORM
AF13  E9ØØ                      SBC     #Ø                ; WITH MVL
AF15  859C                      STA     MVTA+1
                        ;
AF17  2047A9                    JSR     FMOVER            ;GO DO THE VERY FAST MOVE
                        ;
                        ;
AF1A  A5D3                      LDA     VNUM              ; GO GET ORIGNAL DEST
AF1C  2089AB                    JSR     GETVAR            ; STRING
                        ;
AF1F  38                        SEC                       ; DISPL TO END OF
AF2Ø  A5F9                      LDA     ZTEMP3            ; MOVE MINUS DISPL
AF22  E5D4                      SBC     VTYPE+EVSADR      ; TO START OF STRING
AF24  A8                        TAY                       ; IS OUR RESULT LENGTH
AF25  A5FA                      LDA     ZTEMP3+1
AF27  E5D5                      SBC     VTYPE+EVSADR+1
AF29  AA                        TAX
                        ;
AF2A  A9Ø2                      LDA     #Ø2               ; IF THE DESTINATION
AF2C  25B1                      AND     ADFLAG            ; LENGTH WAS IMPLICT
AF2E  FØØF  ^AF3F               BEQ     :XSA5             ; SET NEW LENGTH
AF3Ø  A9ØØ                      LDA     #Ø                ; CLEAR
```

```
AF32   85B1                STA     ADFLAG           ; FLAG
                    ;                                        ELSE FOR EXPLICT LENGTH
AF34   E4D7                CPX     VTYPE+EVSLEN+1   ; IF NEW LENGTH
AF36   9006 ^AF3E          BCC     :XSA6            ; GREATER THAN
AF38   D005 ^AF3F          BNE     :XSA5            ; OLD LENGTH THEN
AF3A   C4D6                CPY     VTYPE+EVSLEN     ; SET NEW LENGTH
AF3C   B001 ^AF3F          BCS     :XSA5            ; ELSE DO NOTHING
AF3E   60           :XSA6  RTS
                    ;
AF3F   84D6         :XSA5    STY      VTYPE+EVSLEN
AF41   86D7                STX     VTYPE+EVSLEN+1
AF43   4C16AC              JMP     RTNVAR
```

AMUL2 — Integer Multiplication of ZTEMP1 by 6

```
AF46                AMUL2
AF46   06F5                ASL     ZTEMP1           ; ZTEMP1 = ZTEMP1*2
AF48   26F6                ROL     ZTEMP1+1
AF4A   A4F6                LDY     ZTEMP1+1         ; SAVE ZTEMP1*2 IN [A,Y]
AF4C   A5F5                LDA     ZTEMP1
AF4E   06F5                ASL     ZTEMP1           ; ZTEMP1 = ZTEMP1*4
AF50   26F6                ROL     ZTEMP1+1
```

AADD — Integer Addition of [A,Y] to ZTEMP1

```
AF52                AADD
AF52   18                  CLC
AF53   65F5         ADC    ADC      ZTEMP1          ; ADD LOW ORDER
AF55   85F5                STA     ZTEMP1
AF57   98                  TYA
AF58   65F6                ADC     ZTEMP1+1         ; ADD HIGH ORDER
AF5A   85F6                STA     ZTEMP1+1
AF5C   60                  RTS                      ; DONE
```

AMUL — Integer Multiplication of ZTEMP1 by DIM2

```
AF5D                AMUL1
AF5D   A900                LDA     #0               ; CLEAR PARTIAL PRODUCT
AF5F   85F7                STA     ZTEMP4
AF61   85F8                STA     ZTEMP4+1
AF63   A010                LDY     #$10             ; SET FOR 16 BITS
                    ;
AF65   A5F5         :AM1   LDA      ZTEMP1          ; GET MULTIPLICAN
AF67                       LSRA                     ; TEST MSB = ON
AF67 +4A                   LSR     A
AF68   900C ^AF76          BCC     :AM3             ; BR IF OFF
                    ;
AF6A   18                  CLC
AF6B   A2FE                LDX     #$FE             ; ADD MULTIPLIER
AF6D   B5F9         :AM2   LDA      ZTEMP4+2,X        ; TO PARTIAL PRODUCT
AF6F   75DA                ADC     VTYPE+EVAD2+2,X
AF71   95F9                STA     ZTEMP4+2,X
AF73   E8                  INX
AF74   D0F7 ^AF6D          BNE     :AM2
                    ;
AF76   A203         :AM3   LDX      #3              ; MULT PRODUCT BY 2
AF78   76F5         :AM4   ROR      ZTEMP1,X
AF7A   CA                  DEX
AF7B   10FB ^AF78          BPL     :AM4
                    ;
AF7D   88                  DEY                      ; TEST MORE BITS
AF7E   D0E5 ^AF65          BNE     :AM1             ; BR IF MORE
                    ;
AF80   60                  RTS                      ; DONE
```

STRCMP — String Compare

```
AF81                STRCMP
AF81   2098AB              JSR     AAPSTR           ; POP STRING WITH ABS ADR
AF84   20B6DD              JSR     MV0TO1           ; MOVE B TO FR1
AF87   2098AB              JSR     AAPSTR           ; POP STRING WITH ABS ADR
```

```
                    ;
AF8A  A2D6          :SC1     LDX      #FRØ-2+EVSLEN    ; GO DEC STR A LEN
AF8C  2ØBCAF                 JSR      ZPADEC
AF8F  Ø8                     PHP                       ; SAVE RTN CODE
AF9Ø  A2E2                   LDX      #FR1-2+EVSLEN    ; GO DEC STR B LEN
AF92  2ØBCAF                 JSR      ZPADEC
AF95  FØ13 ^AFAA             BEQ      :SC2             ; BR STR B LEN = Ø
AF97  28                     PLP                       ; GET STR A COND CODE
AF98  FØØD ^AFA7             BEQ      :SCLT            ; BR STR A LEN = Ø
                    ;
AF9A  AØØØ                   LDY      #Ø               ; COMPARE A BYTE
AF9C  B1D4                   LDA      [FRØ-2+EVSADR],Y ; OF STRING A
AF9E  D1EØ                   CMP      [FR1-2+EVSADR],Y ; TO STRING B
AFAØ  FØØC ^AFAE             BEQ      :SC3             ; BR IF SAME
AFA2  9ØØ3 ^AFA7             BCC      :SCLT            ; BR IF A<B
                    ;
AFA4  A9Ø1          :SCGT    LDA      #1               ; A>B
AFA6  6Ø                     RTS
                    ;
AFA7  A98Ø          :SCLT    LDA      #$8Ø             ; A<B
AFA9  6Ø                     RTS
                    ;
AFAA  28            :SC2     PLP                       ; IF STR A LEN NOT
AFAB  DØF7 ^AFA4             BNE      :SCGT            ; ZERO THEN A>B
AFAD  6Ø            :SCEQ    RTS                       ; ELSE A=B
AFAE  E6D4          :SC3     INC      FRØ-2+EVSADR     ; INC STR A ADR
AFBØ  DØØ2 ^AFB4             BNE      :SC4
AFB2  E6D5                   INC      FRØ-1+EVSADR
AFB4  E6EØ          :SC4     INC      FR1-2+EVSADR     ; INC STR B ADR
AFB6  DØD2 ^AF8A             BNE      :SC1
AFB8  E6E1                   INC      FR1-1+EVSADR
AFBA  DØCE ^AF8A             BNE      :SC1
```

ZPADEC — Decrement a Zero-Page Double Word

```
AFBC                ZPADEC
AFBC  B5ØØ                   LDA      Ø,X              ; GET LOW BYTE
AFBE  DØØ6 ^AFC6             BNE      :ZPAD1           ; BR NOT ZERO
AFCØ  B5Ø1                   LDA      1,X              ; GET HI BYTE
AFC2  FØØ5 ^AFC9             BEQ      :ZPADR           ; BR IF ZERO
AFC4  D6Ø1                   DEC      1,X              ; DEC HIGH BYTE
AFC6  D6ØØ          :ZPAD1   DEC      Ø,X              ; DEC LOW BYTE
AFC8  A8                     TAY                       ; SET NE COND CODE
AFC9  6Ø            :ZPADR   RTS                       ; RETURN
```

Functions

XPLEN — Length Function

```
AFCA                XPLEN
AFCA  2Ø98AB                 JSR      AAPSTR           ; POP STRING WITH ABS ADR
AFCD  A5D6                   LDA      VTYPE+EVSLEN     ; MOVE LENGTH
AFCF  A4D7                   LDY      VTYPE+EVSLEN+1
AFD1                XPIFP
AFD1  85D4                   STA      FRØ              ; TO TOP OF FRØ
AFD3  84D5                   STY      FRØ+1
AFD5  2ØAAD9        XPIFP1   JSR      CVIFP            ; AND CONVERT TO FP
AFD8                XPIFP2
                    ;
AFD8  A9ØØ                   LDA      #Ø               ; CLEAR
AFDA  85D2                   STA      VTYPE            ; TYPE AND
AFDC  85D3                   STA      VNUM             ; NUMBER
AFDE  4CBAAB                 JMP      ARGPUSH          ; PUSH TO STACK AND RETURN
```

XPPEEK — PEEK Function

```
AFE1                XPPEEK
AFE1  2ØE3AB                 JSR      GTINTO           ; GET INT ARG
AFE4  AØØØ                   LDY      #Ø
AFE6  B1D4                   LDA      [FRØ],Y          ; GET MEM BYTE
AFE8  4CD1AF                 JMP      XPIFP            ; GO PUSH AS FP
```

XPFRE — FRE Function

```
AFEB                XPFRE
AFEB   20F2AB          JSR      ARGPOP              ; POP DUMMY ARG
AFEE   38              SEC
AFEF   ADE502          LDA      HIMEM               ; NO FREE BYTES
AFF2   E590            SBC      MEMTOP              ; = HIMEM-MEMTOP
AFF4   85D4            STA      FR0
AFF6   ADE602          LDA      HIMEM+1
AFF9   E591            SBC      MEMTOP+1
AFFB   85D5            STA      FR0+1
AFFD   4CD5AF          JMP      XPIFP1              ; GO PUSH AS FP
```

XPVAL — VAL Function

```
B000                XPVAL
B000   2079BD          JSR      SETSEOL             ; PUT EOL AT STR END
                    ;
B003   A900            LDA      #0                  ; GET NUMERIC TERMINATOR
B005   85F2            STA      CIX                 ; SET INDEX INTO BUFFER = 0
B007   2000D8          JSR      CVAFP               ; CONVERT TO F.P.
```

Restore Character

```
B00A   2099BD          JSR      RSTSEOL             ; RESET END OF STR
                    ;
B00D   90C9 ^AFD8      BCC      XPIFP2
                    ;
                    ;
B00F                :VERR
B00F   201CB9          JSR      ERSVAL
```

XPASC — ASC Function

```
B012                XPASC
B012   2098AB          JSR      AAPSTR              ; GET STRING ELEMENT
```

Get 1>T Byte of String

```
B015   A000            LDY      #0                  ; GET INDEX TO 1ST BYTE
B017   B1D4            LDA      [FR0-2+EVSADR],Y    ; GET BYTE
                    ;
B019   4CD1AF          JMP      XPIFP
                    ;
                    ;
B01C                XPADR
B01C   2098AB          JSR      AAPSTR              ;GET STRING
B01F   4CD5AF          JMP      XPIFP1              ; FINISH
```

XPPDL — Function Paddle

```
B022                XPPDL
B022   A900            LDA      #0                  ; GET DISPL FROM BASE ADDR
B024   F00A ^B030      BEQ      :GRF
```

XPSTICK — Function Joystick

```
B026                XPSTICK
B026   A908            LDA      #8                  ; GET DISP FROM BASE ADDR
B028   D006 ^B030      BNE      :GRF
```

XPPTRIG — Function Paddle Trigger

```
B02A                XPPTRIG
B02A   A90C            LDA      #$0C                ; GET DISPL FROM BASE ADDR
B02C   D002 ^B030      BNE      :GRF
```

XPSTRIG — Function Joystick Trigger

```
B02E                XPSTRIG
B02E   A914            LDA      #$14                ; GET DISP FROM BASE ADDR
                    ;
```

```
B03Ø                    :GRF
B03Ø   48                  PHA
B031   2ØE3AB              JSR    GTINTO          ; GET INTEGER FROM STACK
B034   A5D5                LDA    FRØ+1           ; HIGH ORDER BYTE
B036   DØØE ^BØ46          BNE    :ERGRF          ; SHOULD BE =Ø
B038   A5D4                LDA    FRØ             ; GET #
                        ;
B03A   68                  PLA                    ; GET DISPL FROM BASE
B03B   18                  CLC
B03C   65D4                ADC    FRØ             ; ADD MORE DISPL
B03E   AA                  TAX
                        ;
B03F   BD7ØØ2              LDA    GRFBAS,X        ; GET VALUE
B042   AØØØ                LDY    #Ø
B044   FØ8B ^AFD1          BEQ    XPIFP           ; GO CONVERT & PUSH ON STACK
                        ;
                        ;;
                        ;
BØ46                    :ERGRF
BØ46   2Ø3AB9              JSR    ERVAL
```

XPSTR — STR Function

```
BØ49                    XPSTR
BØ49   2ØF2AB              JSR    ARGPOP          ; GET VALUE IN FRØ
                        ;
BØ4C   2ØE6D8              JSR    CVFASC          ; CONVERT TO ASCII
```

Build String Element

```
BØ4F   A5F3                LDA    INBUFF          ; SET ADDR
BØ51   85D4                STA    FRØ-2+EVSADR ;
BØ53   A5F4                LDA    INBUFF+1
BØ55   85D5                STA    FRØ-1+EVSADR
```

Get Length

```
BØ57   AØFF                LDY    #$FF            ; INIT FOR LENGTH COUNTER
BØ59                    :XSTR1
BØ59   C8                  INY                    ; BUMP COUNT
BØ5A   B1F3                LDA    [INBUFF],Y      ; GET CHAR
BØ5C   1ØFB ^BØ59          BPL    :XSTR1          ; IS MSB NOT ON, REPEAT
BØ5E   297F                AND    #$7F            ; TURN OFF MSB
BØ6Ø   91F3                STA    [INBUFF],Y      ; RETURNS CHAR TO BUFFER
BØ62   C8                  INY                    ; INC TO GET LENGTH
                        ;
BØ63   84D6                STY    FRØ-2+EVSLEN    ; SET LENGTH LOW
                        ;
BØ65   DØ17 ^BØ7E          BNE    :CHR            ; JOIN CHR FUNCTION
```

XPCHR — CHR Function

```
BØ67                    XPCHR
BØ67   2ØF2AB              JSR    ARGPOP          ; GET VALUE IN FRØ
                        ;
BØ6A   2Ø56AD              JSR    CVFPI           ; CONVERT TO INTEGER
BØ6D   A5D4                LDA    FRØ             ; GET INTEGER LOW
BØ6F   8DCØØ5              STA    LBUFF+$4Ø       ; SAVE
```

Build String Element

```
BØ72   A9Ø5                LDA    #(LBUFF+$4Ø)/256  ; SET ADDR
BØ74   85D5                STA    FRØ-1+EVSADR    ; X
BØ76   A9CØ                LDA    #(LBUFF+$4Ø)&255  ; X
BØ78   85D4                STA    FRØ-2+EVSADR    ; X
                        ;
BØ7A   A9Ø1                LDA    #1              ; SET LENGTH LOW
BØ7C   85D6                STA    FRØ-2+EVSLEN    ; X
BØ7E                    :CHR
BØ7E   A9ØØ                LDA    #Ø              ; SET LENGTH HIGH
BØ8Ø   85D7                STA    FRØ-1+EVSLEN    ; X
                        ;
```

```
BØ82  85D3              STA     VNUM                ; CLEAR VARIABLE #
BØ84  A983              LDA     #EVSTR+EVSDTA+EVDIM ; GET TYPE FLAGS
BØ86  85D2              STA     VTYPE               ; SET VARIABLE TYPE
                  ;
BØ88  4CBAAB            JMP     ARGPUSH             ; PUSH ON STACK
```

XPRND — RND Function

```
BØ8B              XPRND
BØ8B  A2A8              LDX     #RNDDIV&255         ; POINT TO 65535
BØ8D  AØBØ              LDY     #RNDDIV/256         ; X
BØ8F  2Ø98DD            JSR     FLD1R               ;MOVE IT TO FR1
                  ;
BØ92  2ØF2AB            JSR     ARGPOP              ; CLEAR DUMMY ARG
                  ;
BØ95  ACØAD2            LDY     RNDLOC              ; GET 2 BYTE RANDOM #
BØ98  84D4              STY     FRØ                 ; X
BØ9A  ACØAD2            LDY     RNDLOC              ; X
BØ9D  84D5              STY     FRØ+1               ; X
BØ9F  2ØAAD9            JSR     CVIFP               ; CONVERT TO INTEGER
BØA2  2Ø4DAD            JSR     FRDIV               ;DO DIVIDE
                  ;
BØA5  4CBAAB            JMP     ARGPUSH             ; PUT ON STACK
                  ;
                  ;
                  ;
BØA8  42Ø655360Ø  RNDDIV  DB      $42,$Ø6,$55,$36,Ø,Ø
      ØØ
```

XPABS — Absolute Value Function

```
BØAE              XPABS
BØAE  2ØF2AB            JSR     ARGPOP              ;GET ARGUMENT
BØB1  A5D4              LDA     FRØ                 ;GET BYTE WITH SIGN
BØB3  297F              AND     #$7F                ;AND OUT SIGN
BØB5  85D4              STA     FRØ                 ;SAVE
BØB7  4CBAAB            JMP     ARGPUSH             ;PUSH ON STACK
```

XPUSR — USR Function

```
BØBA              XPUSR
BØBA  2ØC3BØ            JSR     :USR                ;PUT RETURN ADDR IN CPU STACK
BØBD  2ØAAD9            JSR     CVIFP               ; CONVERT FRØ TO FP
BØCØ  4CBAAB            JMP     ARGPUSH             ; PUSH ON STACK
                  ;
                  ;
                  ;
BØC3              :USR
BØC3  A5BØ              LDA     COMCNT              ;GET COMMA COUNT
BØC5  85C6              STA     ZTEMP2              ;SET AS # OF ARG FOR LOOP
                                                     CONTROL
BØC7              :USR1
BØC7  2ØE3AB            JSR     GTINTO              ; GET AN INTEGER FROM OP STACK
BØCA  C6C6              DEC     ZTEMP2              ;DECR # OF ARGUMENTS
BØCC  3ØØ9 ^BØD7        BMI     :USR2               ;IF DONE THEM ALL, BRANCH
                  ;
BØCE  A5D4              LDA     FRØ                 ;GET ARGUMENT LOW
BØDØ  48                PHA                         ;PUSH ON STACK
BØD1  A5D5              LDA     FRØ+1               ;GET ARGUMENT HIGH
BØD3  48                PHA                         ;PUSH ON STACK
BØD4  4CC7BØ            JMP     :USR1               ;GET NEXT ARGUMENT
BØD7              :USR2
BØD7  A5BØ              LDA     COMCNT              ;GET # OF ARGUMENTS
BØD9  48                PHA                         ;PUSH ON CPU STACK
BØDA  6CD4ØØ            JMP     [FRØ]               ;GO TO USER ROUTINE
```

XPINT — Integer Function

```
BØDD              XPINT
BØDD  2ØF2AB            JSR     ARGPOP              ; GET NUMBER
BØEØ  2ØE6BØ            JSR     XINT                ; GET INTEGER
BØE3  4CBAAB            JMP     ARGPUSH             ; PUSH ON ARGUMENT STACK
```

XINT — Take Integer Part of FR0

```
BØE6                XINT
BØE6   A5D4             LDA     FRØ          ; GET EXPONENT
BØE8   297F             AND     #$7F         ; AND OUT SIGN BIT
BØEA   38               SEC
BØEB   E93F             SBC     #$3F         ; GET LOCATION OF 1ST FRACTION
                                               BYTE
BØED   1ØØ2 ^BØF1       BPL     :XINT1       ; IF > OR = Ø, THEN BRANCH
BØEF   A9ØØ             LDA     #Ø           ; ELSE SET =Ø
                    ;
BØF1                :XINT1
BØF1   AA               TAX                  ; PUT IN X AS INDEX INTO FRØ
BØF2   A9ØØ             LDA     #Ø           ; SET ACCUM TO ZERO FOR ORING
BØF4   A8               TAY                  ; ZERO Y
BØF5                :INT2
BØF5   EØØ5             CPX     #FMPREC      ; IS D.P. LOC > OF = 5?
BØF7   BØØ7 ^B1ØØ       BCS     :XINT3       ; IF YES, LOOP DONE
BØF9   15D5             ORA     FRØM,X       ; OR IN THE BYTE
BØFB   94D5             STY     FRØM,X       ; ZERO BYTE
BØFD   E8               INX                  ; POINT TO NEXT BYTE
BØFE   DØF5 ^BØF5       BNE     :INT2        ; UNCONDITIONAL BRANCH
                    ;
B1ØØ                :XINT3
B1ØØ   A6D4             LDX     FRØ          ; GET EXPONENT
B1Ø2   1Ø14 ^B118       BPL     :XINT4       ; BR IF # IS PLUS
B1Ø4   AA               TAX                  ; GET TOTAL OF ORED BYTES &
                                               SET CC
B1Ø5   FØ11 ^B118       BEQ     :XINT4       ; IF ALL BYTES WERE ZERO
                                               BRANCH
                    ;
                    ;          # IS NEGATIVE AND NOT A WHOLE # [ADD -1]
B1Ø7   A2EØ             LDX     #FR1
B1Ø9   2Ø46DA           JSR     ZF1          ; ZERO FR1
B1ØC   A9CØ             LDA     #$CØ         ; PUT -1 IN FR1
B1ØE   85EØ             STA     FR1          ; X
B11Ø   A9Ø1             LDA     #1           ; X
B112   85E1             STA     FR1+1        ; X
B114   2Ø3BAD           JSR     FRADD        ; ADD IT
B117   6Ø               RTS
B118                :XINT4
B118   4CØØDC           JMP     NORM         ; GO NORMALIZE
```

Transcendental Functions

XPSIN — Sine Function

```
B11B                XPSIN
B11B   2ØF2AB           JSR     ARGPOP       ;GET ARGUMENT
B11E   2ØA7BD           JSR     SIN
B121   BØ3F ^B162       BCS     :TBAD
B123   9Ø3A ^B15F       BCC     :TGOOD
```

XPCOS — Cosine Function

```
B125                XPCOS
B125   2ØF2AB           JSR     ARGPOP       ;GET ARGUMENT
B128   2ØB1BD           JSR     COS
B12B   BØ35 ^B162       BCS     :TBAD
B12D   9Ø3Ø ^B15F       BCC     :TGOOD
```

XPATN — Arc Tangent Function

```
B12F                XPATN
B12F   2ØF2AB           JSR     ARGPOP
B132   2Ø77BE           JSR     ATAN
B135   BØ2B ^B162       BCS     :TBAD
B137   9Ø26 ^B15F       BCC     :TGOOD
```

XPLOG — LOG Function

```
B139                XPLOG
B139  20F2AB             JSR      ARGPOP
B13C  20CDDE             JSR      LOG
B13F  B021  ^B162        BCS      :TBAD
B141  901C  ^B15F        BCC      :TGOOD
```

XPL10 — LOG Base 10

```
B143                XPL10
B143  20F2AB             JSR      ARGPOP
B146  20D1DE             JSR      LOG10
B149  B017  ^B162        BCS      :TBAD
B14B  9012  ^B15F        BCC      :TGOOD
```

XPEXP — EXP Function

```
B14D                XPEXP
B14D  20F2AB             JSR      ARGPOP
B150  20C0DD             JSR      EXP
B153  B00D  ^B162        BCS      :TBAD
B155  9008  ^B15F        BCC      :TGOOD
```

XPSQR — Square Root Function

```
B157                XPSQR
B157  20F2AB             JSR      ARGPOP
B15A  20E5BE             JSR      SQR
B15D  B003  ^B162        BCS      :TBAD
                    ;
                    ;         FALL THREE TO :TGOOD

B15F                :TGOOD
B15F  4CBAAB             JMP      ARGPUSH          ;PUSH ARGUMENT ON STACK
                    ;
                    ;
B162                :TBAD
B162  203AB9             JSR      ERVAL
```

XPPOWER — Exponential Operator [A**B]

```
B165                XPPOWER
B165  2006AC             JSR      ARGP2            ;GET ARGUMENT IN FR0,FR1
B168  A5D4               LDA      FR0              ;IS BASE = 0 ?
B16A  D00B  ^B177        BNE      :N0              ;IF BASE NOT 0, BRANCH
B16C  A5E0               LDA      FR1              ;TEST EXPONENT
B16E  F004  ^B174        BEQ      :P0              ;IF = 0 ; BRANCH
B170  10ED  ^B15F        BPL      :TGOOD           ;IF >0, ANSWER = 0
B172  30EE  ^B162        BMI      :TBAD            ;IF <0, VALUE ERROR
B174                :P0
B174  4C05AD             JMP      XTRUE            ;IF =0, ANSWER = 1
B177                :N0
                    ;
B177  1030  ^B1A9        BPL      :SPEVEN          ; IF BASE + THEN NO SPECIAL
                                                     PROCESS
B179  297F               AND      #$7F             ; AND OUT SIGN BIT
B17B  85D4               STA      FR0              ; SET AS BASE EXPONENT
                    ;
B17D  A5E0               LDA      FR1              ; GET EXPONENT OF POWER
B17F  297F               AND      #$7F             ; AND OUT SIGN BIT
B181  38                 SEC
B182  E940               SBC      #$40             ; IS POWER <1?
B184  30DC  ^B162        BMI      :TBAD            ; IF YES, ERROR
                    ;
B186  A206               LDX      #6               ; GET INDEX TO LAST DIGIT
                    ;
B188  C905               CMP      #5               ; IF # CAN HAVE DECIMAL
B18A  9004  ^B190        BCC      :SP4             ; PORTION, THEN BR
B18C  A001               LDY      #1
B18E  D008  ^B198        BNE      :SP3
B190                :SP4
                    ;
B190  85F5               STA      ZTEMP1           ; SAVE EXP -40
```

```
B192  38               SEC
B193  A9Ø5             LDA    #5             ;GET # BYTES POSSIBLE
B195  E5F5             SBC    ZTEMP1         ; GET # BYTES THAT COULD BE
                                               DECIMAL
B197  A8               TAY                   ; SET COUNTER
                 ;
B198             :SP3
B198  CA               DEX
B199  88               DEY                   ; DEC COUNTER
B19A  FØØ6 ^B1A2       BEQ    :SP2           ; IF DONE GO TEST EVEN/ODD
B19C  B5EØ             LDA    FR1,X          ;GET BYTE OF EXPONENT
B19E  DØC2 ^B162       BNE    :TBAD          ; IF NOT =Ø, THEN VALUE ERROR
B1AØ  FØF6 ^B198       BEQ    :SP3           ; REPEAT
                 ;
B1A2             :SP2
B1A2  AØ8Ø             LDY    #$8Ø           ; GET ODD FLAG
B1A4  B5EØ             LDA    FR1,X          ;GET BYTE OF EXPONENT
B1A6                   LSRA                  ; IS IT ODD[LAST BIT OFF]?
B1A6 +4A               LSR    A
B1A7  BØØ2 ^B1AB       BCS    :POWR          ; IF YES, BR
                 ;
B1A9             :SPEVEN
B1A9  AØØØ             LDY    #Ø
B1AB             :POWR
B1AB  98               TYA
B1AC  48               PHA
```

Save Exponent [from FR1]

```
B1AD  A2Ø5             LDX    #FMPREC        ;GET POINTER INTO FR1
B1AF             :POWR1
B1AF  B5EØ             LDA    FR1,X          ; GET A BYTE
B1B1  48               PHA                   ;PUSH ON CPU STACK
B1B2  CA               DEX                   ;POINT TO NEXT BYTE
B1B3  1ØFA ^B1AF       BPL    :POWR1         ;BR IF MORE TO DO
                 ;
B1B5  2ØD1DE           JSR    LOG1Ø          ;TAKE LOG OF BASE
B1B8  BØA8 ^B162       BCS    :TBAD
```

Pull Exponent into FR1 [from CPU Stack]

```
B1BA  A2ØØ             LDX    #Ø             ;GET POINTER INTO FR1
B1BC  AØØ5             LDY    #FMPREC        ;SET COUNTER
B1BE             :POWR2
B1BE  68               PLA
B1BF  95EØ             STA    FR1,X          ; PUT IN FR1
B1C1  E8               INX                   ;INCR POINTER
B1C2  88               DEY    ;DEC COUNTER
B1C3  1ØF9 ^B1BE       BPL    :POWR2         ;BR IF MORE TO DO
                 ;
B1C5  2Ø47AD           JSR    FRMUL          ;GET LOG OF NUMBER
B1C8  2ØCCDD           JSR    EXP1Ø          ;GET NUMBER
B1CB  BØØ9 ^B1D6       BCS    :EROV
                 ;
B1CD  68               PLA                   ; GET EVEN/ODD FLAG
B1CE  1Ø8F ^B15F       BPL    :TGOOD         ; IF EVEN, GO PUT ON STACK
                 ;
B1DØ  Ø5D4             ORA    FRØ            ; IF ODD MAKE ANSWER-
B1D2  85D4             STA    FRØ            ; X
B1D4  DØ89 ^B15F       BNE    :TGOOD         ; PUSH ON STACK
                 ;
B1D6             :EROV
B1D6  2Ø2AB9           JSR    EROVFL
```

Statements

XDIM & XCOM — Execute DIM and COMMON Statements

```
B1D9                   XDIM
B1D9                   XCOM
                       ;
B1D9  A4A8             :DC1   LDY    STINDEX       ; IF NOT AT
B1DB  C4A7                    CPY    NXTSTD        ; STATEMENT END
B1DD  9001 ^B1E0              BCC    :DC2          ; THEN CONTINUE
B1DF  60                      RTS                  ; RETURN
B1E0  20E0AA           :DC2   JSR    EXEXPR        ; GO SET UP VIA EXECUTE EXPR
B1E3  A5D2                    LDA    VTYPE         ; GET VAR TYPE
B1E5                          RORA                 ; SHIFT DIM BIT TO CARRY
B1E5 +6A                      ROR    A
B1E6  9003 ^B1EB              BCC    :DC3          ; CONTINUE IF NOT YET DIMMED
B1E8  202EB9           :DCERR JSR    ERRDIM        ; ELSE ERROR
                       ;
B1EB  38               :DC3   SEC                  ; TURN ON
B1EC                          ROLA                 ; DIM FLAG
B1EC +2A                      ROL    A
B1ED  85D2                    STA    VTYPE         ; AND RESET
B1EF  302F ^B220              BMI    :DCSTR        ; AND BR IF STRING
                       ;
B1F1  A4F5                    LDY    ZTEMP1        ; INC I1 BY 1
B1F3  A6F6                    LDX    ZTEMP1+1      ; AND SET AS DIM1
B1F5  C8                      INY
B1F6  D003 ^B1FB              BNE    :DC4
B1F8  E8                      INX
B1F9  30ED ^B1E8              BMI    :DCERR        ; BR IF OUT OF BOUNDS
B1FB  84D6             :DC4   STY    VTYPE+EVAD1
B1FD  86D7                    STX    VTYPE+EVAD1+1
B1FF  84F5                    STY    ZTEMP1        ; ALSO PUT BACK ONTO
B201  86F6                    STX    ZTEMP1+1      ; INDEX 1 FOR MULT
                       ;
B203  A497                    LDY    INDEX2        ; INC INDEX 2 BY 1
B205  A698                    LDX    INDEX2+1      ; AND SET AS DIM 2
B207  C8                      INY
B208  D003 ^B20D              BNE    :DC5
B20A  E8                      INX
B20B  30DB ^B1E8              BMI    :DCERR        ; BR IF OUT OF BOUNDS
B20D  84D8             :DC5   STY    VTYPE+EVAD2
B20F  86D9                    STX    VTYPE+EVAD2+1
                       ;
B211  205DAF                  JSR    AMUL1         ; ZTEMP1 = ZTEMP1*D2
B214  2046AF                  JSR    AMUL2         ; ZTEMP1 = ZTEMP1*6
                       ;                             RESULT IS AN ARRAY
                       ;                             SPACE REQD
B217  A4F5                    LDY    ZTEMP1        ; A,Y = LENGTH
B219  A5F6                    LDA    ZTEMP1+1
B21B  30CB ^B1E8              BMI    :DCERR
B21D  4C34B2                  JMP    :DCEXP        ; GO EXPAND
                       ;
B220                   :DCSTR
B220  A900                    LDA    #0            ; SET CURRENT LENGTH =0
B222  85D6                    STA    EVSLEN+VTYPE
B224  85D7                    STA    EVSLEN+1+VTYPE
                       ;
B226  A4F5                    LDY    ZTEMP1        ; MOVE INDEX
B228  84D8                    STY    VTYPE+EVSDIM  ; TO STR DIM
B22A  A5F6                    LDA    ZTEMP1+1      ; [ALSO LOAD A,Y]
B22C  85D9                    STA    VTYPE+EVSDIM+1 ; FOR EXPAND
B22E  D004 ^B234              BNE    :DCEXP        ; INSURE DIM
B230  C000                    CPY    #0            ; NOT ZERO
B232  F0B4 ^B1E8              BEQ    :DCERR        ; FOR STRING
                       ;
B234                   :DCEXP
B234  A28E                    LDX    #ENDSTAR      ; POINT TO END ST & ARRAY
                                                   ; SPACE
B236  2081A8                  JSR    EXPAND        ; GO EXPAND
                       ;
```

```
B239  38              SEC
B23A  A597            LDA    SVESA            ; CALCULATE DISPL INTO
B23C  E58C            SBC    STARP            ; ST/ARRAY SPACE
B23E  85D4            STA    VTYPE+EVSADR     ; AND PUT INTO VALUE BOX
B240  A598            LDA    SVESA+1
B242  E58D            SBC    STARP+1
B244  85D5            STA    VTYPE+EVSADR+1
                ;
B246  2016AC          JSR    RTNVAR           ; RETURN TO VAR VALUE TABLE
B249  4CD9B1          JMP    :DC1             ; AND GO FOR NEXT ONE
```

XPOKE — Execute POKE

```
B24C            XPOKE
B24C  20E0AB          JSR    GETINT           ; GET INTEGER ADDR
B24F  A5D4            LDA    FR0              ; SAVE POKE ADDR
B251  8595            STA    POKADR           ;
B253  A5D5            LDA    FR0+1            ;
B255  8596            STA    POKADR+1         ;
                ;
B257  20E9AB          JSR    GET1INT          ; GET 1 BYTE INTEGER TO POKE
                ;
B25A  A5D4            LDA    FR0              ; GET INTEGER TO POKE
B25C  A000            LDY    #0               ; GET INDEX
B25E  9195            STA    [POKADR],Y       ;GET INDEX
B260  60              RTS
```

XDEG — Execute DEG

```
B261            XDEG
B261  A906            LDA    #DEGON           ; GET DEGREES FLAG
B263  85FB            STA    RADFLG           ; SET FOR TRANSCENDENTALS
B265  60              RTS
```

XRAD — Execute RAD

```
B266            XRAD
B266  A900            LDA    #RADON           ; GET RADIAN FLAG
B268  85FB            STA    RADFLG           ; SET FOR TRANSCENDENTALS
B26A  60              RTS
```

XREST — Execute RESTORE Statement

```
B26B            XREST
B26B  A900            LDA    #0               ; ZERO DATA DISPL
B26D  85B6            STA    DATAD
                ;
B26F  2010B9          JSR    TSTEND           ; TEST END OF STMT
B272  9003 ^B277      BCC    :XR1             ; BR IF NOT END
B274  A8              TAY                     ; RESTORE TO LN=0
B275  F007 ^B27E      BEQ    :XR2
                ;
B277  20D5AB    :XR1  JSR    GETPINT          ; GET LINE NO.
                ;
B27A  A5D5            LDA    FR0+1            ; LOAD LINE NO.
B27C  A4D4            LDY    FR0
                ;
B27E  85B8      :XR2  STA    DATALN+1         ; SET LINE
B280  84B7            STY    DATALN
B282  60              RTS                     ; DONE
```

XREAD — Execute READ Statement

```
B283            XREAD
B283  A5A8            LDA    STINDEX          ; SAVE STINDEX
B285  48              PHA
B286  20C7B6          JSR    XGS              ; SAVE READ STMT VIA GOSUB
                ;
B289  A5B7            LDA    DATALN           ; MOVE DATALN TO TSLNUM
B28B  85A0            STA    TSLNUM
B28D  A5B8            LDA    DATALN+1
B28F  85A1            STA    TSLNUM+1
```

```
B291  20A2A9              JSR     GETSTMT          ; GO FIND TSLNUM
                    ;
B294  A58A                LDA     STMCUR           ; MOVE STMCUR TO INBUFF
B296  85F3                STA     INBUFF
B298  A58B                LDA     STMCUR+1
B29A  85F4                STA     INBUFF+1
                    ;
B29C  2019B7              JSR     XRTN             ; RESTORE READ STMT VIA RETURN
B29F  68                  PLA                      ; GET SAVED STINDEX
B2A0  85A8                STA     STINDEX          ; SET IT
                    ;
B2A2                :XRD1
B2A2  A000                LDY     #0               ; SET CIX=0
B2A4  84F2                STY     CIX              ; SET CIX
B2A6  2007B3              JSR     :XRNT1           ; GET LINE NO. LOW
B2A9  85B7                STA     DATALN           ; SET LINE NO. LOW
B2AB  2005B3              JSR     :XRNT
B2AE  85B8                STA     DATALN+1         ; SET LINE NO. HIGH
B2B0  2005B3              JSR     :XRNT
B2B3  85F5                STA     ZTEMP1           ; SET LINE LENGTH
B2B5                :XRD2
B2B5  2005B3              JSR     :XRNT
B2B8  85F6                STA     ZTEMP1+1         ; SET STMT LENGTH
                    ;
B2BA  2005B3              JSR     :XRNT            ; GET STMT LINE TOKEN
B2BD  C901                CMP     #CDATA           ; IS IT DATA
B2BF  F026 ^B2E7          BEQ     :XRD4            ; BR IF DATA
                    ;
B2C1  A4F6                LDY     ZTEMP1+1         ; GET DISPL TO NEXT STMT
B2C3  C4F5                CPY     ZTEMP1           ; IS IT EOL
B2C5  B005 ^B2CC          BCS     :XRD2A           ; BR IF EOL
B2C7  88                  DEY
B2C8  84F2                STY     CIX              ; SET NEW DISPL
B2CA  90E9 ^B2B5          BCC     :XRD2            ; AND CONTINUE THIS STMT
                    ;
B2CC  84F2          :XRD2A  STY     CIX
B2CE  C6F2                DEC     CIX
                    ;
B2D0  A001          :XRD3   LDY     #1             ; WAS THIS STMT THE
B2D2  B1F3                LDA     [INBUFF],Y       ; DIRECT ONE
B2D4  303D ^B313          BMI     :XROOD           ; BR IF IT WAS [OUT OF DATA]
                    ;
B2D6  38                  SEC
B2D7  A5F2                LDA     CIX              ; INBUFF + CIX + 1
B2D9  65F3                ADC     INBUFF           ; = ADR NEXT PGM LINE
B2DB  85F3                STA     INBUFF
B2DD  A900                LDA     #0
B2DF  85B6                STA     DATAD
B2E1  65F4                ADC     INBUFF+1
B2E3  85F4                STA     INBUFF+1
B2E5  90BB ^B2A2          BCC     :XRD1            ; GO SCAN THIS NEXT LINE
                    ;
B2E7                :XRD4
B2E7  A900                LDA     #0               ; CLEAR ELEMENT COUNT
B2E9  85F5                STA     ZTEMP1
                    ;
B2EB                :XRD5
B2EB  A5F5                LDA     ZTEMP1           ; GET ELEMENT COUNT
B2ED  C5B6                CMP     DATAD            ; AT PROPER ELEMENT
B2EF  B00B ^B2FC          BCS     :XRD7            ; BR IF AT
                    ;                                ELSE SCAN FOR NEXT
B2F1  2005B3        :XRD6   JSR     :XRNT          ; GET CHAR
B2F4  D0FB ^B2F1          BNE     :XRD6            ; BR IF NOT CR OR COMMA
B2F6  B0D8 ^B2D0          BCS     :XRD3            ; BR IF CR
B2F8  E6F5                INC     ZTEMP1           ; INC ELEMENT COUNT
B2FA  D0EF ^B2EB          BNE     :XRD5            ; AND GO NEXT
                    ;
B2FC  A940          :XRD7   LDA     #$40           ; SET READ BIT
B2FE  85A6                STA     DIRFLG
B300  E6F2                INC     CIX              ; INC OVER DATA TOKEN
```

```
B302  4C35B3          JMP     :XINA           ; GO DO IT
                ;
                ;
B305            :XRNT
B305  E6F2            INC     CIX             ; INC INDEX
B307  A4F2      :XRNT1  LDY     CIX           ; GET INDEX
B309  B1F3            LDA     [INBUFF],Y      ; GET CHAR COUNT
B30B  C92C            CMP     #$2C            ; IS IT A COMMA
B30D  18              CLC                     ; CARRY CLEAR FOR COMMA
B30E  F002 ^B312      BEQ     :XRNT2          ; BR IF COMMA
B310  C99B            CMP     #CR             ; IS IT CR
B312  60        :XRNT2  RTS
                ;
B313  2034B9    :XROOD  JSR     ERROOD
```

XINPUT — Execute INPUT

```
B316            XINPUT
                ;
B316  A93F            LDA     #'?'            ; SET PROMPT CHAR
B318  85C2            STA     PROMPT
B31A  203EAB          JSR     GETTOK          ; GET FIRST TOKEN
B31D  C6A8            DEC     STINDEX         ; BACK UP OVER IT
B31F  9005 ^B326      BCC     :XIN0           ; BR IF NOT OPERATOR
B321  2002BD          JSR     GIOPRM          ; GO GET DEVICE NUM
B324  85B4            STA     ENTDTD          ; SET DEVICE NO.
                ;
B326            :XIN0
B326  2051DA          JSR     INTLBF
B329  2089BA          JSR     GLINE           ; GO GET INPUT LINE
B32C  204EB3          JSR     :XITB           ; TEST BREAK
B32F  A000            LDY     #0
B331  84A6            STY     DIRFLG          ; SET INPUT MODE
B333  84F2            STY     CIX             ; SET CIX=0
B335            :XINA
B335  203EAB          JSR     GETTOK          ; GO GET TOKEN
B338  E6A8            INC     STINDEX         ; INC OVER TOKEN
                ;
B33A  A5D2            LDA     VTYPE           ; IS A STR
B33C  3020 ^B35E      BMI     :XISTR          ; BR IF STRING
                ;
B33E  2000D8          JSR     CVAFP           ; CONVERT TO FP
B341  B014 ^B357      BCS     :XIERR
B343  2007B3          JSR     :XRNT1          ; GET END TOKEN
B346  D00F ^B357      BNE     :XIERR          ; ERROR IF NO CR OR COMMA
B348  2016AC          JSR     RTNVAR          ; RETURN VAR
B34B  4C89B3          JMP     :XINX           ; GO FIGURE OUT WHAT TO DO
                                              NEXT
                ;
B34E  20F4A9    :XITB   JSR     TSTBRK        ; GO TEST BREAK
B351  D001 ^B354      BNE     XITBT           ; BR IF BRK
B353  60              RTS                     ; DONE
B354  4C93B7    XITBT   JMP     XSTOP         ; STOP
B357  A900      :XIERR  LDA     #0            ; RESET
B359  85B4            STA     ENTDTD          ; ENTER DVC
B35B  2030B9          JSR     ERRINP          ; GO ERROR
                ;
B35E            :XISTR
B35E  202EAB          JSR     EXPINT          ; INIT EXECUTE EXPR
B361  20BAAB          JSR     ARGPUSH         ; PUSH THE STRING
B364  C6F2            DEC     CIX             ; DEC CIX TO CHAR
B366  A5F2            LDA     CIX             ; BEFORE SOS
B368  85F5            STA     ZTEMP1          ; SAVE THAT CIX
B36A  A2FF            LDX     #$FF            ; SET CHAR COUNT = -1
                ;
B36C  E8        :XIS1   INX                   ; INC CHAR COUNT
B36D  2005B3          JSR     :XRNT           ; GET NEXT CHAR
B370  D0FA ^B36C      BNE     :XIS1           ; BR NOT CR OR COMMA
B372  B004 ^B378      BCS     :XIS2           ; BR IF CR
B374  24A6            BIT     DIRFLG          ; IS IT COMMA, IF NOT READ
B376  50F4 ^B36C      BVC     :XIS1           ; THEN CONTINUE
```

```
                          ;
B378  A4F5               :XIS2  LDY     ZTEMP1         ; GET SAVED INDEX
B37A  A5A8                      LDA     STINDEX        ; SAVE INDEX
B37C  48                        PHA
B37D  8A                        TXA                    ; ACU = CHAR COUNT
B37E  A2F3                      LDX     #INBUFF        ; POINT TO INBUFF
B380  2064AB                    JSR     RISC           ; GO MAKE STR VAR
B383  68                        PLA
B384  85A8                      STA     STINDEX        ; RESTORE INDEX
B386  20A6AE                    JSR     RISASN         ; THEN DO STA ASSIGN
                          ;
B389  24A6               :XINX  BIT     DIRFLG         ; IS THIS READ
B38B  500F ^B39C                BVC     :XIN           ; BR IF NOT
                          ;
B38D  E6B6                      INC     DATAD          ; INC DATA DISPL
B38F  2010B9                    JSR     TSTEND         ; TEST END READ STMT
B392  B00D ^B3A1                BCS     :XIRTS         ; BR IF READ END
                          ;
B394  2007B3             :XIR1  JSR     :XRNT1         ; GET END DATA CHAR
B397  9018 ^B3B1                BCC     :XINC          ; BR IF COMMA
B399  4CD0B2                    JMP     :XRD3          ; GO GET NEXT DATA LINE
                          ;
B39C                     :XIN
B39C  2010B9                    JSR     TSTEND
B39F  9008 ^B3A9                BCC     :XIN1
                          ;
B3A1  2051DA             :XIRTS JSR     INTLBF         ; RESTORE LBUFF
B3A4  A900                      LDA     #0             ; RESTORE ENTER
B3A6  85B4                      STA     ENTDTD         ; DEVICE TO ZERO
B3A8  60                        RTS                    ; DONE
                          ;
B3A9  2007B3             :XIN1  JSR     :XRNT1         ; IF NOT END OF DATA
B3AC  9003 ^B3B1                BCC     :XINC          ; THEN BRANCH
B3AE  4C26B3                    JMP     :XIN0          ; AND CONTINUE
                          ;
B3B1  E6F2               :XINC  INC     CIX            ; INC INDEX
B3B3  4C35B3                    JMP     :XINA          ; AND CONTINUE
```

XPRINT — Execute PRINT Statement

```
B3B6                     XPRINT
B3B6  A5C9                      LDA     PTABW          ; GET TAB VALUE
B3B8  85AF                      STA     SCANT          ; SCANT
B3BA  A900                      LDA     #0             ; SET OUT INDEX = 0
B3BC  8594                      STA     COX
                          ;
B3BE  A4A8               :XPR0  LDY     STINDEX        ; GET STMT DISPL
B3C0  B18A                      LDA     [STMCUR],Y     ; GET TOKEN
                          ;
B3C2  C912                      CMP     #CCOM
B3C4  F053 ^B419                BEQ     :XPTAB         ; BR IF TAB
B3C6  C916                      CMP     #CCR
B3C8  F07C ^B446                BEQ     :XPEOL         ; BR IF EOL
B3CA  C914                      CMP     #CEOS
B3CC  F078 ^B446                BEQ     :XPEOL         ; BR IF EOL
B3CE  C915                      CMP     #CSC
B3D0  F06F ^B441                BEQ     :XPNULL        ; BR IF NULL
B3D2  C91C                      CMP     #CPND
B3D4  F061 ^B437                BEQ     :XPRIOD
                          ;
B3D6  20E0AA                    JSR     EXEXPR         ; GO EVALUATE EXPRESSION
B3D9  20F2AB                    JSR     ARGPOP         ; POP FINAL VALUE
B3DC  C6A8                      DEC     STINDEX        ; DEC STINDEX
B3DE  24D2                      BIT     VTYPE          ; IS THIS A STRING
B3E0  3016 ^B3F8                BMI     :XPSTR         ; BR IF STRING
                          ;
B3E2  20E6D8                    JSR     CVFASC         ; CONVERT TO ASCII
B3E5  A900                      LDA     #0
B3E7  85F2                      STA     CIX
                          ;
B3E9  A4F2               :XPR1  LDY     CIX            ; OUTPUT ASCII CHARACTERS
```

```
B3EB  B1F3            LDA     [INBUFF],Y        ; FROM INBUFF
B3ED  48              PHA                       ; UNTIL THE CHAR
B3EE  E6F2            INC     CIX               ; WITH THE MSB ON
B3F0  205DB4          JSR     :XPRC             ; IS FOUND
B3F3  68              PLA
B3F4  10F3 ^B3E9      BPL     :XPR1
B3F6  30C6 ^B3BE      BMI     :XPR0             ; THEN GO FOR NEXT TOKEN
B3F8                :XPSTR
B3F8  209BAB          JSR     GSTRAD            ; GO GET ABS STRING ARRAY
B3FB  A900            LDA     #0
B3FD  85F2            STA     CIX
B3FF  A5D6          :XPR2C  LDA     VTYPE+EVSLEN    ; IF LEN LOW
B401  D004 ^B407      BNE     :XPR2B            ; NOT ZERO BR
B403  C6D7            DEC     VTYPE+EVSLEN+1    ; DEC LEN HI
B405  30B7 ^B3BE      BMI     :XPR0             ; BR IF DONE
B407  C6D6          :XPR2B  DEC     VTYPE+EVSLEN    ; DEC LEN LOW
                    ;
B409  A4F2          :XPR2   LDY     CIX             ; OUTPUT STRING CHARS
B40B  B1D4            LDA     [VTYPE+EVSADR],Y  ; FOR THE LENGTH
B40D  E6F2            INC     CIX               ; OF THE STRING
B40F  D002 ^B413      BNE     :XPR2A
B411  E6D5            INC     VTYPE+EVSADR+1
B413                :XPR2A
B413  205FB4          JSR     :XPRC1
B416  4CFFB3          JMP     :XPR2C
                    ;
B419                :XPTAB
B419  A494          :XPR3   LDY     COX             ; DO UNTIL COX+1 < SCANT
B41B  C8              INY
B41C  C4AF            CPY     SCANT
B41E  9009 ^B429      BCC     :XPR4
B420  18            :XPIC3  CLC
B421  A5C9            LDA     PTABW             ; SCANT = SCANT+TAB
B423  65AF            ADC     SCANT
B425  85AF            STA     SCANT
B427  90F0 ^B419      BCC     :XPR3
                    ;
B429  A494          :XPR4   LDY     COX             ; DO UNTIL COX = SCANT
B42B  C4AF            CPY     SCANT
B42D  B012 ^B441      BCS     :XPR4A
B42F  A920            LDA     #$20              ; PRINT BLANKS
B431  205DB4          JSR     :XPRC
B434  4C29B4          JMP     :XPR4
                    ;
B437  2002BD        :XPRIOD JSR     GIOPRM          ; GET DEVICE NO.
B43A  85B5            STA     LISTDTD           ; SET AS LIT DEVICE
B43C  C6A8            DEC     STINDEX           ;DEC INDEX
B43E  4CBEB3          JMP     :XPR0             ; GET NEXT TOKEN
                    ;
B441                :XPR4A
B441  E6A8          :XPNULL INC     STINDEX         ; INC STINDEX
B443  4CBEB3          JMP     :XPR0
                    ;
B446                :XPEOL
B446  A4A8          :XPEOS  LDY     STINDEX         ; AT END OF PRINT
B448  88              DEY
B449  B18A            LDA     [STMCUR],Y        ; IF PREV CHAR WAS
B44B  C915            CMP     #CSC              ; SEMI COLON THEN DONE
B44D  F009 ^B458      BEQ     :XPRTN            ; ELSE PRINT A CR
B44F  C912            CMP     #CCOM             ; OR A COMMA
B451  F005 ^B458      BEQ     :XPRTN            ; THEN DONE
B453  A99B            LDA     #CR
B455  205FB4          JSR     :XPRC1            ; THEN DONE
B458                :XPRTN
B458  A900            LDA     #0                ; SET PRIMARY
B45A  85B5            STA     LISTDTD           ; LIST DVC = 0
B45C  60              RTS                       ; AND RETURN
                    ;
                    ;
B45D  297F          :XPRC   AND     #$7F            ; MSB OFF
B45F  E694          :XPRC1  INC     COX             ; INC OUT INDEX
```

```
B461  4C9FBA         JMP    PRCHAR          ; OUTPUT CHAR
                  ;
```

XLPRINT — Print to Printer

```
B464              XLPRINT
B464  A980           LDA    #PSTR&255       ; POINT TO FILE SPEC
B466  85F3           STA    INBUFF          ; X
B468  A9B4           LDA    #PSTR/256       ; X
B46A  85F4           STA    INBUFF+1        ; X
                  ;
B46C  A207           LDX    #7              ; GET DEVICE
B46E  86B5           STX    LISTDTD         ; SET LIST DEVICE
B470  A900           LDA    #0              ; GET AUX 2
B472  A008           LDY    #8              ; GET OPEN TYPE
                  ;
B474  20D1BB         JSR    SOPEN           ; DO OPEN
B477  20B3BC         JSR    IOTEST          ; TEST FOR ERROR
                  ;
B47A  20B6B3         JSR    XPRINT          ; DO THE PRINT
                  ;
B47D  4CF1BC         JMP    CLSYS1          ; CLOSE DEVICE
                  ;
                  ;
                  ;
B480  50          PSTR     DB       'P'
B481  3A9B           DB     ':',CR
```

XLIST — Execute LIST Command

```
B483              XLIST
B483  A000           LDY    #0              ;SET TABLE SEARCH LINE NO
B485  84A0           STY    TSLNUM          ;TO ZERO
B487  84A1           STY    TSLNUM+1
B489  88             DEY
B48A  84AD           STY    LELNUM          ; SET LIST END LINE NO
B48C  A97F           LDA    #$7F            ;TO $7FFF
B48E  85AE           STA    LELNUM+1
B490  8DFE02         STA    $2FE            ; SET NON-DISPLAY MODE
B493  A99B           LDA    #CR             ; POINT CR
B495  209FBA         JSR    PRCHAR
                  ;
B498  20C7B6         JSR    XGS             ; SAVE CURLINE VIA GOSUB
B49B              :XL0
B49B  A4A8           LDY    STINDEX         ;GET STMT INDEX
B49D  C8             INY                    ;INC TO NEXT CHAR
B49E  C4A7           CPY    NXTSTD          ;RT NEXT STMT
B4A0  B02D ^B4CF     BCS    :LSTART         ; BR IF AT, NO PARMS
                  ;
B4A2  A5A8           LDA    STINDEX         ; SAVE STINDEX
B4A4  48             PHA                    ; ON STACK
B4A5  200FAC         JSR    POP1            ; POP FIRST ARGUMENT
B4A8  68             PLA                    ; RESTORE STINDEX TO
B4A9  85A8           STA    STINDEX         ; RE-DO FIRST ARG
B4AB  A5D2           LDA    VTYPE           ; GET VAR TYPE
B4AD  1006 ^B4B5     BPL    :XL1            ; BR IF NOT FILE SPEC STRING
B4AF  20D5BA         JSR    FLIST           ; GO OPEN FILE
B4B2  4C9BB4         JMP    :XL0            ; GO BACK TO AS IF FIRST PARM
                  ;
B4B5              :XL1
B4B5  20D5AB         JSR    GETPINT         ; GO GET START LNO
                  ;
B4B8  85A1           STA    TSLNUM+1
B4BA  A5D4           LDA    FR0             ; MOVE START LNO
B4BC  85A0           STA    TSLNUM          ;TO TSLNUM
                  ;
B4BE  A4A8           LDY    STINDEX         ;GET STMT INDEX
B4C0  C4A7           CPY    NXTSTD          ;AT NEXT STMT
B4C2  F003 ^B4C7     BEQ    :LSE            ; BR IF AT, NO PARMS
                  ;
```

```
B4C4  20D5AB          JSR     GETPINT          ; GO GET LINE NO
                ;
B4C7  A5D4      :LSE    LDA     FRØ            ; MOVE END LINE NO
B4C9  85AD            STA     LELNUM           ;TO LIST END LINE NO
B4CB  A5D5            LDA     FRØ+1            ;
B4CD  85AE            STA     LELNUM+1
                ;
                ;
B4CF            :LSTART
B4CF  20A2A9          JSR     GETSTMT          ;GO FIND FIRST LINE
                ;
B4D2  20E2A9    :LNXT   JSR     TENDST         ;AT END OF STMTS
B4D5  3024 ^B4FB      BMI     :LRTN            ; BR AT END
                ;
B4D7  A001      :LTERNG LDY     #1             ;COMPARE CURRENT STMT
B4D9  B18A            LDA     [STMCUR],Y       ;LINE NO WITH END
B4DB  C5AE            CMP     LELNUM+1         ;LINE NO
B4DD  900B ^B4EA      BCC     :LGO
B4DF  D01A ^B4FB      BNE     :LRTN
B4E1  88              DEY
B4E2  B18A            LDA     [STMCUR],Y
B4E4  C5AD            CMP     LELNUM
B4E6  9002 ^B4EA      BCC     :LGO
B4E8  D011 ^B4FB      BNE     :LRTN
                ;
B4EA  205CB5    :LGO    JSR     :LLINE         ;GO LIST THE LINE
B4ED  20F4A9          JSR     TSTBRK           ; TEST FOR BREAK
B4FØ  D009 ^B4FB      BNE     :LRTN            ; BR IF BREAK
B4F2  20DDA9          JSR     GETLL
B4F5  20D0A9          JSR     GNXTL            ;GO INC TO NEXT LINE
B4F8  4CD2B4          JMP     :LNXT            ;GO DO THIS LINE
                ;
B4FB            :LRTN
B4FB  A5B5            LDA     LISTDTD          ; IF LIST DEVICE
B4FD  F007 ^B506      BEQ     :LRTN1           ; IS ZERO, BR
B4FF  20F1BC          JSR     CLSYSD           ; ELSE CLOSE DEVICE
B502  A900            LDA     #Ø               ; AND RESET
B504  85B5            STA     LISTDTD          ; DEVICE TO ZERO
B506            :LRTN1
B506  8DFE02          STA     $2FE             ; SET DISPLAY MODE
B509  4C19B7          JMP     XRTN             ; THEN RESTORE LIST LINE
                                                 AND RETURN
```

LSCAN — Scan a Table for LIST Token

```
                ;                 ENTRY PARMS
                ;                   X = SKIP LENGTH
                ;                 A,Y = TABLE ADR
                ;               SCANT = TOKEN
                ;
B50C            :LSCAN
B50C  86AA            STX     SRCSKP           ; SAVE SKIP LENGTH
B50E  2030B5          JSR     :LSST            ; SAVE SRC ADR
                ;
B511  A4AA      :LSCØ   LDY     SRCSKP         ; GET SKIP FACTOR
                ;
B513  C6AF            DEC     SCANT            ; DECREMENT SRC COUNT
B515  300E ^B525      BMI     :LSINC           ; BR IF DONE
                ;
B517  B195      :LSC1   LDA     [SRCADR],Y     ; GET CHARACTER
B519  3003 ^B51E      BMI     :LSC2            ; BR IF LAST CHARACTER
B51B  C8              INY                      ; INC TO NEXT
B51C  D0F9 ^B517      BNE     :LSC1            ; BR ALWAYS
B51E  C8        :LSC2   INY                    ; INC TO AFTER LAST CHAR
B51F  2025B5          JSR     :LSINC           ; INC SRC ADR BY Y
B522  4C11B5          JMP     :LSCØ            ; GO TRY NEXT
                ;
B525  18        :LSINC  CLC
B526  98              TYA                      ; Y PLUS
B527  6595            ADC     SRCADR           ; SRCADR
B529  8595            STA     SRCADR           ; IS
```

```
B52B  A8            TAY                         ; NEW
B52C  A596          LDA      SRCADR+1           ; SRCADR
B52E  69ØØ          ADC      #Ø
                   ;
B53Ø  8596         :LSST  STA     SRCADR+1      ; STORE NEW SRCADR
B532  8495          STY      SRCADR             ; AND
B534  6Ø            RTS                         ; RETURN
```

LPRTOKEN — Print a Token

```
B535               LPRTOKEN
B535               :LPRTOKEN
B535  AØFF          LDY      #$FF               ; INITIALIZE INDEX TO ZERO
B537  84AF          STY      SCANT
                   ;
B539  E6AF         :LPT1  INC     SCANT         ; INC INDEX
B53B  A4AF          LDY      SCANT              ; GET INDEX
B53D  B195          LDA      [SRCADR],Y         ; GET TOKEN CHAR
B53F  48            PHA                         ; SAVE CHAR
B54Ø  C99B          CMP      #CR                ; IF ATARI CR
B542  FØØ4 ^B548    BEQ      :LPT1A             ; THEN DON'T AND
B544  297F          AND      #$7F               ; TURN OFF MSB
B546  FØØ3 ^B54B    BEQ      :LPT2              ; BR IF NON-PRINTING
B548               :LPT1A
B548  2Ø9FBA        JSR      PRCHAR             ; GO PRINT CHAR
B54B               :LPT2
B54B  68            PLA                         ; GET CHAR
B54C  1ØEB ^B539    BPL      :LPT1              ; BR IF NOT END CHAR
B54E  6Ø            RTS                         ; GO BACK TO MY BOSS
```

LPTWB — Print Token with Blank Before and After

```
B54F               :LPTWB
B54F  A92Ø          LDA      #$2Ø               ; GET BLANK
B551  2Ø9FBA        JSR      PRCHAR             ; GO PRINT IT
B554  2Ø35B5       :LPTTB JSR     :LPRTOKEN     ; GO PRINT TOKEN
B557  A92Ø         :LPBLNK LDA    #$2Ø          ; GET BLANK
B559  4C9FBA        JMP      PRCHAR             ; GO PRINT IT AND RETURN
                   ;
                   ;
                   ;
```

LLINE — List a Line

```
B55C               LLINE
B55C               :LLINE
B55C  AØØØ          LDY      #Ø
B55E  B18A          LDA      [STMCUR],Y         ; MOVE LINE NO
B56Ø  85D4          STA      FRØ                ; TO FRØ
B562  C8            INY
B563  B18A          LDA      [STMCUR],Y
B565  85D5          STA      FRØ+1
B567  2ØAAD9        JSR      CVIFP              ; CONVERT TO FP
B56A  2ØE6D8        JSR      CVFASC             ; CONVERT TO ASCII
B56D  A5F3          LDA      INBUFF             ; MOVE INBUFF ADR
B56F  8595          STA      SRCADR             ; TO SRCADR
B571  A5F4          LDA      INBUFF+1
B573  8596          STA      SRCADR+1
B575  2Ø54B5        JSR      :LPTTB             ; AND PRINT LINE NO
                   ;
B578               LDLINE
B578  AØØ2          LDY      #2
B57A  B18A          LDA      [STMCUR],Y         ; GET LINE LENGTH
B57C  859F          STA      LLNGTH             ; AND SAVE
B57E  C8            INY
B57F  B18A         :LL1   LDA     [STMCUR],Y    ; GET STMT LENGTH
B581  85A7          STA      NXTSTD             ; AND SAVE AS NEXT ST DISPL
B583  C8            INY                         ; INC TO STMT TYPE
B584  84A8          STY      STINDEX            ; AND SAVE DISPL
B586  2Ø9ØB5        JSR      :LSTMT             ; GO LIST STMT
```

```
B589  A4A7             LDY     NXTSTD         ; DONE LINE
B58B  C49F             CPY     LLNGTH
B58D  90F0 ^B57F       BCC     :LL1           ; BR IF NOT
B58F  60               RTS                    ; ELSE RETURN
```

LSTMT — List a Statement

```
B590                 :LSTMT
B590  2031B6             JSR     :LGCT          ; GET CURRENT TOKEN
B593  C936               CMP     #CILET         ; IF IMP LET
B595  F017 ^B5AE         BEQ     :LADV          ; BR
B597  203DB6             JSR     LSTMC          ; GO LIST STMT CODE
                     ;
B59A  2031B6             JSR     :LGCT          ; GO GET CURRENT TOKEN
B59D  C937               CMP     #CERR          ; BR IF ERROR STMT
B59F  F004 ^B5A5         BEQ     :LDR
B5A1  C902               CMP     #2             ; WAS IT DATA OR REM
B5A3  B009 ^B5AE         BCS     :LADV          ; BR IF NOT
                     ;
B5A5  202FB6         :LDR    JSR     :LGNT      ; OUTPUT DATA/REM
B5A8  209FBA             JSR     PRCHAR         ; THEN PRINT THE CR
B5AB  4CA5B5             JMP     :LDR
                     ;
B5AE  202FB6         :LADV   JSR     :LGNT      ; GET NEXT TOKEN
B5B1  101A ^B5CD         BPL     :LNVAR         ; BR IF NOT VARIABLE
                     ;
B5B3  297F               AND     #$7F           ; TURN OFF MSB
B5B5  85AF               STA     SCANT          ; AND SET AS SCAN COUNT
B5B7  A200               LDX     #0             ; SCAN VNT FOR
B5B9  A583               LDA     VNTP+1         ; VAR NAME
B5BB  A482               LDY     VNTP
B5BD  200CB5             JSR     :LSCAN         ;
B5C0  2035B5         :LS1    JSR     :LPRTOKEN  ; PRINT VAR NAME
B5C3  C9A8               CMP     #$A8           ; NAME END IN LPAREN
B5C5  D0E7 ^B5AE         BNE     :LADV          ; BR IF NOT
B5C7  202FB6             JSR     :LGNT          ; DON'T PRINT NEXT TOKEN
B5CA  4CAEB5             JMP     :LADV          ; IF IT IS A PAREN
                     ;
B5CD                 :LNVAR
B5CD  C90F               CMP     #$0F           ; TOKEN: $0F
B5CF  F018 ^B5E9         BEQ     :LSTC          ; BR IF 0F, STR CONST
                     ;
B5D1  B036 ^B609         BCS     :LOP           ; BR IF TOKEN >$0F
                     ;                                ELSE IT'S NUM CONST
B5D3  204DAB             JSR     NCTOFR0        ; GO MOVE FR0
B5D6  C6A8               DEC     STINDEX        ; BACK INDEX TO LAST CHAR
B5D8  20E6D8             JSR     CVFASC         ; CONVERT FR0 TO ASCII
B5DB  A5F3               LDA     INBUFF         ; POINT SCRADR
B5DD  8595               STA     SRCADR         ; TO INBUFF WHERE
B5DF  A5F4               LDA     INBUFF+1       ; CHAR IS
B5E1  8596               STA     SRCADR+1       ;
B5E3  2035B5         :LSX    JSR     :LPRTOKEN  ; GO PRINT NUMBER
B5E6  4CAEB5             JMP     :LADV          ; GO FOR NEXT TOKEN
                     ;
B5E9  202FB6         :LSTC   JSR     :LGNT      ; GET NEXT TOKEN
B5EC  85AF               STA     SCANT          ; WHICH IS STR LENGTH
B5EE  A922               LDA     #$22           ; PRINT DOUBLE QUOTE CHAR
B5F0  209FBA             JSR     PRCHAR
B5F3  A5AF               LDA     SCANT
B5F5  F00A ^B601         BEQ     :LS3
                     ;
B5F7  202FB6         :LS2    JSR     :LGNT      ; OUTPUT STR CONST
B5FA  209FBA             JSR     PRCHAR         ; CHAR BY CHAR
B5FD  C6AF               DEC     SCANT          ; UNTIL COUNT =0
B5FF  D0F6 ^B5F7         BNE     :LS2
                     ;
B601                 :LS3
B601  A922               LDA     #$22           ; THEN OUTPUT CLOSING
B603  209FBA             JSR     PRCHAR         ; DOUBLE QUOTE
B606  4CAEB5             JMP     :LADV
```

```
B609  38              :LOP   SEC
B60A  E910                 SBC      #$10              ; SUBSTRACT THE 10
B60C  85AF                 STA      SCANT             ; SET FOR SCAN COUNT
B60E  A200                 LDX      #0
B610  A9A7                 LDA      #OPNTAB/256
B612  A0E3                 LDY      #OPNTAB&255
B614  200CB5               JSR      :LSCAN            ; SCAN OP NAME TABLE
B617  2031B6               JSR      :LGCT             ; GO GET CURRENT TOKEN
B61A  C93D                 CMP      #CFFUN            ; IS IT FUNCTION
B61C  B0C5 ^B5E3           BCS      :LSX              ; BR IF FUNCTION
B61E  A000                 LDY      #0
B620  B195                 LDA      [SRCADR],Y        ; GET FIRST CHAR
B622  297F                 AND      #$7F              ; TURN OFF MSB
B624  20F7A3               JSR      TSTALPH           ; TEST FOR ALPHA
B627  B0BA ^B5E3           BCS      :LSX              ; BR NOT ALPHA
B629  204FB5               JSR      :LPTWB            ; LIST ALPHA WITH
B62C  4CAEB5               JMP      :LADV             ; BLANKS FOR AND AFTER
                      ;
B62F                  :LGNT                           ; GET NEXT TOKEN
B62F  E6A8                 INC      STINDEX           ; INC TO NEXT
B631  A4A8            :LGCT   LDY      STINDEX        ; GET DISPL
B633  C4A7                 CPY      NXTSTD            ; AT END OF STMT
B635  B003 ^B63A           BCS      :LGNTE            ; BR IF AT END
B637  B18A                 LDA      [STMCUR],Y        ; GET TOKEN
B639  60                   RTS                        ; AND RETURN
                      ;
B63A  68              :LGNTE  PLA                     ; POP CALLERS ADR
B63B  68                   PLA                        ; AND
B63C  60                   RTS                        ; GO BACK TO LIST LINE
                      ;
B63D                  LSTMC
B63D  85AF                 STA      SCANT             ; SET INSCAN COUNT
B63F  A202                 LDX      #2                ; AND
B641  A9A4                 LDA      #SNTAB/256
B643  A0AF                 LDY      #SNTAB&255        ; STATEMENT NAME TABLE
B645  200CB5               JSR      :LSCAN
B648  4C54B5               JMP      :LPTTB            ; GO LIST WITH FOLLOWING BLANK
```

XFOR — Execute FOR

```
B64B                       LOCAL
B64B                  XFOR
B64B  208AB8               JSR      :SAVDEX           ; SAVE STINDEX
B64E  20E0AA               JSR      EXEXPR            ; DO ASSIGNMENT
B651  A5D3                 LDA      VNUM              ; GET VARIABLE #
B653  0980                 ORA      #$80              ; OR IN HIGH ORDER BIT
B655  48                   PHA                        ; SAVE ON CPU STACK
B656  2025B8               JSR      FIXRSTK           ; FIX RUN STACK
                      *
                      *        BUILD STACK ELEMENT
                      *
B659  A90C                 LDA      #FBODY            ; GET # OF BYTES
B65B  2078B8               JSR      :REXPAN           ; EXPAND RUN STACK
                      ;
B65E  200FAC               JSR      POP1              ; EVAL EXP & GET INTO FR0
                      ;
                      ;        PUT LIMIT [INFR0] ON STACK
                      ;
B661  A2D4                 LDX      #FR0              ;POINT TO FR0
B663  A000                 LDY      #FLIM             ; GET DISPL
B665  208FB8               JSR      :MV6RS            ; GO MOVE LIMIT
                      ;
                      ;        SET DEFAULT STEP
                      ;
B668  2044DA               JSR      ZFR0              ; CLEAR FR0 TO ZEROS
B66B  A901                 LDA      #1                ; GET DEFAULT STEP
B66D  85D5                 STA      FR0+1             ; SET DEFAULT STEP VALUE
B66F  A940                 LDA      #$40              ; GET DEFAULT EXPONENT
B671  85D4                 STA      FR0               ; STORE
                      ;
```

```
                    ;       TEST FOR END OF STMT
                    ;
B673  2010B9           JSR     TSTEND           ; TEST FOR END OF START
B676  B003 ^B67B       BCS     :NSTEP           ; IF YES, WE ARE AT END OF
                                                  STMT
                    ;
                    ;       ELSE GET STEP VALUE
                    ;
B678  200FAC           JSR     POP1             ; EVAL EXP & GET INTO FRØ
B67B                :NSTEP
                    ;
                    ;       PUT STEP [IN FRØ] ON STACK
                    ;
B67B  A2D4             LDX     #FRØ             ; POINT TO FRØ
B67D  AØØ6             LDY     #FSTEP           ; GET DISPL
B67F  208FB8           JSR     :MV6RS           ; GO MOVE STEP
                    ;
B682  68               PLA                      ; GET VARIABLE #
                    ;
                    ;       PSHRSTK - PUSH COMMON PORT OF FOR/GOSUB
                    ;               - ELEMENT ON RUN STACK
                    ;
                    ;       ON ENTRY  A - VARIABLE # OR Ø [FOR GOSUB]
                    ;                 TSLNUM - LINE #
                    ;                 STINDEX - DISPL TO STMT TOKEN +1
B683                PSHRSTK
                    ;
                    ;       EXPAND RUN STACK
                    ;
B683  48               PHA                      ; SAVE VAR # / TYPE
B684  A9Ø4             LDA     #GFHEAD          ; GET # OF BYTES TO EXPAND
B686  2078B8           JSR     :REXPAN          ; EXPAND [OLD TOP RETURN IN
                                                  ZTEMP1]
                    ;
                    ;       PUT ELEMENT ON STACK
                    ;
B689  68               PLA                      ; GET VARIABLE #/TYPE
B68A  AØØØ             LDY     #GFTYPE          ; GET DISPL TO TYPE IN HEADER
B68C  91C4             STA     [TEMPA],Y        ; PUT VAR#/TYPE ON STACK
                    ;
B68E  B18A             LDA     [STMCUR],Y       ; GET LINE # LOW
B69Ø  C8               INY                      ; POINT TO NEXT HEADER BYTE
B691  91C4             STA     [TEMPA],Y        ; PUT LINE # LOW IN HEADER
B693  B18A             LDA     [STMCUR],Y       ; GET LINE # HIGH
B695  C8               INY
B696  91C4             STA     [TEMPA],Y        ; PUT IN HEADER
                    ;
B698  A6B3             LDX     SAVDEX           ; GET SAVED INDEX INTO LINE
B69A  CA               DEX                      ; POINT TO TOKEN IN LINE
B69B  8A               TXA                      ; PUT IN A
B69C  C8               INY                      ; POINT TO DISPL IN HEADER
B69D  91C4             STA     [TEMPA],Y        ; PUT IN HEADER
B69F  6Ø               RTS
```

XGOSUB — Execute GOSUB

```
B6AØ                XGOSUB
B6AØ  2ØC7B6           JSR     XGS              ; GO TO XGS ROUTINE
```

XGOTO — Execute GOTO

```
B6A3                XGOTO
B6A3  2ØD5AB           JSR     GETPINT          ; GET POSTIVE INTEGER IN FRØ
                    ;
                    ;       GET LINE ADRS & POINTERS
                    ;
B6A6                XGO2
B6A6  A5D5             LDA     FRØ+1            ; X
B6A8  85A1             STA     TSLNUM+1         ; X
B6AA  A5D4             LDA     FRØ              ; PUT LINE # IN TSLNUM
B6AC  85AØ             STA     TSLNUM           ; X
```

```
                   ;
B6AE               XGO1
B6AE  2ØA2A9           JSR     GETSTMT         ; LINE POINTERS AND STMT ADDRESS
B6B1  BØØ5 ^B6B8       BCS     :ERLN           ; IF NOT FOUND ERROR
B6B3  68               PLA                     ; CLEAN UP STACK
B6B4  68               PLA
B6B5  4C5FA9           JMP     EXECNL          ; GO TO EXECUTE CONTROL
                   ;
B6B8               :ERLN
B6B8  2ØBEB6           JSR     RESCUR          ; RESTORE STMT CURRENT
                   ;
                   ;
                   ;
B6BB  2Ø28B9           JSR     ERNOLN          ; LINE # NOT FOUND
B6BE               RESCUR
B6BE  A5BE             LDA     SAVCUR          ; RESTORE STMCUR
B6CØ  858A             STA     STMCUR          ; X
B6C2  A5BF             LDA     SAVCUR+1        ; X
B6C4  858B             STA     STMCUR+1        ; X
B6C6  6Ø               RTS
```

XGS — Perform GOSUB [GOSUB, LIST, READ]

```
B6C7               XGS
B6C7  2Ø8AB8           JSR     :SAVDEX         ; GET STMT INDEX
B6CA               XGS1
B6CA  A9ØØ             LDA     #Ø              ; GET GOSUB TYPE
B6CC  4C83B6           JMP     PSHRSTK         ; PUT ELEMENT ON RUN STACK
```

XNEXT — Execute NEXT

```
B6CF               XNEXT
                   ;
                   ;       GET VARIABLE #
                   ;
B6CF  A4A8             LDY     STINDEX         ; GET STMT INDEX
B6D1  B18A             LDA     [STMCUR],Y      ; GET VARIABLE #
B6D3  85C7             STA     ZTEMP2+1        ; SAVE
                   ;
                   ;       GET ELEMENT
                   ;
B6D5               :XN
B6D5  2Ø41B8           JSR     POPRSTK         ; PULL ELEMENT FROM RUN STACK
                   ;                                 VAR#/TYPE RETURN IN A
B6D8  BØ3C ^B716       BCS     :ERNFOR         ; IF AT TOP OF STACK, ERROR
B6DA  FØ3A ^B716       BEQ     :ERNFOR         ; IF TYPE = GOSUB, ERROR
B6DC  C5C7             CMP     ZTEMP2+1        ; DOES STKVAR# = OUR VAR #
B6DE  DØF5 ^B6D5       BNE     :XN
                   ;
                   ;       GET STEP VALUES IN FR1
                   ;
B6EØ  AØØ6             LDY     #FSTEP          ; GET DISPL INTO ELEMENT
B6E2  2Ø9EB8           JSR     :PL6RS          ; GET STEP INTO FR1
                   ;
                   ;       SAVE TYPE OF STEP [+ OR -]
                   ;
B6E5  A5EØ             LDA     FR1             ; GET EXP FR1 [CONTAINS SIGN]
B6E7  48               PHA                     ; PUSH ON CPU STACK
                   ;
                   ;       GET VARIABLE VALUE
                   ;
B6E8  A5C7             LDA     ZTEMP2+1        ; GET VAR #
B6EA  2Ø89AB           JSR     GETVAR          ; GET VARIABLE VALUE
                   ;
                   ;       GET NEW VALUE
                   ;
B6ED  2Ø3BAD           JSR     FRADD           ; ADD STEP TO VALUE
B6FØ  2Ø16AC           JSR     RTNVAR          ; PUT IN VARIABLE TABLE
                   ;
                   ;       GET LIMIT IN FR1
                   ;
```

```
B6F3  A000            LDY     #FLIM           ; GET DISPL TO LIMIT IN ELEMENT
B6F5  209EB8          JSR     :PL6RS          ; GET LIMIT INTO FR1
B6F8  68              PLA                     ; GET SIGN OF STEP
B6F9  1006 ^B701      BPL     :STPPL          ; BR IF STEP +
                  ;
                  ;       COMPARE FOR NEGATIVE STEP
                  ;
B6FB  2035AD          JSR     FRCMP           ; COMPARE VALUE TO LIMIT
B6FE  1009 ^B709      BPL     :NEXT           ; IF VALUE >= LIMIT, CONTINUE
B700  60              RTS                     ; ELSE DONE
                  ;
                  ;       COMPARE FOR POSTIVE STEP
                  ;
B701              :STPPL
B701  2035AD          JSR     FRCMP           ; COMPARE VALUE TO LIMIT
B704  F003 ^B709      BEQ     :NEXT           ; IF = CONTINUE
B706  3001 ^B709      BMI     :NEXT           ; IF < CONTINUE
B708  60              RTS                     ; ELSE RETURN
                  ;
B709              :NEXT
B709  A910            LDA     #GFHEAD+FBODY   ; GET # BYTES IN FOR ELEMENT
B70B  2078B8          JSR     :REXPAND        ; GO PUT IT BACK ON STACK
B70E  2037B7          JSR     :GETTOK         ; GET TOKEN [RETURNS IN A]
B711  C908            CMP     #CFOR           ; IS TOKEN = FOR?
B713  D032 ^B747      BNE     :ERGFD          ; IF NOT IT'S AN ERROR
B715  60              RTS
                  ;
B716              :ERNFOR
B716  2026B9          JSR     ERNOFOR
```

XRTN — Execute RETURN

```
B719              XRTN
B719  2041B8          JSR     POPRSTK         ; GET ELEMENT FROM RUN STACK
B71C  B016 ^B734      BCS     :ERRTN          ; IF AT TOP OF STACK, ERROR
B71E  D0F9 ^B719      BNE     XRTN            ; IF TYPE NOT GOSUB, REPEAT
                  ;
B720  2037B7          JSR     :GETTOK         ; GET TOKEN FROM LINE [IN A]
B723  C90C            CMP     #CGOSUB         ; IS IT GOSUB?
B725  F00C ^B733      BEQ     :XRTS           ; BR IF GOSUB
B727  C91E            CMP     #CON
B729  F008 ^B733      BEQ     :XRTS           ; BR IF ON
B72B  C904            CMP     #CLIST
B72D  F004 ^B733      BEQ     :XRTS           ; BR IF LIST
B72F  C922            CMP     #CREAD          ; MAYBE IT'S READ
B731  D014 ^B747      BNE     :ERGFD          ; IF NOT, ERROR
B733              :XRTS
B733  60              RTS
                  ;
B734              :ERRTN
B734  2020B9          JSR     ERBRTN          ; BAD RETURN ERROR
                  *
                  *       :GETTOK - GET TOKEN POINTED TO BY RUN STACK ELEMENT
                  *
                  *       ON EXIT     A - CONTAINS TOKEN
                  *
B737              :GETTOK
B737  2018B8          JSR     SETLINE         ; SET UP TO PROCESS LINE
B73A  B00B ^B747      BCS     :ERGFD          ; IF LINE # NOT FOUND, ERROR
                  ;
B73C  A4B2            LDY     SVDISP          ; GET DISPL TO TOKEN
B73E  88              DEY                     ; POINT TO NXT STMT DISPL
B73F  B18A            LDA     [STMCUR],Y      ; GET NEXT STMT DISPL
B741  85A7            STA     NXTSTD          ; SAVE
                  ;
B743  C8              INY                     ; GET DISPL TO TOKEN AGAIN
B744  B18A            LDA     [STMCUR],Y      ; GET TOKEN
B746  60              RTS
                  ;
                  ;
B747              :ERGFD
```

```
B747  20BEB6         JSR     RESCUR           ; RESTORE STMT CURRENT
B74A  2022B9         JSR     ERGFDEL
```

XRUN — Execute RUN

```
B74D                XRUN
                    ;
                    ;       TEST FOR END OF STMT
                    ;
B74D  2010B9         JSR     TSTEND           ; CHECK FOR END OF STMT
B750  B003 ^B755     BCS     :NOFILE          ; IF END OF STMT, BR
B752  20F7BA         JSR     FRUN             ; ELSE HAVE FILE NAME
                    ;
B755                :NOFILE
                    ;
                    ;       GET 1ST LINE # OF PROGRAM
                    ;
B755  A900           LDA     #0               ; GET SMALLEST POSSIBLE
                                                LINE NUM
B757  85A0           STA     TSLNUM           ; X
B759  85A1           STA     TSLNUM+1         ; X
B75B  2018B8         JSR     SETLINE          ; SET UP LINE POINTERS
B75E  20E2A9         JSR     TENDST           ; TEST FOR END OF STMT TABLE
B761  3012 ^B775     BMI     :RUNEND          ; IF AT END, BR
B763  20F8B8         JSR     RUNINIT          ; CLEAR SOME STORAGE

                                                   FALL THRU TO CLR
```

XCLR — Execute CLR

```
B766                XCLR
B766  20C0B8         JSR     ZVAR             ; GO ZERO VARS
B769  20AFB8         JSR     RSTPTR           ; GO RESET STACK PTRS
B76C  A900           LDA     #0               ; CLEAR DATA VALUES
B76E  85B7           STA     DATALN
B770  85B8           STA     DATALN+1
B772  85B6           STA     DATAD
B774  60             RTS
                    ;
                    ;
B775                :RUNEND
B775  4C50A0         JMP     SNX1             ;NO PROGRAM TO RUN
```

XIF — Execute IF

```
B778                XIF
B778  200FAC         JSR     POP1             ; EVAL EXP AND GET VALUE
                                                INTO FR0
B77B  A5D5           LDA     FR0M             ; GET 1ST MANTISSA BYTE
B77D  F009 ^B788     BEQ     :FALSE           ; IF = 0, # = 0 AND IS FALSE
                    *
                    *       EXPRESSION TRUE
                    *
B77F  2010B9         JSR     TSTEND           ; TEST FOR END OF STMT
B782  B003 ^B787     BCS     :TREOS           ; IF AT EOS, BRANCH
                    ;
                    ;       TRUE AND NOT EOS
                    ;
B784  4CA3B6         JMP     XGOTO            ; JOIN GOTO
                    ;
                    ;       TRUE AND EOS
                    ;
B787                :TREOS
B787  60             RTS
                    *
                    *       EXPRESSION FALSE
                    *
B788                :FALSE
B788  A59F           LDA     LLNGTH           ; GET DISPL TO END OF LINE
B78A  85A7           STA     NXTSTD           ; SAVE AS DISPL TO NEXT STMT
B78C  60             RTS
```

XEND — Execute END

```
B78D                    XEND
B78D   20A7B7                JSR      STOP
B790   4C50A0                JMP      SNX1
```

XSTOP — Execute STOP

```
B793                    XSTOP
B793   20A7B7                JSR      STOP              ; GO SET UP STOP LINE #
                        ;
                        ;          PRINT MESSAGE
                        ;
B796   206EBD                JSR      PRCR              ; PRINT CR
B799   A9B6                  LDA      #:MSTOP&255       ; SET POINTER FOR MESSAGE
B79B   8595                  STA      SRCADR            ; X
B79D   A9B7                  LDA      #:MSTOP/256       ; X
B79F   8596                  STA      SRCADR+1          ; X
                        ;
B7A1   2035B5                JSR      LPRTOKEN          ; PRINT IT
                        ;
B7A4   4C74B9                JMP      :ERRM2            ; PRINT REST OF MESSAGE
                        ;
                        ;
                        ;
B7A7                    STOP
B7A7   20E2A9                JSR      TENDST            ; GET CURRENT LINE # HIGH
B7AA   3007 ^B7B3            BMI      :STOPEND          ; IF -, THIS IS DIRECT STMT
                        ;                               ; DON'T STOP
B7AC   85BB                  STA      STOPLN+1          ; SAVE LINE # HIGH FOR CON
B7AE   88                    DEY                        ; DEC INDEX
B7AF   B18A                  LDA      [STMCUR],Y        ; GET LINE # LOW
B7B1   85BA                  STA      STOPLN            ; SAVE FOR CON
B7B3                    :STOPEND
B7B3   4C72BD                JMP      SETDZ             ; SET L/D DEVICE =0
                        ;
                        ;
                        ;
B7B6   53544F5050       :MSTOP   DC        'STOPPED '
       4544A0
```

XCONT — Execute Continue

```
B7BE                    XCONT
B7BE   20E2A9                JSR      TENDST            ; IS IT INDIRECT STMT?
B7C1   10F0 ^B7B3            BPL      :STOPEND          ;IF YES, BR
B7C3   A5BA                  LDA      STOPLN            ; SET STOP LINE # AS LINE #
                                                        FOR GET
B7C5   85A0                  STA      TSLNUM            ; X
B7C7   A5BB                  LDA      STOPLN+1          ; X
B7C9   85A1                  STA      TSLNUM+1          ; X
                        ;
B7CB   20A2A9                JSR      GETSTMT           ; GET ADR OF STMT WE
                                                        STOPPED AT
B7CE   20E2A9                JSR      TENDST            ;AT END OF STMT TAB ?
B7D1   30A2 ^B775            BMI      :RUNEND
B7D3   20DDA9                JSR      GETLL             ; GET NEXT LINE ADDR IN CURSTM
B7D6   20D0A9                JSR      GNXTL             ; X
B7D9   20E2A9                JSR      TENDST            ; SEE IF WE ARE AT END OF
                                                        STMT TABLE
B7DC   3097 ^B775            BMI      :RUNEND           ; BR IF MINUS
B7DE   4C1BB8                JMP      SETLN1            ; SET UP LINE POINTERS
```

XTRAP — Execute TRAP

```
B7E1                    XTRAP
B7E1   20E0AB                JSR      GETINT            ; CONVERT LINE # TO POSITIVE
                                                        INT
B7E4   A5D4                  LDA      FR0               ; SAVE LINE # LOW AS TRAP LINE
B7E6   85BC                  STA      TRAPLN            ; IN CASE OF LATER ERROR
B7E8   A5D5                  LDA      FR0+1             ; X
B7EA   85BD                  STA      TRAPLN+1          ; X
B7EC   60                    RTS
```

Source Code

XON — Execute ON

```
B7ED              XON
B7ED  208AB8          JSR     :SAVDEX          ; SAVE INDEX INTO LINE
B7F0  20E9AB          JSR     GET1INT          ; GET 1 BYTE INTEGER
B7F3  A5D4            LDA     FR0              ; GET VALUE
B7F5  F020 ^B817      BEQ     :ERV             ; IF ZERO, FALL THROUGH TO
                                                 NEXT STMT
                  ;
B7F7  A4A8            LDY     STINDEX          ; GET STMT INDEX
B7F9  88              DEY                      ; BACK UP TO GOSUB/GOTO
B7FA  B18A            LDA     [STMCUR],Y       ; GET CODE
B7FC  C917            CMP     #CGTO            ; IS IT GOTO?
B7FE  F003 ^B803      BEQ     :GO              ; IF YES, DON'T PUSH ON
                                                 RUN STACK
                  ;
                  ;
                  ;       THIS IS ON - GOSUB:  PUT ELEMENT ON RUN STACK
                  ;
B800  20CAB6          JSR     XGS1             ; PUT ELEMENT ON RUN STACK
                                               ; FOR RETURN
                  ;
B803              :GO
B803  A5D4            LDA     FR0              ; GET INDEX INTO EXPRESSIONS
B805  85B3            STA     ONLOOP           ; SAVE FOR LOOP CONTROL
B807              :ON1
B807  20D5AB          JSR     GETPINT          ; GET + INTEGER
B80A  C6B3            DEC     ONLOOP           ; IS THIS THE LINE # WE WANT?
B80C  F006 ^B814      BEQ     :ON2             ; IF YES, GO DO IT
                  ;
B80E  2010B9          JSR     TSTEND           ; ARE THERE MORE EXPRESSIONS
B811  90F4 ^B807      BCC     :ON1             ; IF YES, THEN EVAL NEXT ONE
B813  60              RTS                      ; ELSE FALL THROUGH TO
                                                 NEXT STMT
B814              :ON2
B814  4CA6B6          JMP     XGO2             ; JOIN GOTO
                  ;
                  ;
B817              :ERV
B817  60              RTS                      ; FALL THROUGH TO NEXT STMT.
```

Execution Control Statement Subroutines

SETLINE — Set Up Line Pointers

```
                  *       ON ENTRY   TLSNUM - LINE #
                  *
                  *       ON EXIT    STMCUR - CONTAIN PROPER VALUES
                  *                  LLNGTH - X
                  *                  NXTSTM - X
                  *                  CARRY SET BY GETSTMT IF LINE # NOT FOUND
                  *
B818              SETLINE
B818  20A2A9          JSR     GETSTMT          ; GET STMCUR
                  ;
B81B              SETLN1
B81B  A002            LDY     #2               ; GET DISP IN LINE TO LENGTH
B81D  B18A            LDA     [STMCUR],Y       ; GET LINE LENGTH
B81F  859F            STA     LLNGTH           ; SET LINE LENGTH
                  ;
B821  C8              INY                      ; POINT TO NEXT STMT DISPL
B822  84A7            STY     NXTSTD           ; SET NXT STMT DISPL
                  ;
B824  60              RTS
```

FIXRSTK — Fix Run Stack — Remove Old FORs

```
                  *       ON ENTRY   A - VARIABLE # IN CURRENT FOR
                  *
                  *       ON EXIT    RUNSTK CLEAR OF ALL FOR'S
                  *
```

```
B825                FIXRSTK
B825  85C7              STA     ZTEMP2+1          ; SAVE VAR # OF THIS FOR
                    ;
                    ;       SAVE TOP OF RUN STACK
                    ;
B827  2081B8            JSR     :SAVRTOP          ; SAVE TOP OF RUN STACK IN
                                                    ZTEMP1
                    ;
                    ;
B82A                :FIXR
B82A  2041B8            JSR     POPRSTK           ; POP AN ELEMENT FROM RUNSTK
B82D  B008 ^B837        BCS     :TOP              ; IF AT TOP - WE ARE DONE
B82F  F006 ^B837        BEQ     :TOP              ; IF CC = 08 ELEMENT WAS GOSUB
B831  C5C7              CMP     ZTEMP2+1          ; IS STK VAR # = OUR VAR #?
B833  F00B ^B840        BEQ     :FNVAR            ; IF YES, WE ARE DONE
B835  D0F3 ^B82A        BNE     :FIXR             ; ELSE LOOK AT NEXT ELEMENT
                    ;
                    ;       FOR VAR # NOT ON STACK ABOVE TOP OR GOSUB
                    ;             [RESTORE TOP OF STACK]
                    ;
B837                :TOP
B837  A5C4              LDA     TEMPA             ; RESTORE TOPRSTK
B839  8590              STA     TOPRSTK           ; X
B83B  A5C5              LDA     TEMPA+1           ; X
B83D  8591              STA     TOPRSTK+1         ; X
B83F  60                RTS
                    ;
                    ;       FOR VAR # FOUND ON STACK
                    ;
B840                :FNVAR
B840  60                RTS
```

POPRSTK — Pop Element from Run Stack

```
                    *       ON EXIT     A - TYPE OF ELEMENT  OR VAR #
                    *                   X - DISPL INTO LINE OF FOR/GOSUB TOKEN
                    *                   CUSET - CARRY SET STACK WAS EMPTY
                    *                   CARRY CLEAR - ENTRY POPED
                    *                   EQ SET - ELEMENT IS GOSUB
                    *                   TSLNUM - LINE #
                    *
B841                XPOP
B841                POPRSTK
                    ;
                    ;       TEST FOR STACK EMPTY
                    ;
B841  A58F              LDA     RUNSTK+1          ; GET START OF RUN STACK HIGH
B843  C591              CMP     TOPRSTK+1         ; IS IT < TOP OF STACK HIGH
B845  9008 ^B84F        BCC     :NTOP             ; IF YES, WE ARE NOT AT TOP
B847  A58E              LDA     RUNSTK            ; GET START OF RUN STACK LOW
B849  C590              CMP     TOPRSTK           ; IS IT < TOP OF STACK LOW
B84B  9002 ^B84F        BCC     :NTOP             ; IF YES, WE ARE NOT AT TOP
                    ;
B84D  38                SEC                       ; ELSE AT TOP: SET CARRY
B84E  60                RTS                       ; RETURN
                    ;
                    ;       GET 4 BYTE HEADER
                    ;             [COMMON TO GOSUB AND FOR]
                    ;
B84F                :NTOP
B84F  A904              LDA     #GFHEAD           ; GET LENGTH OF HEADER
B851  2072B8            JSR     :RCONT            ; TAKE IT OFF STACK
                    ;
B854  A003              LDY     #GFDISP           ; GET INDEX TO SAVED LINE
                                                    DISPL
B856  B190              LDA     [TOPRSTK],Y       ; GET SAVED LINE DISPL
B858  85B2              STA     SVDISP            ; SAVE
B85A  88                DEY                       ; POINT TO LINE # IN HEADER
B85B  B190              LDA     [TOPRSTK],Y       ; GET LINE # HIGH
B85D  85A1              STA     TSLNUM+1          ; SAVE LINE # HIGH
B85F  88                DEY                       ; GET DISPL TO LINE # LOW
```

```
B860  B190            LDA     [TOPRSTK],Y       ; GET LINE # LOW
B862  85A0            STA     TSLNUM            ; SAVE LINE # LOW
                ;
B864  88              DEY                       ; POINT TO TYPE
B865  B190            LDA     [TOPRSTK],Y       ; GET TYPE
B867  F007  ^B870     BEQ     :FND              ; IF TYPE = GOSUB, SET ELEMENT
                ;
                ;       GET 12 BYTE FOR BODY
                ;
B869  48              PHA                       ; SAVE VAR #
B86A  A90C            LDA     #FBODY            ; GET # BYTES TO POP
B86C  2072B8          JSR     :RCONT            ; POP FROM RUN STACK
B86F  68              PLA                       ; GET VAR #
                ;
B870            :FND
B870  18              CLC                       ; CLEAR CARRY [ENTRY POPPED]
B871  60              RTS
```

:RCONT — Contract Run Stack

```
                *       ON ENTRY   A - # OF BYTES TO SUBTRACT
                *
                *
B872            :RCONT
B872  A8              TAY                       ; Y=LENGTH
B873  A290            LDX     #TOPRSTK          ;X = PTR TO RUN STACK
B875  4CFBA8          JMP     CONTLOW
```

:REXPAN — Expand Run Stack

```
                *       ON ENTRY   A - # OF BYTES TO ADD
                *
                *       ON EXIT    ZTEMP1 - OLD TOPRSTK
                *
B878            :REXPAN
B878  2081B8          JSR     :SAVRTOP          ; SAVE RUN STACK TOP
B87B  A8              TAY                       ; Y=LENGTH
B87C  A290            LDX     #TOPRSTK          ; X=PTR TO TOP RUN STACK
B87E  4C7FA8          JMP     EXPLOW            ; GO EXPAND
```

:SAVRTOP — Save Top of Run Stack in ZTEMP1

```
B881            :SAVRTOP
B881  A690            LDX     TOPRSTK           ; SAVE TOPRSTK
B883  86C4            STX     TEMPA             ; X
B885  A691            LDX     TOPRSTK+1         ; X
B887  86C5            STX     TEMPA+1
B889  60              RTS
```

:SAVDEX — Save Line Displacement

```
B88A            :SAVDEX
B88A  A4A8            LDY     STINDEX           ; GET STMT INDEX
B88C  84B3            STY     SAVDEX            ; SAVE IT
B88E  60              RTS
```

:MV6RS — Move 6-Byte Value to Run Stack

```
                *       ON ENTRY   X - LOCATION TO MOVE FROM
                *                  Y- DISPL FROM ZTEMP1 TO MOVE TO
                *                  ZTEMP1 - LOCATION OF RUN STK ELEMENT
                *
B88F            :MV6RS
B88F  A906            LDA     #6                ; GET # OF BYTES TO MOVE
B891  85C6            STA     ZTEMP2            ; SAVE AS COUNTER
B893            :MV
B893  B500            LDA     0,X               ; GET A BYTE
B895  91C4            STA     [TEMPA],Y         ; PUT ON STACK
B897  E8              INX                       ; POINT TO NEXT BYTE
B898  C8              INY                       ; POINT TO NEXT LOCATION
B899  C6C6            DEC     ZTEMP2            ; DEC COUNTER
B89B  D0F6  ^B893     BNE     :MV               ; IF NOT = 0 DO AGAIN
B89D  60              RTS
```

:PL6RS — Pull 6 Bytes from Run Stack to FR1

```
                    *       ON ENTRY   Y = DISPL FROM TOPRSTK TO MOVE FROM
                    *                  TOPRSTK - START OF ELEMENT
                    *
                    *
B89E                :PL6RS
B89E  A906              LDA     #6               ; GET # OF BYTES TO MOVE
B8A0  85C6              STA     ZTEMP2           ; SAVE AS COUNTER
B8A2  A2E0              LDX     #FR1
B8A4                :PL
B8A4  B190              LDA     [TOPRSTK],Y      ; GET A BYTE
B8A6  9500              STA     0,X              ; SAVE IN Z PAGE
B8A8  E8                INX                      ; INC TO NEXT LOCATION
B8A9  C8                INY                      ; INC TO NEXT BYTE
B8AA  C6C6              DEC     ZTEMP2           ; DEC COUNTER
B8AC  D0F6 ^B8A4        BNE     :PL              ; IF NOT =0, DO AGAIN
B8AE  60                RTS
```

RSTPTR — Reset Stack Pointers [STARP and RUNSTK]

```
                    *
B8AF                RSTPTR
B8AF  A58C              LDA     STARP            ; GET BASE OF STR/ARRAY
                                                   SPACE LOW
B8B1  858E              STA     RUNSTK           ; RESET
B8B3  8590              STA     MEMTOP
B8B5  850E              STA     APHM             ; SET APPLICATION HIMEM
B8B7  A58D              LDA     STARP+1          ; GET BASE STR/ARRAY SPACE
                                                   HIGH
B8B9  858F              STA     RUNSTK+1         ; RESET
B8BB  8591              STA     MEMTOP+1         ; X
B8BD  850F              STA     APHM+1           ; SET APPLICATION HIMEM
B8BF  60                RTS
```

ZVAR — Zero Variable

```
B8C0                ZVAR
                    ;
B8C0  A686              LDX     VVTP             ; MOVE VARIABLE TABLE POINTER
B8C2  86F5              STX     ZTEMP1           ; X
B8C4  A487              LDY     VVTP+1           ; X
B8C6  84F6              STY     ZTEMP1+1         ; X
                    ;
                    ;       ARE WE AT END OF TABLE ?
                    ;
B8C8                :ZVAR1
B8C8  A6F6              LDX     ZTEMP1+1         ; GET NEXT VARIABLE ADDR HIGH
B8CA  E489              CPX     ENDVVT+1         ; IS IT < END VALUE HIGH
B8CC  9007 ^B8D5        BCC     :ZVAR2           ; IF YES, MORE TO DO
B8CE  A6F5              LDX     ZTEMP1           ; GET NEXT VARIABLE ADDR LOW
B8D0  E488              CPX     ENDVVT           ; IS IT < END VALUE LOW
B8D2  9001 ^B8D5        BCC     :ZVAR2           ; IF YES, MORE TO DO
B8D4  60                RTS                      ; ELSE, DONE
                    ;
                    ;       ZERO A VARIABLE
                    ;
B8D5                :ZVAR2
B8D5  A000              LDY     #0               ; TURN OFF
B8D7  B1F5              LDA     [ZTEMP1],Y       ; DIM FLAG
B8D9  29FE              AND     #$FE
B8DB  91F5              STA     [ZTEMP1],Y
B8DD  A002              LDY     #2               ; INDEX PAST VARIABLE HEADER
B8DF  A206              LDX     #6               ; GET # OF BYTES TO ZERO
B8E1  A900              LDA     #0               ; CLEAR A
                    ;
B8E3                :ZVAR3
B8E3  91F5              STA     [ZTEMP1],Y       ; ZERO BYTE
B8E5  C8                INY                      ; POINT TO NEXT BYTE
B8E6  CA                DEX                      ; DEC POINTER
B8E7  D0FA ^B8E3        BNE     :ZVAR3           ; IF NOT = 0, ZERO NEXT BYTE
                    ;
```

```
B8E9  A5F5             LDA      ZTEMP1          ; GET CURRENT VARIABLE
                                                  POINTER LOW
B8EB  18               CLC
B8EC  6908             ADC      #8              ; INCR TO NEXT VARIABLE
B8EE  85F5             STA      ZTEMP1          ; SAVE NEW VARIABLE POINTER
                                                  LOW
B8F0  A5F6             LDA      ZTEMP1+1        ; GET CURRENT VARIABLE
                                                  POINTER HIGH
B8F2  6900             ADC      #0              ; ADD IN CARRY
B8F4  85F6             STA      ZTEMP1+1        ; SAVE NEW VARIABLE POINTER
                                                  HIGH
B8F6  D0D0 ^B8C8       BNE      :ZVAR1          ; UNCONDITIONAL BRANCH
```

RUNINIT — Initialize Storage Locations for RUN

```
B8F8             RUNINIT
B8F8  A000             LDY      #0              ; CLEAR A
B8FA  84BA             STY      STOPLN          ; CLEAR LINE # STOPPED AT
B8FC  84BB             STY      STOPLN+1        ; X
B8FE  84B9             STY      ERRNUM          ; CLEAR ERROR #
B900  84FB             STY      RADFLG          ;CLEAR FLAG TOR TRANSENDENTALS
B902  84B6             STY      DATAD           ;CLEAR DATA POINTERS
B904  84B7             STY      DATALN          ;X
B906  84B8             STY      DATALN+1        ;X
B908  88               DEY
B909  84BD             STY      TRAPLN+1        ; SET TRAP FLAG TO NO TRAP
B90B  8411             STY      BRKBYT          ; SET BRK BYTE OFF [$FF]
B90D  4C41BD           JMP      CLSALL          ; GO CLOSE ALL DEVICES
```

TSTEND — Test for End of Statement

```
                 *       ON EXIT     CC SET
                 *                   CARRY SET - END OF STMT
                 *                   CARRY CLEAR - NOT END OF STMT
                 *
                 *
B910             TSTEND
B910  A6A8             LDX      STINDEX
B912  E8               INX
B913  E4A7             CPX      NXTSTD
B915  60               RTS
```

Error Message Routine

Error Messages

```
B916  E6B9       ERRNSF   INC      ERRNUM         ; FILE NOT SAVE FILE
B918  E6B9       ERRDNO   INC      ERRNUM         ; #DN0 > 7
B91A  E6B9       ERRPTL   INC      ERRNUM         ; LOAD PGM TOO BIG
B91C  E6B9       ERSVAL   INC      ERRNUM         ; STRING NOT VALID
B91E  E6B9       XERR     INC      ERRNUM         ;EXECUTION OF GARBAGE
B920  E6B9       ERBRTN   INC      ERRNUM         ; BAD RETURNS
B922  E6B9       ERGFDE   INC      ERRNUM         ; GOSUB/FOR LINE DELETED
B924  E6B9       ERLTL    INC      ERRNUM         ; LINE TO LONG
B926  E6B9       ERNOFOR  INC      ERRNUM         ; NO MATCHING FOR
B928  E6B9       ERNOLN   INC      ERRNUM         ; LINE NOT FOUND [GOSUB/GOTO]
B92A  E6B9       EROVFL   INC      ERRNUM         ; FLOATING POINT OVERFLOW
B92C  E6B9       ERRAOS   INC      ERRNUM         ; ARG STACK OVERFLOW
B92E  E6B9       ERRDIM   INC      ERRNUM         ; ARRAY/STRING DIM ERROR
B930  E6B9       ERRINP   INC      ERRNUM         ; INPUT STMT ERROR
B932  E6B9       ERRLN    INC      ERRNUM         ;VALUE NOT <32768
B934  E6B9       ERROOD   INC      ERRNUM         ; READ OUT OF DATA
B936  E6B9       ERRSSL   INC      ERRNUM         ; STRING LENGTH ERROR
B938  E6B9       ERRVSF   INC      ERRNUM         ; VARIABLE TABLE FULL
B93A  E6B9       ERVAL    INC      ERRNUM         ; VALUE ERROR
B93C  E6B9       MEMFULL  INC      ERRNUM         ; MEMORY FULL
B93E  E6B9       ERON     INC      ERRNUM         ; NO LINE # FOR EXP IN ON
```

Error Routine

```
B940                ERROR
B940  A900              LDA     #0
B942  8DFE02            STA     DSPFLG              ; FLAG
B945  20A7B7            JSR     STOP                ; SET LINE # STOPPED AT
                    ;
B948  A5BD              LDA     TRAPLN+1            ; GET TRAP LINE # HIGH
B94A  3015 ^B961        BMI     :ERRM1              ; IF NO LINE # PRINT MESSAGE.
                    *
                    *       TRAP SET - GO TO SPECIFIED LINE #
                    *
B94C  85A1              STA     TSLNUM+1            ; SET TRAP LINE # HIGH FOR
                                                      GET STMT
B94E  A5BC              LDA     TRAPLN              ; GET TRAP LINE # LOW
B950  85A0              STA     TSLNUM              ; SET FOR GET STMT
B952  A980              LDA     #$80                ; TURN OFF TRAP
B954  85BD              STA     TRAPLN+1
B956  A5B9              LDA     ERRNUM              ; GET ERROR #
B958  85C3              STA     ERRSAV              ; SAVE IT
B95A  A900              LDA     #0                  ; CLEAR
B95C  85B9              STA     ERRNUM              ; ERROR#
B95E  4CAEB6            JMP     XGO1                ; JOIN GOTO
                    ;
                    *
                    *       NO TRAP - PRINT ERROR MESSAGE
                    *
B961                :ERRM1
```

Print Error Message Part 1 [ERR]**

```
B961  206EBD            JSR     PRCR                ; PRINT CR
B964  A937              LDA     #CERR               ; GET TOKEN FOR ERROR
B966  203DB6            JSR     LSTMC               ; GO PRINT CODE
```

Print Error Number

```
B969  A5B9              LDA     ERRNUM              ; GET ERROR #
B96B  85D4              STA     FR0                 ; SET ERROR # OF FR0 AS INTEGER
B96D  A900              LDA     #0                  ; SET ERROR # HIGH
B96F  85D5              STA     FR0+1               ; X
                    ;
B971  209CB9            JSR     :PRINUM             ; GO PRINT ERROR #
                    ;
                    ;
B974                :ERRM2
B974  20E2A9            JSR     TENDST              ; TEST FOR DIRECT STMT
B977  3019 ^B992        BMI     :ERRDONE            ; IF DIRECT STMT, DONE
```

Print Message Part 2 [AT LINE]

```
B979  A9AE              LDA     #:ERRMS&255         ; SET POINTER TO MSG FOR PRINT
B97B  8595              STA     SRCADR              ; X
B97D  A9B9              LDA     #:ERRMS/256         ; X
B97F  8596              STA     SRCADR+1            ; X
                    ;
B981  2035B5            JSR     LPRTOKEN
```

Print Line Number

```
B984  A001              LDY     #1                  ; SET DISPL
B986  B18A              LDA     [STMCUR],Y          ;GET LINE # HIGH
B988  85D5              STA     FR0+1               ; SET IN FR0 FOR CONVERT
B98A  88                DEY                         ; GET CURRENT LINE # LOW
B98B  B18A              LDA     [STMCUR],Y          ;GET UNUSED LINE # LOW
B98D  85D4              STA     FR0                 ; SET IN FR0 LOW FOR CONVERT
                    ;
B98F  209CB9            JSR     :PRINUM             ; PRINT LINE #
                    ;
                    ;
                    ;
```

```
B992                  :ERRDONE
B992   206EBD            JSR      PRCR             ; PRINT CR
B995   A900              LDA      #0               ; CLEAR A
B997   85B9              STA      ERRNUM           ; CLEAR ERROR #
B999   4C60A0            JMP      SYNTAX
```

Print Integer Number in FR0

```
B99C                  :PRINUM
B99C   20AAD9            JSR      CVIFP            ; CONVERT TO FLOATING POINT
B99F   20E6D8            JSR      CVFASC           ; CONVERT TO ASCII
                      ;
B9A2   A5F3              LDA      INBUFF           ; GET ADR OF # LOW
B9A4   8595              STA      SRCADR           ; SET FOR PRINT ROUTINE
B9A6   A5F4              LDA      INBUFF+1         ; GET ADR OF # HIGH
B9A8   8596              STA      SRCADR+1         ; SET FOR PRINT ROUTINE
B9AA   2035B5            JSR      LPRTOKEN         ; GO PRINT ERROR #
B9AD   60                RTS
                      ;
                      ;
                      ;
B9AE   204154204C     :ERRMS  DC       ' AT LINE '
       494E45A0
```

Execute Graphics Routines

XSETCOLOR — Execute SET COLOR

```
B9B7                  XSETCOLOR
B9B7   20E9AB            JSR      GET1INT          ; GET REGISTER #
B9BA   A5D4              LDA      FR0              ; GET #
B9BC   C905              CMP      #5               ; IS IT <5?
B9BE   B01A ^B9DA        BCS      :ERCOL           ; IF NOT, ERROR
B9C0   48                PHA                       ; SAVE
                      ;
B9C1   20E0AB            JSR      GETINT           ; GET VALUE
                      ;
B9C4   A5D4              LDA      FR0              ; GET VALUE*16+6
B9C6                     ASLA                      ; X
B9C6 +0A                 ASL      A
B9C7                     ASLA                      ; X
B9C7 +0A                 ASL      A
B9C8                     ASLA                      ; X
B9C8 +0A                 ASL      A
B9C9                     ASLA                      ; X
B9C9 +0A                 ASL      A
B9CA   48                PHA                       ; SAVE ON STACKS
B9CB   20E0AB            JSR      GETINT           ; GET VALUE 3
B9CE   68                PLA                       ; GET VALUE 2*16 FROM STACK
B9CF   18                CLC
B9D0   65D4              ADC      FR0              ; ADD IN VALUE 3
B9D2   A8                TAY                       ; SAVE VALUE 2*16 + VALUE 5
B9D3   68                PLA                       ; GET INDEX
B9D4   AA                TAX                       ; PUT IN X
B9D5   98                TYA                       ; GET VALUE
                      ;
B9D6   9DC402            STA      CREGS,X          ;SET VALUE IN REGS
B9D9   60                RTS
                      ;
                      ;
B9DA                  :ERSND
B9DA                  :ERCOL
B9DA   203AB9            JSR      ERVAL
```

XSOUND — Execute SOUND

```
B9DD                  XSOUND
B9DD   20E9AB            JSR      GET1INT          ; GET 1 BYTE INTEGER
B9E0   A5D4              LDA      FR0              ; X
B9E2   C904              CMP      #4               ; IS IT <4?
B9E4   B0F4 ^B9DA        BCS      :ERSND           ; IF NOT, ERROR
```

```
                     ;
B9E6                       ASLA                    ; GET VALUE *2
B9E6 +ØA                   ASL     A
B9E7  48                   PHA
                     ;
B9E8  A9ØØ                 LDA     #Ø              ; SET TO ZERO
B9EA  8DØ8D2               STA     SREG1           ; X
                     ;
B9ED  A9Ø3                 LDA     #3
B9EF  8DØFD2               STA     SKCTL
                     ;
B9F2  2ØEØAB               JSR     GETINT          ; GET EXP2
B9F5  68                   PLA                     ; GET INDEX
B9F6  48                   PHA                     ; SAVE AGAIN
B9F7  AA                   TAX                     ; PUT IN INDEX REG
B9F8  A5D4                 LDA     FRØ             ; GET VALUE
B9FA  9DØØD2               STA     SREG2,X         ; SAVE IT
                     ;
B9FD  2ØEØAB               JSR     GETINT          ; GET EXP3
BAØØ  A5D4                 LDA     FRØ             ; GET 16*EXP3
BAØ2                       ASLA                    ; X
BAØ2 +ØA                   ASL     A
BAØ3                       ASLA                    ; X
BAØ3 +ØA                   ASL     A
BAØ4                       ASLA                    ; X
BAØ4 +ØA                   ASL     A
BAØ5                       ASLA                    ; X
BAØ5 +ØA                   ASL     A
BAØ6  48                   PHA                     ; SAVE IT
                     ;
BAØ7  2ØEØAB               JSR     GETINT          ; GET EXP4
BAØA  68                   PLA                     ; GET 16*EXP3
BAØB  A8                   TAY                     ; SAVE IT
BAØC  68                   PLA                     ; GET INDEX
BAØD  AA                   TAX                     ; PUT IN X
BAØE  98                   TYA                     ; GET EXP3*16
BAØF  18                   CLC
BA1Ø  65D4                 ADC     FRØ             ; GET 16*EXP3+EXP4
BA12  9DØ1D2               STA     SREG3,X         ; STORE IT
BA15  6Ø                   RTS
```

XPOS — Execute POSITION

```
BA16                 XPOS
BA16  2ØEØAB               JSR     GETINT          ; GET INTEGER INTO FRØ
BA19  A5D4                 LDA     FRØ             ; SET X VALUE
BA1B  8555                 STA     SCRX            ; X
BA1D  A5D5                 LDA     FRØ+1           ; X
BA1F  8556                 STA     SCRX+1          ; X
                     ;
BA21  2ØE9AB               JSR     GET1INT         ; SET Y VALUE
BA24  A5D4                 LDA     FRØ             ; X
BA26  8554                 STA     SCRY            ; X
BA28  6Ø                   RTS
```

XCOLOR — Execute COLOR

```
BA29                 XCOLOR
BA29  2ØEØAB               JSR     GETINT          ; GET INTEGER INTO FRØ
BA2C  A5D4                 LDA     FRØ
BA2E  85C8                 STA     COLOR
BA3Ø  6Ø                   RTS
```

XDRAWTO — Execute DRAWTO

```
BA31                 XDRAWTO
BA31  2Ø16BA               JSR     XPOS            ; GET X,Y POSITION
BA34  A5C8                 LDA     COLOR           ; GET COLOR

BA36  8DFBØ2               STA     SVCOLOR         ; SET IT
                     ;
```

```
BA39  A911        LDA    #ICDRAW          ; GET COMMAND
BA3B  A2Ø6        LDX    #6               ; SET DEVICE
BA3D  2ØC4BA      JSR    GLPCX            ; SET THEM
            ;
BA4Ø  A9ØC        LDA    #$ØC             ; SET AUX 1
BA42  9D4AØ3      STA    ICAUX1,X
BA45  A9ØØ        LDA    #Ø               ; SET AUX 2
BA47  9D4BØ3      STA    ICAUX2,X
BA4A  2Ø24BD      JSR    IO7
BA4D  4CB3BC      JMP    IOTEST
```

XGR — Execute GRAPHICS

```
BA5Ø        XGR
BA5Ø  A2Ø6        LDX    #6               ; GET DEVICE
BA52  86C1        STX    IODVC            ;SAVE DEVICE #
BA54  2ØF1BC      JSR    CLSYS1           ; GO CLOSE IT
BA57  2ØEØAB      JSR    GETINT           ; GET INTEGER INTO FRØ
            ;
BA5A  A273        LDX    #SSTR&255        ; SET INBUFF TO POINT
BA5C  AØBA        LDY    #SSTR/256        ; TO FILE SPEC STRING
BA5E  86F3        STX    INBUFF           ; X
BA6Ø  84F4        STY    INBUFF+1         ; X
            ;
BA62  A2Ø6        LDX    #6               ; GET DEVICE #
BA64  A5D4        LDA    FRØ              ;SET SOME BITS FOR GRAPHICS
BA66  29FØ        AND    #$FØ             ;
BA68  491C        EOR    #ICGR            ;
BA6A  A8          TAY                     ;
BA6B  A5D4        LDA    FRØ              ; GET AUX2 [GRAPHICS TYPE]
BA6D  2ØD1BB      JSR    SOPEN            ; OPEN
BA7Ø  4CB3BC      JMP    IOTEST           ; TEST I/O OK
            ;
            ;
            ;
BA73  533A9B      SSTR   DB     'S:',CR
```

XPLOT — Execute PLOT

```
BA76        XPLOT
BA76  2Ø16BA      JSR    XPOS             ; SET X,Y POSITION
            ;
BA79  A5C8        LDA    COLOR            ; GET COLOR
BA7B  A2Ø6        LDX    #6               ; GET DEVICE #
BA7D  4CA1BA      JMP    PRCX             ; GO PRINT IT
```

Input/Output Routines

```
BA8Ø              LOCAL
```

GETLINE — Get a Line of Input

```
            ;     GLINE - GET LINE [PROMPT ONLY]
            ;     GNLINE - GET NEW LINE [CR, PROMPT]
            ;
BA8Ø        GNLINE
BA8Ø  A6B4        LDX    ENTDTD           ; IF ENTER DEVICE NOT ZERO
BA82  DØØE ^BA92  BNE    GLGO             ; THEN DO PROMPT
BA84  A99B        LDA    #CR              ; PUT EOL
BA86  2Ø9FBA      JSR    PUTCHAR
            ;
BA89        GLINE
BA89  A6B4        LDX    ENTDTD           ; IF ENTER DEVICE NOT ZERO
BA8B  DØØ5 ^BA92  BNE    GLGO             ; THEN DON'T PROMPT
BA8D  A5C2        LDA    PROMPT           ; PUT PROMPT
BA8F  2Ø9FBA      JSR    PUTCHAR
            ;
BA92        GLGO
BA92  A6B4        LDX    ENTDTD
BA94  A9Ø5        LDA    #ICGTR
```

```
BA96  20C4BA          JSR     GLPCX
BA99  200ABD          JSR     IO1              ; GO DO I/O
BA9C  4CB3BC          JMP     IOTEST           ; GO TEST RESULT
```

PUTCHAR — Put One Character to List Device

```
BA9F                PRCHAR
BA9F                PUTCHAR
BA9F  A6B5              LDX     LISTDTD          ; GET LIST DEVICE
BAA1                PRCX
BAA1  48                PHA                      ; SAVE IO BYTE
BAA2  20C6BA            JSR     GLPX             ; SET DEVICE
                    ;
BAA5  BD4A03            LDA     ICAUX1,X         ; SET UP ZERO PAGE IOCB
BAA8  852A              STA     ICAUX1-IOCB+ZICB ; X
BAAA  BD4B03            LDA     ICAUX2,X         ; X
BAAD  852B              STA     ICAUX2-IOCB+ZICB ; X
                    ;
BAAF  68                PLA
BAB0  A8                TAY
BAB1  20B8BA            JSR     :PDUM
                    ;
                    ;       RETURN HERE FROM ROUTINE
BAB4  98                TYA                      ; TEST STATUS
BAB5  4CB6BC            JMP     IOTES2
                    ;
                    ;
BAB8                :PDUM
BAB8  BD4703            LDA     ICPUT+1,X        ; GO TO PUT ROUTINE
BABB  48                PHA                      ; X
BABC  BD4603            LDA     ICPUT,X          ; X
BABF  48                PHA                      ; X
BAC0  98                TYA                      ; X
BAC1  A092              LDY     #$92             ;LOAD VALUE FOR CIO ROUTINE
BAC3  60                RTS
                    ;
BAC4  85C0          GLPCX   STA     IOCMD
BAC6                GLPX
BAC6  86C1              STX     IODVC            ; AS I/O DEVICE
BAC8  4CA6BC            JMP     LDDVX            ; LOAD DEVICE X
```

XENTER — Execute ENTER

```
BACB                XENTER
BACB  A904              LDA     #$04             ; OPEN INPUT
BACD  20DDBA            JSR     ELADVC           ; GO OPEN ALT DEVICE
BAD0  85B4              STA     ENTDTD           ; SET ENTER DEVICE
BAD2  4C60A0            JMP     SYNTAX
```

FLIST — Open LIST File

```
BAD5                FLIST
BAD5  A908              LDA     #$08             ; OPEN OUTPUT
BAD7  20DDBA            JSR     ELADVC           ; GO OPEN ALT DEVICE
BADA  85B5              STA     LISTDTD          ; SET LIST DEVICE
BADC  60                RTS                      ; DONE
                    ;
BADD                ELADVC
BADD  48                PHA
BADE  A007              LDY     #7               ; USE DEVICE 7
BAE0  84C1              STY     IODVC            ; SET DEVICE
                    ;
BAE2  20A6BC            JSR     LDDVX            ;BEFORE
BAE5  A90C              LDA     #ICCLOSE         ;GO CLOSE DEVICE
BAE7  2026BD            JSR     IO8              ;OPEN OF NEW ONE
                    ;
BAEA  A003              LDY     #ICOIO           ; CMD IS OPEN
BAEC  84C0              STY     IOCMD            ;
BAEE  68                PLA
BAEF  A000              LDY     #0               ; GET AUX2
BAF1  20FBBB            JSR     XOP2             ; GO OPEN
```

```
BAF4  A9Ø7               LDA     #7               ; LOAD DEVICE
BAF6  6Ø                 RTS                      ; AND RETURN
```

RUN from File

```
BAF7  A9FF         FRUN     LDA      #$FF         ; SET RUN MODE
BAF9  DØØ2 ^BAFD            BNE     :LDØ
```

XLOAD — Execute LOAD Command

```
BAFB               XLOAD
BAFB  A9ØØ                  LDA     #Ø               ; SET LOAD MODE
BAFD  48           :LDØ     PHA                      ; SAVE R/L TYPE
BAFE  A9Ø4                  LDA     #Ø4              ; GO OPEN FOR INPUT
BBØØ  2ØDDBA                JSR     ELADVC           ; THE SPECIFIED DEVICE
BBØ3  68                    PLA                      ; GET R/L TYPE
                   ;
BBØ4               XLOAD1
BBØ4  48                    PHA                      ; SAVE R/L TYPE
BBØ5  A9Ø7                  LDA     #ICGTC           ; CMD IS GET TEXT CHARS
BBØ7  85CØ                  STA     IOCMD
BBØ9  85CA                  STA     LOADFLG          ; SET LOAD IN PROGRESS
                   ;
BBØB  2ØA6BC                JSR     LDDVX            ; LOAD DEVICE X REG
BBØE  AØØE                  LDY     #ENDSTAR-OUTBUFF ; Y=REC LENGTH
BB1Ø  2Ø1ØBD                JSR     IO3              ; GO GET TABLE BLOCK
BB13  2ØB3BC                JSR     IOTEST           ; TEST I/O
BB16  AD8ØØ5                LDA     MISCRAM+OUTBUFF  ; IF FIRST 2
BB19  ØD81Ø5                ORA     MISCRAM+OUTBUFF+1 ; BYTES NOT ZERO
BB1C  DØ38 ^BB56            BNE     :LDFER           ; THEN NOT SAVE FILE
                   ;
BB1E  A28C                  LDX     #STARP           ; START AT STARP DISPL
BB2Ø  18           :LD1     CLC
BB21  A58Ø                  LDA     OUTBUFF          ; ADD LOMEM TO
BB23  7DØØØ5                ADC     MISCRAM,X        ; LOAD TABLE DISPL
BB26  A8                    TAY
BB27  A581                  LDA     OUTBUFF+1
BB29  7DØ1Ø5                ADC     MISCRAM+1,X
                   ;
BB2C  CDE6Ø2                CMP     HIMEM+1          ; IF NEW VALUE NOT
BB2F  9ØØA ^BB3B            BCC     :LD3             ; LESS THEN HIMEM
BB31  DØØ5 ^BB38            BNE     :LD2             ; THEN ERROR
BB33  CCE5Ø2                CPY     HIMEM
BB36  9ØØ3 ^BB3B            BCC     :LD3
BB38  4C1AB9       :LD2     JMP      ERRPTL
                   ;
BB3B  95Ø1         :LD3     STA      1,X             ; ELSE SET NEW TABLE VALUE
BB3D  94ØØ                  STY     Ø,X
BB3F  CA                    DEX                      ; DECREMENT TO PREVIOUS TBL
                                                       ENTRY
BB4Ø  CA                    DEX
BB41  EØ82                  CPX     #VNTP            ; IF NOT AT LOWER ENTRY
BB43  BØDB ^BB2Ø            BCS     :LD1             ; THEN CONTINUE
                   ;
BB45  2Ø88BB                JSR     :LSBLK           ; LOAD USER AREA
BB48  2Ø66B7                JSR     XCLR             ; EXECUTE CLEAR
BB4B  A9ØØ                  LDA     #Ø               ; RESET LOAD IN PROGRESS
BB4D  85CA                  STA     LOADFLG          ; X
BB4F  68                    PLA                      ; LOAD R/S STATUS
BB5Ø  FØØ1 ^BB53            BEQ     :LD4             ; BR IF LOAD
BB52  6Ø                    RTS                      ; RETURN TO RUN
BB53               :LD4
BB53  4C5ØAØ                JMP     SNX1             ;GO TO SYNTAX
                   ;
BB56               :LDFER
BB56  A9ØØ                  LDA     #Ø               ; RESET LOAD IN PROGRESS
BB58  85CA                  STA     LOADFLG          ; X
BB5A  2Ø16B9                JSR     ERRNSF           ; NOT SAVE FILE
```

XSAVE — Execute SAVE Command

```
BB5D                XSAVE
BB5D  A9Ø8              LDA     #Ø8                ; GO OPEN FOR OUTPUT
BB5F  2ØDDBA            JSR     ELADVC             ; THE SPECIFIED DEVICE
                    ;
BB62                XSAVE1
BB62  A9ØB              LDA     #ICPTC             ; I/O CMD IS PUT TEXT CHARS
BB64  85CØ              STA     IOCMD              ; SET I/O CMD
                    ;
BB66  A28Ø              LDX     #OUTBUFF           ; MOVE RAM TABLE PTRS
BB68  38            :SV1    SEC                    ; [OUTBUFF THRU ENSTAR]
BB69  B5ØØ              LDA     Ø,X                ; TO LBUFF
BB6B  E58Ø              SBC     OUTBUFF            ; AS DISPLACEMENT
BB6D  9DØØØ5            STA     MISCRAM,X          ; FROM LOW MEM
BB7Ø  E8                INX
BB71  B5ØØ              LDA     Ø,X
BB73  E581              SBC     OUTBUFF+1
BB75  9DØØØ5            STA     MISCRAM,X
BB78  E8                INX
BB79  EØ8E              CPX     #ENDSTAR
BB7B  9ØEB ^BB68        BCC     :SV1
                    ;
BB7D  2ØA6BC            JSR     LDDVX              ; OUTPUT LBUFF
BB8Ø  AØØE              LDY     #ENDSTAR-OUTBUFF   ; FOR PROPER LENGTH
BB82  2Ø1ØBD            JSR     IO3
BB85  2ØB3BC            JSR     IOTEST             ; TEST GOOD I/O
```

LSBLK — LOAD or SAVE User Area as a Block

```
BB88                :LSBLK
BB88  2ØA6BC            JSR     LDDVX              ; LOAD DEVICE X REG
BB8B  A582              LDA     VNTP               ; SET VAR NAME TBL PTR
BB8D  85F3              STA     INBUFF             ; AS START OF BLOCK ADR
BB8F  A583              LDA     VNTP+1
BB91  85F4              STA     INBUFF+1
BB93  AC8DØ5            LDY     MISCRAM+STARP+1    ; A,Y = BLOCK LENGTH
BB96  88                DEY
BB97  98                TYA
BB98  AC8CØ5            LDY     MISCRAM+STARP
BB9B  2Ø12BD            JSR     IO4                ; GO DO BLOCK I/O
BB9E  2ØB3BC            JSR     IOTEST
BBA1  4CF1BC            JMP     CLSYS1             ;GO CLOSE DEVICE
                    ;
```

XCSAVE — Execute CSAVE

```
BBA4                XCSAVE
BBA4  A9Ø8              LDA     #8                 ; GET OPEN FOR OUTPUT
BBA6  2ØB6BB            JSR     COPEN              ; OPEN CASSETTE
                    ;
BBA9  4C62BB            JMP     XSAVE1             ; DO SAVE
```

XCLOAD — Execute CLOAD

```
BBAC                XCLOAD
BBAC  A9Ø4              LDA     #4                 ; GET OPEN FOR OUTPUT
BBAE  2ØB6BB            JSR     COPEN              ; OPEN CASSETTE
                    ;
BBB1  A9ØØ              LDA     #Ø                 ; GET LOAD TYPE
BBB3  4CØ4BB            JMP     XLOAD1             ; DO LOAD
                    ;
```

COPEN — OPEN Cassette

```
                    *       ON ENTRY:  A - TYPE OF OPEN [IN OR OUT]
                    *       ON EXIT:   A - DEVICE #7
                    *
BBB6                COPEN
BBB6  48                PHA                        ;
BBB7  A2CE              LDX     #:CSTR&255
BBB9  86F3              STX     INBUFF
```

```
BBBB  A2BB                LDX     #:CSTR/256
BBBD  86F4                STX     INBUFF+1
                    ;
BBBF  A207                LDX     #7
BBC1  68                  PLA
BBC2  A8                  TAY                       ; SET COMMAND TYPE
BBC3  A980                LDA     #$80              ; GET AUX 2
                    ;
BBC5  20D1BB              JSR     SOPEN             ; GO OPEN
BBC8  20B3BC              JSR     IOTEST
BBCB  A907                LDA     #7                ; GET DEVICE
BBCD  60                  RTS
                    ;
                    ;
                    ;
BBCE  433A9B        :CSTR    DB        'C:',CR
```

SOPEN — OPEN System Device

```
                    *       ON ENTRY    X - DEVICE
                    *                   Y - AUX1
                    *                   A - AUX2
                    *                   INBUFF - POINTS TO FILE SPEC
                    *
BBD1                SOPEN
BBD1  48                  PHA                       ; SAVE AUX2
BBD2  A903                LDA     #ICOIO            ; GET COMMAND
BBD4  20C4BA              JSR     GLPCX             ; GET DEVICE/COMMAND
BBD7  68                  PLA                       ; SET AUX2 & AUX 1
BBD8  9D4B03              STA     ICAUX2,X          ; X
BBDB  98                  TYA
BBDC  9D4A03              STA     ICAUX1,X
                    ;
BBDF  2019BD              JSR     IO5               ; DO COMMAND
BBE2  4C51DA              JMP     INTLBF            ; RESET INBUFF
```

XXIO — Execute XIO Statement

```
BBE5                XXIO
BBE5  2004BD              JSR     GIOCMD            ; GET THE COMMAND BYTE
BBE8  4CEDBB              JMP     XOP1              ; CONTINUE AS IF OPEN
```

XOPEN — Execute OPEN Statement

```
BBEB                XOPEN
BBEB  A903                LDA     #ICOIO            ; LOAD OPEN CODE
BBED  85C0          XOP1      STA       IOCMD
BBEF  209FBC              JSR     GIODVC            ; GET DEVICE
                    ;
BBF2  2004BD              JSR     GIOCMD            ; GET AUX1
BBF5  48                  PHA
BBF6  2004BD              JSR     GIOCMD            ; GET AUX2
BBF9  A8                  TAY                       ; AUX2 IN Y
BBFA  68                  PLA                       ; AUX1 IN A
BBFB                XOP2
BBFB  48                  PHA                       ; SAVE AUX1
BBFC  98                  TYA
BBFD  48                  PHA                       ; SAVE AUX2
                    ;
BBFE  20E0AA              JSR     EXEXPR            ; GET FS STRING
BC01  2079BD              JSR     SETSEOL           ; GIVE STRING AN EOL
                    ;
BC04  20A6BC              JSR     LDDVX             ; LOAD DEVICE X REG
BC07  68                  PLA
BC08  9D4B03              STA     ICAUX2,X          ; SET AUX 2
BC0B  68                  PLA                       ; GET AUX 1
BC0C  9D4A03              STA     ICAUX1,X          ;
BC0F  200ABD              JSR     IO1               ; GO DO I/O
                    ;
BC12  2099BD              JSR     RSTSEOL           ; RESTORE STRING EOL
```

```
BC15  2051DA          JSR     INTLBF
BC18  4CB3BC          JMP     IOTEST             ; GO TEST I/O STATUS
```

XCLOSE — Execute CLOSE

```
BC1B                XCLOSE
BC1B  A90C            LDA     #ICCLOSE           ; CLOSE CMD
```

GDVCIO — General Device I/O

```
BC1D                GDVCIO
BC1D  85C0            STA     IOCMD              ; SET CMD
BC1F  209FBC          JSR     GIODVC             ; GET DEVICE
BC22  2024BD        GDIO1   JSR    IO7           ; GO DO I/O
BC25  4CB3BC          JMP     IOTEST             ; GO TEST STATUS
```

XSTATUS — Execute STATUS

```
BC28                XSTATUS
BC28  209FBC          JSR     GIODVC             ; GET DEVICE
BC2B  A90D            LDA     #ICSTAT            ; STATUS CMD
BC2D  2026BD          JSR     IO8                ; GO GET STATUS
BC30  20FBBC          JSR     LDIOSTA            ; LOAD STATUS
BC33  4C2DBD          JMP     ISVAR1             ; GO SET VAR
```

XNOTE — Execute NOTE

```
BC36                XNOTE
BC36  A926            LDA     #$26               ; NOTE CMD
BC38  201DBC          JSR     GDVCIO             ; GO DO
BC3B  BD4C03          LDA     ICAUX3,X           ; GET SECTOR N/. LOW
BC3E  BC4D03          LDY     ICAUX4,X           ; AND HI
BC41  202FBD          JSR     ISVAR              ; GO SET VAR
BC44  20A6BC          JSR     LDDVX              ; GET DEVICE X REG
BC47  BD4E03          LDA     ICAUX5,X           ; GET DATA LENGTH
BC4A  4C2DBD          JMP     ISVAR1             ; GO SET VAR
```

XPOINT — Execute POINT

```
BC4D                XPOINT
BC4D  209FBC          JSR     GIODVC             ; GET I/O DEVICE NO.
BC50  20D5AB          JSR     GETPINT            ; GET SECTOR NO.
BC53  20A6BC          JSR     LDDVX              ; GET DEVICE X
BC56  A5D4            LDA     FR0                ; SET SECTOR NO.
BC58  9D4C03          STA     ICAUX3,X
BC5B  A5D5            LDA     FR0+1
BC5D  9D4D03          STA     ICAUX4,X
BC60  20D5AB          JSR     GETPINT            ; GET DATA LENGTH
BC63  20A6BC          JSR     LDDVX              ; LOAD DEVICE X
BC66  A5D4            LDA     FR0                ; GET AL
BC68  9D4E03          STA     ICAUX5,X           ; SET DATA LENGTH
BC6B  A925            LDA     #$25               ; SET POINT CMD
BC6D  85C0            STA     IOCMD
BC6F  4C22BC          JMP     GDIO1              ; GO DO
```

XPUT — Execute PUT

```
BC72                XPUT
BC72  209FBC          JSR     GIODVC             ; GET DEVICE #
                    ;
BC75  20E0AB          JSR     GETINT             ; GET DATA
BC78  A5D4            LDA     FR0                ; X
BC7A  A6C1            LDX     IODVC              ; LOAD DEVICE #
BC7C  4CA1BA          JMP     PRCX               ; GO PRINT
```

XGET — Execute GET

```
BC7F                XGET
BC7F  209FBC          JSR     GIODVC             ; GET DEVICE
                    ;
BC82                GET1
BC82  A907            LDA     #ICGTC             ; GET COMMAND
BC84  85C0            STA     IOCMD              ; SET COMMAND
```

```
BC86  A001              LDY     #1              ; SET BUFF LENGTH=1
BC88  2010BD            JSR     IO3             ; DO IO
BC8B  20B3BC            JSR     IOTEST          ; TEST I/O
BC8E  A000              LDY     #0              ; GET CHAR
BC90  B1F3              LDA     [INBUFF],Y      ; X
BC92  4C2DBD            JMP     ISVAR1          ; ASSIGN VAR
```

XLOCATE — Execute LOCATE

```
BC95              XLOCATE
BC95  2016BA            JSR     XPOS            ; GET X,Y POSITION
BC98  A206              LDX     #6              ; GET DEVICE #
BC9A  20C6BA            JSR     GLPX            ; X
                  ;
BC9D  D0E3 ^BC82        BNE     GET1            ; GO GET
```

GIODVC — Get I/O Device Number

```
BC9F              GIODVC
BC9F  2002BD            JSR     GIOPRM          ; GET PARM
BCA2  85C1              STA     IODVC           ; SET AS DEVICE
BCA4  F00A ^BCB0        BEQ     DNERR           ; BR IF DVC=0
```

LDDVX — Load X Register with I/O Device Offset

```
BCA6              LDDVX
BCA6  A5C1              LDA     IODVC           ; GET DEVICE
BCA8                    ASLA                    ; MULT BY 16
BCA8 +0A                ASL     A
BCA9                    ASLA
BCA9 +0A                ASL     A
BCAA                    ASLA
BCAA +0A                ASL     A
BCAB                    ASLA
BCAB +0A                ASL     A
BCAC  AA                TAX                     ; PUT INTO X
BCAD  3001 ^BCB0        BMI     DNERR           ; BR DN0>7
BCAF  60                RTS                     ; AND RETURN
BCB0  2018B9      DNERR JSR     ERRDNO
```

IOTEST — Test I/O Status

```
BCB3              IOTEST
BCB3  20FBBC            JSR     LDIOSTA         ; LOAD I/O STATUS
BCB6              IOTES2
BCB6  3001 ^BCB9        BMI     SICKIO          ; BR IF BAD
BCB8  60                RTS                     ; ELSE RETURN
BCB9              SICKIO
BCB9  A000              LDY     #0              ; RESET DISPLAY FLAG
BCBB  8CFE02            STY     DSPFLG
                  ;
BCBE  C980              CMP     #ICSBRK         ; IF BREAK
BCC0  D00A ^BCCC        BNE     :SIO1           ; SIMULATE ASYNC
BCC2  8411              STY     BRKBYT          ; BREAK
BCC4  A5CA              LDA     LOADFLG         ;IF LOAD FLAG SET
BCC6  F003 ^BCCB        BEQ     :SIOS           ;
BCC8  4C00A0            JMP     COLDSTART       ;DO COLDSTART
BCCB              :SIOS
BCCB  60                RTS
                  ;
BCCC  A4C1        :SIO1 LDY     IODVC           ; PRE-LOAD I/O DEVICE
BCCE  C988              CMP     #$88            ; WAS ERROR EOF
BCD0  F00F ^BCE1        BEQ     :SIO4           ; BR IF EOF
BCD2  85B9        :SIO2 STA     ERRNUM          ; SET ERROR NUMBER
                  ;
BCD4  C007              CPY     #7              ; WAS THIS DEVICE #7
BCD6  D003 ^BCDB        BNE     :SIO3           ; BR IF NOT
BCD8  20F1BC            JSR     CLSYSD          ; CLOSE DEVICE 7
                  ;
BCDB  2072BD      :SIO3 JSR     SETDZ           ; SET L/D DEVICE = 0
BCDE  4C40B9            JMP     ERROR           ; REPORT ERROR
                  ;
```

```
BCE1  C007          :SIO4   CPY    #7           ; WAS EOF ON DEVICE 7
BCE3  D0ED ^BCD2       BNE    :SIO2             ; BR IF NOT
BCE5  A25D             LDX    #EPCHAR           ; WERE WE IN ENTER
BCE7  E4C2             CPX    PROMPT            ;
BCE9  D0E7 ^BCD2       BNE    :SIO2             ; BR NOT ENTER
BCEB  20F1BC           JSR    CLSYSD            ; CLOSE DEVICE 7
BCEE  4C53A0           JMP    SNX2              ; GO TO SYNTAX
                    ;
```

CLSYSD — Close System Device

```
BCF1                CLSYSD
                    ;
BCF1  20A6BC        CLSYS1  JSR    LDDVX
BCF4  F00B ^BD01       BEQ    NOCD0             ; DON'T CLOSE DEVICE0
BCF6  A90C             LDA    #ICCLOSE          ; LOAD CLOSE CORD
BCF8  4C26BD           JMP    IO8               ; GO CLOSE
```

LDIOSTA — Load I/O Status

```
BCFB                LDIOSTA
BCFB  20A6BC           JSR    LDDVX             ; GET DEVICE X REG
BCFE  BD4303           LDA    ICSTA,X           ; GET STATUS
BD01                NOCD0
BD01  60               RTS                      ; RETURN
```

GIOPRM — Get I/O Parameters

```
BD02                GIOPRM
BD02  E6A8             INC    STINDEX           ; SKIP OVER #
BD04  20D5AB        GIOCMD  JSR    GETPINT      ; GET POSITIVE INT
BD07  A5D4             LDA    FR0               ; MOVE LOW BYTE TO
BD09  60               RTS
```

I/O Call Routine

```
BD0A  A0FF          IO1     LDY    #255         ;BUFL = 255
BD0C  D002 ^BD10       BNE    IO3
BD0E  A000          IO2     LDY    #0           ; BUFL = 0
BD10  A900          IO3     LDA    #0           ; BUFL < 256
BD12  9D4903        IO4     STA    ICBLH,X      ; SET BUFL
BD15  98               TYA
BD16  9D4803           STA    ICBLL,X
BD19  A5F4          IO5     LDA    INBUFF+1     ; LOAD INBUFF VALUE
BD1B  A4F3             LDY    INBUFF
BD1D  9D4503        IO6     STA    ICBAH,X      ; SE BUF ADR
BD20  98               TYA
BD21  9D4403           STA    ICBAL,X
BD24  A5C0          IO7     LDA    IOCMD        ; LOAD COMMAND
BD26  9D4203        IO8     STA    ICCOM,X      ; SET COMMAND
BD29  2056E4           JSR    CIO               ;GO DO I/O
BD2C  60               RTS                      ; DONE
```

ISVAR — I/O Variable Set

```
BD2D                ISVAR1
BD2D  A000             LDY    #0                ; GET HIGH ORDER BYTE
BD2F                ISVAR
BD2F  48               PHA                      ; PUSH INT VALUE LOW
BD30  98               TYA
BD31  48               PHA                      ; PUSH INT VALUE HI
BD32  200FAC           JSR    POP1              ; GET VARIABLE
BD35  68               PLA
BD36  85D5             STA    FR0+1             ; SET VALUE LOW
BD38  68               PLA
BD39  85D4             STA    FR0               ; SET VALUE HI
BD3B  20AAD9           JSR    CVIFP             ; CONVERT TO FP
BD3E  4C16AC           JMP    RTNVAR            ; AND RETURN TO TABLE
```

CLSALL — CLOSE All IOCBs [except 0]

```
BD41                 CLSALL
                     ;
                     ; TURN OFF SOUND
                     ;
BD41  A900               LDA     #0
BD43  A207               LDX     #7
BD45                 :CL
BD45  9D00D2             STA     SREG3-1,X
BD48  CA                 DEX
BD49  D0FA ^BD45         BNE     :CL
                     ;
BD4B  A007               LDY     #7              ; START AT DEVICE 7
BD4D  84C1               STY     IODVC
BD4F  20F1BC         CLALL1  JSR     CLSYSD      ; CLOSE DEVICE
BD52  C6C1               DEC     IODVC           ; DEC DEVICE #
BD54  D0F9 ^BD4F         BNE     CLALL1          ; BR IF NOT ZERO
BD56  60                 RTS
```

PREADY — Print READY Message

```
BD57                 PREADY
BD57  A206               LDX     #RML-1          ; GET READY MSG LENGTH-1
BD59  86F2           PRDY1   STX     CIX         ; SET LEN REM
BD5B  BD67BD             LDA     RMSG,X          ; GET CHAR
BD5E  209FBA             JSR     PRCHAR          ; PRINT IT
BD61  A6F2               LDX     CIX             ; GET LENGTH
BD63  CA                 DEX
BD64  10F3 ^BD59         BPL     PRDY1           ; BR IF MORE
BD66  60                 RTS
BD67  9B59444145     RMSG    DB      CR,'YDAER',CR
      529B
      = 0007         RML     EQU     *-RMSG
```

PRCR — Print Carriage Return

```
BD6E  A200           PRCR    LDX     #0          ; SET FOR LAST CHAR
BD70  F0E7 ^BD59         BEQ     PRDY1           ; AND GO DO IT
```

SETDZ — Set Device 0 as LIST/ENTER Device

```
BD72  A900           SETDZ   LDA     #0
BD74  85B4               STA     ENTDTD
BD76  85B5               STA     LISTDTD
BD78  60                 RTS
```

SETSEOL — Set an EOL [Temporarily] after a String EOL

```
BD79                 SETSEOL
BD79  2098AB             JSR     AAPSTR          ; GET STRING WITH ABS ADR
BD7C  A5D4               LDA     FR0-2+EVSADR    ; PUT IT'S ADR
BD7E  85F3               STA     INBUFF          ; INTO INBUFF
BD80  A5D5               LDA     FR0-1+EVSADR
BD82  85F4               STA     INBUFF+1
                     ;
BD84  A4D6               LDY     FR0-2+EVSLEN    ; GET LENGTH LOW
BD86  A6D7               LDX     FR0-1+EVSLEN    ; IF LEN < 256
BD88  F002 ^BD8C         BEQ     :SSE1           ; THEN BR
BD8A  A0FF               LDY     #$FF            ; ELSE SET MAX
                     ;
BD8C  B1F3           :SSE1   LDA     [INBUFF],Y  ; GET LAST STR CHAR+1
BD8E  8597               STA     INDEX2          ; SAVE IT
BD90  8498               STY     INDEX2+1        ; AND IT'S INDEX
BD92  A99B               LDA     #CR             ; THEN REPLACE WITH EOL
BD94  91F3               STA     [INBUFF],Y
BD96  8592               STA     MEOLFLG         ; INDICATE MODIFIED EOL
BD98  60                 RTS                     ; DONE
                     ;
BD99                 RSTSEOL                     ; RESTORE STRING CHAR
BD99  A498               LDY     INDEX2+1        ; LOAD INDEX
```

```
BD9B  A597              LDA     INDEX2          ; LOAD CHAR
BD9D  91F3              STA     [INBUFF],Y      ; DONE
BD9F  A900              LDA     #0              ;
BDA1  8592              STA     MEOLFLG         ; RESET EOL FLAG
BDA3  60                RTS                     ; DONE
BDA4  = 0001      PATCH    DS      PATSIZ
```

SIN[X] and COS[X]

```
                  ;
BDA5  38          SINERR  SEC       ;ERROR - SET CARRY
BDA6  60                RTS
                  ;
                  ;
BDA7  A904        SIN     LDA     #4            ; FLAG SIN[X] ENTRY RIGHT NOW
BDA9  24D4              BIT     FR0
BDAB  1006 ^BDB3        BPL     BOTH
BDAD  A902              LDA     #2              ; SIN[-X]
BDAF  D002 ^BDB3        BNE     BOTH
BDB1  A901        COS     LDA     #1            ;FLAG COS[X] ENTRY
BDB3  85F0        BOTH    STA     SGNFLG
BDB5  A5D4              LDA     FR0             ; FORCE POSITIVE
BDB7  297F              AND     #$7F
BDB9  85D4              STA     FR0
BDBB  A95F              LDA     #PIOV2&$FF
BDBD  18                CLC
BDBE  65FB              ADC     DEGFLG
BDC0  AA                TAX
BDC1  A0BE              LDY     #PIOV2/$100
BDC3  2098DD            JSR     FLD1R
BDC6  2028DB            JSR     FDIV            ; X/[PI/2] OR X/90
BDC9  9001 ^BDCC        BCC     SINF7
BDCB  60          SINOVF  RTS                   ; OVERFLOW
BDCC              SINF7
BDCC  A5D4              LDA     FR0
BDCE  297F              AND     #$7F            ; CHECK EXPONENT
BDD0  38                SEC
BDD1  E940              SBC     #$40
BDD3  302B ^BE00        BMI     SINF3           ; QUADRANT 0 - USE AS IS
BDD5  C904        SINF6   CMP     #FPREC-2      ; FIND QUAD NO & REMAINDER
BDD7  10CC ^BDA5        BPL     SINERR          ; OUT OF RANGE
BDD9  AA                TAX                     ; X->LSB OR FR0
BDDA  B5D5              LDA     FR0+1,X         ; LSB
BDDC  85F1              STA     XFMFLG
BDDE  2910              AND     #$10            ; CHECK 10'S DIGIT
BDE0  F002 ^BDE4        BEQ     SINF5
BDE2  A902              LDA     #2              ; ODD - ADD 2 TO QUAD #
BDE4  18          SINF5   CLC
BDE5  65F1              ADC     XFMFLG
BDE7  2903              AND     #3              ; QUADRANT = 0,1,2,3
BDE9  65F0              ADC     SGNFLG          ; ADJUST FOR SINE VS COSINE
BDEB  85F0              STA     SGNFLG
BDED  86F1              STX     XFMFLG          ; SAVE DEC PT LOC
BDEF  20B6DD            JSR     FMOVE           ; COPY TO FR1
BDF2  A6F1              LDX     XFMFLG
BDF4  A900              LDA     #0
BDF6  95E2        SINF1   STA     FR1+2,X       ; CLEAR FRACTION
BDF8  E8                INX
BDF9  E003              CPX     #FPREC-3
BDFB  90F9 ^BDF6        BCC     SINF1
BDFD  2060DA            JSR     FSUB            ; LEAVE REMAINDER
BE00  46F0        SINF3   LSR     SGNFLG        ; WAS QUAD ODD
BE02  900D ^BE11        BCC     SINF4           ; NO
BE04  20B6DD            JSR     FMOVE           ; YES - USE 1.0 - REMAINDER
BE07  A271              LDX     #FPONE&$FF
BE09  A0BE              LDY     #FPONE/$100
BE0B  2089DD            JSR     FLD0R
BE0E  2060DA            JSR     FSUB
BE11              SINF4                         ; NOW DO THE SERIES THING
BE11  A2E6              LDX     #FPSCR&$FF      ; SAVE ARG
BE13  A005              LDY     #FPSCR/$100
```

```
BE15  20A7DD          JSR    FSTØR
BE18  20B6DD          JSR    FMOVE              ;X->FR1
BE1B  20DBDA          JSR    FMUL               ;X**2->FRØ
BE1E  BØ85 ^BDA5      BCS    SINERR
BE2Ø  A9Ø6            LDA    #NSCF
BE22  A241            LDX    #SCOEF&$FF
BE24  AØBE            LDY    #SCOEF/$1ØØ
BE26  204ØDD          JSR    PLYEVL             ; EVALUATE P[X**2]
BE29  A2E6            LDX    #FPSCR&$FF
BE2B  AØØ5            LDY    #FPSCR/$1ØØ
BE2D  2098DD          JSR    FLD1R              ; X-> FR1
BE3Ø  2ØDBDA          JSR    FMUL               ; SIN[X] = X*P[X**2]
BE33  46FØ            LSR    SGNFLG             ; WAS QUAD 2 OR 3?
BE35  9009 ^BE4Ø      BCC    SINDON             ; NO - THRU
BE37  18              CLC                       ; YES
BE38  A5D4            LDA    FRØ                ; FLIP SIGN
BE3A  FØØ4 ^BE4Ø      BEQ    SINDON             ; [UNLESS ZERO]
BE3C  498Ø            EOR    #$8Ø
BE3E  85D4            STA    FRØ
BE4Ø  6Ø        SINDON RTS                      ;RETURN
BE41  BDØ3551499 SCOEF   .BYTE  $BD,$Ø3,$55,$14,$99,$39 ; -.ØØØØØ354149939
      39
BE47  3EØ16Ø4427   .BYTE  $3E,$Ø1,$6Ø,$44,$27,$52 ; Ø.ØØØ16Ø442752
      52
BE4D  BE46817543   .BYTE  $BE,$46,$81,$75,$43,$55 ; -.ØØ4681754355
      55
BE53  3FØ7969262   .BYTE  $3F,$Ø7,$96,$92,$62,$39 ; Ø.Ø796926239
      39
BE59  BF645964Ø8   .BYTE  $BF,$64,$59,$64,$Ø8,$67 ; -.645964Ø867
      67
BE5F  4ØØ157Ø796 PIOV2   .BYTE  $4Ø,$Ø1,$57,$Ø7,$96,$32 ;PI/2
      32
      = ØØØ6     NSCF    EQU    (*-SCOEF)/FPREC
BE65  4Ø9ØØØØØØØ   .BYTE  $4Ø,$9Ø,Ø,Ø,Ø,Ø  ; 9Ø DEG
      ØØ
BE6B  3FØ1745329 PIOV18  .BYTE  $3F,$Ø1,$74,$53,$29,$25 ;PI/18Ø
      25
BE71  4ØØ1ØØØØØØ FPONE   .BYTE  $4Ø,1,Ø,Ø,Ø,Ø   ; 1.Ø
      ØØ
```

ATAN[X] — Arctangent

```
BE77  A9ØØ        ATAN   LDA    #Ø              ; ARCTAN[X]
BE79  85FØ               STA    SGNFLG          ; SIGN FLAG OFF
BE7B  85F1               STA    XFMFLG          ; & TRANSFORM FLAG
BE7D  A5D4               LDA    FRØ
BE7F  297F               AND    #$7F
BE81  C94Ø               CMP    #$4Ø            ; CHECK X VS 1.Ø
BE83  3Ø15 ^BE9A         BMI    ATAN1           ; X<1.Ø - USE SERIES DIRECTLY
BE85  A5D4               LDA    FRØ             ; X>=1.Ø - SAVE SIGN & TRANSFORM
BE87  298Ø               AND    #$8Ø
BE89  85FØ               STA    SGNFLG          ; REMEMBER SIGN
BE8B  E6F1               INC    XFMFLG
BE8D  A97F               LDA    #$7F
BE8F  25D4               AND    FRØ
BE91  85D4               STA    FRØ             ; FORCE PLUS
BE93  A2EA               LDX    #FP9S&$FF
BE95  AØDF               LDY    #FP9S/$1ØØ
BE97  2Ø95DE             JSR    XFORM           ; CHANGE ARG TO [X-1]/[X+1]
BE9A              ATAN1
BE9A  A2E6               LDX    #FPSCR&$FF      ; ARCTAN[X], -1<X<1 BY SERIES
                                                ; OF APPROXIMATIONS
BE9C  AØØ5               LDY    #FPSCR/$1ØØ
BE9E  2ØA7DD             JSR    FSTØR           ;X->FSCR
BEA1  2ØB6DD             JSR    FMOVE           ; X->FR1
BEA4  2ØDBDA             JSR    FMUL            ; X*X->FRØ
BEA7  BØ39 ^BEE2         BCS    ATNOUT          ; Ø'FLOW
BEA9  A9ØB               LDA    #NATCF
BEAB  A2AE               LDX    #ATCOEF&$FF
BEAD  AØDF               LDY    #ATCOEF/$1ØØ
```

```
BEAF  2040DD           JSR    PLYEVL            ;P[X*X]
BEB2  B02E ^BEE2       BCS    ATNOUT
BEB4  A2E6             LDX    #FPSCR&$FF
BEB6  A005             LDY    #FPSCR/$100
BEB8  2098DD           JSR    FLD1R             ;X->FR1
BEBB  20DBDA           JSR    FMUL              ;X*P[X*X]
BEBE  B022 ^BEE2       BCS    ATNOUT            ; 0'FLOW
BEC0  A5F1             LDA    XFMFLG            ; WAS ARG XFORM'D
BEC2  F010 ^BED4       BEQ    ATAN2             ; NO
BEC4  A2F0             LDX    #PIOV4&$FF        ; YES-ADD ARCTAN [1.0] = PI/4
BEC6  A0DF             LDY    #PIOV4/$100
BEC8  2098DD           JSR    FLD1R
BECB  2066DA           JSR    FADD
BECE  A5F0             LDA    SGNFLG            ; GET ORG SIGN
BED0  05D4             ORA    FR0
BED2  85D4             STA    FR0               ; ATAN[-X] = - ATAN[X]
BED4  A5FB       ATAN2 LDA      DEGFLG          ; RADIANS OR DEGREES
BED6  F00A ^BEE2       BEQ    ATNOUT            ; RAD - FINI
BED8  A26B             LDX    #PIOV18&$FF       ; DEG - DIVIDE BY PI/180
BEDA  A0BE             LDY    #PIOV18/$100
BEDC  2098DD           JSR    FLD1R
BEDF  2028DB           JSR    FDIV
BEE2  60         ATNOUT RTS
```

SQR[X] — Square Root

```
                 ;
BEE3  38         SQRERR SEC                     ;SET FAIL
BEE4  60               RTS
                 ;
BEE5  A900       SQR   LDA      #0
BEE7  85F1             STA    XFMFLG
BEE9  A5D4             LDA    FR0
BEEB  30F6 ^BEE3       BMI    SQRERR
BEED  C93F             CMP    #$3F
BEEF  F017 ^BF08       BEQ    FSQR              ; X IN RANGE OF APPROX - GO DO
BEF1  18               CLC
BEF2  6901             ADC    #1
BEF4  85F1             STA    XFMFLG            ; NOT IN RANGE - TRANSFORM
BEF6  85E0             STA    FR1               ; MANTISSA = 1
BEF8  A901             LDA    #1
BEFA  85E1             STA    FR1+1
BEFC  A204             LDX    #FPREC-2
BEFE  A900             LDA    #0
BF00  95E2       SQR1  STA      FR1+2,X
BF02  CA               DEX
BF03  10FB ^BF00       BPL    SQR1
BF05  2028DB           JSR    FDIV              ; X/100**N
BF08             FSQR                           ;SQR[X], 0.1<=X<1.0
BF08  A906             LDA    #6
BF0A  85EF             STA    SQRCNT
BF0C  A2E6             LDX    #FSCR&$FF
BF0E  A005             LDY    #FSCR/$100
BF10  20A7DD           JSR    FST0R             ;STASH X IN FSCR
BF13  20B6DD           JSR    FMOVE             ;X->FR1
BF16  A293             LDX    #FTWO&$FF
BF18  A0BF             LDY    #FTWO/$100
BF1A  2089DD           JSR    FLD0R             ;2.0->FR0
BF1D  2060DA           JSR    FSUB              ;2.0-X
BF20  A2E6             LDX    #FSCR&$FF
BF22  A005             LDY    #FSCR/$100
BF24  2098DD           JSR    FLD1R             ;X->FR1
BF27  20DBDA           JSR    FMUL              ;X*[2.0-X] :1ST APPROX
BF2A  A2EC       SQRLP LDX      #FSCR1&$FF
BF2C  A005             LDY    #FSCR1/$100
BF2E  20A7DD           JSR    FST0R             ;Y->FSCR1
BF31  20B6DD           JSR    FMOVE             ;Y->FR1
BF34  A2E6             LDX    #FSCR&$FF
BF36  A005             LDY    #FSCR/$100
BF38  2089DD           JSR    FLD0R
```

```
BF3B  2028DB          JSR     FDIV              ;X/Y
BF3E  A2EC            LDX     #FSCR1&$FF
BF40  A005            LDY     #FSCR1/$100
BF42  2098DD          JSR     FLD1R
BF45  2060DA          JSR     FSUB              ;[X/Y]-Y
BF48  A26C            LDX     #FHALF&$FF
BF4A  A0DF            LDY     #FHALF/$100
BF4C  2098DD          JSR     FLD1R
BF4F  20DBDA          JSR     FMUL              ;0.5*[[X/Y]-Y]=DELTAY
BF52  A5D4            LDA     FR0               ;DELTA 0.0
BF54  F00E ^BF64      BEQ     SQRDON
BF56  A2EC            LDX     #FSCR1&$FF
BF58  A005            LDY     #FSCR1/$100
BF5A  2098DD          JSR     FLD1R
BF5D  2066DA          JSR     FADD              ;Y=Y+DELTA Y
BF60  C6EF            DEC     SQRCNT            ; COUNT & LOOP
BF62  10C6 ^BF2A      BPL     SQRLP
BF64  A2EC      SQRDON LDX    #FSCR1&$FF        ; DELTA = 0 - GET Y BACK
BF66  A005            LDY     #FSCR1/$100
BF68  2089DD          JSR     FLD0R
                ;      WAS ARG TRANSFORMED
BF6B  A5F1            LDA     XFMFLG
BF6D  F023 ^BF92      BEQ     SQROUT            ; NO FINI
BF6F  38              SEC
BF70  E940            SBC     #$40
BF72  18              CLC                       ; YES - TRANSFORM RESULT
BF73                  RORA                      ; DIVIDE EXP BY 2
BF73 +6A              ROR     A
BF74  18              CLC
BF75  6940            ADC     #$40
BF77  297F            AND     #$7F
BF79  85E0            STA     FR1
BF7B  A5F1            LDA     XFMFLG
BF7D                  RORA
BF7D +6A              ROR     A
BF7E  A901            LDA     #1                ; MANTISSA = 1
BF80  9002 ^BF84      BCC     SQR2              ; WAS EXP ODD OR EVEN
BF82  A910            LDA     #$10              ; ODD - MANT = 10
BF84  85E1      SQR2   STA     FR1+1
BF86  A204            LDX     #FPREC-2
BF88  A900            LDA     #0
BF8A  95E2      SQR3   STA     FR1+2,X          ; CLEAR REST OF MANTISSA
BF8C  CA              DEX
BF8D  10FB ^BF8A      BPL     SQR3
BF8F  20DBDA          JSR     FMUL              ; SQR[X] = SQR[X/100**N]
                                                  * [10**N]
BF92  60        SQROUT RTS
BF93  4002000000 FTWO  .BYTE  $40,2,0,0,0,0     ; 2.0
      00
```

Floating Point

```
BF99  = D800          ORG     FPORG
D800                  LOCAL
```

ASCIN — Convert ASCII Input to Internal Form

```
                *      ON ENTRY   INBUFF - POINTS TO BUFFER WITH ASCII
                *                 CIX - INDEX TO 1ST BYTE OF #
                *
                *      ON EXIT    CC SET - CARRY SET IF NOT #
                *                          CARRY CLEAR OF #
                *
                *
D800            AFP
D800            CVAFP
D800            ASCIN
D800  20A1DB          JSR     SKPBLANK
D803  20BBDB          JSR     :TSTCHAR          ; SEE IF THIS COULD BE A NUMBER
D806  B039 ^D841      BCS     :NONUM            ; BR IF NOT A NUMBER
```

```
                    ;
                    ;         SET INITIAL VALUES
                    ;
D8Ø8  A2ED              LDX     #EEXP              ; ZERO 4 VALUES
D8ØA  AØØ4              LDY     #4                 ; X
D8ØC  2Ø48DA            JSR     ZXLY               ; X
D8ØF  A2FF              LDX     #$FF
D811  86F1              STX     DIGRT              ; SET TO $FF
                    ;
D813  2Ø44DA            JSR     ZFRØ               ; CLEAR FRØ
                    ;
D816  FØØ4 ^D81C        BEQ     :IN2               ; UNCONDITIONAL BR
                    ;
                    ;
D818                :IN1
D818  A9FF              LDA     #$FF               ; SET 1ST CHAR FLAG TO NON
                                                     ZERO
D81A  85FØ              STA     FCHRFLG            ; X
                    ;
D81C                :IN2
D81C  2Ø94DB            JSR     :GETCHAR           ; GET INPUT CHAR
D81F  BØ21 ^D842        BCS     :NON1              ; BR IF CHAR NOT NUMBER
                    ;
                    ;
                    ;         IT'S A NUMBER
                    ;
D821  48                PHA                        ; SAVE ON CPU STACK
D822  A6D5              LDX     FRØM               ; GET 1ST BYTE
D824  DØ11 ^D837        BNE     :INCE              ; INCR EXPONENT
                    ;
D826  2ØEBDB            JSR     NIBSHØ             ; SHIFT FRØ ONE NIBBLE LEFT
                    ;
D829  68                PLA                        ; GET DIGIT ON CPU STACK
D82A  Ø5D9              ORA     FRØM+FMPREC-1      ; OR INTO LAST BYTE
D82C  85D9              STA     FRØM+FMPREC-1      ; SAVE AS LAST BYTE
                    ;
                    ;         COUNT CHARACTERS AFTER DECIMAL POINT
                    ;
D82E  A6F1              LDX     DIGRT              ; GET # OF DIGITS RIGHT
D83Ø  3ØE6 ^D818        BMI     :IN1               ; IF = $FF, NO DECIMAL POINT
D832  E8                INX                        ; ADD IN THIS CHAR
D833  86F1              STX     DIGRT              ; SAVE
D835  DØE1 ^D818        BNE     :IN1               ; GET NEXT CHAR
                    ;
                    ;
                    ;         INCREMENT # OR DIGIT MORE THAN 9
                    ;
                    ;
D837                :INCE
D837  68                PLA                        ; CLEAR CPU STACK
D838  A6F1              LDX     DIGRT              ; HAVE DP?
D83A  1ØØ2 ^D83E        BPL     :INCE2             ; IF YES, DON'T INCR E COUNT
D83C  E6ED              INC     EEXP               ; INCR EXPONENT
D83E                :INCE2
D83E  4C18D8            JMP     :IN1               ; GET NEXT CHAR
                    ;
                    ;
D841                :NONUM
D841  6Ø                RTS                        ; RETURN FAIL
                    ;
                    ;         NON-NUMERIC IN NUMBER BODY
                    ;
D842                :NON1
D842  C92E              CMP     #'.'               ; IS IT DECIMAL POINT?
D844  FØ14 ^D85A        BEQ     :DP                ; IF YES, PROCESS IT
D846  C945              CMP     #'E'               ; IS IT E FOR EXPONENT?
D848  FØ19 ^D863        BEQ     :EXP               ; IF YES, DO EXPONENT
                    ;
D84A  A6FØ              LDX     FCHRFLG            ; IS THIS THE 1ST CHAR
D84C  DØ68 ^D8B6        BNE     :EXIT              ; IF NOT, END OF NUMERIC INPUT
D84E  C92B              CMP     #'+'               ; IS IT PLUS?
```

```
D85Ø  FØC6 ^D818       BEQ     :IN1              ; GO FOR NEXT CHAR
D852  C92D             CMP     #'-'              ; IS IT MINUS?
D854  FØØØ ^D856       BEQ     :MINUS
                   ;
                   ;
D856               :MINUS
D856  85EE             STA     NSIGN             ; SAVE SIGN FOR LATER
D858  FØBE ^D818       BEQ     :IN1              ; UNCONDITIONAL BRANCH FOR
                                                   NEXT CHAR
                   ;
D85A               :DP
D85A  A6F1             LDX     DIGRT             ; IS DIGRT STILL = FF?
D85C  1Ø58 ^D8B6       BPL     :EXIT             ; IF NOT, ALREADY HAVE DP
D85E  E8               INX                       ; INCR TO ZERO
D85F  86F1             STX     DIGRT             ; SAVE
D861  FØB5 ^D818       BEQ     :IN1              ; UNCONDITIONAL BR FOR NEXT
                                                   CHAR
                   ;
D863               :EXP
D863  A5F2             LDA     CIX               ; GET INDEX
D865  85EC             STA     FRX               ; SAVE
D867  2Ø94DB           JSR     :GETCHAR          ; GET NEXT CHAR
D86A  BØ37 ^D8A3       BCS     :NON2             ; BR IF NOT NUMBER
                   ;
                   ;       IT'S A NUMBER IN AN EXPONENT
                   ;
D86C               :EXP2
D86C  AA               TAX                       ; SAVE 1ST CHAR OF EXPONENT
D86D  A5ED             LDA     EEXP              ; GET # OF CHAR OVER 9
D86F  48               PHA                       ; SAVE IT
D87Ø  86ED             STX     EEXP              ; SAVE 1ST CHAR OF EXPONENT
D872  2Ø94DB           JSR     :GETCHAR          ; GET NEXT CHAR
                   ;
                   ;
D875  BØ17 ^D88E       BCS     :EXP3             ; IF NOT # NO SECOND DIGIT
D877  48               PHA                       ; SAVE SECOND DIGIT
                   ;
D878  A5ED             LDA     EEXP              ; GET 1ST DIGIT
D87A                   ASLA                      ; GET DIGIT * 1Ø
D87A +ØA               ASL     A
D87B  85ED             STA     EEXP              ; X
D87D                   ASLA                      ; X
D87D +ØA               ASL     A
D87E                   ASLA                      ; X
D87E +ØA               ASL     A
D87F  65ED             ADC     EEXP              ; X
D881  85ED             STA     EEXP              ; SAVE
D883  68               PLA                       ; GET SECOND DIGIT
D884  18               CLC
D885  65ED             ADC     EEXP              ; GET EXPONENT INPUTTED
D887  85ED             STA     EEXP              ; SAVE
                   ;
D889  A4F2             LDY     CIX               ; INC TO NEXT CHAR
D88B  2Ø9DDB           JSR     :GCHR1            ; X
                   ;
                   ;
D88E               :EXP3
D88E  A5EF             LDA     ESIGN             ; GET SIGN OF EXPONENT
D89Ø  FØØ9 ^D89B       BEQ     :EXP1             ; IF NO SIGN, IT IS +
D892  A5ED             LDA     EEXP              ; GET EXPONENT ENTERED
D894  49FF             EOR     #$FF              ; COMPLEMENT TO MAKE MINUS
D896  18               CLC                       ; X
D897  69Ø1             ADC     #1                ; X
D899  85ED             STA     EEXP              ; SAVE
D89B               :EXP1
D89B  68               PLA                       ; GET # DIGITS MORE THAN 9
D89C  18               CLC                       ; CLEAR CARRY
D89D  65ED             ADC     EEXP              ; ADD IN ENTERED EXPONENT
D89F  85ED             STA     EEXP              ; SAVE EXPONENT
D8A1  DØ13 ^D8B6       BNE     :EXIT             ; UNCONDITIONAL BR
```

```
                         ;
                         ;       NON-NUMERIC IN EXPONENT
                         ;
D8A3                     :NON2
D8A3  C92B                   CMP     #'+'                ; IS IT PLUS?
D8A5  F006 ^D8AD             BEQ     :EPLUS              ; IF YES BR
D8A7  C92D                   CMP     #'-'                ; IS IT A MINUS?
D8A9  D007 ^D8B2             BNE     :NOTE               ; IF NOT, BR
                         ;
                         ;
D8AB                     :EMIN
D8AB  85EF                   STA     ESIGN               ; SAVE EXPONENT SIGN
D8AD                     :EPLUS
D8AD  2094DB                 JSR     :GETCHAR            ; GET CHARACTER
D8B0  90BA ^D86C             BCC     :EXP2               ; IF A #, GO PROCESS EXPONENT
                         ;
                         ;
                         ;
                         ;       E NOT PART OF OUR #
                         ;
D8B2                     :NOTE
D8B2  A5EC                   LDA     FRX                 ; POINT TO 1 PAST E
D8B4  85F2                   STA     CIX                 ; RESTORE CIX
                         ;
                         ;       FALL THRU TO EXIT
                         ;
                         ;       WHOLE # HAS BEEN INPUTTED
                         ;
D8B6                     :EXIT
                         ;
                         ;       BACK UP ONE CHAR
                         ;
D8B6  C6F2                   DEC     CIX                 ; DECREMENT INDEX
                         ;
                         ;
                         ;       CALCULATE POWER OF 10 = EXP - DIGITS RIGHT
                         ;       WHERE EXP = ENTERED EXPONENT [COMPLEMENT OF -]
                         ;               + # DIGITS MORE THAN 9
                         ;
D8B8  A5ED                   LDA     EEXP                ; GET EXPONENT
D8BA  A6F1                   LDX     DIGRT               ; GET # DIGITS RIGHT OF DECIMAL
D8BC  3005 ^D8C3             BMI     :EXIT1              ; NO DECIMAL POINT
D8BE  F003 ^D8C3             BEQ     :EXIT1              ; # OF DIGITS AFTER D.P.=0
D8C0  38                     SEC                         ; GET EXP - DIGITS RIGHT
D8C1  E5F1                   SBC     DIGRT               ; X
                         ;
                         ;       SHIFT RIGHT ALGEBRAIC TO DIVIDE BY 2 = POWER OF 100
                         ;
D8C3                     :EXIT1
D8C3  48                     PHA
D8C4                         ROLA                        ; SET CARRY WITH SIGN OF
                                                           EXPONENT
D8C4 +2A                     ROL     A
D8C5  68                     PLA                         ; GET EXPONENT AGAIN
D8C6                         RORA                        ; SHIFT RIGHT
D8C6 +6A                     ROR     A
D8C7  85ED                   STA     EEXP                ; SAVE POWER OF 100
D8C9  9003 ^D8CE             BCC     :EVEN               ; IF NO CARRY # EVEN
                         ;
D8CB  20EBDB                 JSR     NIBSH0              ; ELSE SHIFT 1 NIBBLE LEFT
D8CE                     :EVEN
D8CE  A5ED                   LDA     EEXP                ; ADD 40 FOR EXCESS 64 + 4
                                                           FOR NORM
D8D0  18                     CLC                         ; X
D8D1  6944                   ADC     #$44                ; X
D8D3  85D4                   STA     FR0                 ; SAVE AS EXPONENT
                         ;
D8D5  2000DC                 JSR     NORM                ; NORMALIZE NUMBER
D8D8  B00B ^D8E5             BCS     :IND2               ; IF CARRY SET, IT'S AN ERROR
                         ;
```

```
                    ;       SET MANTISSA SIGH
                    ;
D8DA  A6EE              LDX    NSIGN             ; IS SIGN OF # MINUS?
D8DC  F006 ^D8E4        BEQ    :INDON            ; IF NOT, BR
                    ;
D8DE  A5D4              LDA    FRØ               ; GET EXPONENT
D8EØ  Ø98Ø              ORA    #$8Ø              ; TURN ON MINUS # BIT
D8E2  85D4              STA    FRØ               ; SET IN FRØ EXP
D8E4                :INDON
D8E4  18                CLC                      ; CLEAR CARRY
D8E5                :IND2
D8E5  6Ø                RTS
```

FPASC — Convert Floating Point to ASCII

```
                    *       ON ENTRY   FRØ - # TO CONVERT
                    *
                    *       ON EXIT    INBUFF - POINTS TO START OF #
                    *                  HIGH ORDER BIT OF LAST BYTE IS ON
                    *
                    *
D8E6                CVFASC
D8E6                FASC
D8E6  2Ø51DA            JSR    INTLBF            ;SET INBUFF TO PT TO LBUFF
                    ;
D8E9  A93Ø              LDA    #'Ø'              ; GET ASCII ZERO
D8EB  8D7FØ5            STA    LBUFF-1           ; PUT IN FRONT OF LBUFF
                    ;
                    ;       TEST FOR E FORMAT REQUIRED
                    ;
D8EE  A5D4              LDA    FRØ               ; GET EXPONENT
D8FØ  FØ28 ^D91A        BEQ    :EXPØ             ; IF EXP = Ø, # = Ø, SO BR
D8F2  297F              AND    #$7F              ; AND OUT SIGN
D8F4  C93F              CMP    #$3F              ; IS IT LESS THAN 3F
D8F6  9Ø28 ^D92Ø        BCC    :EFORM            ; IF YES, E FORMAT REQUIRED
D8F8  C945              CMP    #$45              ; IF IT IS > 44
D8FA  BØ24 ^D92Ø        BCS    :EFORM            ; IF YES, E FORMAT REQUIRED
                    *
                    *       PROCESS NOT E FORMAT
                    *
D8FC  38                SEC                      ; SET CARRY
D8FD  E93F              SBC    #$3F              ; GET DECIMAL POSITION
                    ;
D8FF  2Ø7ØDC            JSR    :CVFRØ            ; CONVERT FRØ TO ASCII CHAR
                    ;
D9Ø2  2ØA4DC            JSR    :FNZERO           ; FIND LAST NON-ZERO CHARACTER
D9Ø5  Ø98Ø              ORA    #$8Ø              ; TURN ON HIGH ORDER BIT
D9Ø7  9D8ØØ5            STA    LBUFF,X           ; STORE IT BACK IN BUFFER
                    ;
D9ØA  AD8ØØ5            LDA    LBUFF             ; GET 1ST CHAR IN LBUFF
D9ØD  C92E              CMP    #'.'              ; IS IT DECIMAL?
D9ØF  FØØ3 ^D914        BEQ    :FN6              ; BR IF YES
D911  4C88D9            JMP    :FN5              ; ELSE JUMP
D914                :FN6
D914  2ØC1DC            JSR    :DECINB           ; DECIMAL INBUFF
D917  4C9CD9            JMP    :FN4              ; DO FINAL ADJUSTMENT
                    *
                    *       EXPONENT IS ZERO - # IS ZERO
                    *
                    *
D91A                :EXPØ
D91A  A9BØ              LDA    #$8Ø+$3Ø          ; GET ASCII Ø WITH MSB = 1
D91C  8D8ØØ5            STA    LBUFF             ; PUT IN BUFFER
D91F  6Ø                RTS
                    *
                    *       PROCESS E FORMAT
                    *
D92Ø                :EFORM
D92Ø  A9Ø1              LDA    #1                ; GET DECIMAL POSITION
D922  2Ø7ØDC            JSR    :CVFRØ            ; CONVERT FRØ TO ASCII IN
                                                 LBUFF
```

```
                   ;
D925  20A4DC          JSR     :FNZERO         ; GET RID OF TRAILING ZEROS
D928  E8              INX                     ; INCR INDEX
D929  86F2            STX     CIX             ; SAVE INDEX TO LAST CHAR
                   ;
                   ;     ADJUST EXPONENT
                   ;
D92B  A5D4            LDA     FRØ             ; GET EXPONENT
D92D                  ASLA                    ; MULT BY 2 [GET RID OF
                                                SIGN TOO]
D92D +ØA              ASL     A
D92E  38              SEC
D92F  E98Ø            SBC     #$4Ø*2          ; SUB EXCESS 64
                   ;
D931  AE8ØØ5          LDX     LBUFF           ; GET 1ST CHAR IN LBUFF
D934  EØ3Ø            CPX     #'Ø'            ; IS IT ASCII Ø?
D936  FØ17 ^D94F      BEQ     :EF1
                   ;
                   ;     PUT DECIMAL AFTER 1ST CHAR [IT'S AFTER 2ND NOW]
                   ;
D938  AE81Ø5          LDX     LBUFF+1         ; SWITCH D.P. + 2ND DIGIT
D93B  AC82Ø5          LDY     LBUFF+2         ; X
D93E  8E82Ø5          STX     LBUFF+2         ; X
D941  8C81Ø5          STY     LBUFF+1         ; X
                   ;
                   ;
D944  A6F2            LDX     CIX             ; IF CIX POINTS TO D.P.
D946  EØØ2            CPX     #2              ; THEN INC
D948  DØØ2 ^D94C      BNE     :NOINC          ; X
D94A  E6F2            INC     CIX             ; X
                   ;
D94C               :NOINC
D94C  18              CLC                     ; X
D94D  69Ø1            ADC     #1              ; X
                   ;
                   ;     CONVERT EXP TO ASCII
                   ;
D94F               :EF1
D94F  85ED            STA     EEXP            ; SAVE EXPONENT
D951  A945            LDA     #'E'            ; GET ASCII E
D953  A4F2            LDY     CIX             ; GET POINTER
D955  209FDC          JSR     :STCHAR         ; STORE CHARACTER
D958  84F2            STY     CIX             ; SAVE INDEX
                   ;
                   ;
D95A  A5ED            LDA     EEXP            ; GET EXPONENT
D95C  1ØØB ^D969      BPL     :EPL            ; BR IF PLUS
                   ;
                   ;     EXPONENT IS MINUS - COMPLEMENT IT
                   ;
D95E  A9ØØ            LDA     #Ø              ; SUBTRACT FROM Ø TO
                                                COMPLEMENT
D96Ø  38              SEC                     ; X
D961  E5ED            SBC     EEXP            ; X
D963  85ED            STA     EEXP
                   ;
D965  A92D            LDA     #'-'            ; GET A MINUS
D967  DØØ2 ^D96B      BNE     :EF2
                   ;
D969               :EPL
D969  A92B            LDA     #'+'            ; GET A PLUS
D96B               :EF2
D96B  209FDC          JSR     :STCHAR         ; STORE A CHARACTER
                   ;
D96E  A2ØØ            LDX     #Ø              ; SET COUNTER FOR # OF TENS
D97Ø  A5ED            LDA     EEXP            ; GET EXPONENT
                   ;
D972               :EF3
D972  38              SEC
D973  E9ØA            SBC     #1Ø             ; SUBTRACT 1Ø
```

```
D975  9003 ^D97A      BCC     :EF4              ; IF < 0, BRANCH
D977  E8              INX                       ; INCR # OF 10'S
D978  D0F8 ^D972      BNE     :EF3              ; BR UNCONDITIONAL
                   ;
D97A               :EF4
D97A  18              CLC                       ; ADD BACK IN 10
D97B  690A            ADC     #10               ; X
D97D  48              PHA                       ; SAVE
                   ;
D97E  8A              TXA                       ; GET # OF 10'S
D97F  209DDC          JSR     :STNUM            ; PUT 10'S IN EXP IN BUFFER
D982  68              PLA                       ; GET REMAINDER
D983  0980            ORA     #$80              ; TURN ON HIGH ORDER BIT
D985  209DDC          JSR     :STNUM            ; PUT IN BUFFER
                   ;
                   ;    FINAL ADJUSTMENT
                   ;
D988               :FN5
D988  AD8005          LDA     LBUFF             ; GET 1ST BYTE IN LBUFF
                                                  [OUTPUT]
D98B  C930            CMP     #'0'              ; IS IT ASCII 0?
D98D  D00D ^D99C      BNE     :FN4              ; IF NOT BR
                   ;
                   ;    INCREMENT INBUFF TO POINT TO NON-ZERO
                   ;
D98F  18              CLC                       ; ADD 1 TO INBUFF
D990  A5F3            LDA     INBUFF            ; X
D992  6901            ADC     #1                ; X
D994  85F3            STA     INBUFF            ; X
D996  A5F4            LDA     INBUFF+1          ; X
D998  6900            ADC     #0                ; X
D99A  85F4            STA     INBUFF+1          ; X
D99C               :FN4
D99C  A5D4            LDA     FR0               ; GET EXPONENT OF #
D99E  1009 ^D9A9      BPL     :FADONE           ; IF SIGN +, WE ARE DONE
                   ;
D9A0  20C1DC          JSR     :DECINB           ; DECR INBUFF
D9A3  A000            LDY     #0                ; GET INDEX
D9A5  A92D            LDA     #'-'              ; GET ASCII -
D9A7  91F3            STA     [INBUFF],Y        ; SAVE - IN BUFFER
                   ;
D9A9               :FADONE
D9A9  60              RTS
```

IFP — Convert Integer to Floating Point

```
                   *      ON ENTRY   FR0 - CONTAINS INTEGER
                   *
                   *      ON EXIT    FR0 - CONTAINS FLOATING POINT #
                   *
                   *
D9AA               CVIFP
D9AA               IFP
                   ;
                   ;      MOVE INTEGER AND REVERSE BYTES
                   ;
D9AA  A5D4            LDA     FR0               ; GET INTEGER LOW
D9AC  85F8            STA     ZTEMP4+1          ; SAVE AS INTEGER HIGH
D9AE  A5D5            LDA     FR0+1             ; GET INTEGER HIGH
D9B0  85F7            STA     ZTEMP4            ; SAVE AS INTEGER LOW
                   ;
D9B2  2044DA          JSR     ZFR0              ; CLEAR FR0
D9B5  F8              SED                       ; SET DECIMAL MODE
                   *
                   *      DO THE CONVERT
                   *
D9B6  A010            LDY     #16               ; GET # BITS IN INTEGER
D9B8               :IFP1
D9B8  06F8            ASL     ZTEMP4+1          ; SHIFT LEFT INTEGER LOW
D9BA  26F7            ROL     ZTEMP4            ; SHIFT LEFT INTEGER HIGH
```

```
                                                   ; CARRY NOW SET IF THERE WAS A
                                                     BIT
D9BC  A2Ø3              LDX      #3              ; BIGGEST INTEGER IS 3 BYTES
D9BE               :IFP2
                   ;
                   ;        DOUBLE # AND ADD IN 1 IF CARRY SET
                   ;
D9BE  B5D4              LDA      FRØ,X           ; GET BYTE
D9CØ  75D4              ADC      FRØ,X           ; DOUBLE [ADDING IN CARRY
                                                   FROM SHIFT
D9C2  95D4              STA      FRØ,X           ; SAVE
D9C4  CA                DEX                      ; DECREMENT COUNT OF FRØ BYTES
D9C5  DØF7 ^D9BE        BNE      :IFP2           ; IF MORE TO DO, DO IT
                   ;
D9C7  88                DEY                      ; DECR COUNT OF INTEGER DIGITS
D9C8  DØEE ^D9B8        BNE      :IFP1           ; IF MORE TO DO, DO IT
D9CA  D8                CLD                      ; CLEAR DECIMAL MODE
                   ;
                   ;        SET EXPONENT
                   ;
D9CB  A942              LDA      #$42            ; INDICATE DECIMAL AFTER LAST
                                                   DIGIT
D9CD  85D4              STA      FRØ             ; STORE EXPONENT
                   ;
D9CF  4CØØDC            JMP      NORM            ; NORMALIZE
                   ;
```

FPI — Convert Floating Point to Integer

```
                   *        ON ENTRY    FRØ - FLOATING POINT NUMBER
                   *
                   *        ON EXIT     FRØ - INTEGER
                   *
                   *
                   *        CC SET   CARRY CLEAR - NO ERROR
                   *                 CARRY SET - ERROR
                   *
                   *
D9D2               FPI
                   ;
                   ;        CLEAR INTEGER
                   ;
D9D2  A9ØØ              LDA      #Ø              ; CLEAR INTEGER RESULT
D9D4  85F7              STA      ZTEMP4
D9D6  85F8              STA      ZTEMP4+1
                   ;
                   ;        CHECK EXPONENT
                   ;
D9D8  A5D4              LDA      FRØ             ; GET EXPONENT
D9DA  3Ø66 ^DA42        BMI      :ERVAL          ; IF SIGN OF FP# IS -, THEN
                                                   ERROR
D9DC  C943              CMP      #$43            ; IS FP# TOO BIG TO BE INTEGER
D9DE  BØ62 ^DA42        BCS      :ERVAL          ; IF YES, THEN ERROR
D9EØ  38                SEC                      ; SET CARRY
D9E1  E94Ø              SBC      #$4Ø            ; IS FP# LESS THAN 1?
D9E3  9Ø3F ^DA24        BCC      :ROUND          ; IF YES, THEN GO TEST FOR
                                                   ROUND
                   ;
                   ;        GET # OF DIGITS TO CONVERT = [EXPONENT -4Ø+1]*2
                   ;        [A CONTAINS EXPONENT -4Ø]
                   ;        [CARRY SET]
                   ;
D9E5  69ØØ              ADC      #Ø              ; ADD IN CARRY
D9E7                    ASLA                     ; MULT BY 2
D9E7 +ØA                ASL      A
D9E8  85F5              STA      ZTEMP1          ; SAVE AS COUNTER
                   *
                   *        DO CONVERT
                   *
D9EA               :FPI1
                   ;
```

```
                        ;          MULT INTEGER RESULT BY 1Ø
                        ;
D9EA  205ADA               JSR     :ILSHFT             ; GO SHIFT ONCE LEFT
D9ED  BØ53 ^DA42           BCS     :ERVAL              ; IF CARRY SET THEN # TOO BIG
                        ;
D9EF  A5F7                 LDA     ZTEMP4              ; SAVE INTEGER *2
D9F1  85F9                 STA     ZTEMP3              ; X
D9F3  A5F8                 LDA     ZTEMP4+1            ; X
D9F5  85FA                 STA     ZTEMP3+1            ; X
                        ;
D9F7  205ADA               JSR     :ILSHFT             ; MULT BY *2
D9FA  BØ46 ^DA42           BCS     :ERVAL              ; # TOO BIG
D9FC  205ADA               JSR     :ILSHFT             ; MULT BY *2 [NOW * 8 IN ZTEMP4]
D9FF  BØ41 ^DA42           BCS     :ERVAL              ; BR IF # TOO BIG
                        ;
DAØ1  18                   CLC                         ; ADD IN * 2 TO = *1Ø
DAØ2  A5F8                 LDA     ZTEMP4+1            ; X
DAØ4  65FA                 ADC     ZTEMP3+1            ; X
DAØ6  85F8                 STA     ZTEMP4+1            ; X
DAØ8  A5F7                 LDA     ZTEMP4              ; X
DAØA  65F9                 ADC     ZTEMP3              ; X
DAØC  85F7                 STA     ZTEMP4              ; X
DAØE  BØ32 ^DA42           BCS     :ERVAL              ; IF CARRY SET ERROR
                        ;
                        ;
                        ;          ADD IN NEXT DIGIT
                        ;
DA1Ø  2ØB9DC               JSR     :GETDIG             ; GET DIGIT IN A
DA13  18                   CLC
DA14  65F8                 ADC     ZTEMP4+1            ; ADD IN DIGIT
DA16  85F8                 STA     ZTEMP4+1            ; X
DA18  A5F7                 LDA     ZTEMP4              ; X
DA1A  69ØØ                 ADC     #Ø                  ; X
DA1C  BØ24 ^DA42           BCS     :ERVAL              ; BR IF OVERFLOW
DA1E  85F7                 STA     ZTEMP4              ;X
                        ;
DA2Ø  C6F5                 DEC     ZTEMP1              ; DEC COUNTER OF DIGITS TO DO
DA22  DØC6 ^D9EA           BNE     :FPI1               ; IF MORE TO DO, DO IT
                        ;
                        ;          ROUND IF NEEDED
                        ;
DA24                    :ROUND
DA24  2ØB9DC               JSR     :GETDIG             ; GET NEXT DIGIT IN A
DA27  C9Ø5                 CMP     #5                  ; IS DIGIT <5?
DA29  9ØØD ^DA38           BCC     :NR                 ; IF YES, DON'T ROUND
DA2B  18                   CLC                         ; ADD IN 1 TO ROUND
DA2C  A5F8                 LDA     ZTEMP4+1            ; X
DA2E  69Ø1                 ADC     #1                  ; X
DA3Ø  85F8                 STA     ZTEMP4+1            ; X
DA32  A5F7                 LDA     ZTEMP4              ; X
DA34  69ØØ                 ADC     #Ø                  ; X
DA36  85F7                 STA     ZTEMP4              ; X
                        ;
                        ;          MOVE INTEGER TO FRØ
                        ;
DA38                    :NR
DA38  A5F8                 LDA     ZTEMP4+1            ; GET INTEGER LOW
DA3A  85D4                 STA     FRØ                 ; SAVE
DA3C  A5F7                 LDA     ZTEMP4              ; GET INTEGER HIGH
DA3E  85D5                 STA     FRØ+1               ; SAVE
                        ;
DA4Ø  18                   CLC                         ; CLEAR CC FOR GOOD RETURN
DA41  6Ø                   RTS
                        ;
                        ;
DA42                    :ERVAL
DA42  38                   SEC                         ; SET CARRY FOR ERROR RETURN
DA43  6Ø                   RTS

                        *          ZFRØ - ZERO FRØ
                        *
                        *          ZF1 - ZERO 6 BYTES AT LOC X
```

```
                    *
                    *       ZXLY - ZERO PAGE ZERO LOC X FOR LENGTH Y
                    *
                    ;
DA44                ZFRØ
DA44  A2D4              LDX      #FRØ              ; GET POINTER TO FR1
                    ;
DA46                ZF1
DA46  AØØ6              LDY      #6                ; GET # OF BYTES TO CLEAR
DA48                ZXLY
DA48  A9ØØ              LDA      #Ø                ; CLEAR A
DA4A                :ZF2
DA4A  95ØØ              STA      Ø,X               ; CLEAR A BYTE
DA4C  E8                INX                        ; POINT TO NEXT BYTE
DA4D  88                DEY                        ; DEC COUNTER
DA4E  DØFA ^DA4A        BNE      :ZF2              ; LOOP
DA5Ø  6Ø                RTS
                    ;
                    ;
                    ;
                    ;
                    ;       INTLBF - INIT LBUFF INTO INBUFF
                    ;
DA51                INTLBF
DA51  A9Ø5              LDA      #LBUFF/256
DA53  85F4              STA      INBUFF+1
DA55  A98Ø              LDA      #LBUFF&255
DA57  85F3              STA      INBUFF
DA59  6Ø                RTS
                    *
                    *       :ILSHFT - SHIFT INTEGER IN ZTEMP4 LEFT ONCE
                    *
DA5A                ILSHFT
DA5A                :ILSHFT
DA5A  18                CLC                        ; CLEAR CARRY
DA5B  26F8              ROL      ZTEMP4+1          ; SHIFT LOW
DA5D  26F7              ROL      ZTEMP4            ; SHIFT HIGH
DA5F  6Ø                RTS
```

Floating Point Routines

FADD — Floating Point Add Routine

```
                                   ADDS VALUES IN FRØ AND FR1
                    *
                    *       ON ENTRY   FRØ & FR1 - CONTAIN # TO ADD
                    *
                    *       ON EXIT    FRØ - RESULT
```

FSUB — Floating Point Subtract Routine

```
                    *              SUBTRACTS FR1 FROM FRØ
                    *
                    *       ON ENTRY   FRØ & FR1 - CONTAIN # TO SUBTRACT
                    *
                    *       ON EXIT    FRØ - RESULT
                    *
                    *       BOTH RETURN WITH CC SET:
                    *              CARRY SET IF ERROR
                    *              CARRY CLEAR IF NO ERROR
                    *
                    *
DA6Ø                FSUB
DA6Ø  A5EØ              LDA      FR1               ; GET EXPONENT OF FR1
DA62  498Ø              EOR      #$8Ø              ; CHANGE SIGN OF MANTISSA
DA64  85EØ              STA      FR1               ; SAVE EXPONENT
                    ;
                    ;
                    ;
DA66                FADD
DA66                :FRADD
```

```
DA66  A5E0           LDA     FR1          ; GET EXPONENT FR1
DA68  297F           AND     #$7F         ; TURN OFF MANTISSA SIGN BIT
DA6A  85F7           STA     ZTEMP4       ; SAVE TEMPORARILY
DA6C  A5D4           LDA     FRØ          ; GET EXPONENT FRØ
DA6E  297F           AND     #$7F         ; TURN OFF MANTISSA SIGN BIT
DA7Ø  38             SEC                  ; CLEAR CARRY
DA71  E5F7           SBC     ZTEMP4       ; SUB EXPONENTS
DA73  1Ø1Ø ^DA85     BPL     :NSWAP       ; IF EXP[FRØ]>= EXP[FR1],
                                            NO SWAP
                   ;
                   ;     SWAP FRØ AND FR1
                   ;
DA75  A2Ø5           LDX     #FMPREC      ; GET INDEX
                   ;
DA77               :SWAP
DA77  B5D4           LDA     FRØ,X        ; GET BYTE FROM FRØ
DA79  B4EØ           LDY     FR1,X        ; GET BYTE FROM FR1
DA7B  95EØ           STA     FR1,X        ; PUT FRØ BYTE IN FR1
DA7D  98             TYA                  ; GET FR1 BYTE
DA7E  95D4           STA     FRØ,X        ; PUT FR1 BYTE IN FRØ
DA8Ø  CA             DEX                  ; DEC INDEX
DA81  1ØF4 ^DA77     BPL     :SWAP        ; IF MORE TO DO, GO SWAP
DA83  3ØE1 ^DA66     BMI     :FRADD       ; UNCONDITIONAL
                   ;
DA85               :NSWAP
DA85  FØØ7 ^DA8E     BEQ     :NALIGN      ; IF DIFFERENCE = Ø, ALREADY
                                            ALIGNED
DA87  C9Ø5           CMP     #FMPREC      ; IS DIFFERENCE < # OF BYTES
DA89  BØ19 ^DAA4     BCS     :ADDEND      ; IF NOT, HAVE RESULT IN FRØ
                   ;
                   ;
DA8B  2Ø3EDC         JSR     RSHFT1       ; SHIFT TO ALIGN
                   ;
                   ;     TEST FOR LIKE SIGN OF MANTISSA
                   ;
DA8E               :NALIGN
DA8E  F8             SED                  ; SET DECIMAL MODE
DA8F  A5D4           LDA     FRØ          ; GET FRØ EXPONENT
DA91  45EØ           EOR     FR1          ; EOR WITH FR1 EXPONENT
DA93  3Ø1E ^DAB3     BMI     :SUB         ; IF SIGNS DIFFERENT - SUBTRACT
                                          ; ELSE ADD
                   ;
                   ;     ADD FRØ & FR1
                   ;
DA95  A2Ø4           LDX     #FMPREC-1    ; GET POINTER FOR LAST BYTE
DA97  18             CLC                  ; CLEAR CARRY
DA98               :ADD1
DA98  B5D5           LDA     FRØM,X       ; GET BYTE OF FRØ
DA9A  75E1           ADC     FR1M,X       ; ADD IN BYTE OF FR1
DA9C  95D5           STA     FRØM,X       ; STORE
DA9E  CA             DEX                  ; DEC POINTER
DA9F  1ØF7 ^DA98     BPL     :ADD1        ; ADD NEXT BYTE
                   ;
DAA1  D8             CLD                  ; CLEAR DECIMAL MODE
DAA2  BØØ3 ^DAA7     BCS     :ADD2        ; IF THERE IS A CARRY, DO IT
DAA4               :ADDEND
DAA4  4CØØDC         JMP     NORM         ; GO NORMALIZE
                   ;
                   ;     ADD IN FIND CARRY
                   ;
DAA7               :ADD2
DAA7  A9Ø1           LDA     #1           ; GET 1 TIMES TO SHIFT
DAA9  2Ø3ADC         JSR     RSHFTØ       ; GO SHIFT
                   ;
DAAC  A9Ø1           LDA     #Ø1          ; GET CARRY
DAAE  85D5           STA     FRØM         ; ADD IN CARRY
DABØ  4CØØDC         JMP     NORM
                   ;
                   ;     SUBTRACT FR1 FROM FRØ
                   ;
DAB3               :SUB
DAB3  A2Ø4           LDX     #FMPREC-1    ; GET POINTER TO LAST BYTE
DAB5  38             SEC                  ; SET CARRY
```

```
                     ;
DAB6                 :SUB1
DAB6  B5D5              LDA     FRØM,X         ; GET FRØ BYTE
DAB8  F5E1              SBC     FR1M,X         ; SUB FR1 BYTE
DABA  95D5              STA     FRØM,X         ; STORE
DABC  CA                DEX                    ; DEC POINTER
DABD  1ØF7 ^DAB6        BPL     :SUB1          ; SUB NEXT BYTE
                     ;
DABF  9ØØ4 ^DAC5        BCC     :SUB2          ; IF THERE IS A BORROW DO IT
DAC1  D8                CLD                    ; CLEAR DECIMAL MODE
DAC2  4CØØDC            JMP     NORM
                     ;
                     ;      TAKE COMPLEMENT SIGN
                     ;
DAC5                 :SUB2
DAC5  A5D4              LDA     FRØ            ; GET EXPONENT
DAC7  498Ø              EOR     #$8Ø           ; CHANGE SIGN OF MANTISSA
DAC9  85D4              STA     FRØ            ; PUT IT BACK
                     ;
                     ;      COMPLEMENT MANTISSA
                     ;
DACB  38                SEC                    ; SET CARRY
DACC  A2Ø4              LDX     #FMPREC-1      ; GET INDEX COUNTER
DACE                 :SUB3
DACE  A9ØØ              LDA     #Ø             ; GET ZERO
DADØ  F5D5              SBC     FRØM,X         ; COMPLEMENT BYTE
DAD2  95D5              STA     FRØM,X         ; STORE
DAD4  CA                DEX                    ; MORE TO DO
DAD5  1ØF7 ^DACE        BPL     :SUB3          ; BR IF YES
                     ;
DAD7  D8                CLD                    ; CLEAR DECIMAL MODE
DAD8  4CØØDC            JMP     NORM           ; GO NORMALIZE
```

FMUL — Multiply FR0 by FR1

```
                     *      ON ENTRY   # ARE IN FRØ AND FR1
                     *
                     *      ON EXIT    FRØ - CONTAINS PRODUCT
                     *      RETURN WITH CC SET
                     *                 CARRY SET IF ERROR
                     *                 CARRY CLEAR IF NO ERROR
                     *
                     *
                     *
DADB                 FMUL
                     ;
                     ;      SET UP EXPONENT
                     ;
DADB  A5D4              LDA     FRØ            ; GET EXP FRØ
DADD  FØ45 ^DB24        BEQ     MEND3          ; IF = Ø, DONE
DADF  A5EØ              LDA     FR1            ; GET FR1 EXP
DAE1  FØ3E ^DB21        BEQ     MEND2          ; IF =Ø, ANSWER =Ø
                     ;
DAE3  2ØCFDC            JSR     MDESUP         ; DO COMMON SET FOR EXPONENT
DAE6  38                SEC                    ; SET CARRY
DAE7  E94Ø              SBC     #$4Ø           ; SUB EXCESS 64
DAE9  38                SEC                    ; SET CARRY TO ADD 1
DAEA  65EØ              ADC     FR1            ; ADD 1 + FR1 EXP TO FRØ EXP
DAEC  3Ø38 ^DB26        BMI     :EROV          ;IF - THEN OVERFLOW
                     ;
                     ;      FINISH MULTIPLY SET UP
                     ;
DAEE  2ØEØDC            JSR     MDSUP          ; DO SET UP COMMON TO DIVIDE
                     ;
                     *
                     *      DO THE MULTIPLY
                     *
DAF1                 :FRM
                     ;
                     ;      GET # OF TIMES TO ADD IN MULTIPLICAND
                     ;
```

```
DAF1  A5DF               LDA     FRE+FMPREC        ; GET LAST BYTE OF FRE
DAF3  29ØF               AND     #$ØF              ; AND OUT HIGH ORDER NIBBLE
DAF5  85F6               STA     ZTEMP1+1          ; SET COUNTER FOR LOOP CONTROL
                   ;
                   ;          ADD IN FR1
                   ;
DAF7               :FRM1
DAF7  C6F6               DEC     ZTEMP1+1          ; DEC MULT COUNTER
DAF9  3ØØ6 ^DBØ1         BMI     :FRM2             ; IF - THIS LOOP DONE
DAFB  2ØØ1DD             JSR     FRA1Ø             ; ADD FR1 TO FRØ [6 BYTES]
DAFE  4CF7DA             JMP     :FRM1             ; REPEAT
                   ;
                   ;          GET # OF TIMES TO ADD IN MULTIPLICAND * 1Ø
                   ;
DBØ1               :FRM2
DBØ1  A5DF               LDA     FRE+FMPREC        ; GET LAST BYTE OF FRE
DBØ3                     LSRA                      ; SHIFT OUT LOW ORDER NIBBLE
DBØ3 +4A                 LSR     A
DBØ4                     LSRA                      ; X
DBØ4 +4A                 LSR     A
DBØ5                     LSRA                      ; X
DBØ5 +4A                 LSR     A
DBØ6                     LSRA                      ; X
DBØ6 +4A                 LSR     A
DBØ7  85F6               STA     ZTEMP1+1          ; SAVE AS COUNTER
                   ;
                   ;          ADD IN FR2
                   ;
DBØ9               :FRM3
DBØ9  C6F6               DEC     ZTEMP1+1          ; DECREMENT COUNTER
DBØB  3ØØ6 ^DB13         BMI     :NXTB             ; IF -, DO NEXT BYTE
DBØD  2ØØ5DD             JSR     FRA2Ø             ; ADD FR2 TO FRØ [6 BYTES]
DB1Ø  4CØ9DB             JMP     :FRM3             ; REPEAT
                   ;
                   ;          SET UP FOR NEXT SET OF ADDS
                   ;
DB13               :NXTB
                   ;
                   ;          SHIFT FRØ/FRE RIGHT ONE BYTE
                   ;                  [THEY ARE CONTIGUOUS]
                   ;
DB13  2Ø62DC             JSR     RSHFØE            ;SHIFT FRØ/FRE RIGHT
                   ;
                   ;          TEST FOR # OF BYTES SHIFTED
                   ;
DB16  C6F5               DEC     ZTEMP1            ; DECREMENT LOOP CONTROL
DB18  DØD7 ^DAF1         BNE     :FRM              ; IF MORE ADDS TO DO, DO IT
                   ;
                   ;          SET EXPONENT
                   ;
DB1A               MDEND
DB1A  A5ED               LDA     EEXP              ; GET EXPONENT
DB1C  85D4               STA     FRØ               ; STORE AS FRØ EXP
                   ;
                   ;
DB1E               MEND1
DB1E  4CØ4DC             JMP     NORM1             ; NORMALIZE
                   ;
                   ;
                   ;
DB21               MEND2
DB21  2Ø44DA             JSR     ZFRØ              ; CLEAR FRØ
DB24               MEND3
DB24  18                 CLC                       ; CLEAR CARRY FOR GOOD RTN
DB25  6Ø                 RTS
                   ;
                   ;
                   ;
DB26               :EROV
DB26  38                 SEC                       ; SET CARRY FOR ERROR ROUTINE
DB27  6Ø                 RTS                       ; RETURN
```

FDIV — Floating Point Divide

```
                   *         ON ENTRY    FRØ - DIVIDEND
                   *                     FR1 - DIVISOR
                   *
                   *         ON EXIT     FRØ - QUOTIENT
                   *
                   *         RETURNS WITH CC SET:
                   *                CARRY CLEAR - ERROR
                   *                CARRY SET - NO ERROR
                   *
                   *
DB28               FDIV
                   ;
                   ;         DO DIVIDE SET UP
                   ;
DB28  A5EØ               LDA      FR1                ; GET FR1 EXP
DB2A  FØFA ^DB26         BEQ      :EROV              ; IF =Ø, THEN OVERFLOW
DB2C  A5D4               LDA      FRØ                ; GET EXPONENT FRØ
DB2E  FØF4 ^DB24         BEQ      MEND3              ; IF = Ø, THEN DONE
                   ;
DB3Ø  20CFDC             JSR      MDESUP             ; DO COMMOM PART OF EXP SET UP
                   ;
DB33  38                 SEC
DB34  E5EØ               SBC      FR1                ; SUB FR1 EXP FROM FRØ EX
DB36  18                 CLC
DB37  694Ø               ADC      #$4Ø               ; ADD IN EXCESS 64
DB39  3ØEB ^DB26         BMI      :EROV              ; IF MINUS THEN OVERFLOW
                   ;
DB3B  2ØEØDC             JSR      MDSUP              ; DO SETUP COMMON FOR MULT
DB3E  E6F5               INC      ZTEMP1             ;LOOP 1 MORE TIME FOR DIVIDE
DB4Ø  4C4EDB             JMP      :FRD1              ; SKIP SHIFT 1ST TIME THROUGH
                   ;
      = ØØD9       QTEMP    EQU     FRØ+FMPREC
DB43               :NXTQ
                   ;
                   ;         SHIFT FRØ/FRE LEFT ONE BYTE
                   ;                [THEY ARE CONTIGUOUS]
                   ;
DB43  A2ØØ               LDX      #Ø                 ; GET POINTER TO BYTE TO MOVE
DB45               :NXTQ1
DB45  B5D5               LDA      FRØ+1,X            ; GET BYTE
DB47  95D4               STA      FRØ,X              ; MOVE IT LEFT ONE BYTE
                   ;
DB49  E8                 INX                         ; POINT TO NEXT BYTE
DB4A  EØØC               CPX      #FMPREC*2+2        ; HAVE WE DONE THEM ALL?
DB4C  DØF7 ^DB45         BNE      :NXTQ1             ; IF NOT, BRANCH
                   *
                   *         DO DIVIDE
                   *
DB4E               :FRD1
                   ;
                   ;         SUBTRACT FR2 [DIVISOR * 2] FROM FRE [DIVIDEND]
                   ;
                   ;
DB4E  AØØ5               LDY      #FMPREC            ; SET LOOP CONTROL
DB5Ø  38                 SEC                         ; SET CARRY
DB51  F8                 SED                         ; SET DECIMAL MODE
DB52               :FRS2
DB52  B9DAØØ             LDA      FRE,Y              ; GET A BYTE FROM FRE
DB55  F9E6ØØ             SBC      FR2,Y              ; SUB FR2
DB58  99DAØØ             STA      FRE,Y              ; STORE RESULT
DB5B  88                 DEY                         ; DEC COUNTER
DB5C  1ØF4 ^DB52         BPL      :FRS2              ; BR IF MORE TO DO
DB5E  D8                 CLD                         ; CLEAR DECIMAL MODE
                   ;
DB5F  9ØØ4 ^DB65         BCC      :FAIL              ; IF RESULT <Ø [FRE < FR2] BR
                   ;
DB61  E6D9               INC      QTEMP              ; INCR # TIMES SUB [QUOTIENT]
                   ;
```

```
DB63  DØE9 ^DB4E       BNE     :FRD1             ; SUB AGAIN
                      ;
                      ;      SUBTRACT OF FR2 DIDN'T GO
                      ;
DB65                  :FAIL
DB65  200FDD           JSR     FRA2E             ; ADD FR2 BACK TO FRØ
                      ;
                      ;      SHIFT LAST BYTE OF QUOTIENT ONE NIBBLE LEFT
                      ;
DB68  Ø6D9             ASL     QTEMP             ; SHIFT 4 BITS LEFT
DB6A  Ø6D9             ASL     QTEMP             ; X
DB6C  Ø6D9             ASL     QTEMP             ; X
DB6E  Ø6D9             ASL     QTEMP             ; X
DB7Ø                  :FRD2
                      ;
                      ;      SUBTRACT FR1 [DIVISOR] FROM FRE [DIVIDEND]
                      ;
                      ;
DB7Ø  AØØ5             LDY     #FMPREC           ; SET LOOP CONTROL
DB72  38               SEC                       ; SET CARRY
DB73  F8               SED                       ; SET DECIMAL MODE
DB74                  :FRS1
DB74  B9DAØØ           LDA     FRE,Y             ; GET A BYTE FROM FRE
DB77  F9EØØØ           SBC     FR1,Y             ; SUB FR1
DB7A  99DAØØ           STA     FRE,Y             ; STORE RESULT
DB7D  88               DEY
DB7E  1ØF4 ^DB74       BPL     :FRS1             ; BR IF MORE TO DO
DB8Ø  D8               CLD                       ; CLEAR DECIMAL MODE
                      ;
DB81  9ØØ4 ^DB87       BCC     :FAIL2            ; IF RESULT < Ø [FRE < FR1] BR
                      ;
DB83  E6D9             INC     QTEMP             ; INCR # TIMES SUB [QUOTIENT]
                      ;
DB85  DØE9 ^DB7Ø       BNE     :FRD2             ; SUB AGAIN
                      ;
                      ;      SUBTRACT OF FR1 DIDN'T GO
                      ;
DB87                  :FAIL2
DB87  2009DD           JSR     FRA1E             ; ADD FR1 BACK TO FRØ
                      ;
DB8A  C6F5             DEC     ZTEMP1            ; DEC LOOP CONTROL
DB8C  DØB5 ^DB43       BNE     :NXTQ             ; GET NEXT QUIOTIENT BYTE
                      ;
DB8E  2062DC           JSR     RSHFØE            ;SHIFT RIGHT FRØ/FRE TO CLEAR
                                                  EXP
DB91  4C1ADB           JMP     MDEND             ; JOIN MULT END UP CODE
```

:GETCHAR — Test Input Character

```
                      *      ON ENTRY   INBUFF - POINTS TO BUFFER WITH INPUT
                      *                 CIX - POINTS TO CHAR IN BUFFER
                      *
                      *      ON EXIT    CIX - POINTS TO NEXT CHAR
                      *                 CC - CARRY CLEAR IF CHAR IS NUMBER
                      *                      CARRY SET IF CHAR NOT NUMBER
                      *
DB94                  :GETCHAR
DB94  20AFDB           JSR     TSTNUM            ; GO TEST FOR NUMBER
DB97  A4F2             LDY     CIX               ; GET CHARACTER INDEX
DB99  9ØØ2 ^DB9D       BCC     :GCHR1            ; IF CHAR = NUM, SKIP
                      ;
DB9B  B1F3             LDA     [INBUFF],Y        ; GET CHARACTER
                      ;
DB9D                  :GCHR1
DB9D  C8               INY                       ; POINT TO NEXT CHAR
DB9E  84F2             STY     CIX               ; SAVE INDEX
DBAØ  6Ø               RTS
                      ;
                      ;SKPBLANK-SKIP BLANKS
                      ;      STARTS AT CIX AND SCANS FOR NON BLANKS
                      ;
```

```
DBA1                SKBLANK
DBA1                SKPBLANK
DBA1  A4F2              LDY      CIX              ;GET CIX
DBA3  A920              LDA      #$20             ;GET A BLANK
                    ;
DBA5  D1F3          :SB1    CMP      [INBUFF],Y       ;IS CHAR A BLANK
DBA7  D003 ^DBAC        BNE      :SBRTS           ;BR IF NOT
DBA9  C8                INY                       ;INC TO NEXT
DBAA  D0F9 ^DBA5        BNE      :SB1             ;GO TEST
                    ;
DBAC  84F2          :SBRTS  STY      CIX              ;SET NON BLANK INDEX
DBAE  60                RTS                       ;RETURN
                    ;
                    ; TSTNUM-TEST CHAR AT CIX FOR NUM
                    ;        - RTNS CARRY SET IF NUM
DBAF                TSTNUM
DBAF  A4F2              LDY      CIX              ;GET INDEX
DBB1  B1F3              LDA      [INBUFF],Y       ;AND GET CHAR
DBB3  38                SEC
DBB4  E930              SBC      #$30             ;SUBTRACT ASCLT ZERO
DBB6  9018 ^DBD0        BCC      :TSNFAIL         ;BR CHAR<ASCLT ZERO
DBB8  C90A              CMP      #$0A             ;TEST GT ASCLT 9
DBBA  60                RTS                       ;DONE
```

:TSTCHAR — Test to See if This Can Be a Number

```
                    *        ON EXIT    CC - CARRY SET IF NOT A #
                    *                        CARRY CLEAR IF A #
                    *
DBBB                :TSTCHAR
DBBB  A5F2              LDA      CIX              ; GET INDEX
DBBD  48                PHA                       ; SAVE IT
DBBE  2094DB            JSR      :GETCHAR         ; GET CHAR
DBC1  901F ^DBE2        BCC      :RTPASS          ; IF = #8 RETURN PASS
                    ;
DBC3  C92E              CMP      #'.'             ; IF = D.P., OK SO FAR
DBC5  F014 ^DBDB        BEQ      :TSTN
DBC7  C92B              CMP      #'+'             ; IF = +8 OK SO FAR
DBC9  F007 ^DBD2        BEQ      :TSTN1
DBCB  C92D              CMP      #'-'             ; IF = -8 OK SO FAR
DBCD  F003 ^DBD2        BEQ      :TSTN1
                    ;
                    ;
DBCF                :RTFAIL
DBCF  68                PLA                       ; CLEAR STACK
DBD0  38            :TSNFAIL SEC                  ;SET FAIL
DBD1  60                RTS
                    ;
                    ;
DBD2                :TSTN1
DBD2  2094DB            JSR      :GETCHAR         ; GET CHAR
DBD5  900B ^DBE2        BCC      :RTPASS          ; IF #, RETURN PASS
DBD7  C92E              CMP      #'.'             ; IS IT D.P.
DBD9  D0F4 ^DBCF        BNE      :RTFAIL          ; IF NOT, RETURN FAIL
DBDB                :TSTN
DBDB  2094DB            JSR      :GETCHAR         ; ELSE GET NEXT CHAR
DBDE  9002 ^DBE2        BCC      :RTPASS          ; IF #, RETURN PASS
DBE0  B0ED ^DBCF        BCS      :RTFAIL          ; ELSE, RETURN FAIL
                    ;
                    ;
DBE2                :RTPASS
DBE2  68                PLA                       ; RESTORE CIX
DBE3  85F2              STA      CIX              ; X
DBE5  18                CLC                       ; CLEAR CARRY
DBE6  60                RTS                       ; RETURN PASS
```

NIBSH0 — Shift FR0 One Nibble Left

```
                    *        NIBSH2 - SHIFT FR2 ONE NIBBLE LEFT
                    *
DBE7                NIBSH2
DBE7  A2E7              LDX      #FR2+1           ; POINT TO 1ST MANTISSA BYTE
```

```
DBE9  DØØ2 ^DBED        BNE     :NIB1
                  ;
DBEB              NIBSHØ
DBEB  A2D5              LDX     #FRØM               ; POINT TO MANTISSA OF FRØ
DBED              :NIB1
DBED  AØØ4              LDY     #4                  ; GET # OF BITS TO SHIFT
DBEF              :NIBS
DBEF  18                CLC                         ; CLEAR CARRY
DBFØ  36Ø4              ROL     4,X                 ; ROLL
DBF2  36Ø3              ROL     3,X                 ; X
DBF4  36Ø2              ROL     2,X                 ; X
DBF6  36Ø1              ROL     1,X                 ; X
DBF8  36ØØ              ROL     Ø,X                 ; X
DBFA  26EC              ROL     FRX                 ; SAVE SHIFTED NIBBLE
                  ;
DBFC  88                DEY                         ; DEC COUNT
DBFD  DØFØ ^DBEF        BNE     :NIBS               ; IF NOT = Ø, REPEAT
DBFF  6Ø                RTS
```

NORM — Normalize Floating Point Number

```
DCØØ              NORM
DCØØ  A2ØØ              LDX     #Ø                  ; GET ZERO
DCØ2  86DA              STX     FRØ+FPREC           ; FOR ADD NORM SHIFT IN A ZERO
DCØ4              NORM1
DCØ4  A2Ø4              LDX     #FMPREC-1           ; GET MAX # OF BYTES TO SHIFT
DCØ6  A5D4              LDA     FRØ                 ; GET EXPONENT
DCØ8  FØ2E ^DC38        BEQ     :NDONE              ; IF EXP=Ø, # =Ø
DCØA              :NORM
DCØA  A5D5              LDA     FRØM                ; GET 1ST BYTE OF MANTISSA
DCØC  DØ1A ^DC28        BNE     :TSTBIG             ; IF NOT = Ø THEN NO SHIFT
                  ;
                  ;         SHIFT 1 BYTE LEFT
                  ;
DCØE  AØØØ              LDY     #Ø                  ; GET INDEX FOR 1ST MOVE BYTE
DC1Ø              :NSH
DC1Ø  B9D6ØØ            LDA     FRØM+1,Y            ; GET MOVE BYTE
DC13  99D5ØØ            STA     FRØM,Y              ; STORE IT
DC16  C8                INY
DC17  CØØ5              CPY     #FMPREC             ; ARE WE DONE
DC19  9ØF5 ^DC1Ø        BCC     :NSH                ; IF NOT SHIFT AGAIN
                  ;
                  ;
                  ;         DECREMENT EXPONENT
                  ;
DC1B  C6D4              DEC     FRØ                 ; DECREMENT EXPONENT
                  ;
DC1D  CA                DEX                         ; DEC COUNTER
DC1E  DØEA ^DCØA        BNE     :NORM               ; DO AGAIN IF NEEDED
                  ;
                  ;
                  ;
DC2Ø  A5D5              LDA     FRØM                ; IS MANTISSA STILL Ø
DC22  DØØ4 ^DC28        BNE     :TSTBIG             ; IF NOT, SEE IF TOO BIG
DC24  85D4              STA     FRØ                 ; ELSE ZERO EXP
DC26  18                CLC
DC27  6Ø                RTS
                  ;
DC28              :TSTBIG
DC28  A5D4              LDA     FRØ                 ; GET EXPONENT
DC2A  297F              AND     #$7F                ; AND OUT SIGN BIT
DC2C  C971              CMP     #49+64              ; IS IT < 49+64?
DC2E  9ØØ1 ^DC31        BCC     :TSTUND             ; IF YES, TEST UNDERFLOW
DC3Ø  6Ø                RTS                         ; SO RETURN
DC31              :TSTUND
DC31  C9ØF              CMP     #-49+64             ; IS IT >=-49+64?
DC33  BØØ3 ^DC38        BCS     :NDONE              ; IF YES, WE ARE DONE
DC35  2Ø44DA            JSR     ZFRØ                ; ELSE # IS ZERO
                  ;
DC38              :NDONE
DC38  18                CLC                         ; CLEAR CARRY FOR GOOD RETURN
DC39  6Ø                RTS
```

RSHFT0 — Shift FR0 Right/Increment Exponent

RSHFT1 — Shift FR1 Right/Increment Exponent

```
                    *       ON ENTRY    A - # OF PLACES TO SHIFT
                    *
                    *
DC3A                RSHFTØ
DC3A  A2D4              LDX     #FRØ            ; POINT TO FRØ
DC3C  DØØ2 ^DC4Ø        BNE     :RSH
                    ;
DC3E                RSHFT1
DC3E  A2EØ              LDX     #FR1            ; POINT TO FR1
                    ;
DC4Ø                :RSH
DC4Ø  86F9              STX     ZTEMP3          ; SAVE FR POINTER
DC42  85F7              STA     ZTEMP4          ; SAVE # OF BYTES TO SHIFT
DC44  85F8              STA     ZTEMP4+1        ; SAVE FOR LATER
                    ;
DC46                :RSH2
DC46  AØØ4              LDY     #FMPREC-1       ; GET # OF BYTES TO MOVE
DC48                :RSH1
DC48  B5Ø4              LDA     4,X             ; GET CHAR
DC4A  95Ø5              STA     5,X             ; STORE CHAR
DC4C  CA                DEX                     ; POINT TO NEXT BYTE
DC4D  88                DEY                     ; DEC LOOP CONTROL
DC4E  DØF8 ^DC48        BNE     :RSH1           ; IF MORE TO MOVE, DO IT
DC5Ø  A9ØØ              LDA     #Ø              ; GET 1ST BYTE
DC52  95Ø5              STA     5,X             ; STORE IT
                    ;
DC54  A6F9              LDX     ZTEMP3          ; GET FR POINTER
DC56  C6F7              DEC     ZTEMP4          ; DO WE NEED TO SHIFT AGAIN?
DC58  DØEC ^DC46        BNE     :RSH2           ; IF YES, DO IT
                    ;
                    ;       FIX EXPONENT
                    ;
DC5A  B5ØØ              LDA     Ø,X             ; GET EXPONENT
DC5C  18                CLC
DC5D  65F8              ADC     ZTEMP4+1        ; SUB # OF SHIFTS
DC5F  95ØØ              STA     Ø,X             ; SAVE NEW EXPONENT
DC61  6Ø                RTS
```

RSHF0E — Shift FR0/FRE 1 Byte Right [They Are Contiguous]

```
DC62                RSHFØE
DC62  A2ØA              LDX     #FMPREC*2       ; GET LOOP CONTROL
                    ;
DC64                :NXTB1
DC64  B5D4              LDA     FRØ,X           ; GET A BYTE
DC66  95D5              STA     FRØ+1,X         ; MOVE IT OVER 1
                    ;
DC68  CA                DEX                     ; DEC COUNTER
DC69  1ØF9 ^DC64        BPL     :NXTB1          ; MOVE NEXT BYTE
DC6B  A9ØØ              LDA     #Ø              ; GET ZERO
DC6D  85D4              STA     FRØ             ; SHIFT IT IN
DC6F  6Ø                RTS
```

:CVFR0 — Convert Each Byte in FR0 to 2 Characters in LBUFF

```
                    *
                    *       ON ENTRY    A - DECIMAL POINT POSITION
                    *
                    *
DC7Ø                :CVFRØ
DC7Ø  85F7              STA     ZTEMP4          ; SAVE DECIMAL POSITION
                    ;
DC72  A2ØØ              LDX     #Ø              ; SET INDEX INTO FRØM
DC74  AØØØ              LDY     #Ø              ; SET INDEX INTO OUTPUT
                                                  LINE [LBUFF]
                    ;
                    ;       CONVERT A BYTE
                    ;
```

```
DC76                    :CVBYTE
DC76  2093DC                 JSR    :TSTDP            ; PUT IN D.P. NOW?
DC79                    :CVB1
DC79  38                     SEC                      ; DECREMENT DECIMAL POSITION
DC7A  E901                   SBC    #1                ; X
DC7C  85F7                   STA    ZTEMP4            ; SAVE IT
                        ;
                        ;        DO 1ST DIGIT
                        ;
DC7E  B5D5                   LDA    FRØM,X            ; GET FROM FRØ
DC8Ø                         LSRA                     ; SHIFT OUT LOW ORDER BITS
DC8Ø +4A                     LSR    A
DC81                         LSRA                     ; TO GET 1ST DIGIT
DC81 +4A                     LSR    A
DC82                         LSRA                     ; X
DC82 +4A                     LSR    A
DC83                         LSRA                     ; X
DC83 +4A                     LSR    A
DC84  209DDC                 JSR    :STNUM            ; GO PUT # IN BUFFER
                        ;
                        ;        DO SECOND DIGIT
                        ;
DC87  B5D5                   LDA    FRØM,X            ; GET NUMBER FROM FRØ
DC89  29ØF                   AND    #$ØF              ; AND OUT HIGH ORDER BITS
DC8B  209DDC                 JSR    :STNUM            ; GO PUT # IN BUFFER
                        ;
DC8E  E8                     INX                      ; INCR FRØ POINTER
DC8F  EØØ5                   CPX    #FMPREC           ; DONE LAST FRØ BYTE?
DC91  9ØE3 ^DC76             BCC    :CVBYTE           ; IF NOT, MORE TO DO
                        ;
                        ;        PUT IN DECIMAL POINT NOW?
                        ;
DC93                    :TSTDP
DC93  A5F7                   LDA    ZTEMP4            ; GET DECIMAL POSITION
DC95  DØØ5 ^DC9C             BNE    :TST1             ; IF NOT = Ø RTN
DC97  A92E                   LDA    #'.'              ; GET ASCII DECIMAL POINT
DC99  209FDC                 JSR    :STCHAR           ; PUT D.P. IN BUFFER
DC9C                    :TST1
DC9C  6Ø                     RTS
```

:STNUM — Put ASCII Number in LBUFF

```
                        *        ON ENTRY   A - DIGIT TO BE CONVERTED TO ASCII
                        *                       AND PUT IN LBUFF
                        *                   Y - INDEX IN LBUFF
```

:STCHAR — Store Character in A in LBUFF

```
DC9D                    :STNUM
DC9D  Ø93Ø                   ORA    #$3Ø              ; CONVERT TO ASCII
DC9F                    :STCHAR
DC9F  9980Ø5                 STA    LBUFF,Y           ; PUT IN LBUFF
DCA2  C8                     INY                      ; INCR LBUFF POINTER
DCA3  6Ø                     RTS
```

:FNZER0 — Find Last Non-zero Character in LBUFF

```
                        *        ON EXIT    A - LAST CHAR
                        *                   X - POINT TO LAST CHAR
                        *
DCA4                    :FNZERØ
DCA4  A2ØA                   LDX    #1Ø               ; POINT TO LAST CHAR IN LBUFF
                        ;
DCA6                    :FN3
DCA6  BD8ØØ5                 LDA    LBUFF,X           ; GET THE CHARACTER
DCA9  C92E                   CMP    #'.'              ; IS IT DECIMAL?
DCAB  FØØ7 ^DCB4             BEQ    :FN1              ; IF YES, BR
DCAD  C93Ø                   CMP    #'Ø'              ; IS IT ZERO?
DCAF  DØØ7 ^DCB8             BNE    :FN2              ; IF NOT, BR
DCB1  CA                     DEX                      ; DECREMENT INDEX
DCB2  DØF2 ^DCA6             BNE    :FN3              ; UNCONDITIONAL BR
```

```
                    ;
                    ;
DCB4                :FN1
DCB4  CA                DEX                     ; DECREMENT BUFFER INDEX
DCB5  BD8005            LDA     LBUFF,X         ; GET LAST CHAR
DCB8                :FN2
DCB8  60                RTS
```

:GETDIG -- Get Next Digit from FR0

```
                    *       ON ENTRY   FR0 - #
                    *
                    *       ON EXIT    A - DIGIT
                    *
                    *
DCB9                :GETDIG
DCB9  20EBDB            JSR     NIBSH0          ; SHIFT FR0 LEFT ONE NIBBLE
                    ;
DCBC  A5EC              LDA     FRX             ; GET BYTE CONTAINING
                                                  SHIFTED NIBBLE
DCBE  290F              AND     #$0F            ; AND OUT HIGH ORDER NIBBLE
DCC0  60                RTS
```

:DECINB — Decrement INBUFF

```
DCC1                :DECINB
DCC1  38                SEC                     ; SUBTRACT ONE FROM INBUFF
DCC2  A5F3              LDA     INBUFF          ; X
DCC4  E901              SBC     #1              ; X
DCC6  85F3              STA     INBUFF          ; X
DCC8  A5F4              LDA     INBUFF+1        ; X
DCCA  E900              SBC     #0              ; X
DCCC  85F4              STA     INBUFF+1        ; X
DCCE  60                RTS
```

MDESUP — Common Set-up for Multiply and Divide Exponent

```
                    *       ON EXIT    FR1 - FR1 EXP WITH OUT SIGN
                    *                  A - FR0 EXP WITHOUT SIGN
                    *                  FRSIGN - SIGN FOR QUOTIENT
                    *
DCCF                MDESUP
DCCF  A5D4              LDA     FR0             ; GET FR0 EXPONENT
DCD1  45E0              EOR     FR1             ; GET FR1 EXPONENT
DCD3  2980              AND     #$80            ; AND OUT ALL BUT SIGN BIT
DCD5  85EE              STA     FRSIGN          ; SAVE SIGN
                    ;
DCD7  06E0              ASL     FR1             ; SHIFT OUT SIGN IN FR1 EXP
DCD9  46E0              LSR     FR1             ; RESTORE FR1 EXP WITHOUT SIGN
DCDB  A5D4              LDA     FR0             ; GET FR0 EXP
DCDD  297F              AND     #$7F            ; AND OUT SIGN BIT
DCDF  60                RTS
```

MDSUP — Common Set-up for Multiply and Divide

```
                    *       ON ENTRY   A - EXPONENT
                    *                  CC - SET BY ADD OR SUB TO GET A
                    *
                    *
DCE0                MDSUP
DCE0  05EE              ORA     FRSIGN          ; OR IN SIGN BIT
DCE2  85ED              STA     EEXP            ; SAVE EXPONENT FOR LATER
DCE4  A900              LDA     #0              ; CLEAR A
DCE6  85D4              STA     FR0             ; CLEAR FR0 EXP
DCE8  85E0              STA     FR1             ; CLEAR FR0 EXP
                    ;
                    ;
DCEA  2028DD            JSR     MVFR12          ; MOVE FR1 TO FR2
                    ;
DCED  20E7DB            JSR     NIBSH2          ; SHIFT FR2 1 NIBBLE LEFT
DCF0  A5EC              LDA     FRX             ; GET SHIFTED NIBBLE
```

```
DCF2  290F              AND    #$0F           ; AND OUT HIGH ORDER NIBBLE
DCF4  85E6              STA    FR2            ; STORE TO FINISH SHIFT
                   ;
DCF6  A905              LDA    #FMPREC        ; SET LOOP CONTROL
DCF8  85F5              STA    ZTEMP1         ; X
                   ;
DCFA  2034DD            JSR    MVFR0E         ; MOVE FR0 TO FRE
DCFD  2044DA            JSR    ZFR0           ; CLEAR FR0
                   ;
DD00  60                RTS
                   ;
```

FRA

```
                   *      FRA10 - ADD FR1 TO FR0 [6 BYTES]
                   *
                   *      FRA20 - ADD FR2 TO FR0 [6 BYTES]
                   *
                   *      FRA1E - ADD FR1 TO FRE
                   *
                   *      FRA2E - ADD FR2 TO FRE
                   *
DD01               FRA10
DD01  A2D9              LDX    #FR0+FMPREC    ; POINT TO LAST BYTE OF SUM
DD03  D006 ^DD0B        BNE    :F1
                   ;
DD05               FRA20
DD05  A2D9              LDX    #FR0+FMPREC
DD07  D008 ^DD11        BNE    :F2
                   ;
DD09               FRA1E
DD09  A2DF              LDX    #FRE+FMPREC
DD0B               :F1
DD0B  A0E5              LDY    #FR1+FMPREC
DD0D  D004 ^DD13        BNE    :FRA
DD0F               FRA2E
DD0F  A2DF              LDX    #FRE+FMPREC
DD11               :F2
DD11  A0EB              LDY    #FR2+FMPREC
                   ;
                   ;
DD13               :FRA
DD13  A905              LDA    #FMPREC        ; GET VALUE FOR LOOP CONTROL
DD15  85F7              STA    ZTEMP4         ; SET LOOP CONTROL
DD17  18                CLC                   ; CLEAR CARRY
DD18  F8                SED                   ; SET DECIMAL MODE
DD19               :FRA1
DD19  B500              LDA    0,X            ; GET 1ST BYTE OF
DD1B  790000            ADC    0,Y            ; ADD
DD1E  9500              STA    0,X            ; STORE
DD20  CA                DEX                   ; POINT TO NEXT BYTE
DD21  88                DEY                   ; POINT TO NEXT BYTE
DD22  C6F7              DEC    ZTEMP4         ; DEC COUNTER
DD24  10F3 ^DD19        BPL    :FRA1          ; IF MORE TO DO, DO IT
DD26  D8                CLD                   ; CLEAR DECIMAL MODE
DD27  60                RTS
```

MVFR12 — Move FR1 to FR2

```
DD28               MVFR12
DD28  A005              LDY    #FMPREC        ; SET COUNTER
DD2A               :MV2
DD2A  B9E000            LDA    FR1,Y          ; GET A BYTE
DD2D  99E600            STA    FR2,Y          ; STORE IT
                   ;
DD30  88                DEY                   ; DEC COUNTER
DD31  10F7 ^DD2A        BPL    :MV2           ; IF MORE TO MOVE, DO IT
DD33  60                RTS
```

MVFR0E — Move FR0 to FRE

```
DD34                MVFRØE
DD34  AØØ5              LDY      #FMPREC
DD36                :MV1
DD36  B9D4ØØ            LDA      FRØ,Y
DD39  99DAØØ            STA      FRE,Y
                    ;
DD3C  88                DEY
DD3D  1ØF7  ^DD36       BPL      :MV1
DD3F  6Ø                RTS
```

Polynomial Evaluation

```
                    *       Y=A[Ø]+A[1]*X+A[2]*X**2+...+A[N]*X**N,N>Ø
                    *        =[[...[A[N]*X+A[N-1]]*X+...+A[2]]*X+A[1]]*X+A[Ø]
                    *       INPUT: X IN FRØ, N+1 IN A-REG
                    *       REG [X,Y]->A[N]...A[Ø]
                    *       OUTPUT  Y IN FRØ
                    *       USES FPTR2, PLYCNT, PLYARG
                    *       CALLS FSTØR, FMOVE, FLD1R, FADD, FMUL
DD4Ø  86FE          PLYEVL  STX      FPTR2         ;SAVE POINTER TO COEFF'S
DD42  84FF              STY      FPTR2+1
DD44  85EF              STA  PLYCNT
DD46  A2EØ              LDX      #PLYARG&$FF
DD48  AØØ5              LDY      #PLYARG/$1ØØ
DD4A  2ØA7DD            JSR      FSTØR         ;SAVE ARG
DD4D  2ØB6DD            JSR      FMOVE         ;ARG->FR1
DD5Ø  A6FE              LDX      FPTR2
DD52  A4FF              LDY      FPTR2+1
DD54  2089DD            JSR      FLDØR         ;COEF->FRØ [INIT SUM]
DD57  C6EF              DEC      PLYCNT
DD59  FØ2D  ^DD88       BEQ      PLYOUT        ;DONE ?
DD5B  2ØDBDA        PLYEV1  JSR      FMUL      ; SUM * ARG
DD5E  BØ28  ^DD88       BCS      PLYOUT        ; Ø'FLOW
DD6Ø  18                CLC
DD61  A5FE              LDA      FPTR2         ;BUMP COEF POINTER
DD63  69Ø6              ADC      #FPREC
DD65  85FE              STA      FPTR2
DD67  9ØØ6  ^DD6F       BCC      PLYEV2
DD69  A5FF              LDA      FPTR2+1       ;ACROSS PAGE
DD6B  69ØØ              ADC      #Ø
DD6D  85FF              STA      FPTR2+1
DD6F  A6FE          PLYEV2  LDX      FPTR2
DD71  A4FF              LDY      FPTR2+1
DD73  2Ø98DD            JSR      FLD1R         ;GET NEXT COEF
DD76  2Ø66DA            JSR      FADD          ;SUM*ARG + COEF
DD79  BØØD  ^DD88       BCS      PLYOUT        ; Ø'FLOW
DD7B  C6EF              DEC      PLYCNT
DD7D  FØØ9  ^DD88       BEQ      PLYOUT        ;DONE ?
DD7F  A2EØ              LDX      #PLYARG&$FF
DD81  AØØ5              LDY      #PLYARG/$1ØØ
DD83  2Ø98DD            JSR      FLD1R         ;GET ARG AGAIN
DD86  3ØD3  ^DD5B       BMI      PLYEV1        ; [=JMP]
DD88  6Ø            PLYOUT  RTS
```

Floating Load/Store

```
                    *       LOAD FRØ FROM [X,Y]  X=LSB, Y=MSB, USES FLPTR [PGØ]
DD89  86FC          FLDØR   STX      FLPTR         ; SET FLPTR => [X,Y]
DD8B  84FD              STY      FLPTR+1
DD8D  AØØ5          FLDØP   LDY      #FPREC-1      ;# BYTES ENTER HERE W/FLPTR SET
DD8F  B1FC          FLDØ1   LDA      [FLPTR],Y     ; MOVE
DD91  99D4ØØ            STA      FRØ,Y
DD94  88                DEY
DD95  1ØF8  ^DD8F       BPL      FLDØ1         ; COUNT & LOOP
DD97  6Ø                RTS
                    *
                    *       LOAD FR1 FROM [X,Y] OR [FLPTR]
DD98  86FC          FLD1R   STX      FLPTR         ; FLPTR=>[X,Y]
```

```
DD9A  84FD             STY     FLPTR+1
DD9C  A005        FLD1P    LDY     #FPREC-1        ; # BYTES ENTER W/FLPTR SET
DD9E  B1FC        FLD11    LDA     [FLPTR],Y       ; MOVE
DDA0  99E000           STA     FR1,Y
DDA3  88               DEY
DDA4  10F8 ^DD9E       BPL     FLD11               ; COUNT & LOOP
DDA6  60               RTS
                  *
                  *        STORE FR0 IN [X,Y] OR [FLPTR]
DDA7  86FC        FST0R    STX     FLPTR
DDA9  84FD             STY     FLPTR+1
DDAB  A005        FST0P    LDY     #FPREC-1        ; ENTRY W/FLPTR SET
DDAD  B9D400      FST01    LDA     FR0,Y
DDB0  91FC             STA     [FLPTR],Y
DDB2  88               DEY
DDB3  10F8 ^DDAD       BPL     FST01
DDB5  60               RTS
                  *
                  *        MOVE FR0 TO FR1
                  *
DDB6              MV0TO1
DDB6  A205        FMOVE    LDX     #FPREC-1
DDB8  B5D4        FMOVE1   LDA     FR0,X
DDBA  95E0             STA     FR1,X
DDBC  CA               DEX
DDBD  10F9 ^DDB8       BPL     FMOVE1
DDBF  60               RTS
```

EXP[X] and EXP10[X]

```
DDC0  A289        EXP      LDX     #LOG10E&$FF       ; E**X = 10**[X*LOG10[E]]
DDC2  A0DE             LDY     #LOG10E/$100
DDC4  2098DD           JSR     FLD1R
DDC7  20DBDA           JSR     FMUL
DDCA  B07F ^DE4B       BCS     EXPERR
DDCC  A900        EXP10    LDA     #0              ; 10**X
DDCE  85F1             STA     XFMFLG              ; CLEAR TRANSFORM FLAG
DDD0  A5D4             LDA     FR0
DDD2  85F0             STA     SGNFLG              ; REMEMBER ARG SGN
DDD4  297F             AND     #$7F                ; ; & MAKE PLUS
DDD6  85D4             STA     FR0
DDD8  38               SEC
DDD9  E940             SBC     #$40
DDDB  3026 ^DE03       BMI     EXP1                ; X<1 SO USE SERIES DIRECTLY
                  *        10**X = 10**[I+F] = [10**I] * [10**F]
DDDD  C904             CMP     #FPREC-2
DDDF  106A ^DE4B       BPL     EXPERR              ; ARG TOO BIG
DDE1  A2E6             LDX     #FPSCR&$FF
DDE3  A005             LDY     #FPSCR/$100
DDE5  20A7DD           JSR     FST0R               ; SAVE ARG
DDE8  20D2D9           JSR     FPI                 ; MAKE INTEGER
DDEB  A5D4             LDA     FR0
DDED  85F1             STA     XFMFLG              ; SAVE MULTIPLIER EXP IN XFORM
DDEF  A5D5             LDA     FR0+1               ; CHECK MSB
DDF1  D058 ^DE4B       BNE     EXPERR              ; SHOULD HAVE NONE
DDF3  20AAD9           JSR     IFP                 ; NOW TURN IT BACK TO FLPT
DDF6  20B6DD           JSR     FMOVE
DDF9  A2E6             LDX     #FPSCR&$FF
DDFB  A005             LDY     #FPSCR/$100
DDFD  2089DD           JSR     FLD0R               ; GET ARG BACK
DE00  2060DA           JSR     FSUB                ; ARG - INTEGER PART = FRACTION
                  *        NOW HAVE FRACTION PART OF ARG [F] IN FR0,
                  *        INTEGER PART [I]
                  *        IN XFMFLG.  USE SERIES APPROX FOR
                  *        10**F, THEN MULTIPLY BY 10**I
DE03              EXP1
DE03  A90A             LDA     #NPCOEF
DE05  A24D             LDX     #P10COF&$FF
DE07  A0DE             LDY     #P10COF/$100
```

```
DEØ9   2040DD             JSR      PLYEVL           ;P[X]
DEØC   20B6DD             JSR      FMOVE
DEØF   20DBDA             JSR      FMUL             ;P[X]*P[X]
DE12   A5F1               LDA      XFMFLG           ; DID WE TRANSFORM ARG
DE14   FØ23 ^DE39         BEQ      EXPSGN           ; NO SO LEAVE RESULT ALONE
DE16   18                 CLC
DE17                      RORA                      ; I/2
DE17 +6A                  ROR      A
DE18   85EØ               STA      FR1              ; SAVE AS EXP-TO-BE
DE1A   A9Ø1               LDA      #1               ; GET MANTISSA BYTE
DE1C   9ØØ2 ^DE2Ø         BCC      EXP2             ; CHECK BIT SHIFTED OUT OF A
DE1E   A91Ø               LDA      #$1Ø             ; I WAS ODD - MANTISSA = 1Ø
DE2Ø   85E1        EXP2     STA      FR1+1
DE22   A2Ø4               LDX      #FPREC-2
DE24   A9ØØ               LDA      #Ø
DE26   95E2        EXP3     STA      FR1+2,X          ; CLEAR REST OF MANTISSA
DE28   CA                 DEX
DE29   1ØFB ^DE26         BPL      EXP3
DE2B   A5EØ               LDA      FR1              ; BACK TO EXPONENT
DE2D   18                 CLC
DE2E   694Ø               ADC      #$4Ø             ; BIAS IT
DE3Ø   BØ19 ^DE4B         BCS      EXPERR           ; OOPS...IT'S TOO BIG
DE32   3Ø17 ^DE4B         BMI      EXPERR
DE34   85EØ               STA      FR1              ; FR1 = 1Ø**I
DE36   2ØDBDA             JSR      FMUL             ; [1Ø**I]*[1Ø**F]
DE39   A5FØ        EXPSGN   LDA      SGNFLG           ; WAS ARG<Ø
DE3B   1ØØD ^DE4A         BPL      EXPOUT           ; NO-DONE
DE3D   2ØB6DD             JSR      FMOVE            ; YES-INVERT RESULT
DE4Ø   A28F               LDX      #FONE&$FF
DE42   AØDE               LDY      #FONE/$1ØØ
DE44   2089DD             JSR      FLDØR
DE47   2028DB             JSR      FDIV
DE4A   6Ø          EXPOUT   RTS                       ; [PANT, PANT - FINISHED::]
DE4B   38          EXPERR   SEC                       ; FLAG ERROR
DE4C   6Ø                 RTS                       ; & QUIT
DE4D   3D17941900  P1ØCOF   .BYTE    $3D,$17,$94,$19,Ø,Ø ;Ø.ØØØØ179419
       ØØ
DE53   3D573305ØØ         .BYTE    $3D,$57,$33,$Ø5,Ø,Ø ;Ø.ØØØØ5733Ø5
       ØØ
DE59   3EØ5547662         .BYTE    $3E,$Ø5,$54,$76,$62,Ø ;Ø.ØØØ5547662
       ØØ
DE5F   3E32196227         .BYTE    $3E,$32,$19,$62,$27,Ø ;Ø.ØØ32176227
       ØØ
DE65   3FØ168603Ø         .BYTE    $3F,$Ø1,$68,$6Ø,$3Ø,$36 ;Ø.Ø1686Ø3Ø36
       36
DE6B   3FØ732Ø327         .BYTE    $3F,$Ø7,$32,$Ø3,$27,$41 ;Ø.Ø732Ø32741
       41
DE71   3F25433456         .BYTE    $3F,$25,$43,$34,$56,$75 ;Ø.2543345675
       75
DE77   3F6627373Ø         .BYTE    $3F,$66,$27,$37,$3Ø,$5Ø ;Ø.66273735Ø
       5Ø
DE7D   4ØØ1151292         .BYTE    $4Ø,$Ø1,$15,$12,$92,$55 ;1.15129255
       55
DE83   3F99999999         .BYTE    $3F,$99,$99,$99,$99,$99 ;Ø.999999999
       99
       = ØØØA      NPCOEF   EQU      (*-P1ØCOF)/FPREC
DE89   3F43429448  LOG1ØE   .BYTE    $3F,$43,$42,$94,$48,$19  ; LOG1Ø[E]
       19
DE8F   4ØØ1ØØØØØØ  FONE     .BYTE    $4Ø,1,Ø,Ø,Ø,Ø   ; 1.Ø
       ØØ
```

Z = [X-C]/[X + C]

```
DE95   86FE        XFORM    STX      FPTR2
DE97   84FF               STY      FPTR2+1
DE99   A2EØ               LDX      #PLYARG&$FF
DE9B   AØØ5               LDY      #PLYARG/$1ØØ
DE9D   2ØA7DD             JSR      FSTØR            ;STASH X IN PLYARG
DEAØ   A6FE               LDX      FPTR2
DEA2   A4FF               LDY      FPTR2+1
```

```
DEA4  2098DD          JSR     FLD1R
DEA7  2066DA          JSR     FADD                ;X+C
DEAA  A2E6            LDX     #FPSCR&$FF
DEAC  A005            LDY     #FPSCR/$100
DEAE  20A7DD          JSR     FSTØR
DEB1  A2EØ            LDX     #PLYARG&$FF
DEB3  A005            LDY     #PLYARG/$100
DEB5  2089DD          JSR     FLDØR
DEB8  A6FE            LDX     FPTR2
DEBA  A4FF            LDY     FPTR2+1
DEBC  2098DD          JSR     FLD1R
DEBF  2060DA          JSR     FSUB                ;X-C
DEC2  A2E6            LDX     #FPSCR&$FF
DEC4  A005            LDY     #FPSCR/$100
DEC6  2098DD          JSR     FLD1R
DEC9  2028DB          JSR     FDIV                ; [X-C]/[X+C] = Z
DECC  60              RTS
```

LOG10[X]

```
DECD  A901            LOG     LDA     #1          ;REMEMBER ENTRY POINT
DECF  D002 ^DED3        BNE     LOGBTH
DED1  A900            LOG10   LDA     #0          ; CLEAR FLAG
DED3  85F0            LOGBTH  STA     SGNFLG      ; USE SGNFLG FOR LOG/LOG10
                                                    MARKER
DED5  A5D4                    LDA     FRØ
DED7  1002 ^DEDB              BPL     LOG5
DED9  38              LOGERR  SEC
DEDA  60                      RTS
DEDB                  LOG5
                      *       WE WANT X = F*[10**Y], 1<F<10
                      *       10**Y HAS SAME EXP BYTE AS X
                      *       & MANTISSA BYTE = 1 OR 10
DEDB  A5D4            LOG1    LDA     FRØ
DEDD  85EØ                    STA     FR1
DEDF  38                      SEC
DEEØ  E940                    SBC     #$40
DEE2                          ASLA
DEE2 +0A                      ASL     A
DEE3  85F1                    STA     XFMFLG      ; REMEMBER Y
DEE5  A5D5                    LDA     FRØ+1
DEE7  29F0                    AND     #$F0
DEE9  D004 ^DEEF              BNE     LOG2
DEEB  A901                    LDA     #1
DEED  D004 ^DEF3              BNE     LOG3
DEEF  E6F1            LOG2    INC     XFMFLG      ; BUMP Y
DEF1  A910                    LDA     #$10
DEF3  85E1            LOG3    STA     FR1+1       ; SET UP MANTISSA
DEF5  A204                    LDX     #FPREC-2    ; CLEAR REST OF MANTISSA
DEF7  A900                    LDA     #0
DEF9  95E2            LOG4    STA     FR1+2,X
DEFB  CA                      DEX
DEFC  10FB ^DEF9              BPL     LOG4
DEFE  2028DB                  JSR     FDIV        ; X = X/[10**Y] - S.B.
                                                    IN [1,10]
DF01                  FLOG10                      ;;LOG10[X],1<=X<=10
DF01  A266                    LDX     #SQR10&$FF
DF03  AØDF                    LDY     #SQR10/$100
DF05  2095DE                  JSR     XFORM       ;Z = [X-C]/[X+C],C*C = 10
DF08  A2E6                    LDX     #FPSCR&$FF
DFØA  A005                    LDY     #FPSCR/$100
DFØC  20A7DD                  JSR     FSTØR       ;SAVE Z
DFØF  20B6DD                  JSR     FMOVE
DF12  20DBDA                  JSR     FMUL        ; Z*Z
DF15  A90A                    LDA     #NLCOEF
DF17  A272                    LDX     #LGCOEF&$FF
DF19  AØDF                    LDY     #LGCOEF/$100
DF1B  2040DD                  JSR     PLYEVL      ; P[Z*Z]
DF1E  A2E6                    LDX     #FPSCR&$FF
DF20  A005                    LDY     #FPSCR/$100
DF22  2098DD                  JSR     FLD1R
```

```
DF25  20DBDA          JSR    FMUL            ; Z*P[Z*Z]
DF28  A26C            LDX    #FHALF&$FF
DF2A  A0DF            LDY    #FHALF/$100
DF2C  2098DD          JSR    FLD1R
DF2F  2066DA          JSR    FADD            ; 0.5 + Z*P[Z*Z]
DF32  20B6DD          JSR    FMOVE
DF35  A900            LDA    #0
DF37  85D5            STA    FR0+1
DF39  A5F1            LDA    XFMFLG
DF3B  85D4            STA    FR0
DF3D  1007 ^DF46      BPL    LOG6
DF3F  49FF            EOR    #-1             ; FLIP SIGN
DF41  18              CLC
DF42  6901            ADC    #1
DF44  85D4            STA    FR0
DF46              LOG6
DF46  20AAD9          JSR    IFP             ; LEAVES FR1 ALONE
DF49  24F1            BIT    XFMFLG
DF4B  1006 ^DF53      BPL    LOG7
DF4D  A980            LDA    #$80            ; FLIP AGAIN
DF4F  05D4            ORA    FR0
DF51  85D4            STA    FR0
DF53              LOG7
DF53  2066DA          JSR    FADD            ; LOG[X] = LOG[X] +Y
DF56              LOGOUT
DF56  A5F0            LDA    SGNFLG
DF58  F00A ^DF64      BEQ    LOGDON          ;WAS LOG10, NOT LOG
DF5A  A289            LDX    #LOG10E&255     ; LOG[X]/LOG10[E]
DF5C  A0DE            LDY    #LOG10E/$100
DF5E  2098DD          JSR    FLD1R
DF61  2028DB          JSR    FDIV
DF64  18          LOGDON  CLC
DF65  60              RTS
DF66  4003162277  SQR10   .BYTE   $40,$03,$16,$22,$77,$66 ;SQUARE ROOT OF 10
      66
DF6C  3F50000000  FHALF   .BYTE   $3F,$50,0,0,0,0      ; 0.5
      00
DF72  3F49155711  LGCOEF  .BYTE   $3F,$49,$15,$57,$11,$08 ;0.4915571108
      08
DF78  BF51704947      .BYTE   $BF,$51,$70,$49,$47,$08 ;-0.5170494708
      08
DF7E  3F39205761      .BYTE   $3F,$39,$20,$57,$61,$95 ;0.3920576195
      95
DF84  BF04396303      .BYTE   $BF,$04,$39,$63,$03,$55 ;-0.0439630355
      55
DF8A  3F10093012      .BYTE   $3F,$10,$09,$30,$12,$64 ;0.1009301264
      64
DF90  3F09390804      .BYTE   $3F,$09,$39,$08,$04,$60   ; 0.0939080460
      60
DF96  3F12425847      .BYTE   $3F,$12,$42,$58,$47,$42 ;0.1242584742
      42
DF9C  3F17371206      .BYTE   $3F,$17,$37,$12,$06,$08   ; 0.1737120608
      08
DFA2  3F28952971      .BYTE   $3F,$28,$95,$29,$71,$17 ;0.28957117
      17
DFA8  3F86858896      .BYTE   $3F,$86,$85,$88,$96,$44 ;0.8685889644
      44
      = 000A      NLCOEF  EQU     (*-LGCOEF)/FPREC
DFAE  3E16054449  ATCOEF  .BYTE   $3E,$16,$05,$44,$49,0 ;0.0016054449
      00
DFB4  BE95683845      .BYTE   $BE,$95,$68,$38,$45,0 ;-0.009568345
      00
DFBA  3F02687994      .BYTE   $3F,$02,$68,$79,$94,$16 ;0.0268799416
      16
DFC0  BF04927890      .BYTE   $BF,$04,$92,$78,$90,$80 ;-0.0492789080
      80
DFC6  3F07031520      .BYTE   $3F,$07,$03,$15,$20,0 ;0.0703152000
      00
DFCC  BF08922912      .BYTE   $BF,$08,$92,$29,$12,$44 ;-0.0892291244
      44
DFD2  3F11084009      .BYTE   $3F,$11,$08,$40,$09,$11 ;0.1108400911
      11
```

```
DFD8  BF14283156       .BYTE   $BF,$14,$28,$31,$56,$Ø4 ;-Ø.14283156Ø4
      Ø4
DFDE  3F19999877       .BYTE   $3F,$19,$99,$98,$77,$44 ;Ø.1999987744
      44
DFE4  BF33333331       .BYTE   $BF,$33,$33,$33,$31,$13   ; -Ø.3333333113
      13
DFEA  3F99999999  FP9S    .BYTE   $3F,$99,$99,$99,$99,$99  ; Ø.999999999
      99
      = ØØØB      NATCF   EQU     (*-ATCOEF)/FPREC
DFFØ  3F78539816  PIOV4   .BYTE   $3F,$78,$53,$98,$16,$34 ; PI/4 = ARCTAN[1.Ø]
      34
```

Atari Cartridge Vectors

```
DFF6  = BFF9           ORG     CRTGI
BFF9              SCVECT
BFF9  6Ø               RTS
BFFA  ØØAØ             DW      COLDSTART      ; COLDSTART ADDR
BFFC  ØØ               DB      Ø              ; CART EXISTS
BFFD  Ø5               DB      5              ; FLAG
BFFE  F9BF             DW      SCVECT  ; COLDSTART ENTRY ADDR
```

End of BASIC

```
CØØØ                   END
```

Macros in Source Code

The following is a listing of the macros used in this source listing. You will be able to tell when a macro was used by a plus (+) sign to the left of the hex code produced in column two by the assembler.

```
ASLA:   MACRO
%L      ASL     A
        ENDM
RORA:   MACRO
%L      ROR     A
        ENDM
LSRA:   MACRO
%L      LSR     A
        ENDM
ROLA:   MACRO
%L      ROL     A
        ENDM
FDB:    MACRO
%L      DW      REV (%1)
        IF      '=%2' <> '='
        DW      REV (%2)
        IF      '=%3' <> '='
        DW      REV (%3)
        IF      '=%4' <> '='
        DW      REV (%4)
        IF      '=%5' <> '='
        DW      REV (%5)
        ENDIF
        ENDIF
        ENDIF
        ENDIF
        ENDM
LOCAL:  MACRO
        PROC
        ENDM
BYTE:   MACRO
        IF      '%1' = '='
%L      DB      $80+(((%2-*)&$7F) XOR $40 )
        ELSE
        IF      '%1' = '@@'
%L      DW      ( %2 )
        ELSE
%L      DB      %1
        ENDIF
        ENDIF
        ENDM
```

Syntax Table Macro

```
; THIS MACRO IS USED TO SIMULATE THE ACTION OF THE ORIGINAL
; ASSEMBLER IN HANDLING SPECIAL SYNTAX TABLE PSEUDO OPS AND
; OPERANDS
;
; THE 'SYN' MACRO EXAMINES UP TO 4 ARGUMENTS FOR CERTAIN SPECIAL
; CASE NAMES.
;
; IF THE NAME 'JS' IS FOUND, IT GENERATES A SPECIAL 'RELATIVE
;       SYNTAX JSR' TO THE LABEL FOUND IN THE NEXT PARAMETER
```

```
;
; IF THE NAME 'AD' IS FOUND, IT GENERATES A WORD ADDRESS OF
;       THE LABEL FOUND IN THE NEXT PARAMETER
;
; ANY OTHER NAME IS ASSUMED TO BE A SIMPLE BYTE VALUE
SYN:    MACRO
:SYAR2  SET     '=%2'<>'='
:SYAR3  SET     '=%3'<>'='
:SYAR4  SET     '=%4'<>'='
        IF      '%1' = 'JS'
%L      DB      $8Ø+(((%2-*)&$7F) XOR $4Ø )
:SYAR2  SET     Ø
        ELSE
          IF    '%1' = 'AD'
%L        DW    (%2)
:SYAR2    SET   Ø
          ELSE
%L        DB    %1
          ENDIF
        ENDIF

      IF        :SYAR2
        IF      '%2' = 'JS'
        DB      $8Ø+(((%3-*)&$7F) XOR $4Ø )
:SYAR3  SET     Ø
        ELSE
          IF    '%2' = 'AD'
          DW    (%3)
:SYAR3    SET   Ø
          ELSE
          DB    %2
          ENDIF
        ENDIF
      ENDIF

      IF        :SYAR3
        IF      '%3' = 'JS'
        DB      $8Ø+(((%4-*)&$7F) XOR $4Ø )
:SYAR4  SET     Ø
        ELSE
          IF    '%3' = 'AD'
          DW    (%4)
:SYAR4    SET   Ø
          ELSE
          DB    %3
          ENDIF
        ENDIF
      ENDIF

      IF        :SYAR4
        IF      '%4' = 'JS'
        DB      $8Ø+(((%5-*)&$7F) XOR $4Ø )
        ELSE
          IF    '%4' = 'AD'
          DW    (%5)
          ELSE
          DB    %4
          ENDIF
        ENDIF
      ENDIF

        ENDM
```

The Bugs in Atari BASIC

Yes, it's true. There are some bugs in Atari BASIC. Of course, that's not surprising, since Atari released the product as ROM without giving the authors a chance to do second-round bug-fixing. But what hurts, a little, is that most of the fixes for the bugs have been known since June of 1979.

As this book is being written, rumor has it that at last Atari is in the final stages of releasing a new version of the BASIC ROMs. Unfortunately, these modified ROMs will appear too late for us to comment upon them in this edition. On the other hand, there are supposed to be fewer than twenty fixes implemented (which isn't a bad record for a product as mature as Atari BASIC), so those of you who are willing to PEEK around a bit can use this listing as at least a road map to the new ROMs.

In any case, though, we thought it would be appropriate to mention a few of the bugs we know about, show you why they exist, and tell how we fixed them back there in the summer of '79.

The Editing and String Bug

In the course of editing a BASIC program, sometimes the system loses all or part of the program, or it simply hangs. Often, even SYSTEM RESET will not return control to the user.

Also, string assignments that involve the movement of exact multiples of 256 bytes do not move the bytes properly. For example, A$=B$(257,512) would actually move bytes 513 through 768 of B$ into bytes 257 through 512 of A$, even if neither string were DIMensioned to those values.

Both of these are really the same bug. And both are caused because we strove to be a little too efficient.

There are many ways to move strings of bytes using the 6502's instruction set. The simplest and most-used methods, though, are excruciatingly slow. So Paul and Kathleen invented a super-fast set of move-memory routines, one for moving up in memory (EXPAND, at $A881) and one for moving down in memory (CONTRACT, at $A8FD). Unfortunately, the routines are very complex (which is what makes them fast) and difficult to interface with properly. And so a bug crept into CONTRACT.

Take a look at the code of FMOVER ($A947). When we get here, we expect MVLNG to contain the *complement* of the least significant byte of the move length while MVLNG + 1 contains its most significant byte. But look what happens if the original move length was, for example, $200. The complement of the least significant byte ($00) is still zero ($00), so the BEQ to :CONT4 occurs immediately.

But by then, the X register contains the number of pages to move plus one (X would contain 3 in this example), so we increment it (it becomes 2) and go to label :CONT3, where we bump the high-order byte of both the source and destination addresses. Ah, but therein lies the rub! We haven't yet done anything with the first values in those source and destination addresses, so we have effectively skipped 256 bytes of each!

The solution is to replace the BEQ :CONT4 at $A94E with the following code:

```
DEX
BNE :CONT2
RTS
```

Do you see the difference? If we enter with MVLNG equal to zero, we immediately move 256 bytes (at :CONT2) *before* ever attempting to change the source and destination addresses.

And this fix works, honest. We've been using it like this for over two years in BASIC A+.

Minus Zero

Taking the unary minus of a number (A=0 : PRINT -A) can result in garbage. Usually, this garbage will not affect subsequent calculations, but it does print strangely. And how did this come about?

We simply forgot to take into consideration the fact that zero doesn't really have a sign. Look at the code for the unary minus operator (XPUMINUS, at $ACA8). Do you see the problem? We simply invert the most significant bit (the sign bit) of the floating point number in FR0.

What we should have coded would be something like this:

```
 LDA  FR0
 BEQ  :NOINVERT
 EOR  #$80
 STA  FR0
:NOINVERT
```

Luckily, this is not too severe a problem to the BASIC user (one can always use "PRINT 0-A" instead of "PRINT -A"), but just think — it only cost two bytes to fix this bug.

LOCATE and GET

The GET statement does not reinitialize its buffer pointer, so it can do nasty things to memory if used directly after a statement which has changed the system buffer pointer. For example, GET can change the line number of a DATA statement if it is used after a READ. Also, the same problem exists for the LOCATE statement, since it calls GET.

From BASIC, the easiest solution is to use a function or statement which is known to reset the pointer. Coding "XX=STR$(0)" works just fine, as does PRINTing any number.

Within the source listing, the problem exists at location $BC82, label GET1. If the code had simply read as follows, there would be no bug:

```
GET1
    JSR  INTLBF ; reset buffer pointer
    LDA #ICGTC ; continue as before
```

INPUT and READ

Using either an INPUT or READ statement without a following variable does *not* cause a syntax error (as it should). Then, attempting to execute a statement such as 20 INPUT can cause total system lock-up.

The solution from BASIC? Be careful and don't do it.

And this is one bug that we will not show the fix for, simply because it's too long and involved. We will, however, point to labels :SINPUT and :SREAD (at locations $A6F4 and $A6F5) in the Syntax Tables and show *why* the bug exists.

Note that the :SINPUT does a syntax call (SYN JS,) to the :OPD syntax, which looks for — but does *not* insist upon — a file number specifier (#<numeric expression>). Then the syntax joins with :SREAD, which looks for zero or more variables.

Oops! Zero or more? Shouldn't that be one or more? That's where the problem lies.

Do *Not* Use NOT

In all too many cases, the use of the NOT operator is guaranteed to get you in trouble. If you don't believe it, try this: PRINT NOT NOT 1.

The explanation of why the bug occurs is too lengthy to give in detail here; suffice it to say that the precedence of NOT is wrong. Remember the Operator Precedence Table we displayed in Chapter 8 of Part 2? Look at what you got for the go-onto-stack and come-off-stack precedence values for NOT.

Or look at location $AC57, the NOT entry in OPRTAB. NOT uses a 7 for both its precedence values. But wait a minute. If two operators have the same apparent precedence (as in NOT NOT A or even A + B + C), the expression executor will pop the first one off the stack and execute it. But with a unary operator, there is nothing to execute yet.

And the same bug exists for both unary minus and unary plus, so - -3 and + +5 don't execute properly. Of course, since unary plus doesn't really do anything, it doesn't matter. In the case of unary minus, though, all but the last minus sign in a string of minus signs is ignored (that is, - -3 produces -3 as a result, instead of +3, as it should). But, by an incredible coincidence, the damage that unary minus causes is invisible to Execute Expression as a whole and only produces the error noted.

The fix? Well, if we want to leave NOT where it is in the order of things, the only way is to restructure the whole precedence table. But if we are willing to accord it a very high precedence, like unary plus and minus, we can fix it — and plus and minus — by changing the bytes at $AC57, $AC64, and $AC65 to $DC. And, thanks to the differing go-onto-stack and come-off-stack values, we can stack as many NOTs, pluses, or minuses as we want.

Are these all the bugs we know about that can be fixed easily? No. But these are the easiest to understand or the easiest to fix, and we thought they were instructive.

Of course, unless you have an EPROM board and burner handy, you may not be able to take advantage of these fixes.

But at least now you may be able to work around them as you program with good old buggy-version Atari BASIC.

And take heart. Remember Richard's Rule: Any nontrivial piece of software has bugs in it. And the corollary: Any piece of software which is bug-free is trivial.

Labels and Hexadecimal Addresses

	Label	Address
	AADD	AF52
	AAPSTR	AB98
n	ADC	AF53
	ADFLAG	ØØB1
n	AFP	D8ØØ
	AMUL1	AF5D
	AMUL2	AF46
	APHM	ØØØE
	ARGOPS	ØØ8Ø
	ARGP2	ACØ6
	ARGPOP	ABF2
	ARGPUS	ABBA
	ARGSTK	ØØ8Ø
	ARSLVL	ØØAA
	ARSTKX	ØØAA
n	ASCIN	D8ØØ
	ASLA	mac
	ATAN	BE77
	ATAN1	BE9A
	ATAN2	BED4
	ATCOEF	DFAE
	ATEMP	ØØAF
	ATNOUT	BEE2
	BININT	ØØD4
	BOTH	BDB3
	BRKBYT	ØØ11
	BYELOC	E471
n	BYTE	mac
	C	ØØ44
	BYELOC	E471
n	BYTE	mac
	C	ØØ44
	CAASN	ØØ2D
	CACOM	ØØ3C
	CADR	ØØ43
	CALPRN	ØØ38
	CAND	ØØ2A
	CASC	ØØ4Ø
	CCHR	ØØ3E
	CCOM	ØØ12
	CCR	ØØ16
	CDATA	ØØØ1
	CDIV	ØØ27
	CDLPRN	ØØ39
n	CDOL	ØØ13
n	CDQ	ØØ1Ø
	CDSLPR	ØØ3B
	CEOS	ØØ14
	CEQ	ØØ22
	CERR	ØØ37
	CEXP	ØØ23
	CFFUN	ØØ3D
	CFLPRN	ØØ3A
	CFOR	ØØØ8
	CGE	ØØ1F
	CGOSUB	ØØØC
	CGS	ØØ18
	CGT	ØØ21
	CGTO	ØØ17
	CILET	ØØ36
	CIO	E456
	CIX	ØØF2
	CLALL1	BD4F
	CLE	ØØ1D
	CLEN	ØØ42
	CLIST	ØØØ4
	CLPRN	ØØ2B
	CLSALL	BD41
	CLSYS1	BCF1
	CLSYSD	BCF1
	CLT	ØØ2Ø
	CMINUS	ØØ26
	CMUL	ØØ24
	CNE	ØØ1E
	CNFNP	ØØ44
	CNOT	ØØ28
	COLD1	AØØ8
	COLDST	AØØØ
	COLOR	ØØC8
	COMCNT	ØØBØ
	CON	ØØ1E
	CONTLO	A8FB
	CONTRA	A8FD
	COPEN	BBB6
	COR	ØØ29
	COS	BDB1
	COX	ØØ94
	CPC	ØØ9D
	CPLUS	ØØ25
	CPND	ØØ1C
	CR	ØØ9B
	CREAD	ØØ22
	CREGS	Ø2C4
	CRPRN	ØØ2C
	CRTGI	BFF9
	CSASN	ØØ2E
	CSC	ØØ15
	CSEQ	ØØ34
	CSGE	ØØ31
	CSGT	ØØ33
	CSLE	ØØ2F
	CSLPRN	ØØ37
	CSLT	ØØ32
	CSNE	ØØ3Ø
	CSOE	ØØ11
	CSROP	ØØ1D
	CSTEP	ØØ1A
	CSTR	ØØ3D
	CTHEN	ØØ1B
	CTO	ØØ19
	CUMINU	ØØ36
	CUPLUS	ØØ35
	CUSR	ØØ3F
	CVAFP	D8ØØ
	CVAL	ØØ41
	CVFASC	D8E6
	CVFPI	AD56
	CVIFP	D9AA
	DATAD	ØØB6
	DATALN	ØØB7
n	DCBORG	Ø3ØØ
	DEGFLG	ØØFB
	DEGON	ØØØ6
	DIGRT	ØØF1
	DIRFLG	ØØA6
	DNERR	BCBØ
	DOSLOC	ØØØA
	DSPFLG	Ø2FE
	ECSIZE	ØØA4
	EEXP	ØØED
	ELADVC	BADD
	ENDSTA	ØØ8E
	ENDVVT	ØØ88
	ENTDTD	ØØB4
	EPCHAR	ØØ5D
	ERBRTN	B92Ø
	ERGFDE	B922
	ERLTL	B924
	ERNOFO	B926
	ERNOLN	B928
n	ERON	B93E
	EROVFL	B92A
	ERRAOS	B92C
	ERRDIM	B92E
	ERRDNO	B918
	ERRINP	B93Ø
	ERRLN	B932
	ERRNSF	B916
	ERRNUM	ØØB9
	ERROOD	B934
	ERROR	B94Ø
	ERRPTL	B91A
	ERRSAV	ØØC3
	ERRSSL	B936
	ERRVSF	B938
	ERSVAL	B91C
	ERVAL	B93A
	ESIGN	ØØEF
	EVAADR	ØØØ2
	EVAD1	ØØØ4
	EVAD2	ØØØ6
n	EVARRA	ØØ4Ø
	EVDIM	ØØØ1
n	EVNUM	ØØØ1
	EVSADR	ØØØ2
	EVSCAL	ØØØØ
	EVSDIM	ØØØ6
	EVSDTA	ØØØ2
	EVSLEN	ØØØ4
	EVSTR	ØØ8Ø
n	EVTYPE	ØØØØ
n	EVVALU	ØØØ2
	EXECNL	A95F
	EXECNS	A962
	EXEXPR	AAEØ
	EXOPOP	ABØB
	EXP	DDCØ
	EXP1	DEØ3
	EXP1Ø	DDCC
	EXP2	DE2Ø
	EXP3	DE26
	EXPAND	A881
	EXPERR	DE4B
	EXPINT	AB2E
	EXPLOW	A87F
	EXPOUT	DE4A
	EXPSGN	DE39
	EXSVOP	ØØAB
	EXSVPR	ØØAC
	FADD	DA66
n	FASC	D8E6
	FBODY	ØØØC
	FCHRFL	ØØFØ
	FDB	mac
	FDIV	DB28
	FHALF	DF6C
	FIXRST	B825
	FLDØ1	DD8F
n	FLDØP	DD8D
	FLDØR	DD89
	FLD1l	DD9E
n	FLD1P	DD9C
	FLD1R	DD98
	FLIM	ØØØØ
	FLIST	BAD5
n	FLOG1Ø	DFØ1
	FLPTR	ØØFC
	FMOVE	DDB6
	FMOVE1	DDB8
	FMOVER	A947
	FMPREC	ØØØ5
	FMUL	DADB
n	FNTAB	A829
	FONE	DE8F
	FP9S	DFEA
	FPI	D9D2
	FPONE	BE71
	FPORG	D8ØØ
	FPREC	ØØØ6
	FPSCR	Ø5E6
	FPSCR1	Ø5EC
	FPTR2	ØØFE
	FRØ	ØØD4
	FRØM	ØØD5
	FR1	ØØEØ
	FR1M	ØØE1
	FR2	ØØE6
	FRA1Ø	DDØ1
	FRA1E	DDØ9
	FRA2Ø	DDØ5
	FRA2E	DDØF
	FRADD	AD3B

Appendix C

	FRCMP	AD35
	FRCMPP	AD32
	FRDIV	AD4D
	FRE	ØØDA
	FRMUL	AD47
	FRSIGN	ØØEE
	FRSUB	AD41
	FRUN	BAF7
	FRX	ØØEC
	FSCR	Ø5E6
	FSCR1	Ø5EC
	FSQR	BFØ8
	FSTØ1	DDAD
n	FSTØP	DDAB
	FSTØR	DDA7
	FSTEP	ØØØ6
	FSUB	DA6Ø
	FTWO	BF93
	GDIO1	BC22
	GDVCIO	BC1D
	GET1	BC82
	GET1IN	ABE9
	GETINT	ABEØ
	GETLL	A9DD
n	GETPIØ	ABD8
	GETPIN	ABD5
	GETSTM	A9A2
	GETTOK	AB3E
	GETVAR	AB89
	GFDISP	ØØØ3
	GFHEAD	ØØØ4
n	GFLNO	ØØØ1
	GFTYPE	ØØØØ
	GIOCMD	BDØ4
	GIODVC	BC9F
	GIOPRM	BDØ2
	GLGO	BA92
	GLINE	BA89
	GLPCX	BAC4
	GLPX	BAC6
n	GNLINE	BA8Ø
	GNXTL	A9DØ
	GRFBAS	Ø27Ø
	GSTRAD	AB9B
	GTINTO	ABE3
	GVVTAD	AC28
	HIMEM	Ø2E5
	HMADR	Ø2E5
n	IBUFFX	ØØA9
	ICAUX1	Ø34A
	ICAUX2	Ø34B
	ICAUX3	Ø34C
	ICAUX4	Ø34D
	ICAUX5	Ø34E
	ICBAH	Ø345
	ICBAL	Ø344
	ICBLH	Ø349
	ICBLL	Ø348
	ICCLOS	ØØØC
	ICCOM	Ø342
n	ICDDC	ØØØE
n	ICDNO	Ø341
	ICDRAW	ØØ11
n	ICFREE	ØØFF
n	ICGBC	ØØØ6
n	ICGBR	ØØØ4
	ICGR	ØØ1C
	ICGTC	ØØØ7
	ICGTR	ØØØ5
n	ICHID	Ø34Ø
	ICLEN	ØØ1Ø
n	ICMAX	ØØØE
n	ICOIN	ØØØ1
	ICOIO	ØØØ3
n	ICOOUT	ØØØ2
n	ICPBC	ØØØA
n	ICPBR	ØØØ8
	ICPTC	ØØØB
n	ICPTR	ØØØ9
	ICPUT	Ø346
	ICSBRK	ØØ8Ø
n	ICSDER	ØØ83
n	ICSDNR	ØØ81
n	ICSEOF	ØØØ3
n	ICSIVC	ØØ84
n	ICSIVN	ØØ86
n	ICSNED	ØØ82
n	ICSNOP	ØØ85
n	ICSOK	ØØØ1
	ICSTA	Ø343
	ICSTAT	ØØØD
n	ICSTR	ØØØ2
n	ICSWPE	ØØ87
	IFP	D9AA
n	ILSHFT	DA5A
	INBUFF	ØØF3
	INDEX2	ØØ97
	INTLBF	DA51
	IO1	BDØA
n	IO2	BDØE
	IO3	BD1Ø
	IO4	BD12
	IO5	BD19
n	IO6	BD1D
	IO7	BD24
	IO8	BD26
	IOCB	Ø34Ø
	IOCBOR	Ø34Ø
	IOCMD	ØØCØ
	IODVC	ØØC1
	IOTES2	BCB6
	IOTEST	BCB3
	ISVAR	BD2F
	ISVAR1	BD2D
n	LBPR1	Ø57E
n	LBPR2	Ø57F
	LBUFF	Ø58Ø
	LDDVX	BCA6
	LDIOST	BCFB
	LDLINE	B578
	LELNUM	ØØAD
	LGCOEF	DF72
	LISTDT	ØØB5
	LLINE	B55C
	LLNGTH	ØØ9F
	LMADR	Ø2E7
	LOADFL	ØØCA
	LOCAL	mac
	LOG	DECD
n	LOG1	DEDB
	LOG1Ø	DED1
	LOG1ØE	DE89
	LOG2	DEEF
	LOG3	DEF3
	LOG4	DEF9
	LOG5	DEDB
	LOG6	DF46
	LOG7	DF53
	LOGBTH	DED3
	LOGDON	DF64
n	LOGERR	DED9
n	LOGOUT	DF56
	LOMEM	ØØ8Ø
	LPRTOK	B535
	LSRA	mac
	LSTMC	B63D
	MAXCIX	ØØ9F
	MDEND	DB1A
	MDESUP	DCCF
	MDSUP	DCEØ
	MEMFUL	B93C
	MEMTOP	ØØ9Ø
n	MEND1	DB1E
	MEND2	DB21
	MEND3	DB24
	MEOLFL	ØØ92
	MISCR1	Ø48Ø
	MISCRA	Ø5ØØ
	MVØTO1	DDB6
	MVFA	ØØ99
	MVFRØE	DD34
	MVFR12	DD28
	MVLNG	ØØA2
	MVTA	ØØ9B
	NATCF	ØØØB
	NCTOFR	AB4D
	NIBSHØ	DBEB
	NIBSH2	DBE7
	NLCOEF	ØØØA
	NOCDØ	BDØ1
	NORM	DCØØ
	NORM1	DCØ4
	NPCOEF	ØØØA
	NSCF	ØØØ6
	NSIGN	ØØEE
	NXTSTD	ØØA7
	ONLOOP	ØØB3
	OPETAB	AA7Ø
	OPNTAB	A7E3
	OPRTAB	AC3F
	OPSTKX	ØØA9
	OUTBUF	ØØ8Ø
	P1ØCOF	DE4D
n	PATCH	BDA4
	PATSIZ	ØØØ1
	PIOV18	BE6B
	PIOV2	BE5F
	PIOV4	DFFØ
	PLYARG	Ø5EØ
	PLYCNT	ØØEF
	PLYEV1	DD5B
	PLYEV2	DD6F
	PLYEVL	DD4Ø
	PLYOUT	DD88
	POKADR	ØØ95
	POP1	ACØF
	POPRST	B841
	PRCHAR	BA9F
	PRCR	BD6E
	PRCX	BAA1
	PRDY1	BD59
	PREADY	BD57
	PROMPT	ØØC2
	PSHRST	B683
	PSTR	B48Ø
	PTABW	ØØC9
	PUTCHA	BA9F
	QTEMP	ØØD9
	RADFLG	ØØFB
	RADON	ØØØØ
	RESCUR	B6BE
	RISASN	AEA6
	RISC	AB64
	RML	ØØØ7
	RMSG	BD67
	RNDDIV	BØA8
	RNDLOC	D2ØA
	ROLA	mac
	ROM	AØØØ
	RORA	mac
	RSHFØE	DC62
	RSHFTØ	DC3A
	RSHFT1	DC3E
	RSTPTR	B8AF
	RSTSEO	BD99
	RTNVAR	AC16
	RUNINI	B8F8
	RUNSTK	ØØ8E
	SAVCUR	ØØBE
	SAVDEX	ØØB3
	SCANT	ØØAF
	SCOEF	BE41
	SCRX	ØØ55
	SCRY	ØØ54
	SCVECT	BFF9
	SEARCH	A462
	SETDZ	BD72
	SETLIN	B818
	SETLN1	B81B
	SETSEO	BD79
	SGNFLG	ØØFØ
	SICKIO	BCB9
	SIN	BDA7
	SINDON	BE4Ø
	SINERR	BDA5
	SINF1	BDF6
	SINF3	BEØØ
	SINF4	BE11
	SINF5	BDE4
n	SINF6	BDD5
	SINF7	BDCC
n	SINOVF	BDCB
	SIX	Ø48Ø
	SKBLAN	DBA1
	SKCTL	D2ØF
	SKPBLA	DBA1
	SNTAB	A4AF
	SNX1	AØ5Ø
	SNX2	AØ53
	SNX3	AØ5D
	SOPEN	BBD1
	SOX	Ø481
	SPC	Ø482
	SQR	BEE5
	SQR1	BFØØ
	SQR1Ø	DF66
	SQR2	BF84
	SQR3	BF8A
	SQRCNT	ØØEF
	SQRDON	BF64
	SQRERR	BEE3
	SQRLP	BF2A
	SQROUT	BF92
	SRCADR	ØØ95
	SRCNXT	A49Ø
	SRCSKP	ØØAA
	SREG1	D2Ø8
	SREG2	D2ØØ
	SREG3	D2Ø1
	SSTR	BA73
	STACK	Ø48Ø
	STARP	ØØ8C
	STENUM	ØØAF
	STETAB	AAØØ
	STINDE	ØØA8
	STKLVL	ØØA9
	STMCUR	ØØ8A

Appendix C

	STMLBD	00A7
	STMSTR	00A8
	STMTAB	0088
	STOP	B7A7
	STOPLN	00BA
	STRCMP	AF81
	SVCOLO	02FB
	SVDISP	00B2
	SVESA	0097
	SVONTC	00B0
	SVONTL	00B2
	SVONTX	00B3
	SVVNTP	00AD
	SVVVTE	00B1
	SYN	mac
	SYNTAX	A060
	TEMPA	00C4
	TENDST	A9E2
n	TESTRT	A9E7
	TOPRST	0090
	TRAPLN	00BC
	TSCOX	00AB
	TSLNUM	00A0
	TSTALP	A3F7
	TSTBRK	A9F4
	TSTEND	B910
	TSTNUM	DBAF
	TVNUM	00D3
	TVSCIX	00AC
	TVTYPE	00D2
	VNTD	0084
	VNTP	0082
	VNUM	00D3
	VTYPE	00D2
	VVTP	0086
	WARMFL	0008
	WARMST	A04D
	WVVTPT	009D
	XBYE	A9E8
	XCLOAD	BBAC
	XCLOSE	BC1B
	XCLR	B766
	XCMP	AD26
	XCOLOR	BA29
	XCOM	B1D9
	XCONT	B7BE
	XCSAVE	BBA4
	XDATA	A9E7
	XDEG	B261
	XDIM	B1D9
	XDOS	A9EE
	XDPSLP	AD82
	XDRAWT	BA31
	XEND	B78D
	XENTER	BACB
	XERR	B91E
	XFALSE	AD00
	XFMFLG	00F1
	XFOR	B64B
	XFORM	DE95
	XGET	BC7F
	XGO1	B6AE
	XGO2	B6A6
	XGOSUB	B6A0
	XGOTO	B6A3
	XGR	BA50
	XGS	B6C7
	XGS1	B6CA
	XIF	B778
	XINPUT	B316
	XINT	B0E6
	XITBT	B354
	XLET	AAE0
	XLIST	B483
	XLOAD	BAFB
	XLOAD1	BB04
	XLOCAT	BC95
	XLPRIN	B464
	XNEW	A00C
	XNEXT	B6CF
	XNOTE	BC36
	XON	B7ED
	XOP1	BBED
	XOP2	BBFB
	XOPEN	BBEB
	XPAASN	AD5F
	XPABS	B0AE
	XPACOM	AD79
	XPADR	B01C
	XPALPR	AD86
	XPAND	ACE3
	XPASC	B012
	XPATN	B12F
	XPCHR	B067
	XPCOS	B125
	XPDIV	AC9F
	XPDLPR	AD82
	XPEQ	ACDC
	XPEXP	B14D
	XPFLPR	AD7B
	XPFRE	AFEB
	XPGE	ACD5
	XPGT	ACCC
	XPIFP	AFD1
	XPIFP1	AFD5
	XPIFP2	AFD8
	XPINT	B0DD
	XPL10	B143
	XPLE	ACB5
	XPLEN	AFCA
	XPLOG	B139
	XPLOT	BA76
	XPLPRN	AB1F
	XPLT	ACC5
	XPMINU	AC8D
	XPMUL	AC96
	XPNE	ACBE
	XPNOT	ACF9
	XPOINT	BC4D
	XPOKE	B24C
	XPOP	B841
	XPOR	ACEE
	XPOS	BA16
	XPPDL	B022
	XPPEEK	AFE1
	XPPLUS	AC84
	XPPOWE	B165
	XPPTRI	B02A
	XPRINT	B3B6
	XPRND	B08B
	XPRPRN	AD7B
n	XPSEQ	ACDC
	XPSGE	ACD5
	XPSGN	AD19
	XPSGT	ACCC
	XPSIN	B11B
	XPSLE	ACB5
	XPSLPR	AE26
	XPSLT	ACC5
	XPSNE	ACBE
	XPSQR	B157
	XPSTIC	B026
	XPSTR	B049
	XPSTRI	B02E
	XPUMIN	ACA8
	XPUPLU	ACB4
	XPUSH	AD16
	XPUSR	B0BA
	XPUT	BC72
	XPVAL	B000
	XRAD	B266
	XREAD	B283
	XREM	A9E7
	XREST	B26B
	XRTN	B719
	XRUN	B74D
	XSAASN	AEA3
	XSAVE	BB5D
	XSAVE1	BB62
	XSETCO	B9B7
	XSOUND	B9DD
	XSTATU	BC28
	XSTOP	B793
	XTF	AD09
	XTI	AD07
	XTRAP	B7E1
	XTRUE	AD05
	XXIO	BBE5
	ZF1	DA46
	ZFP	00D2
	ZFR0	DA44
	ZICB	0020
	ZPADEC	AFBC
	ZPG1	0080
	ZTEMP1	00F5
	ZTEMP2	00C6
	ZTEMP3	00F9
	ZTEMP4	00F7
	ZVAR	B8C0
	ZXLY	DA48

Index

Symbols

Numbers

A

Index

F

Index

X

Y

Z

If you've enjoyed the articles in this book, you'll find the same style and quality in every monthly issue of **COMPUTE!** Magazine. Use this form to order your subscription to **COMPUTE!**

For Fastest Service,
Call Our **Toll-Free** US Order Line
800-334-0868
In NC call 919-275-9809

COMPUTE!

P.O. Box 5406
Greensboro, NC 27403

My Computer Is:
☐ PET ☐ Apple ☐ Atari ☐ VIC ☐ Other ______ ☐ Don't yet have one...

☐ $20.00 One Year US Subscription
☐ $36.00 Two Year US Subscription
☐ $54.00 Three Year US Subscription

Subscription rates outside the US:
☐ $25.00 Canada
☐ $38.00 Europe, Australia, New Zealand/Air Delivery
☐ $48.00 Middle East, North Africa, Central America/Air Mail
☐ $68.00 Elsewhere/Air Mail
☐ $25.00 International Surface Mail (lengthy, unreliable delivery)

Name ______________________

Address ______________________

City ______________ State ______ Zip ______

Country ______________________

Payment must be in US Funds drawn on a US Bank; International Money Order, or charge card.

☐ Payment Enclosed ☐ VISA
☐ MasterCard ☐ American Express

Acct. No. ______________ Expires ___ / ___

15-9